Involved Fathering and Men's Adult Development

Provisional Balances

Involved Fathering and Men's Adult Development

Provisional Balances

Rob Palkovitz
University of Delaware

LAWRENCE ERLBAUM ASSOCIATES, PUBLISHERS
2002 Mahwah, NJ London

Lawrence Erlbaum Associates, Inc., Publishers
10 Industrial Avenue
Mahwah, NJ 07430

Cover design by Kathryn Houghtaling Lacey

Photograph of W. Dean McClanahan and Jason D. McClanahan by Rob Palkovitz.

Library of Congress Cataloging-in-Publication Data

Palkovitz, Robin Joseph, 1954–
Involved fathering and men's adult development : provisional balances / Rob J. Palkovitz.
p. cm.
Includes bibliographical references and index.
ISBN 0-8058-3564-4 (cloth : alk. paper)
ISBN 0-8058-3565-2 (pbk. : alk. paper)
1. Fathers—Psychology. 2. Fatherhood—Psychological aspects. 3. Parenting—Psychological aspects. 4. Developmental psychology. 5. Adult Development. I. Title.
HQ756 .P35 2002
306.874'2—dc21 2001057762
CIP

Books published by Lawrence Erlbaum Associates are printed on acid-free paper, and their bindings are chosen for strength and durability.

Printed in the United States of America
10 9 8 7 6 5 4 3 2 1

This book is warmly dedicated to I. Joseph Palkovitz, my Dad. Dad, I am thankful for the heritage of faith, love, provision, care, closeness, learning, opportunity, and fun that you have created and nurtured for me and your grandchildren. You have always been ahead of the times, a "new involved father" for decades.

Contents

III: The Social Domain

IV: The Work Domain

V: Summary, Evaluations, and Applications

Acknowledgments

This book would not have been possible without the support, collaboration, and encouragement of many people. First, and foremost, I want to sincerely thank the men who so generously shared their time and their fathering stories. Your willingness to talk about fathering and your lives provided the heart of this book. Each story has made a difference. I sincerely wish you the best as your lives and fathering relationships continue to develop.

Barbara and Philip Newman played a major role in the genesis of this project by stimulating and focusing my interest in the relationships between parenting and adult development through their professional writing and subsequent conversations. Their enthusiasm and encouragement for this project is of inestimable value to me. Thanks for your generativity!

The University of Delaware supported this project through numerous phases and channels: semester-long sabbatical leaves in 1991 and 1998, funding through the General University Research Fund in 1993, and funding from the College of Human Resources and the Department of Individual and Family Studies. Dene Klinzing, Dean of the College of Human Resources, and John Cavanaugh, Chair of the Department of Individual and Family Studies at the time, provided support and encouragement when the transcription process seemed overwhelming. Steven DeCherney of the Medical Research Institute of Delaware provided generous support in the form of research space and recruitment, scheduling, and transcription assistance. This project would not have been possible without each of these important sources of support and encouragement.

A number of colleagues have also shaped the development and progress of this book in significant ways. Much of the project conceptualization and data analysis has been positively shaped by ongoing discussion and interaction with Kerry Daly, Glen Palm, Shawn Christiansen, Alan Hawkins, David Dollahite, Ralph LaRossa, Kay Pasley, Michael Farrell, and Barbara and Philip Newman. I have copresented at conferences and coauthored articles from this data set with Glen Palm, Shawn Christiansen, Marcella Copes, and Tara Woolfolk. Their insights and friendship have been a gold mine.

Tamara Hareven's friendship, scholarship, example, and encouragement has also made significant contributions to my progress on this book.

I have also been fortunate to have some outstanding experiences with both graduate and undergraduate students in seminars and independent research projects where aspects of this project and data analysis benefited from discussion and class projects. Those students are David Appleby, Dianne Baker, Brooke Bollinger, Shawn Christiansen, Charlene Clark, Christian Dunn, Chris Fraser, Erin Kramer Holmes, Jason Latshaw, Loren Marks, Jen Molinaro, David Murray, and Tara Woolfolk. Loren Marks read through the penultimate draft of the book and made invaluable suggestions and careful editorial recommendations. His enthusiasm, positivism, and encouragement were a Godsend. My thanks to Thomas Crescenzo for his computer expertise and help with the preliminary cover design.

I would also like to thank Judi Amsel of Lawrence Erlbaum Associates for believing in this project when it was a book prospectus. The Editorial Team at Lawrence Erlbaum, Bill Webber, Senior Acquisitions Editor, Nadine Simms, Senior Book Production Editor, and Karen Kinney, Copy Editor, has my gratitude for their efficient professionalism, editing, and support in preparing the manuscript for publication.

Finally, my friends and family have shaped and supported this project through its various phases. Bruce Latshaw and Tom Hilferty—your words of encouragement and your prayers were much needed and felt. Judy—I wouldn't be here without you. Your love, support, encouragement, and example have kept me going. Thanks for the fun and for keeping me relatively balanced. After all of this work, I owe you and the guys a significant fun binge. Nathan, Collin, Ian, and Shane—you are amazing! You have taught me so much and have brought an overflow of joy and fulfillment to my life and career. You are each a unique blessing. J.C.—you and your Dad continue be the ultimate example of provision and balance. None of this would have been possible without you. Thanks.

—Rob Palkovitz

Preface

All the parents I know say that their lives are different because they have children. If you carefully listen to them, you realize that they are not just talking about their schedules, energy levels, or the need to navigate a sea of toys and clutter as they walk through the house. Parents who have invested in caring for their children feel have become different people as a result of involvement with their children. Involvement in the ongoing care of their growing and changing children fosters development in parents. Involvement in parenting provides a powerful and pervasive context for adults' development as they continually adapt to the new needs, challenges, and abilities of their children.

Researchers have extensively studied the effects of parenting styles and parent involvement on child development, and the professional literature speaks as though some relatively firm conclusions can be drawn. It is known that authoritative parenting styles, warmth, and moderate parental control are beneficial to children's development. Researchers have elaborated on the types of environments and interactions that enhance children's lives. In short, they know that particular patterns of parenting enhance child development while other patterns present challenges or defecits that children must overcome if they are going to reach their developmental potential.

There is no comparable knowledge of the effects of parenting on adult development. Professional literature on this topic is limited to a handful of theoretical statements, and a more extensive sprinkling of anecdotal accounts. There are surprisingly few data-based research studies, most of which were designed to focus on something else (i.e., a specific variable) and consider parenting as a tangential issue. Although every parent will tell you that having children has caused them to develop differently than they would have had they never had children, contemporary texts on life-span or adult development and family studies are nearly silent with regard to the relations between active engagement in parenting roles and adult development outcomes.

I first became aware of this curious gap in knowledge during a sabbatical leave in spring 1991. I characterize the relative void of research as curious, because well over 90% of all persons become parents, and a vast majority of parents devote significant amounts of time (18 or more years) and energy (how is this quantified?) to engagement in parenting roles. Developmental psychologists have long recognized that contexts of development significantly influence developmental outcomes. So why is it that such a normative and pervasive context of adult development is virtually ignored in scholarly pursuits?

From a scientific perspective, there are two primary sets of barriers working against the study of such a universal and powerful shaper of adult development. First, the study of young adulthood is a "frontier" area. Although researchers have amassed significant knowledge of prenatal development, infancy, childhood, adolescence, and senescence, relatively little is known about middle age, and the least is known about developmental change during young adulthood. There are numerous exceptions, but it is during young adulthood that most people make the transition to parenthood. Whereas the transition to parenthood is viewed to be a significant life-course transition, it is often viewed as a relatively short-term adjustment. The long-term and cumulative effects of parenting are not often studied. Further, the parenting folklore asserts that parenting is natural. Why should anyone study something so normal and natural?

Perhaps the greatest barrier has to do with contemporary biases about how researchers define and study "truth." Controlled experimental research is frequently heralded as the pinnacle of inquiry because of its power to illuminate causal relationships. It is unethical to conduct experimental research to conclusively demonstrate a causal relation between parenting and adult development. It would be unthinkable to randomly assign people to parent and nonparent comparison groups and to trace their development across time. Another confound is that parenting roles are embedded within and permeated by other roles. At the same time that a man is a father, he may be a son, a husband, a brother, a provider, an employee, a mentor, a neighbor, a citizen, a community leader, and so on. Further, as men parent, they also age and experience the effects of other relationships, education, culture, and other significant shapers of developmental outcomes. Given such a complex array of variables, how can anyone be sure that changes attributed to parental involvement are not more directly the result of maturing, learning, or some other factor? In short, all of this adds up to low priority scores for grant proposals targeted toward studying a phenomenon so normative, natural, powerful, pervasive, and elusive.

To me, these challenges make the topic all the more intriguing. Since spring 1991, I have systematically read the available literature, conceptualized possible relations between parenting and adult development, written and presented theory papers on this topic, and designed and conducted the study represented in this book.

Recent debates on the role of values in researchers' approaches to studying a phenomenon consider whether or not it is important for investigators to disclose their beliefs, values, and biases that are likely to influence the design, execution, and analyses of their research data. Although there is not a clear consensus in regard to these issues, I personally subscribe to the view that researchers are inevitably biased (i.e., nonobjective) in their inquiries, and an increase in intellectual honesty is achieved as scholars examine their own training and values, and the effects these may exert on their work. Further, if the known influences are explicitly stated, it gives readers an understanding of the lens(es) through which the study was designed, the data were collected and analyzed, and the report written. I believe that such disclosure, although previously viewed to be "unscientific" or "anti-intellectual," allows a greater degree of evaluation and objectivity on the part of both researcher and reader. For these reasons, I will briefly describe some factors that have undoubtedly shaped my approach to the topics of this book.

First, I know that my research on fathering has been indelibly influenced by the fact that I am an actively engaged father. My academic interest in fathering can be directly traced to my graduate school days, when after 5 years of "steady dating" and 3 years of marriage, my wife and I were expecting our first child as I was selecting a dissertation topic. Because of the coursework I had taken, I was supposed to be an "expert" in child development, yet I came to the unsettling realization that there was much I did not know about how to be a father. I decided to study father involvement in infancy, hoping to find a "job description" for my new role as a dad. Our first son was born months before my dissertation was completed, but this launched a 20-plus year pursuit of fathering research. That research has continuously been paralleled, tempered, challenged, shaped, and qualified by my active engagement, with my wife, in coparenting our four sons (currently ages 12, 15, 19, and 22).

The tensions of having qualifications as a "father research expert" sometimes present a daunting task in trying to be a good dad. There have been many times while working on fathering research in general, and this book in particular, that the tensions to find the balance between being a productive and responsible worker and an engaged father loomed large. For example, part of the time that I was working on the analyses for this book, I was on sabbatical leave. During a nice spring week, I was camping with Judy, my wife, and Ian and Shane, our two youngest sons. The trip was a mix of work and leisure. While they were engaged in home schooling activities, I was reading interview transcripts. I was feeling the need to accomplish much in regard to the analyses, as the end of my sabbatical leave was rapidly approaching. I went off to work in my favorite "office" atmosphere (sitting by a trout stream with rocks, hemlocks, rhododendrons, and moving water). I was reading fathers' comments about their own fathers and how little time their dads had spent with them (data that eventually contributed to chap. 9). Many of the men's statements were filled with bitterness, resentment, and an abiding hurt that left a weighted sense of the importance of regularly engaging with kids as they grow up. I clearly realized that over time, when my kids think back to our working camping trip, they would not reflect on it and say, "Gee, it was a great trip—Dad knocked out analyses for two chapters!" I was torn between feeling the pressure to make progress on the book and being the kind of dad they will remember as somebody who took the time to "fool around" with them and focus on their interests even when I was busy. So when the morning's work was done, I packed my transcripts away and we spent the afternoon hiking and wading in the streams. We discovered some wonderfully refreshing things, in addition to numbing pools at the foot of cascading waterfalls that afternoon. Now when I reflect on that working camping trip, there will be some warm memories of shared times that will far outlast the value of an afternoon of analytic progress. I have also had a heightened appreciation for the extent to which my academic work on fathering has been greatly shaped and enriched by my involvement in my sons' lives.

As I have designed and conducted this study, I have reflected on how I have been shaped as a person by being a dad who is involved in the life of my family. I realize that my perceptions are not objective, and I could never conclusively demonstrate that developmental changes are causally related to fathering, but I have a sense that because I am a dad I have become somewhat less selfish, more playful, less egocentric, and more sensitive to the feelings and perspectives of others. I have purposed to be less of a workaholic and more flexible. Partly because of interactions with my children, I have become more of a man of faith, health, love, patience, and laughter. I am more open to trying new things than I used to be. Because of the encouragement and teaching of my sons, I have taken up guitar playing—something I had always wanted to do, but never invested the time to learn. Through my interactions with my kids, I have become more aware of my faults, limitations, and things that trigger negative reactions. I have become more invested in facilitating the development of the next generation of children and teens in our community, and more engaged in volunteer work with foster children and orphans. I have grown to be more connected to and appreciative of my own Dad. I have come to see that little things really do make a big difference, and I am more invested in doing those little things. Through my involvement as a dad, I have come to a practical understanding that roles have a way of drawing you into consistency when you do not feel consistent. You feel the pull to do expected things for your kids or wife, "because you're the dad." When we invest in being a dad, the role exerts a pressure that is beyond the self and makes us better people than we would have ever become apart from the role. I have seen that the "costs" of engaged fathering include reduced individuality, decreased freedom, greater responsibility, increased stress, less predictability, and some loss of "order." The benefits are in depth of relationship, richness of memories, and the joys of watching as your children grow and develop into unique and capable adults.

In short, for much of my career development and much of my personal growth, I am forever grateful for and indebted to my children for what I have learned through the opportunity to be involved with them. I know, in ways that surpass the theories and data of developmental textbooks, that fathering changes men's adult development. Reflecting on my own adult development has created some dissatisfaction with our current capabilities as social scientists.

It has concerned me for some time that it is often the case that textbooks on life-span development or family studies present a broad array of theories and data, yet students can complete introductory courses without anything beyond a general understanding of why they are the way they are. Somehow, textbook presentations of theories and data are a bit too sterile, or they are so general that they fail to capture the unique realities of the daily lives and incremental changes that people experience in their own lives and in their families as they enact different roles and go about the business (and pleasures) of everyday life. Even the best of boxed vignettes do not offer the depth of analysis necessary to nurture significant levels of self-understanding in students.

My training as a developmental psychologist has contributed to my perception of and appreciation for the continuity of development despite maturation and role changes. At the simplest level, with a notable exception or two that are not central to this discussion, I subscribe to the eloquent developmental theory of song writer/performer Paul Simon: "After changes upon changes, we are more or less the same." This statement captures the time-tested and empirically supported balance between continuity and discontinuity, consistency and change.

With these musings as a backdrop, it should come as no surprise that I would view my development as a research scientist to have its genesis in childhood interests and characteristics. I see my current academic foci as grounded in earlier experiences. I would say that after changes upon changes in terms of methodologies and topics of interest and even disciplinary alignment, as a researcher, I am more or less the same as I was as a child.

As a child, I was a model builder. I can still remember the interest and excitement I experienced on one summer evening as John, a family friend, showed me the models he had recently completed. That night I decided to pursue model building. Although I experimented with ships and planes, and had an intricate layout of HO gauge trains and cars, I had my baptism into model building with car models. At first, because of lack of experience, confidence, and patience, I built them "right out of the box," carefully following all of the directions. Later, in my development as a model builder, I created elaborate multicolored paint schemes to make the finished models look more realistic. The climax of my childhood model building career was characterized by adding realistic touches, like mud around the wheel wells (*real* mud, not painted mud), glue or heat-induced dents in doors, and my masterpiece of reality, small pieces of trash in the back seat. In retrospect, I recognize that I viewed the models as a representation of a perceived reality. I have some meticulous friends, but I have seen few cars that maintain their showroom appearance over time. Perhaps that is why I did not like the sterile and uniform nature of the out of the box models. In my experience, real cars have real mud, real scratches and dents, and real trash.

On further reflection, I recognize that I am still a model builder, and my career as a researcher has not been much different than my metamorphosis as a childhood model builder. As an undergraduate and early in my graduate training, I was happy to be a consumer of out of the box theories to explain, predict, and control developmental phenomena. At first exposure to developmental theories, I admired them with a wide-eyed appreciation that resembled my impressions of John's car models. However, it was not long before I began to realize that the theories of life-span development were much like unaltered car models, reasonably capable of representing the generalized showroom state, but not particularly detailed as far as representing the character-giving alterations that come with the unique individual histories of real change over time. I began to reflect on friends' and acquaintances' real-world experiences and to collect data that brought alterations to out of the box models, modifying existing representations of individual and family development as people pass milestones, take scenic detours, and deal with road hazards in their distinctively personal styles. These are the characteristics that add unique individual differences to people's paths to maturity and build character and practical wisdom that defies mass production of one model or universal theorizing.

Because my undergraduate and graduate training also included a healthy dose of ethology (the study of animal behavior), I have logged many hours in conducting observational studies of different species. I have seen the differences in the behaviors of animals in their natural environments versus laboratory and even man made "ecologically friendly" settings. As a result, I have come to value real-world data, and models and theories that can encompass and handle their "reality." I have come to recognize that there is a world of difference between theories and models based on sterile experimental designs and those grounded in the unpredictability of everyday "life in the trenches."

As a developmental scholar, I recognize that I am still a model builder at heart, and I continue to value models that capture my understanding of the real world. I do not see myself as particularly theoretical, at least in a formal sense. Although I have read (and taught) extensively in different theories of life-span development and family studies, and I frequently serve as a presenter or discussant in an annual theory construction conference, I have not fully embraced any single theory or family of theories as particularly comprehensive in its explanation of the complexities of human or family development. I have not yet found a theory that is simultaneously general enough to explain the diversity of human experience and specific enough to offer detailed renderings of individuals' unique and complex developmental histories. I view theories as imperfect representations of reality, but expect that they should present a reasonable rendering of the reality they are intended to symbolize. To date, I have not found any theories that satisfactorily explain the effects of parenting on adult development, and the unique accumulations of "mud, dents, and trash" (or positive custom enhancements) that parents experience along the road to maturity as they engage with their children as they grow and develop.

Perhaps, for all of these reasons, my research has recently shifted from quantitative analyses and has gravitated toward interviews and qualitative methodologies. I want to know the details and interrelations between what everyday fathers think and feel and believe about themselves as dads and the effects their children are having on their development. Analyses of interview data are uniquely suited to allow a researcher, who is so invested, to build realistic models that represent unique custom alterations while simultaneously having real mud on the fenders, dents in the doors, and trash in the back seat. It is also possible for innovators to dabble in areas where out of the box models do not exist, to create their own models from scratch (e.g., in areas like the relations between father involvement in raising children and the development of men's faith, morality, and values). I have yet to craft a fully elaborated developmental theory from my qualitative studies, however, I would like to think that I am making progress toward building some decent models by qualifying or altering existing theories and models, and by building some models from scratch. By analyzing the discourse of study participants, it is possible to find some universal themes of involved fathers (the production-line showroom-type model) and yet to represent "custom" touches of individual developmental histories. Again, in this regard, as a researcher, after many changes, I am more or less the same as I was as a child.

Finally, as a "dad in the trenches," I am often acutely aware of the difficulties of simultaneously trying to juggle all of the responsibilities of being a father, husband, professor, provider, friend, and active community participant. Many days, it is difficult to keep a perspective on what really matters versus the distractions that cry for attention. For years, I have actively and consciously struggled with balance. The balances I achieve in any of these roles and their various facets is always tentative, shifting, and my best shot at what is needed given the resources and demands at the time. Balance was a universal and pressing theme that emerged as I interviewed 40 diverse men who were all struggling with balancing the various demands of active lives. I resisted accepting this as a central unifying theme for this book for over a year of analyzing the transcripts because I knew the pervasiveness of balance issues in my own life. After careful consideration and thorough examination for other themes, and with reassuring encouragement from graduate and undergraduate students who worked with portions of the data set in courses, balance emerged as the unifying theme. As men work through the issues of being involved fathers, providers, and so on, the balances achieved are truly provisional, making their contributions to adult development all the more elusive. As Pipher (1999) states in *Another Country,* "Balancing needs is tricky" (p. 24).

It is my hope that this book will provide its readers with a realistic and useful beginning point to bring a synthesis of developmental theories, family studies perspectives, and men's insights about fathering that will enhance academic understanding of fathering and adult development. However, I am equally invested in having this book spark reflective and practical application for fathers and families, whether readers are academicians, practitioners, policymakers or fathers in the trenches!

I

Foundations for Understanding Fathering and Development

Chapter 1

The Effects of Parenting on Adult Development: What the Theories and Data Tell Us

The child is father to the man.

—William Wordsworth

Wordsworth's observation and wisdom suggested that the child is father to the man. Wordsworth (1802/1992) briefly and eloquently stated the premise of this book nearly two centuries ago: In assuming responsibility for actively fathering a child, engagement in the roles of fathering exerts a developmental pull on a father that catalyzes his growth into maturity and new levels of adult development. By engaging in active fathering across time, men mature differently than they would if they were not fathers. Fathers' involvement with their children provides a pervasive and rich context for developmental change and maturity that is distinct from and that provides different developmental outcomes from not being an actively involved father. Interestingly, although fathers are able to address the perceived developmental consequences of fathering, in comparison to other aspects of human development and family studies, social scientists have not devoted significant time or energy to studying the relations between fathering and men's adult development.

At the risk of stating an obvious, yet often forgotten or overlooked fact, fathers are only fathers because of relationships. There is no such thing as a father independent of relationships. A father is only a father in relation to a child, yet father–child relationships are not isolated from the effects of other relationships, and the array of different types of father–child relationships is quite diverse. A man becomes a biological father as a result of a relationship with the child's birth mother. Biological fathering is the result of a biological act with differing degrees of planning, intentionality, emotion, and commitment across different relationships. However, becoming a social father, making the transition to fatherhood (P. A. Cowan, 1991), is a different process involving different functions and dynamics (Daniels & Weingarten, 1988). Doherty, Kouneski, and Erickson (1998, p. 278) asserted that sociological and historical analyses clearly establish that, beyond insemination, fathering is "fundamentally a social construction," with each cohort shaping its cultural ideal of fathers. Garbarino (2000) observed that people are currently reinventing social fatherhood. Social fathering is a decision that can be made independent of biological status. To embrace social fathering, a man must engage in a significant reorganization of both identity and role enactment (P. A. Cowan, 1991). LaRossa (1988) noted the discrepancy between the ideals that cohorts set forth (the culture of fatherhood) and the ways that fathering roles are actually enacted (the conduct of fatherhood). According to Lamb (2000, p. 37):

> In any pluralistic society, various conceptions of the father's role coexist, so that while journalists and filmmakers in the United States have been lauding active and nurturant fathering for the last 10 years, many citizens continue to hold very different conceptions of fathering. In addition, one must recognize that fathers fill many roles, and the relative importance of each varies from one cultural context to another. Thus, active fathering must be viewed in the context of the multiple activities that fathers undertake for and with their children (for example, breadwinning, sex-role modeling, moral guidance, emotional support of mothers).

Demographic analyses would indicate that social fatherhood by nonbiological fathers is increasing as a growing array of men are being perceived to have fatherlike roles in children's lives, in part, because increasing numbers of biological fathers are disengaging from their children or were never actively involved (Marsiglio, Day, & Lamb, 2000, p. 273).

Good fathering across time is a commitment that reflects an ongoing set of decisions that have behavioral, cognitive, and affective components (Palkovitz, 1997), as well as developmental consequences for both fathers and their children (Palkovitz, 1996a). Demographic data reveal that a social father is most often in a relationship with the child's mother, at least initially. But oftentimes, changes in the relationship with the child's mother bring significant changes in the father–child relationship. This is true whether the mother to whom the father is relating is the birth mother, a stepmother, or a mother figure to the child. So, whereas fathers are fathers in relation to one or more children, the father–child relationship varies by fathering context and is influenced by the changing nature of other relationships.

The assertion that fathering has developmental consequences for men does not refer to the biological act of procreating a child. It is engagement in social fathering, involvement in relationships with children (whether or not you are the biological father), relating to them, taking responsibility for them, entering into their world, planning for their future, providing for them, protecting them, and wanting them to prosper in their own development that challenges adult males to grow into a new level of maturity. It is fathers' ongoing exposure to alternative perspectives, contingencies, emotions, demands, interactions, wishes, desires, fears, hurts, dreams, friendships, and needs that pull men toward new levels of developmental functioning. When a man commits his life to fathering, in many regards, the child becomes father to the man.

As men apply themselves to active engagement in fathering, they immerse themselves into a rapidly changing and complex array of shifting conditions. When men view "good fathering" as an ideal to subscribe to, it brings a different set of circumstances and therefore different developmental outcomes than deciding not to engage in fathering. Involved fathers do develop differently than men who do not engage in fathering. In a four-decade study of fathering, Snarey (1993) stated: "Most men today want to be good fathers. Many also have come to see that fathering is potentially the most satisfying and probably the most demanding task that the life cycle has to offer them. They sense that the experiences of child rearing are about as enjoyable, and about as difficult, as life usually gets" (p. 311).

The biological act of fathering a child is neither necessary nor sufficient to foster men's maturity. However, the evidence garnered in this book demonstrates that, from fathers' perspectives, active engagement in social fathering roles—direct ongoing interaction with and responsibility for raising children—creates a rich and pervasive context for men's adult development. Although there are costs of involved fathering, men who apply themselves to regular, ongoing responsibility for and interaction with their children reap benefits in terms of their own perceived health, happiness, purpose, and development.

Arguably, this characterization sounds like a uniformly positive endorsement of father involvement. That is not the intention. There are seen cases where a father's style and/or level of involvement is detrimental to his children's development. Fathers who are abusive, substance dependent, or unpredictably vacillating between warmth and harshness, and those who are consistently detached or absent, create developmental deficits for their children to overcome. Based on such observations, more father involvement is not a panacea for all families. Most people know some families where either or both parents would benefit from greater involvement from the other partner. In contrast, in some observed families, either or both parents would benefit from less involvement from the other partner. Similarly, what is best for an individual parent or child may not be best for each of the family members or the good of society. So although greater involvement is not always better, this book does argue that greater involvement has greater potential to affect the development of all persons associated with the relationship.

As different aspects of father involvement and men's adult development are systematically presented and discussed, this book attempts to represent the perceptions and experiences of 40 diverse fathers who embraced father involvement, and who perceived that ongoing commitment to have altered the course of their development as people. It is my attempt to understand, from a contextually sensitive position as a scholar of life-span development and life-course perspectives, how men in the sample viewed father involvement to influence their lives. The aim is to convey their stories as accurately as possible and to place their perceptions and their words into a developmental framework so that social scientists, as policymakers, and as developing people, can better understand what a commitment to fathering affords men as they develop, as well as what father involvement does for children, families, and their communities.

This presentation is not to be used to as an argument for the necessity of fathering as a vehicle for men's maturity. First, this sample only consisted of men who were active fathers. The study did not include a comparison group of men who are child free by choice or circumstance. No doubt, each reader knows a number of men who are not actively fathering, and who are as developmentally advanced, well adjusted, and fully functional as any involved fathers. Some child-free men are model citizens, and have been generative through their contributions to work, the arts, philanthropy, volunteer service, political involvement, religious commitment, and countless other contributions to society. On the contrary, there are men who have conceived children, and who are not mature, productive, well-adjusted individuals. They are biological fathers, but they have not fully embraced social fathering. Some of the most distressing problems in contemporary society are related to "players" who father multiple children and abandon them and their mothers, providing little or no support for either. Less dramatic, but far more prevalent, are cases where men who have fathered children show little direct engagement in their daily lives. They throw themselves fully into the world of work or into other adult activities and do not directly interact with their children to any significant extent. They may justify their lack of direct contact and engagement with their children by their commitment to economic provision, but nonetheless, they leave an atmosphere of neglect and abandonment for their children to work through. By various criteria (see, e.g., Allport, 1961; Erikson, 1980; Farrell & Rosenberg, 1981; Gilligan, 1982; Heath, 1991; Snarey, 1993), these men are not particularly mature. Each reader can also think of families they know where a father's involvement is less than optimal for different family members. As a developmentalist and a family scholar, I am aware of cases that fit these categories. Thus, as a social scientist, I am fully convinced that father involvement is neither necessary nor sufficient to foster adult men's development. However, from interviewing these 40 diverse fathers, each with his own challenges and struggles as men trying to be good dads, I am convinced that men view father involvement to be pivotal in shaping their lives and maturity. That is the story I hope to convey through this book.

Empirical research on fathering in the 1970s and 1980s concluded that men's positive involvement in children's lives yields positive results for children's development (Pleck, 1997). More recently, it has become evident that good fathering is good for mothers and marriages. For example, Parke and Brott (1999) reported that the more support mothers get from involved fathers, the happier they are in their marriages. Snarey (1993) found that a father's involvement during earlier adulthood was related to men's successful midlife attainment of a stable marriage and positively correlated with marital satisfaction. It has also been established that good fathering is good for communities in that father involvement in childrearing and moral education is associated with lower school drop out rates and lower juvenile crime rates (McKeown, Ferguson, & Rooney, 1998). Data also indicate that fathers' involvement with their children is frequently associated with fathers' participation in community organizations (A. Rossi, 1984; Snarey, 1993). The data presented in this book indicate that good fathering is good for fathers as well. Good fathering has the potential to foster men's adult development and is perceived by fathers to yield gains in social, emotional, physical health, and career development.

Understanding that fathering is not the only pathway to generativity, and that there are fallacies in adopting a universal "more is better" approach to father involvement, it should be recognized that good fathering is accompanied by different developmental paths in men, and is associated with positive developmental outcomes for children, partners, families, and communities. In short, good fathering is good for everyone.

A REVIEW OF PERTINENT PROFESSIONAL LITERATURE

For nearly 50 years, developmental psychologists and family scholars have posited that parenting facilitates adult development. Erikson (1950) originated the notion of *generativity*, simply defined as the ability to care for the next generation. He asserted that parenting, the most common route to generativity, is a major role in adulthood characterized by numerous occasions and requirements for personal reorganization and maturation (Erikson, 1968). Erikson (1964, p. 130) depicted parenthood as "the first, and for many, the prime generative encounter." More recently, Eriksonian theorists have explicitly described parenthood as a necessary, but not sufficient, condition for the achievement of generativity (cf. Anthony & Benedek, 1970; Farrell & Rosenberg, 1981, Snarey, 1993). Simply stated, parenting has been broadly identified as the chief catalyst of adult development, but the particulars of causal links between parenting and adult development have not been detailed, particularly through empirical research.

During the past 20 years, numerous reports have been published in the professional literature to more solidly substantiate the theoretical relation between parenting and adult development (see, e.g., Hawkins, Christiansen, Sargent, & Hill, 1993; Palkovitz, 1996a). Parke (1981, p. 11) stated that "fathering ... may be good for men" in a developmental sense. Daniels and Weingarten (1988, p. 36) described parenthood as a "powerful generator of development," stating that it "affects those who become engaged in it in profound and particular ways." P. R. Newman and B. M. Newman (1988, p. 313) proposed probable causal links between involvement in parenting and development during adulthood, asserting that "if any new experiences of adulthood were to produce a period of openness to new learning and to stimulate new coping strategies, parenting must certainly be a prime candidate." Cowan (1988, p. 14) noted that whereas it is inappropriate to view fatherhood as a developmental stage, there is "merit to considering fatherhood as an opportunity for increased differentiation and integration, a qualitative developmental change that can be summarized using ... [Allport's 1961] ... concept of maturity." Colarusso and Neimiroff (1982, p. 317) stated that "it is clear that the experience of fatherhood during midlife is potentially a strong stimulus to continued adult development." The European Commission Network on Childcare (1993) suggested that the impact of children on fathers' development could be just as significant as the impact of fathers on the development of children. In an examination of the relations between parenting and adult development, Palkovitz (1996a) hypothesized that "parents engaging in greater involvement with their children will show greater developmental change in comparison to parents who are less involved in child rearing or adults not involved in raising children" (p. 573). Although this type of reasoning is widespread and congruous with developmental theory, empirical research specifically designed to test such claims is rare.

Ambert (1992, p. 5) interjected that "while the topics of reciprocity of effect and child effect were brought in two decades ago, the general literature merely pays lip service to them." The viewpoints expressed in the professional developmental literature mirror the nearly unanimous position of layperson parents: They are confident that they are very different people than they would have been had they never had children (Palkovitz, 1994). What is even more interesting than Ambert's observation of superficial coverage of child effects on parents is the fact that no data are available to conclusively support the position that parenting causes the development of adults.

Contemporary demography substantiates the fact that American men are less likely to be fathers than in the past, and are more likely to have fewer children and to have less leisure time (that could be spent with families) than men in the past 50 years (Johnson, 1992). Despite these trends, fathering is still the most prevalent developmental context of adult men around the world. Developmentalists have long recognized that contextual elements exert substantial influence on developmental outcomes. Since over 90% of all people invest a significant portion of their adult time and energy focused on various aspects of parenting children, it seems that it would be fruitful to study the effects of parenting on adult development. Although there is a considerable theoretical base, and a prevalent understanding by professionals and laypersons alike that the experiences of parenting significantly affect daily lives, until recently, the long-term developmental consequences of parenting have been largely ignored.

Long-term, qualitative, developmental outcome effects have seldom been explicated to advance beyond theoretical or anecdotal analyses. A majority of the research data available to address this important issue tend to be bivariate in nature, derived from cross-sectional designs, and incapable of dispelling a reinterpretation in favor of reciprocal or multivariate influence.

The assertion that fathering is a significant generator of adult male development forfeits some of its attraction when the plausible developmental contributions of other socializing influences are appraised (e.g., marriage, work, community involvement, social networks). Further complicating the issue is the fact that fatherhood and its associated roles are permeable. The role of father overlaps with and is penetrated by roles in other competing and interrelated trajectories and contexts of development (see chap. 3, this vol.). Parenting behavior, cognitions, and emotions are intercontingent with behavior, cognitions, and emotions in the world of work, other relationships, and a range of responsibilities indirectly related or unrelated to fathering (Palkovitz, 1996a). Simply stated, parenting does not occur in a contextual vacuum. Parenting represents a complex set of ongoing transitions and developmental processes extending across time, exhibiting varied configurations of investment at different times, and concomitant with other ongoing role prescriptions, life-course transitions, and investments of men's time, attention, and energy. As the following review demonstrates, the current database is unable to substantiate that it is fathering per se, rather than aging or simultaneous investments and transitions within other domains, that is responsible for developmental change in men. How is it possible to be sure that it is parenting and not aging, maturation, or the effects of marriage, education, or other factors that accounts for observed developments in fathers?

The answers to these questions have important implications for furthering an understanding of developmental mechanisms in general and adult development in particular. The remainder of this chapter elaborates on what is and is not known in reference to the previous questions. It briefly reviews selected research findings regarding parenting and development and sets the stage for a research design for the study presented in the remainder of this book.

Before continuing, it is important to state two disclaimers: First, this analysis is not intended to be an exhaustive formulation of relevant theoretical positions and research findings. Selected portions of the literature have been examined to develop the central premises that adult development is profoundly influenced by the events, contexts, and experiences associated with parenting, and that these experiences alter the course, quality, and texture of developmental trajectories throughout adulthood, producing a divergent path in comparison to nonparents. Even if parents and nonparents do not function at different levels of maturity or complexity, they are likely to experience development differently. From a parent's vantage point, these experiential differences represent distinctly different paths through the life course. Second, this review is not intended to indicate that either parenting or childlessness is superior to or more preferable than the other. It is intended to stimulate focused scientific inquiry into the different developmental trajectories that parents and nonparents traverse.

PARENTING AND ADULT DEVELOPMENT: A SELECTED REVIEW

As previously stated, it is assumed that fathers who engage in greater amounts of involvement with their children will manifest more developmental change as compared to men who are less involved in childrearing or fathers who are not at all involved in raising children. Being a father has uniquely different meanings to different individuals, and the ways in which individual fathers envision, enact, integrate, and differentiate their roles varies considerably. Clearly, all fathers are not equally involved in the care of their children (Palkovitz, 1980, 1984, 1997). Keep in mind that there is great diversity in the fathering relationships defined here. When "fathers" are discussed as though fathers are a homogenous group, it masks the great diversity of fathers, their contexts of being involved, the developmental characteristics they have, the challenges they face, and their responses to these variables at any given time, as well as patterns across time.

When cataloging variability in contexts for fathering relationships and involvement, the listing is considerable. Fathers vary by residential status (co-residential, nonresidential but living in the nearby area, nonresidential living far away) (Mott, 1990; Seltzer, 1991; Seltzer & Bianchi, 1988), educational level (which effects egalitarianism and knowledge of child development and developmentally appropriate practice), employment status (from unemployed, voluntarily or non; part time; full time; holding multiple jobs; blue collar; white collar; hours of nonwork time; security of employment) (Christiansen & Palkovitz, 2001; Teachman, Call, & Carver, 1994), income (adequacy, percentage of family income contributed and total family income; other support obligations, such as alimony or child support from previous relationships), relationship with own father (primacy of modeling vs. reworking, warmth vs. emotional distance, etc.) (Sachs, 1983; Snarey, 1993), marital status (cohabiting, married, separated, divorced, remarried, re-cohabiting) (Pasley & Minton, 1997), marital quality (C. P. Cowan & P. A. Cowan, 1987; Cox, Owen, Lewis, & Henderson, 1989), supports and hindrances toward involvement (Allen & Hawkins, 1999; C. P. Cowan & P. A. Cowan, 1987), personality (Palkovitz, 1980), health, type of fathering relationship (biological, stepparenting, adoptive, fictive kin, early timing, on time, late timing), types (and blends) of involvement engaged in (engagement, accessibility, responsibility) (Lamb, Pleck, & Levine, 1987; Pleck, 1997), predominant parenting style (authoritarian, authoritative, indulgent-permissive, indifferent-uninvolved) (Baumrind, 1975), beliefs about the fathers' role (Palkovitz, 1980, 1984), cultural background (Hewlett, 2000), ethnicity (McAdoo, 1988, 1993), individual skill levels (Palkovitz, 1980), and motivation (Lamb, 2000). This list is not exhaustive, but it does represent variables that are frequently reported in various studies of father involvement, and begins to show the multidimensional aspect of fathering and the complexity of the issues under investigation.

There is a small but growing body of literature considering the effects of children on their parents. Table 1.1 summarizes reported or assumed differences between parents and nonparents appearing in selected segments of the professional literature. For the purpose of condensing and organizing the information in the most useful manner, findings have been arranged into categories of development that relate to the different domains of development: self, social, and work. As the reader can readily observe, reported or assumed differences between parents and nonparents are indeed substantial. Specifically, compiling these citations in this manner shows that the professional literature asserts that, in comparison to nonparents, parents experience a different set of ongoing circumstances and environmental stimulation and are reported to manifest different patterns of cognitive, personality, emotional, and affective development. Parents are portrayed as having increased social-cognitive awareness, more clear and explicit values, greater connection to their own developmental histories, and a higher magnitude of change in health habits than nonparent peers. Parents are also said to perceive that they hold a greater degree of responsibility than nonparents. However, the linkages between reported differences, existing empirical data, and theories of adult development are, for the most part, unelaborated. Snarey (1993, p. 117) stated:

> The actual dynamics by which parental generativity may promote fathers' personal maturity are, of course, very complex and not fully understood. Part of the process, however, seems to hinge on a father becoming bonded, committed to a child who periodically makes demands upon him which he simply is not prepared to meet. The resulting disequilibrium promotes the development of increased complexity in the father's cognitive, emotional, and behavioral repertoire in order to meet the basic needs of this one for whom he would willingly sacrifice all.

TABLE 1.1

Relations Between Parenting and Adult Development

Cognitive Development	*Emotional/Affective Development*
Discrepancies between competencies and expectations[I,O]	Regulation of emotion[c,H,I,K,l,O]
Disequilibrium and Reorganization of thinking[c,O]	Expansion of caring[b,f,I,O]
Engagement in more probabilistic thinking[I,O]	Depth of commitment[l]
Engagement in more contingency- based thinking[I]	Empathy[H,I,l]
More dialectical thinking[J,I]	Emotional reactivity[I,O]
More anticipation of the future[I,O]	
Increased competence in problem solving[c]	**Responsibility[b,D,K,O]**
Social Cognition	**Values Made More Clear and Explicit[b,H,I,K,O,q]**
Expansion of consciousness[I,O]	Philosophy of life[l]
Greater allocentrism, improved perspective-taking ability[a,c,H,I,K,O]	Religious beliefs/faith[O]
Greater self-awareness[h,l,q]	Moral issues[b,l,O]
Personality Development[c]	*Childlike Qualities and Connection to the Early Years[c,H,K,l,O]*
Locus of control[a,c,l]	
General trait changes (e.g., patience, control, altruism, flexibility)[O]	**Changes in Health Habits[H,K]**
Competence/self-esteem[c,H,J,l,O,P,q]	
Maturity in identity[C,H,J]	Dietary changes[A,O]
Vital commitment[C]	Changes in exercise[O]
Generativity[e,g,K,O,R]	Changes in substance use/abuse[O]
Gender-typing[b,C,M,N,O,P]	Changes in sleep[O]
Changes in Health Habits[H,K]	

Notes: Superscripted letters correspond to the references listed below. Capitalized letters indicate supportive data and lowercase letters indicate that the citation is for theoretical, speculative, or anecdotal evidence

[a]Aljadir (1988); [b]Ambert (1992); [c]P. Cowan (1988); [d]Daniels & Weingarten (1988); [e]Erikson (1968); [f]Gutmann (1975); [g]Hawkins et al. (1993); [h]Heath (1978); [i]Heath (1991); [j]Hoffman & Mannis (1979); [k]Hooker & Fiese (1993); [l]P. R. Newman & B. M. Newman (1988); [m]Palkovitz (1980); [n]Palkovitz (1984); [o]Palkovitz (1994); [p]Palkovitz & Copes (1988); [q]Parke (1981); [r]Snarey (1993).

Empirical Findings

There are a number of empirical studies that report relations between parental involvement and adult development outcomes. In a pioneering longitudinal study of men during early adulthood, Heath (1978) noted changes in fathers' attitudes and values during their child's gestation, but little evidence of continuing effects of fatherhood on men's maturing. Heath (1978) speculated that the lack of enduring effects was because fathers' participation in caring for infants during their first year was too minimal. This assertion is consistent with the hypothesis (Palkovitz, 1996a) that changes in parental development are positively related to involvement with children. Of particular interest, Heath (1978) reported that fathers in his study consistently demonstrated greater degrees of maturity and psychological health than a comparison group of married men who were not fathers. Although the data suggest that fatherhood may facilitate maturation, the finding cannot be viewed to be conclusive. Small sample size, lack of representativeness, and lack of specialized measures precludes ruling out other factors such as occupational contributions to maturity. According to Heath (1978), "Another factor may be that paternal competence among American professionals is just not central to one's identity, particularly in the early years of marriage and career" (p. 277). This statement supports the notion that it is the salience of the parental role that determines the extent of its effect on adult development. Further, the maturing effects were nominal and did not appear to have enduring qualities.

P. A. Cowan (1991) also submitted that parenthood has an effect on adults' maturity and elaborates that maturity can be operationalized in terms of differentiation and integration, concluding that it should be feasible to construct measures of maturity based on these constructs and existing work. In a vein convergent to Cowan's, Heath (1991) wrote extensively in regard to maturity. Specifically, Heath stated that

> while individuals walk seemingly idiosyncratic and diverse paths to maturing, their trek can be described similarly. The paths lead to minds and characters (interpersonal skills, values, and self-concepts) that are more reflectively aware, other-centered, well integrated, stable and autonomous. They lead in the same direction for persons of any age, sex, and cultural background. (p. 116)
>
> Fatherhood may further a man's maturing and that if it does, its probable principal effects are to increase his awareness of himself, his values, and familial relationships, the allocentric quality of his values and family relationships, and the acceptance and integration of his emotional needs. (p. 276)

Despite the contributions of Cowan and Heath, the relation between father involvement and men's developmental maturity has not been systematically studied. Given the relatively high levels of conceptualization in these areas, it appears to be a fruitful place to direct empirical efforts. These characteristics of maturity represent constructs that can be explored through open-ended interviews.

A. S. Rossi (1980) reviewed literature on differences in life priorities between men and women in adulthood and concluded that the "first priority has been to family for women, to work for men" (p. 26). Although this synopsis can surely be rebutted by innumerable individual exceptions and the fact that it reflects cohort effects, other family scholars have concurred with the direction of differences. Thurnher (1974) found that the major midlife transition for a majority of women coincides with the transition to the empty nest, whereas for men it is associated with termination of careers. Dinnerstein (1976; quoted in Hawkins et al., 1993, p. 546) connected gender, parental investment, and developmental differences in this manner: "The process of nurturing life is the most profoundly transforming experience in the range of human possibilities. Because women have this experience and men generally don't, we live and think and love across a great gap of understanding." Writers who have elaborated the construct of the nurturant father (e.g., A. Coleman & L. Coleman, 1988; Pruett, 1989; Russell, 1978) would take exception to the absolute manner in which gender differences have been represented by the previous statement.

A number of empirical investigations have discovered positive relations between parental involvement and various components of developmental maturity. Cross-sectional data from the Oakland Growth Study were interpreted by Speicher-Dubin (1982) to show a positive relation between fathers' caregiving involvement and men's moral development. Longitudinal data concerning relations between fathers' engagement in child care and men's functioning also reflected positive relationships in Vaillant's (1977) 35-year study of college men (Snarey et al., 1987), Sachs' (1983) transition to parenthood study with a matched comparison group of nonfathers, and Pruett's (1989) study of nurturing males. In cross-cultural comparisons, Gutmann (1991) found that parents in several cultures demonstrate less selfishness and more responsibility as they are involved in childrearing activities over time.

Snarey's (1993) book, summarizing a four-decade, longitudinal intergenerational study of father–child relationships, details the connections between men's differing fathering experiences and influences on marriage, occupational advancement, and generativity. It is the most comprehensive longitudinal study to date. For these purposes, there appears to be a growing body of evidence to suggest that varying patterns of paternal involvement differentially relate to men's status during midlife.

Bidirectionally sensitive, sequence-dependent research investigating the relations between parent and child interaction, behavior, and development have been conducted since the mid-1970s. Research conducted in this manner captures the interdependent nature of parent and child behavior, rejecting the notion that socialization is a one-way process. However, most studies conducted from this perspective focus on tightly prescribed behaviors and employ mocroanalytic techniques to study a span of seconds or minutes as opposed to major portions of the life span. In separate literature reviews, Peterson and Rollins (1987) and Ambert (1992) noted that though research studies conducted from the bidirectional perspective of parent–child socialization offer distinct advantages over unidirectional models, they are characterized by a number of flaws that need to be addressed. Specifically, most empirical studies have been limited to the infancy period, and later development has been neglected. A more serious inadequacy has been the failure of researchers to designate and elaborate theoretical concepts that clarify the nature, the antecedents, and the consequences of reciprocal interaction (Osofsky & Connors, 1979). As a result, a majority of bidirectional research has been limited to a narrow range of methodological issues, and the description of behavior sequences without sufficient concern for conceiving the developmental implications of the interaction. Although it is recognized that the relationship between parents and children influences the development of both (Belsky, 1984), the developmental consequences of parent–child relationships are even more elusive to study than the direct effects of parent–child interactions.

THE NEED FOR CONCEPTUAL ADVANCEMENTS

Peterson and Rollins (1987, p. 496) noted the superficiality of conceptual bases in addressing the relations between parenting and adult development. They suggested that the most productive tactic for scholars to advance understanding would be to "develop sound theories, to use sensitizing concepts, and to be realistically restrictive in the questions that they ask. Although various methodologies and statistics can be used to acquire and to summarize data, scholars ultimately must develop the concepts that give this information meaning. The latter task is the goal, whereas the former is only the means."

In order to follow this recommendation, there is much foundational work to be realized in regard to identification of principal issues and determination of suitable research methodologies for securing and evaluating the germane data. These are the underlying issues that motivated the design and implementation of the study reported here. After reviewing the literature described earlier, an exploratory study was conducted to investigate the perceived relations between fathers' involvement in childrearing and their adult development.

Interdisciplinary Issues

A significant component of the challenge in clarifying relations between fathering and men's adult development is associated with the fact that this field of inquiry is at the crossroads of disciplines; the pivotal issues remain somewhere in the interface between life-span development and family science. The field is not yet in the position where the disciplines share sufficient literatures, theories, nomenclatures, and methodologies to the degree required for substantive interdisciplinary integration. Developmentalists are inclined to focus on functional changes that occur in individuals (Baltes, 1979, 1987). Family sociologists (e.g., Hill & Mattessich, 1979) and life-course theorists (e.g., Elder, 1985, Hareven, 1977) focus on transitions made by families in the processes of reorganization and change (P. Cowan, 1988). To satisfactorily address the relations between parenting and adult development, it is imperative to employ theories and methods from each of these specialties. In seeking to link the disciplines, there are numerous barriers: finding collectively valued levels of analyses, suitable nomenclature, and acceptable data collection and analysis techniques.

Intradisciplinary Issues

Further obstacles lie within intradisciplinary dissentions concerning appropriate theoretical constructs, methodologies, and measures. For example, developmentalists do not agree on the characteristics of development that differentiate it from change. Dixon, Lerner, and Hultsch (1991, pp. 287–288) stated that "the concept of development is an essentially contested one, for which profound differences among models exist and for which there can be no final or absolute solution. ... There are no criteria (or very few stringent criteria) by which to distinguish development from change." Dixon et al. (1991) concluded that "it is immediately apparent, then, that the concept of development is what may be called (with no pejorative intent) an ill-defined, fuzzy, or blurred concept" (p. 287).

Part of the "fuzziness" results from the absolute volume and interactive complexity of factors influencing developmental outcomes. Lerner and Spanier (1978, p. 4) summarized Riegel's (1976) position that "development arises from a confluence of constantly changing inner-biological, individual-psychological, physical-environmental, and sociocultural-historical processes that are reciprocally embedded one in the other." This results in a "recognition that change can only be described through a pluralistic approach ... on both an empirical and a theoretical level behavior change processes should be seen as interdependent" (Lerner & Spanier, 1978, p. 6). Lerner and Spanier (1978) concluded that developmental explanations dictate enumeration of relationships between current behaviors and antecedent and/or concurrent conditions. The emphasis is on which variables account for intraindividual and interindividual change and how they do so. The examination of the relations between fathering and men's adult development has not yet realized this stage of refinement.

There is comparable variability in *what* family scholars are willing to call a life-course transition and in selection of appropriate criteria to demonstrate when and how transitions have occurred. Some approaches link transitions directly to events: "Occurrence represents the first and most basic property of a transition" (Elder, 1991, p. 33). Others propose that true transitions require inner and outer adjustments in the individual in response to life events (P. A. Cowan, 1991). P. A. Cowan (1991) also made the notable distinction that a developmental transition requires a restructuring of one's sense of self and one's assumptive world. The affective domain becomes involved through changes in inner coping. According to Cowen, "Transitions involve a qualitative shift in perceptions of oneself and the world, and an imbalance usually, but not always, followed by rebalance in our emotional equilibrium " (p. 15). Cowan additionally recognized that "concrete observable external actions and readjustments of adaptive behavior" (p. 15) should also accompany a true transition. Transitions include role adaptations. Yet, there is disagreement regarding measures suitable to capture these processes.

Nock (1982) thoroughly reviewed life-cycle approaches to family development. In doing so, he showed that it is routine to highlight an individual's progress through differing developmental tasks (Havinghurst, 1953) or the family's adaptations to differing phases of the life cycle (Rodgers, 1973). P. Cowan (1988, p. 21) noted that "in the simple life-cycle model, the mere fact that one becomes a parent advances men to a new developmental phase," yet this does little to specify how development has taken place, or even what has developed. These issues are crystalized by P. Cowan's (1988, p. 13)

> realization that my colleagues and I have been participating in research that provides extensive documentation of parents' negative changes and distress during the transition to parenthood, ... but which has not yet systematically investigated *development* in new fathers and mothers. This omission does not stem from deliberate oversight. It follows from the fact that there are reasonably good instruments for assessing problems and stress, but *we lack clear concepts of what developmental change should look like, and we lack instruments for assessing when that change has occurred.* (emphasis added)

P. Cowan further asserted that "there is no consensus about the markers that signal developmental progress as distinct from simple change in life circumstances [and that] ... very different types of markers have been used to answer these questions, each implying a different conceptualization of adult development" (1988, p. 21). Before expecting to see substantive increases in the ability to specify the relations between fathering and men's adult development, it is necessary to identify specific dependent variables where changes in development attributable to father involvement are expected. A likely place to begin is in interviewing fathers regarding the alleged changes summarized in Table 1.1.

POSSIBLE RELATIONS BETWEEN PARENTAL INVESTMENT AND ADULT DEVELOPMENT

Because adult development is multidimensional, multidirectional, and increasingly divergent between individuals with increasing age (Baltes, 1987), it is difficult to causally link any developmental "outcome" to a specific precursor (Hultsch & Plemons, 1979). An adult's developmental status is influenced by a multitude of variables, including the relationship the adult has with any child(ren) or a spouse or partner, the extent of that individual's investment in the development of a career, the individual's dedication to particular ideologies and opinions, personality characteristics, and genetic endowment.

Because there is a direct relation between the degree of investment in any given context and the influence that context will exert in terms of developmental outcomes, the developmental impact of parenting will be directly related to its cumulative salience in relation to other contexts of development. Yet it cannot be assumed that the level of fathers' involvement will predict the overall direction of development, it will merely effect the magnitude of developmental change. As elaborated in theoretical presentations (Palkovitz, 1994, 1996a), and as substantiated throughout this book, the direction of influence is likely to be different for various attributes, domains, and measures.

Analyses of the relations between father involvement and men's adult development require exploratory research because of the likely differences within and across domains. There is an abundance of theoretically and anecdotally based citations in the professional literature, but it is time to substantiate the claimed relationships between fathering and adult development by collecting data focused on specific perceived changes within each of the suggested areas of developmental difference. If we were to ask "what does a particular pattern of father involvement mean for the developmental status of a given father?", then the composite result would reflect some gains, some losses (Uttal & Perlmutter, 1989), and different developmental trajectories across and within domains across time (see Fig. 1.1). For example, in an individual case, decreased paternal involvement in children's lives following a divorce may be associated with decreases in self-esteem and reduced emotional expressiveness and simultaneous increases in risk-taking behavior and sex-typing. Furthermore, it would be ill advised to attribute these differences to changes in parental involvement per se. Perhaps concomitant changes associated with divorce, depression, residential relocation, and role changes are more directly related to changes in developmental status than is the changed level of father involvement.

Although it may be possible to describe general patterns of development associated with different levels of father involvement, it is important to identify and appreciate interindividual differences, a foundational focus

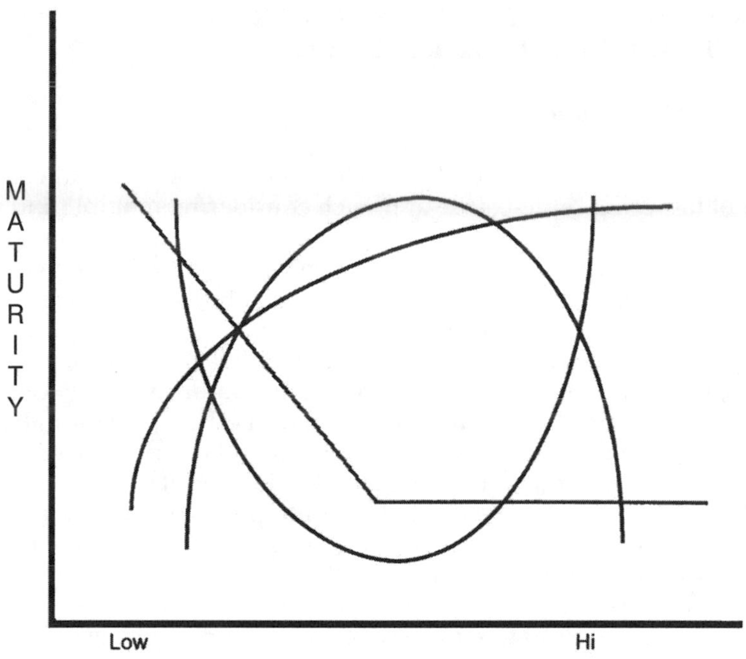

FIG. 1.1. Theoretical relationships between parental involvement and development. *Note:* Each trajectory could represent a composite score from different domains (e.g., self, family, work, social) or specific categories or measures within domains (e.g., marital communication, marital satisfaction, sexuality, sense of group membership).

of life-span developmental psychology. Existent literature demonstrates that the same pattern of parental involvement is likely to yield different developmental outcomes in persons varying from one another by age (Cooney, Pedersen, Indelicato, & Palkovitz, 1993), timing of transition to fatherhood (Cooney et al., 1993), race (Cazenave, 1979), ethnicity (Shelton & John, 1993), culture (Hewlett, 2000), gender (Hawkins et al., 1993; A. S. Rossi & P. H. Rossi, 1992), socioeconomic status (Conger et al., 1990; Stier & Tienda, 1993), educational attainment (Barnett, 1994), and historical period or cohort (LaRossa, 1988). By studying a diverse group of fathers representing different circumstances and contexts of father involvement, it is possible to look for universal patterns of development in involved fathers and start to understand the relations between contextual variability and individual differences in development.

TOWARD A PRESCRIPTION FOR FURTHER CONCEPTUALIZATION AND RESEARCH

Life-Course Contributions

In order to satisfactorily depict the developmental processes and consequences of fathering, a life-course approach considering multiple and interdependent trajectories is useful. The developmental trajectories of separate domains (e.g., self, social, work) may be modified in noticeably different manners by the same level of father involvement (see Fig. 1.1). Further, different aspects within the same domain may be differentially effected by the level of father involvement. Because it is constrained by time and energy expenditures, father involvement is mutually influenced by and exerts influence on concurrent investment in other trajectories (e.g., work, marriage, community involvement). Further, because development of any system is most prone to environmental influences at the time of most rapid change, it can be assumed that transition points within a fathering career are the most fruitful to examine (e.g., transition to parenthood, the child's entry into alternate caregiving, the child's entry into and out of educational systems, or the parents' exit or reentry into work settings).

These assumptions lead to some testable hypotheses. If the experiences of fathering exert a developmental influence, then fathers who sustain relatively involved and active roles during times of rapid developmental transition in themselves or their family systems would be expected to be most greatly affected by the experiences of fathering. Further, those who consistently and cumulatively have demonstrated the greatest involvement in role enactment would be expected to show the greatest amount of developmental difference from nonparents. As conceptualized, Fig. 1.2 shows that father involvement mediates the relation between a wide array of variables. Specifically, father involvement is influenced by and, in turn, influences other roles in which men engage. Some roles and demands may facilitate father involvement (e.g., some aspects of spouse roles, work roles, community involvement) while other factors compete or interfere with father involvement (e.g., other aspects of spouse roles, work roles, community involvement). Similarly, there are bidirectional influences between father involvement and other modifying conditions (e.g., family form, family functioning, cohort effects, social support, etc.), individual parental characteristics (e.g., sensitivity to child signals, expressivity, coping skills, self-concept, etc.), and the characteristics of individual children (age, gender, developmental status, personality, etc.). Likewise, there is a reciprocal influence between father involvement and adult development outcomes in cognitive, personality, emotional, affective, and physical realms of development. The relations between these variables can be expected to vary across individual, family, and historical time (Hareven, 1977).

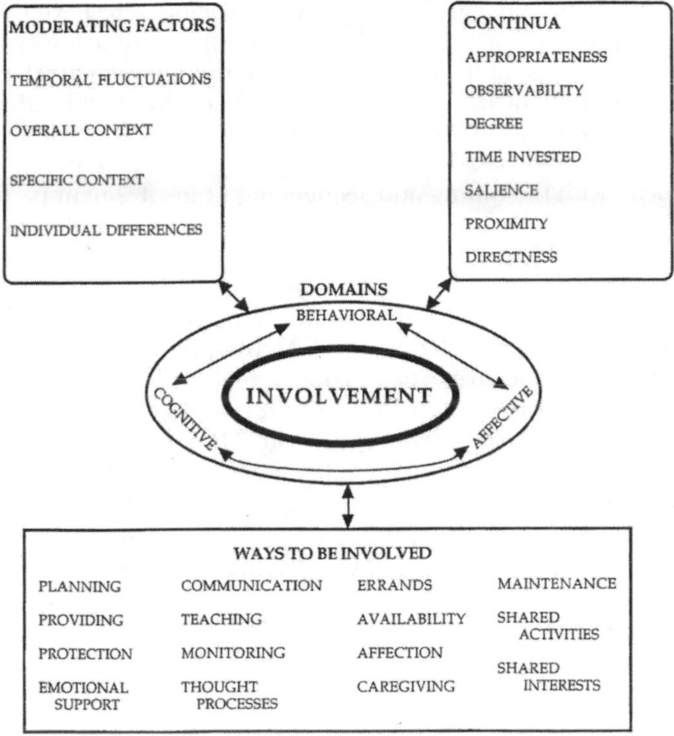

FIG. 1.2. A conceptual model of involvement

Life-Cycle Contributions

An engrossing possibility is that the transition to parenthood and subsequent milestones in child development and the emerging parent–child relationship simply serve as "marker events," or impending deadlines, thus providing an organizational context, sequencing, and timing for fostering adult development that may otherwise occur more randomly and with greater flexibility in timing. Because the life events related to parenthood have concomitant social prescriptions and norms, parenting may serve a regulating function in adult development. As parents enact the roles associated with caring for children of different ages and developmental abilities, different skills and levels of direct oversight and involvement are needed. As children grow and develop, they require different types and levels of father involvement and fathers are likely to be differentially effected by enactment of parental roles.

Although life-cycle perspectives of family development have been thoroughly criticized (see White, 1991), it is still useful to outline life-cycle stages on the basis of the age of the oldest child. As fathers are engaged in and assume responsibility for the development of their oldest child, they face a new, never before encountered set of requirements. In order to suitably carry out parental roles, individual fathers must develop a minimum set of competencies with the timing and sequencing of involvement patterns determined by family transitional events and children's developmental capabilities.

Erikson's theory of psychosocial development (sometimes referred to as a life-cycle theory) is not considered a life-cycle approach in the sense of family science, but one of its central constructs, the epigenetic principle, affords a useful perspective. The epigenetic principle states that development is governed by the interaction of biological maturation and cultural prescriptions for each stage of development. The expectations of different levels and types of father involvement during different phases of the child's life cycle would parallel age- (stage-) appropriate prescriptions of the epigenetic principle. Cultural prescriptions inform fathers of appropriate fathering behavior toward children of different ages and developmental capabilities.

CONCLUSIONS

The study of the relations between fathering and men's adult development presents a challenging arena in which to attempt to synthesize life-span, life-course, and life-cycle perspectives into an integrated whole. Integrative problems exist in both units and levels of analysis, methodologies, and statistical precision. However, it is through attempts to meet challenges that theoretical syntheses are achieved, or new, overshadowing theories are formulated (Kuhn, 1962). It is to that end that the effects of parenting on adult development must be reexamined.

This area of inquiry is in the pre-paradigm stage. There is a substantial amount of theoretical discourse regarding the relations between fathering and men's adult development, but the data-based understanding of the relations between parenting and adult development is in its infancy. Significant efforts need to be invested in studying developmental consequences of involved fathering. Advancements in this area have the potential to facilitate interdisciplinary integration across life-span, life-course, and life-cycle approaches to development. In addition, empirical research in this area can facilitate understanding of the complex interplay of multiple roles, contexts, and investments in parenting and adult development. Given the continuing prevalence of parenting as a context of adult development, and the salience that parenting holds in most parents' identity and daily lives, it makes sense to invest significant resources into understanding the relations between parenting and adult development. In the words of Parke and Brott (1999, p. 3), "Every generation has its scapegoat for contemporary ills. ... Now it seems to be the absence of fathers in the family. It's hard to pick up a newspaper or magazine without encountering a story about the continuing deterioration of the American family and how the absence of the father is at least partly responsible." Given the prevalence of this argument, it is time to collect data concerning the costs and benefits of involved fathering for men. Certainly, exploratory qualitative research will yield data that will stimulate further interest, theoretical debate, model development, and empirical research in this area. Thus, the study described in the next chapter was designed to begin to address the issues raised in this introductory chapter.

Chapter **2**

A Research Plan: Forty Fathers, Their Situations, and What They Can Tell Us

This chapter describes the purposeful design of a research study consisting of an extensive open-ended interview with a sample of 40 diverse fathers discussing their perceptions of the effects of fathering on their development and life course. The interview schedule was designed to systematically explore areas within the self, social, and work domains that theoretical, anecdotal, and empirical evidence reviewed in chapter 1 indicated as areas of change associated with involved fathering.

RATIONALE AND DEVELOPMENTAL HISTORY OF THE DESIGN OF THIS STUDY

The study represented in this book had its genesis over 15 years ago—although I did not know it then. Marvin Sussman and I were co-editing a volume on *The Transition to Parenthood* (Palkovitz & Sussman, 1988) when I received a draft of a most provocative chapter from Barbara and Philip Newman. In the chapter, which ultimately was included in the book as the chapter "Parenthood and Adult Development," Newman and Newman made many fascinating observations regarding changes they experienced and attributed to active engagement in raising their children. The chapter represented a synthesis of theory and reflective analysis that, in my opinion, was highly original scholarship. However, as an editor, my job was to require the authors to place appropriate disclaimers in their chapter. They needed to point out that the developmental outcome effects that they attributed to parent involvement could possibly come through other contexts or experiences. Simply stated, although the possible relationships were thought provoking, the chapter did not present data that would allow causal inferences to be made. Further, whereas their chapter was quite intellectually stimulating, it did not incorporate empirical research findings to the same degree as other chapters in the volume. When I contacted them with these concerns, Newman and Newman responded that they had not included empirical underpinnings because they did not exist, and obligingly inserted some cautionary statements about the theoretical, anecdotal, and personally experiential nature of their chapter.

That chapter, and subsequent conversations with the Newmans, sparked an interest that eventually led to the design of this study. Specifically, I spent my next sabbatical leave reading all of the professional literature that I could find that was applicable to the relation between parenting and adult development. Empirical studies were scarce, indeed. The literature that I could amass was highly anecdotal, incidental, or theoretical. Through intensive reading during a sabbatical leave in spring 1991, I became aware that there was almost no empirical literature to support the popular notion that the contexts of parenting bring developmental changes to adults. In the process of analyzing why this is the case, I discovered a number of conceptual and methodological shortcomings in the existing literature. As a result, I have centered my recent scholarly efforts on refining and expanding the conceptual base, and on designing measures and collecting data that examine men's perceptions of the relations between involvement in fathering and adult development.

I assembled the available literature and began to hypothesize about the relation between parenting and adult development. My first presentation of this material occurred at the Conference on Human Development in Atlanta in spring 1992 (Palkovitz, 1992a). My paper ("Parenting as a Generator of Adult Development: Is the Child Parent to the Adult?") was slotted in a session with three empirical studies focusing primarily on adolescent development. My paper was the fourth 15-minute presentation in the session, and was distinctly different from the three prior presentations in a number of ways. First, whereas the other three presentations focused on adolescent development, my paper focused on adult development. Second, I did not have empirical findings to present. I reviewed the existing literature and hypothesized about possible relations between parenting and adult development. Third, although the previous papers had been followed by spirited question and answer sessions, mine was followed by silence. My read was that the other papers were quite successfully presented and well received—mine was not. I would have shelved the project, but I had already committed to revise it and to submit it to a theory conference.

In fall 1992, I was invited to present a paper to an interdisciplinary group of family scholars at the Center for the Study of the Family at the University of Delaware. With hesitation, I decided to again risk presenting a version of the paper that I had given at the Conference on Human Development. I developed it further and presented it to the center fellows. The interdisciplinary team of scholars at the center showed a significantly higher degree of interest, provided valuable feedback, and asked provocative questions. Encouraged, I revised the paper further and prepared to present it to the Theory Construction and Research Methodology (TCRM) preconference of the National Council on Family Relations in November 1992 (Palkovitz, 1992b).

For readers unfamiliar with the character and format of this annual preconference, it is notably different than traditional conference formats. First, the papers submitted are acknowledged as works in progress. Second, the papers are distributed to discussants for detailed review. At the conference, the actual paper is never presented. Discussants offer their comments and the authors respond to the comments. Following that exchange, the audience, who is provided with and expected to read the papers in advance, offers comments and questions. The TCRM preconcerence is known for spirited and constructive discussion.

Largely based on my TCRM experience, I was encouraged to further revise and submit the developing article to the *Journal of Social and Personal Relationships,* where further editorial comments and reviews brought greater development and advancement of my thinking. Most notably, I was encouraged to make explicit hypotheses regarding the relation between parenting and adult development.

The first assumption that I developed and explored is that the degree of developmental change attributable to fathering is related to the amount of fathers' active involvement in childrearing. However, it is unlikely that the relation between parenting and adult development is linear or simple. In essence, I (Palkovitz, 1996a) argued that although there may be significant causal relations between parenting and adult development, we do not have a clear conceptualization of what the change may look like. Various models are elaborated concerning possible relations between involvement in parenting and adult development.

Second, if there is a documentable relation between involvement in parenting and adult development, then it is necessary to have reliable and valid measures of involvement. A review of available tools showed that contemporary measures focus almost exclusively on behavioral involvement taking place in discrete in-person interactions. However, limiting conceptualization and measurement of involvement to such characteristics overlooks what I believe to be the majority of change-producing contexts. As a result, I presented a reconceptualization of father involvement at the National Council on Family Relations (NCFR) in 1994 and subsequently published the paper as a chapter in an edited volume on generative fathering (Palkovitz, 1997). I have since collaborated with Alan Hawkins in writing about needed changes in father involvement measures (Hawkins & Palkovitz, 1999) and have served as a panel moderator and discussant at several symposia on father involvement, mostly at NCFR annual conferences and theory construction preconferences.

The basic question, "Does fatherhood as an experience influence mens' development as adults?" was the staring point for this study. Despite the recognition that the bidirectional nature of parent–child relationships is important (Bell, 1968), there have been few systematic attempts to outline the impacts of parenthood on men (Ambert, 1992; Palkovitz, 1996a). This study began as an initial exploration of men's perceptions of their own experiences of fatherhood and how fatherhood has taken their adult lives in new directions.

Combining the reconceptualizations of potential developmental changes and involvement, I designed an in-depth qualitative interview project where 40 fathers with diverse backgrounds were questioned concerning their perceptions of the relations between fathering and adult development. The interview schedule specifically targeted salient developmental domains suggested by my reconceptualizations and reviews of the professional literature. I balanced questioning between cognitive, emotional, social, work, family, and personal domains. The interview schedule for the project (see Appendix 1) closely paralleled and expanded areas reviewed in Table 1.1 (see chap. 1, this vol.). The interviews yielded more than 1,000 pages of transcripts.

SAMPLE

The 40 fathers who participated in the interviews were recruited through newspapers in a suburban area in the eastern United States. The purpose of the sample was to include a diverse group of men that encompassed a wide range of fathering contexts. The sample included 23% non- Caucasian fathers and also represented diversity in marital history, family structure, residential status, education, occupational achievement and status, degree of paternal involvement in childrearing, and father's age at time of first child's birth. These variables were not used to exert systematic control in regard to the study questions, but to begin to identify and understand patterns in contextual influences on fathering as it facilitates men's adult development.

To qualify for inclusion in the sample, fathers could have children of any age and the children could be biological, adopted, stepchildren, or fictive kin. The fathers could either be co-resident or living in another household. All men in the sample had at least one biological child, and the average father in the sample had two biological children (M = 1.98, SD = .83). Ten of the 40 men fathered a total of 19 stepchildren (range 1–4, M = 1.90 stepchildren per stepfather). The average age of first-born biological children was 10.00 years (SD = 6.23), and the average age at the time of men's transitions to fatherhood was 26.15 years (SD = 5.03 years).

Previous research has documented that timing of men's transition to parenthood is associated with different patterns of father involvement and adjustment (Cooney et al., 1993). Therefore, for analytic purposes, fathers were divided into early timing (ET), ontime (OT), and late timing (LT) groupings. Arbitrary, but conventional criteria were employed to divide men into ET, OT, and LT groups. Men who were within one standard deviation of the mean age for making the transition to fatherhood were considered OT (age 22–31 years at birth of first child, *N* = 28, or 70% of the sample). Those one standard deviation below the mean (men age 21 and younger) at the transition to fatherhood and those one standard deviation above (men age 32 and above) were considered to be ET (*N* = 7, or 18% of the sample) and LT fathers (*N* = 5, or 13% of the sample), respectively. A summary of the demographic characteristics of the sample is presented in Table 2.1. A brief demographic and contextual sketch for each study participant is provided in Appendix 2.

Each study participant was assigned a unique first name pseudonym to protect his privacy. By reading biographic and demographic summaries of each participant in Appendix 2, the reader can gain a fuller sense of each father's life circumstances. As quotations are cited throughout the remainder of the text to substantiate thematic analyses, pseudonyms are consistently provided for each quote. Thus, by referring to the participant quote index and looking up the full set of quotes for each father, readers can reconstruct a more complete sense of each interview.

PROCEDURES

All interviews were conducted, by myself, in a face-to-face setting. Most fathers (*N* = 35) were interviewed in an office space at a medical research center. For the convenience of the remaining five fathers, interviews were conducted at their home or office. Fathers were greeted at the site of data collection and given a demographic and health questionnaire to complete. Following that, each father participated in a 60- to 90-minute interview examining his perceptions of the specific effects of fatherhood on marriage (or relationships with significant others), sexuality, relationships with other relatives, friendships, work history, community involvement, morality, religious beliefs and practices, values, household location, household organization, health practices, emotional experience, emotional expression, paternal roles, patterns of paternal involvement, and preparation for fatherhood. The interview schedule is provided in Appendix 1.

All interviews were audiotaped, and transcribed verbatim. Interview questions and responses were assigned alphanumeric codes to allow sorting transcripts via computer. Specifically, unique codes were created for each question, and included subject identification numbers. Thus, transcripts could be searched by question codes, and respondents' remarks could be sorted by question and or subject number. This allowed manipulation of the data set so that completed transcripts could be analyzed for emergent themes.

Completed transcripts were analyzed for emergent themes. I engaged in data analyses without preconceived categories of themes or theories to classify men's responses to interview topics. However, I am a father of four

TABLE 2.1

Demographic Characteristics

AGE[1]	*NUMBER*[2]	*INCOME*[3]	*NUMBER*
20–25	5	0–10	4
26–30	6	10–20	4
31–35	10	20–30	5
36–40	9	30–40	7
41–45	10	40–50	8
		50–60	3
		60–70	3
ETHNICITY	*NUMBER*	70–80	3
WHITE	31	80–90	2
AFRICAN AMERICAN	8	90–100	0
HISPANIC	1	100+	1

EDUCATION LEVEL	*NUMBER*	*TIMING*[4]	*NUMBER*
LESS THAN HIGH SCHOOL	1	ET ($\leq$ 21)	7
HIGH SCHOOL/GED	8	OT (22–31)	28
SOME COLLEGE	15	LT ($\geq$ 32)	5
2-YEAR COLLEGE DEGREE	5		
4-YEAR COLLEGE DEGREE	5		
GRADUATE COURSEWORK	5		
MASTER'S DEGREE	1		
DOCTORAL COURSEWORK	1		
Ph.D.	1		

[1]Age of respondent in years
[2]Number of respondents in category (total N = 40)
[3]Gross Family Income, reported in bands of $10,000
[4]Age at first transition to fatherhood

sons (currently age 12–22 years old), trained as a developmental psychologist, and have been studying fathering and development for over 20 years. Undoubtedly, the contexts of my personal career and father-role development exerted influence in the analytic process (see an expanded discussion of possible researcher biases in the preface).

LIMITATIONS OF THE STUDY

It must be noted that although this sample is a diverse group of fathers in terms of context and composition, the group is unrepresentative in that all of the men in the study are "involved" fathers, at least to the extent that they have assumed responsibility for their children to varying degrees. In this regard, the sample is atypical. Each father viewed himself to be involved with his child(ren), and to have responsibility for fostering his children's development. Although there were both coresidential and nonresidential fathers, biological and social fathers, early timing and late timing dads, well-educated men of significant position and accomplishment, laborers, high school dropouts, married men, cohabitors, and many other variations in living arrangement, age, and life circumstance, the overriding commonality for men in the sample was that they perceived themselves to be involved with their children.

This makes the sample unrepresentative of the larger population, where some men are immature and/or dysfunctional to the point where impending fatherhood does not change them—they do not accept responsibility and give themselves over to the ongoing forging that can take place through continued father involvement. Clearly, biological fathers who are sperm donors or cut and run fathers after a one-night stand or short relationship do not experience the same degree of developmental pull from fathering that continually involved fathers do. After conducting this study, I can say nothing regarding fathers who do not play involved roles in their children's lives. Without a commitment to responsibility, involvement would not exist. Men who make this "first cut" place themselves into a different trajectory than those who see the responsibilities of fathering as too limiting or too demanding, and as a consequence, "cut and run." Admittedly, none of the men in this sample fit the latter pattern. Each of the men in the sample made a commitment to involved fatherhood in one way or another.

Although the sample represented a great deal of diversity in terms of men's career development, age, SES, education, marital and family history, and ethnicity, the sample cannot be considered to be representative. The men in this study had decided to assume responsibility for fathering and to maintain relatively high degrees of investment or involvement in their children's lives, even when not co-resident. As such, the sample is biased toward responsible, involved fathers.

Second, as is the case with any self-report data, there is always the concern that the men in the sample are not expressing an objective view of their developmental pathways. Even so, Tim provided an important perspective on this issue:

> It's been a wild year. And even if it's not the kid that's changed me, if I think it's the kid that's changed me that's what's really important, isn't it?

Like Tim, some argue that a person's construction of reality significantly influences their experience whether or not there is a close correspondence between their perceptions and more objective assessments of the situation. Self-report studies are also vulnerable to demand characteristics and social desirability exerting significant influences in respondent's statements. Interviewers and researchers who interpret qualitative data need to be sensitive to the presence of demand characteristics.

Perhaps a greater concern is that no triangulating data were collected by interviewing participant's children or spouses, or through observational methods. This was a choice that I made at the outset of the study in order to devote maximum resources to collecting extensive interview data from as diverse a sample of fathers as possible.

A majority of the questions required retrospective assessment from the participants, and no data were collected longitudinally. In addition, there was no comparison group of men who had not fathered children. Given these limitations, it is important to recognize that the data presented here represent involved fathers' stated perceptions of the effect of fathering on men's adult development. Because no longitudinal data with comparison groups are available, it is important not to make specific causal attributions, but to see this as an exploratory study that brings qualitative empirical support to the anecdotally and theoretically salient perspective that fathering affects adult male development.

The most important feature of the data presented in this book is the ability to examine men's perceptions of the effects of fathering on both everyday life (from a life-course perspective) and personal development (from a life-span perspective), while highlighting theoretically important issues and the interface between the two approaches. Moreover, although the sample is not representative in the demographic sense, a particular strength of this study is having a purposefully designed data set from a diverse sample of men (residential and nonresidential fathers, biological and stepfathers, African American as well as Caucasian fathers, high school dropouts to PhDs, and men from every socioeconomic stratum, never married, married, divorced and widowed fathers, primary caregiving fathers, fathers who were incarcerated, fathers with restraining orders, men fighting for custody of their children, unemployed fathers, dual career family men, gender-role traditionalists and egalitarian men, men for whom religious faith is a central defining construct, and atheists or agnostics). By summarizing major theoretical and experiential accounts in the fathers' own voices—their experiences and perceptions of the interfaces between fulfilling fathering roles and their own development—both professionals and men experiencing or anticipating these roles will gain understanding of the dynamic relations between fathering and early adult development. Using various qualitative analytic approaches, I will be able to explore important themes and constructs—issues that will make sense to "dads in the trenches," yet bring empirical support and refinement to theoretically salient issues in both life-span development and family studies.

The remaining chapters present numerous quotations from study participants, along with my analytic and interpretive commentary in an attempt to present the stories of the 40 fathers who shared their fathering experiences. Analyses and integration with existing theories and empirical findings are offered to help advance an understanding of the relations between involved fathering and men's adult development.

Chapter 3

Men's Construction of the Fathering Role: Balancing the Demands of What It Means to Be a Dad Today

Over the last 30 or so years, an extensive and eclectic literature on fathering has evolved. The field, particularly in the past decade, has been characterized by rapid proliferation of a diverse array of articles and books addressing fathers' roles (Dienhart, 1998), the relation between father involvement in childrearing and child outcome effects (Lamb, 1997), and various patterns of paternal involvement and father absence (Ihinger-Tallman, Pasley, & Biehler, 1993; W. B. Johnson, 1993). Until now, there has not been a reciprocal focus on the effects of fathering on men's adult development.

Interestingly, the professional literature presents starkly contrasting views in changing trends in fatherhood. One perspective suggests that, in comparison to recent history, there is a new, increased level of father involvement, variously labeled "nurturant fathering," "generative fathering," "egalitarian fathering," "positively involved fathering," or "responsible fathering," among other descriptors. A more accurate portrayal, in the historical sense, would be that some patterns of contemporary involved fathering mirror a return to patterns of father involvement prevalent in colonial America when fathers were recognized to have primary responsibility for children's welfare (Palkovitz, 1996b). The comparable role today is portrayed in what both professional and popular media refer to as a "new breed" of fathers: men who have increased commitment to engagement in fathering roles, while at the same time being successful as providers and participants in their communities.

Yet, these images come at a time when independent sources of demographic data document that American men are now less likely than in recent decades to become fathers at all. The same data show that when men do become fathers, there is a tendency for men to have fewer children. It is also true that significant numbers of men spend less time in households with children, and experience less "leisure time" (that could be spent with children) than in the past 50 years (R. C. Johnson, 1992). Demographic data indicate that divorce, mother-headed households, and defaults on court-ordered alimony and child support payments have reached or are near all-time highs (Whitehead, 1993; Zinsmeister, 1991). Some observers of social phenomena have interpreted these indicators to suggest that contemporary patterns of fatherhood are far from reflective of the new breed of fathers, and are, in fact, indicative of a fathering deficiency. Indeed, contemporary discourse frequently centers on father absence as a crisis in the state of the nation's families. How can the starkly contrasting "new involved father" and the "fatherless America" perspectives be reconciled? Is there a balanced view of fatherhood between the extremes? How do men engaged in fathering roles discuss the enactment of and challenges and barriers to those roles?

By briefly reviewing historical documentation concerning paternal roles and levels of father involvement in family matters and childrearing, and by comparing historical data with patterns of father involvement described by study participants, this chapter describes some changes in different constructions of the fathers' role across historical time, and describes different aspects of fathering roles and involvement patterns using the self-reports of contemporary fathers.

CHANGING ROLES OF FATHERS

There are significant questions concerning the ability to accurately assess the degree of change that has occurred in levels of paternal involvement across history in the United States. Whereas there are broad characterizations portraying primary emphases within fathers' roles, and some generalizations that can be made concerning typical patterns of involvement in different eras during U.S. historical development, it is virtually impossible to make detailed, meaningful comparisons between contemporary patterns of father involvement and those of the past. Although scholars and popular press writers are quick to do so, there are numerous factors that inhibit the ability to accurately assess anything beyond macrolevel changes in fathering across time.

Despite the last decade's proliferation of fathering literature, in comparison to writings on mothering or parenting in general, fathering literature is relatively sparse, particularly within past eras. Recent contributions have begun to correct for this shortage, but researchers vary in their opinion of whether there is a sufficiently solid basis for delineating the degree of change in roles in American fatherhood across time. LaRossa (1988) was cautious concerning social scientists' abilities to assess historical changes in fatherhood: "Only a few scholars have systematically conceptualized the changing father hypothesis, and no one to date has marshaled the historical evidence needed to adequately test the hypothesis" (p. 451).

Since then, LaRossa (1997) devoted concerted study to chronicling the modernization of fatherhood. Although his efforts have yielded superb historical scholarship covering some eras of fatherhood, because of gaps in similarly detailed analyses of other eras and the lack of representative samples of fathers from different historical periods, overall, things are not much better in terms of assessing the degree of change in fathering roles across time. Other scholars suggest that there is sufficient evidence to address the degree of change in paternal roles and participation: "A brief examination of the literature shows, first, that there has been a stream of papers on fathers over the past fifty years which repeatedly claim that little has been written on the topic" (Lewis & O'Brien, 1987, p. 3).

Most scholars would agree, however, that this enterprise is not without peril. There is a notable difference between being able to describe changes in predominant themes of fathering and making quantitatively meaningful assessments regarding historical variation in levels of paternal involvement. Demos (1982) addressed the complexities of describing changes in fatherhood across historical periods by stating that "a vast gulf of change separates early American fathers from their counterparts today. The differences embrace underlying goals and values; prescribed methods and styles of practice; the shape and quality of personal interaction; and the larger configuration of domestic life" (p. 426).

LaRossa (1997, p. 21) warned that whereas it is necessary to understand modern fatherhood in the context of the history of fatherhood,

> strictly speaking, however, there is no such thing as "the" history of fatherhood; rather, there are histories of fatherhoods, with an accent on the plural. In the nineteenth century, for example, the strain of fatherhood that might be found in a northern industrial state differed from the strain of fatherhood that might be found in a southern agricultural community. Likewise, the strain of fatherhood among the Anglo-Saxons in Boston differed from the strain of fatherhood among the Chinese or Italian immigrants in Philadelphia or among African slaves in Atlanta. Even these categories minimize the contradictions within locales and groups- consider the differences from one city block to the next, or from one family line to another.

In other words, whereas there may be patterns evident in predominant fathering roles across epochs or regions, there are significant variations in ways that individuals perceive and walk out those role prescriptions (Palkovitz, 1988). LaRossa's caution was stated in a parallel manner by Linton (quoted in Guttman, 1991, p. 1): "In some ways each man is like all other men; in some ways, each man is like some other men; and in some ways, each man is like no other men." The literature regarding fatherhood, whether historical reports or contemporary observations, cover each of these three levels of observation: Some make general statements about fathers as though all fathers conform to the description as prescription; some focus on a particular subgroup (e.g., teen fathers, fathers in dual-wage families, primary caregiving fathers) or style of fathering (e.g., traditional, authoritative, androgynous) to highlight the typical characteristics within groups or to make comparisons between groups; and some of the literature is comprised of individual case histories. There is a degree of validity to a generalized discussion of "fathers" because all fathers share some universal characteristics. Yet, any literature reviewed about "fathers" minimizes consideration of unique individual variations. When considering subgroups of fathers, keep in mind that men who may be categorized within the same general classification (e.g., early timing fathers) will have unique histories, developmental trajectories, interaction styles, and involvement levels, varying broadly on variables other than the target variable that triggered their classification into a subgroup. Descriptions of different styles or types of fathers are "ideal types" in the Weberian usage:

> They are not ideal in the normative sense, however; neither are they accurate descriptions of reality. As a heuristic device, ideal types represent logical exaggerations of reality; as such they serve as a basis for comparison and potential measurement of concrete trends. The polar types of "traditional" and "androgynous" father serve as a point of reference for the empirical assessment of the social reality: the "typical" father. (Horna & Lupri, 1987, p. 55)

A goal of this chapter is to summarize historical trends in fatherhood and to focus on contemporary roles of fathers, so remember that any generalized statements are precarious at best, and wrong at worst, when applied to the individual level. Lewis and O'Brien (1987) asserted:

> The variations between individual fathers can themselves be considerable. Such a finding emerges within relatively homogenous communities irrespective of whether mothers ... fathers ... or children ... are the source of data collection. It is also evident in cross-cultural comparisons. ... The very heterogeneity of fathering roles, ... invalidates general statements about "the father." (p. 6)

Also recognize that historical shifts are in progress, both at societal and individual (developmental) levels. Any transition from one model of fathering to another may be incomplete. The tendency is to describe fathering styles as fixed, but they are, in reality, varied and dynamic (Horna & Lupri, 1987). It is also the case that although fathers may have a predominant fathering style, no father actually practices the style as a pure type. That is, he likely blends elements of other paternal styles into his overall pattern of fathering. Further, movement or development through various styles of fathering may be more the rule than the exception. The paternal style manifested at any given point of data collection or analysis depends on the context, individual father's assessments of the balance of requirements and resources, and the relative importance individual fathers assign to the various roles they enact (e.g., breadwinning, gender-role modeling, moral guidance, nurturance) toward their children (Palkovitz, 1997).

To present an acceptably accurate representation of historical changes in American fatherhood, it is necessary to include a discussion of predominant cultural, ideological, political, and economic forces affecting fatherhood at each point of comparison. Such a commission is clearly beyond the scope of this brief examination, but several excellent reviews have been written, and when read together, present a thorough and convergent picture of the various forces that have shaped fatherhood in the United States from the colonial period to the present.[1]

The previous discussion allows for some cautious, generalized statements concerning predominant role patterns of fathers across different historical periods in the United States in order to can understand the roots of contemporary trends in paternal roles. It is acknowledged that there was significant variability within and across these general patterns of father involvement, but they supply a useful foundation to understand patterns of contemporary fathering in the United States.

Fatherhood in Colonial America

Puritan men were the authors of the first handbooks on childrearing in the United States, and served as the principal instructors of their children. Colonial fatherhood "involved a remarkable amount of daily care, companionship [and] concern" (Zinsmeister, 1991, p. 3). Although responsibility centered on moral teaching (Lamb, 1987; Pleck, 1987, 1997), discipline, training children for life's work, provision of material needs, control of family property, and veto power in concerns of courtship and marriage were also integral in the father's role (Rotundo, 1985). Fathers also discharged major functions as models, psychologists, companions, and caregivers (Demos, 1982), especially with older children. Although there were differences in the relative distribution of responsibilities between mothers and fathers toward their children that varied by age of the child, fathers were commonly considered to be the primary parent:

> There is no question that colonial mothers, as their counterparts today, provided most of the caretaking that infants and young children received. But fathers were nonetheless thought to have far greater responsibility for, and influence on, their children. Prescriptions for parents were addressed almost entirely to fathers: the responsibilities of mothers were rarely mentioned. (Pleck, 1987, p. 84)

Demos (1982) appreciated that such descriptions give little room for individual variability in performance or role enactment over time. However, he asserted that "almost everywhere fatherhood displayed the same active,

[1]Interested readers are encouraged to pursue a more complete presentation than can be provided here by reading Degler (1980); Demos (1982, 1986), Gerson (1993), Griswold (1993, 1997), La Rossa (1997), Marsh (1990), Pleck (1987, 1997), and Rotundo (1985, 1993).

integrated orientation. And in this, there was little apparent change through the several generations of our 'colonial period'" (p. 431).

The Industrial Age Father

Perhaps the most dependable finding across historical analyses of fatherhood is the following: Since the time of the Industrial Revolution, fathers have increasingly devoted time and energies in employment away from the home setting (see, e.g., Bernard, 1981; Demos, 1982; Pleck, 1987; Rotundo, 1985).

Rotundo documented shifts in American society and roles during the 19th century. He summarized changes in family responsibilities in the following manner:

> At the same time that the traditional ideas of patriarchy fell into decline, a new notion of womanhood emerged: a belief that women were inherently moral, more spiritual, and more tender than men. ... Despite the decline of patriarchy and the expanded importance of mothers within the nineteenth-century family, middle-class fathers still had a significant role to play. More than ever before, the man was *the* provider in the family. That, in turn, reinforced his role as "head of the household." (Rotundo, 1985, pp. 10–11, emphasis in original)

For the first time in American history, mothers were now regarded as the primary parent beyond the infancy period. Culturewide reforms in gender-role stereotypes led to redefinitions and renegotiations of appropriate roles for men and women in regard to employment and family life. Demos (1982) explained:

> Certain key elements of premodern fatherhood dwindled and disappeared (father as teacher, father as moral overseer, father as companion), while others were profoundly transformed (father as counselor, father as model). ... Although fatherhood on these terms was hardly insubstantial, it diverged in obvious and important ways from the earlier pattern. For one thing, it became part-time ... for another, it opened some distance from the everyday workings of the household ... preeminently for one reason. Beginning in the first decades of the nineteenth century, and increasingly thereafter, men were drawn out of their families toward income producing work. (p. 433)

During the Industrial Age, the most significant change in fathers' roles was an increased emphasis on the father as breadwinner or provider (Christiansen & Palkovitz, 2001):

> Of course, fathers had always been involved in the provision of goods and services to their families; but before the nineteenth century such activity was embedded in a larger matrix of domestic sharing. With modernization, it

> became "differentiated" as the chief, if not the exclusive, province of adult men. Now, for the first time, the central activity of fatherhood was sited outside one's immediate household. Now being fully a father meant being separated from one's children for a considerable part of each working day. (Demos, 1982, p. 434)

Rotundo (1985) submitted that the segregation of the father's work from the home took him outside of the "emotional currents" of the home, deterred the ability to develop deep intimacy with his children, and supplanted the traditional authority of fathers. These are characteristics that are lamented in relation to "traditional" fathers today.

Fatherhood in the 20th Century

The image of *father as provider* was more robust at the turn of the 20th century than ever before, conferring on individual fathers special status, respect, deference, and familial love (Demos, 1982). In the leading conception of the good provider role, a man's primary responsibility was his job, rendering the family to subordinate significance (Scanzoni, 1975). In fact, Bernard (1981, p. 4) maintained that, in the 20th century, "success in the good provider role came to define masculinity itself." Two world wars and an economic depression had societal and international impacts on the conduct of fatherhood:

> The Depression attacked, and sometimes shattered, fathers in their central role as providers; but the role itself survived until the return of better times, and flourished thereafter. The wars separated millions of fathers from their families for months or years at a stretch, but the ensuing peacetimes brought a renewal (even a reinforcement) of traditional arrangements. ... Two changes, recently begun and still in progress, deserve special notice here. ... The first is the entry of women—most strikingly, of married women with small children—into the working world outside the home. The second is the growing incidence of divorce and thus of single parenthood (even, in a small proportion of cases, of single *father*hood). (Demos, 1982, p. 444, emphasis in original)

Rotundo (1985, p. 15) agreed with this appraisal, noting that the economic growth following World War II reestablished fathers to their positions as providers and "heads of households." He further noted that in the revival of modern fatherhood, the opposing trends of father absence and father involvement gained renewed momentum (Rotundo, 1985) and carried over into contemporary bipolarization of patterns of fathering.

Pleck (1987, 1997) chronicled yet another period in the social history of fatherhood in the 20th century, noting that from the end of World War II to the mid-1970s, although breadwinning and moral guardianship continued to be important, principal emphasis was focused on fathers as sex-role models, particularly for their sons. Around the mid-1970s, an emerging view of fathers as active, nurturant, caretaking parents predominated (Lamb, 1987; Pleck, 1987, 1997).

Contemporary Fatherhood

Although very much in transition, the good provider role is still central in contemporary men's accounts of fatherhood (Christiansen & Palkovitz, 2001), and as acknowledged in the introduction to this chapter, the bipolar trends of father absence and involvement are continuing (Horna & Lupri, 1987). Restructuring of the social base and the new ideal of what a man should be has laid the basis for a new style of fatherhood variously labeled "involved fatherhood," "highly participant" fatherhood, "androgynous fatherhood," or "new fatherhood" (Palkovitz, 1996b). These characterizations of fatherhood, especially prevalent among the well-educated and families of the middle class and above, originated within the past decade and a half (Palkovitz, Christiansen, & Dunn, 1998), and have only begun to take hold. As such, a full description of this style of fatherhood is not possible. But, according to Rotundo (1985),

> this emerging form of fatherhood can at least be outlined. As part of the evolving style, a good father is an active participant in the details of day-to-day child care. He involves himself in a more intimate and expressive way with his children, and he plays a larger part in the socialization process that his male forebears had long since abandoned to their wives. In short, the new style of parenting blurs the distinctions between fatherhood and motherhood. ... Within this style, a good father avoids sex-typing his children and makes as little distinction as possible between sons and daughters. ... Androgynous Fatherhood, then, involves a substantial recasting of American manhood, womanhood, and family life. It demands new emotional styles; it entails different notions of male and female; and it requires men to surrender substantial authority to their wives in return for a greater measure of involvement with their children. (p. 17)

Despite earlier precautions stated against generalizing about fathers, it can still be said that alongside of the much-heralded androgynous father, or the "new father" of the 1990s, father-breadwinner (Christiansen & Palkovitz, 2001) and father as gender-role model remain as significant competitors for subscribers among fathers. Still,

> the critique of the distant bread-winning father is intensifying further. A new image, summed up in the term "the new father," is clearly on the rise in print and broadcast media. This new father differs from older images of involved fatherhood in several key respects: he is present at the birth; he is involved with his children as infants, not just when they are older; he participates in the

actual day-to-day work of child care and not just play; he is involved with his daughters as much as his sons. (Pleck, 1987, p. 93)

Yet, for all of the attention that the popular and professional media have focused on the new father, many wonder about the extent to which this man actually exists (Palkovitz, 1996b). Lamb (1987, p. 3) asserted that "rhetorical exchanges concerning the new fatherhood abound; unfortunately, rhetoric continues to outpace serious analysis." LaRossa (1988) counseled that the idea that fathers have fundamentally changed qualifies as a folk belief. Specifically, attempts to empirically chronicle involvement patterns of contemporary fathers in comparison to mothers show significant, although shrinking, gaps between men's and women's contributions to childrearing (Lamb et al., 1987; Pleck, 1997):

> The discrepancy between the actual pace of change in men and the profusion of profathering imagery has led some to dismiss the image of the new, involved father as only media "hype." While this element clearly exists, it is also important to recognize that the new father is not *all* hype. This image, like the dominant images of earlier periods, is ultimately rooted in structural forces and structural change. Wives *are* more often employed, and do less in the family when they are; men *are* spending more time in the family, both absolutely and relative to women (husbands' proportion of the total housework and child care rose from 20% to 30% between 1965 and 1981 ...). If the distant father-breadwinner has a social structural base, so too does the new father. (Pleck, 1987, p. 94, emphases in original)

CULTURE/CONDUCT DISTINCTIONS

LaRossa differentiated between the dominant imagery of fatherhood and the actual execution of paternal roles by use of the terms "culture of fatherhood" and "conduct of fatherhood," respectively (LaRossa, 1988; LaRossa & Reitzes, 1993). Specifically, this distinction can account for the differences in rates of change between the ideological shifts (culture) and the behaviors (conduct) of fatherhood. Whereas this refinement in the conceptualization of fatherhood has allowed theoretical and analytical power absent before LaRossa's contribution, it has not ended the perpetual debate about the reality of the conjectured change that has taken place in American fatherhood. If anything, these concepts have provided an increased level of conceptual analysis to the debate:

> Has fatherhood changed in the wake of the social and economic changes that have taken place in America since the turn of the century? Although the evidence is scant, it would appear that the answer to this question is both yes and no. Yes, fatherhood has changed if one looks at the culture of fatherhood—the ideologies surrounding men's parenting. No, fatherhood has not changed (at least significantly), if one looks at the

conduct of fatherhood—how fathers behave vis-a-vis their children. (LaRossa, 1988, p. 451)

Because the idealized image of fatherhood prescribes higher levels and greater ranges of involvement than are realized in practice, the resulting dissonance can yield powerful feelings of ambivalence, frustration, and guilt in both fathers and mothers. If the predominant culture of fatherhood is prescribing higher levels of participation than are being achieved, then what factors can explain the chasm between the culture and the conduct of fatherhood? These issues were explored in the interviews with study participants. The next section presents a summary of their responses to issues concerning various aspects of the fathering role.

WHAT TODAY'S DADS HAVE TO SAY ABOUT FATHERING ROLES

Overview of Findings

Fathers in the sample spontaneously described the multidimensional nature of fathering. Besides the multiple facets of fatherhood, there were a few themes concerning paternal roles that came through strongly, both in terms of frequency of expression and strength of expression. It was interesting to note that although some of the themes were prevalent, there was great individual variability in the ways the themes were expressed. For example, only 38% fathers directly discussed *loving* their children, or making their children feel loved. However, when the theme of love was expanded to include terms like *caring, understanding,* and *being their best friend,* love became the most frequently expressed theme within the role of fatherhood (voiced by 68% of the men in some manner). The other prevalent themes expressed included *provider* (63%), *being there* for your child(ren) (47%), and *model/teacher/moral guide* (50%). Beyond these prevalent themes, each with historical roots as described earlier, small numbers of men or individuals expressed idiosyncratic variations on these themes.

A large proportion of the sample discussed the *role-sharing* aspects of parenting (Dienhart, 1998; Dollahite & Hawkins, 1998) before being specifically questioned about the differences between men's and women's roles. Reflecting much of the discourse of contemporary society, there was nearly an even split in the number of fathers who believed that outside of bearing children and nursing them, there are essentially no differences between what fathers and mothers can do with their children and those men who enumerated unique differences between mothers' and fathers' roles with children. Although the question was posed in a rather absolutistic manner (Do you think that there are certain things that a mother (father) can do with her/his child that a father (mother) can't?), even role-sharing fathers voiced limitations or subtle differences in roles between mothers and fathers. Each theme is developed more fully and representative quotes are provided so that the reader can understand how the fathers themselves construct fathering roles.

The Multiple Facets of Fathering Roles

A major theme that came through in study participants' conversations was the fact that the father's role is "multifaceted" and "complex." Perhaps this was best voiced by Clifford in a response to the question, "In everyday terms, what makes a good father?": "That could be a million different things I guess." There was a recognition that each of the aspects of the role needed to have sufficient expression in everyday activities, or the household would be out of balance, experiencing a deficiency. In talking through the various aspects of involved fatherhood, there was considerable acknowledgment that there is significant convergence between paternal and maternal roles (and they are both multifaceted). There was also the recognition that it was difficult to view facets of fatherhood individually—they are all part of the same role, and the expression (or lack of expression) of each facet effects the overall texture of the role. Individual facets were recognized to be interdependent on one another, and interdependent on supports and conditions, such as the roles adequately fulfilled by others in their children's lives. For example, the responses of men who had highly functional spouses or partners differed significantly from those who did not have a coparent.

In responding to the prompt, "Describe your pattern of involvement with your child," Roger replied:

> I think mine, mine is everything, a provider, teacher, it's almost like I don't have an individual role.

It was difficult for Roger to focus on any particular aspect of fathering. Rather, he voiced that he needed to be engaged in "everything." Similarly, Ned's comments showed an awareness of the interdependent and multiple facets of involved fathering:

> To be a good father you have to be all those things. You have to wear many hats. You have to be there for them. You have to let them know that no matter what they do that you're still going to love them. So it's a real tough question.

Obviously, the question was not too "tough" for Ned to answer. It is likely that Ned sees that to adequately fill the multiple role demands of fathering, considerable effort must be expended. Although not many men explicitly stated that fathering roles are multifaceted, the notion was implicit in each respondent's comments. No father in the sample expressed fewer than four different aspects of fathering, and most discussed six or more components of fathering roles.

Fathering and Providing

When questioned in an open-ended manner concerning the role of fathers, men in the sample spontaneously mentioned providing more than any other single element of the fathering role. This indicates that the "good provider" role—which emerged during the industrial age and became the predominant fathering role of the early 20th century, only to be characterized as lacking in comparison to the "new nurturant" father—still looms large in engaged fathers' self-descriptions of their roles (see Christiansen & Palkovitz, 2001). Because the relation between fathering, providing, and the work domain is highlighted in chapter 11, those themes are not developed in detail here. However, it is important to note that providing is often viewed in a much broader sense than in the economic realm. This is consistent with the idea that economic provision is no longer "enough" for fathers to do. This theme is well represented by Colin's description of the father's role:

> To provide a safe environment, to provide a healthy environment, to give the child's life a sense of consistency, a sense that things are going to be here tomorrow just like they are today, that you're going to be here tomorrow just like you are today, to be a teacher and teach the child love, among other things. ... There's so many things.

Colin's statement reflects the idea that fathers should play an active role in providing economic support as well as structure and input into the overall physical and emotional environment. Thus, fathers' providing goes well beyond finances. Jeff similarly described a broad sense of provision. He began by talking about physical provision, but he quickly acknowledged moral, spiritual, and other dimensions of provision:

> Well, the father needs to do everything in his power to physically provide for his family. That is, to try to set the best example that you can both morally, spiritually and will-wise in responsibility, and that sort of thing. To try to provide—to try to enable, to try to provide opportunity for your children to be exposed to things so that they can make their decision. Try to pray that they make the right decisions because you can't force them, but to be a positive influence.

Jeff sees provision as including opportunities for children to make real choices and decisions in a supportive environment. These examples document that fathers do not necessarily view provision in the narrow sense of economics (Christiansen & Palkovitz, 2001). Some fathers are acutely aware that they help establish a fountainhead of emotional, moral, and spiritual resources that benefit or hinder their children. Implicit in these comments is the realization that if they do not provide positive influences in these areas, their children will suffer lack or harm.

The most common way to discuss the provider was in the more traditional economic sense, however, some important issues were raised by study participants. Craig talked through the concept that he had not planned to be the provider, and there were no specific, explicit agreements made to say "that's the way it will be." Structural barriers, specifically wage inequities, dictate that men are more likely to carry a greater proportion of the economic provision burdens than their wives (Palkovitz, 1987). Whereas wage inequity is illegal, and is prevalently renounced as unjust, it remains pervasive in contemporary society. Specifically, a woman working the same job as a man, at the same level of experience and competency, earns approximately 74% of the wages paid to a male in the same circumstances (CareerWomen.com, 1998). Thus, if other choice points dictate that it is in the best interest of the family for one person to be the economic provider so that another caregiver can focus time and consistent attention on childrearing, then economic reality says that the sole provider is most likely to be the male partner. Craig said:

> Well, I am the provider because it's the way things worked out, it wasn't planned. My wife has had a few decent jobs but it always seems that she's the one that ends up staying home to take care of the kids. So I'm obviously the provider there.

Although the proportion of families with two wage earners has increased dramatically in the past three decades, it is still the case that some men experience and express guilt if their female partners need to work in order to provide and keep up what they view to be an appropriate lifestyle.

Father Love

Study participants discussed the need for fathers to show love to their children. However, fatherly love is not just expressed toward children. The expression of love toward a spouse or partner is seen by some fathers to be a part of their fatherly role. As stated in the introduction to the data from the study participants presented earlier in this chapter, love was not explicitly mentioned by a majority of the dads. However, in expanding the construct to include understanding, caring, and being the child's best friend, love became the single most prevalent theme. It may be that a masculine means of expressing love is framed in these other terms. Even those fathers who talked about the necessity to demonstrate love to their children often couched the discussion in terms of "strong love," "bear hugs," or other phrases that gave permission for masculine men to express nurturance and love.

In response to the question, "What makes a good father?", Glen replied:

> What makes a good father? Wish I had the answer. ... I think it's kind of what I would call strong love. That it's there, it's free flowing, it comes out. Not a day

> goes by where I don't tell my daughter, "Have I told you that you're the bestest daughter in the whole wide world today, and that I love you very much?" And it doesn't matter whether we have a good day or an absolutely rotten day together.

Glen referred to this as "strong" love, but he characterized it in very tender terms and emphasized that it is there in abundance, unconditionally and tenderly expressed. Similarly, Greg used the term "bear hugs" to characterize his frequent expressions of affection and made it clear that this was physical affection that should not just flow from fathers to daughters, but to sons as well:

> For me every day I try to give the kids kind of like a bear hug, and again I don't care if anybody's got boys or girls but let them know they're loved. That's important to start off the day.

A bit of the struggle to be consistently emotionally available and affectionately expressive came through in Greg's statement that he "tries" to dispense these hugs everyday. Ken was more comfortable in being able to express his affection without needing to couch it in traditional male terms. He spontaneously discussed that his perspective may not be the most traditional, but that it did not matter to him:

> And I guess the other thing I've strongly believed was that the father needs to show a lot of love. That's the role of the father ... to show love. And that may not be real traditional because I think a lot of people believe ... that it's the mother's role to show love and the father's role is to discipline. I think each parent shows the whole thing. And so what I wanted to show was love and affirmation and acceptance.

Ken's statement of love and affirmation and acceptance was among the most explicit. For Ken, this style of relating to his children had been a conscious decision. His statement reflected an understanding that children need father love, affirmation and acceptance to be demonstrated on a regular basis. Later the discussion turned to other dad's ways of talking through related issues. Although they did not specifically mention the word "love" in their comments, they were caring, emotionally engaged, and sensitive men who felt the need to connect with their children in this manner. In responding to the question of what makes a good dad, Robert said:

> A good father to me is someone who is willing to sit down and listen to their children.

These aspects of listening and being available for talking through issues was a way for fathers to express love, concern, and connection to their children. Adam discussed a different aspect of being a good father. Again, although not explicitly using the term love, Adam's description of a good father is characterized by a loving sensitivity and understanding:

> I think a good listener, a lot of patience, and ... I think an ability to understand where your children are at and how they think as opposed to where you're at and how you're thinking about what they're involved in. You know trying to understand the mentality of ... like a nine-year-old as opposed to you being a forty-year-old or something like that. You know there is a generation gap there and people tend to think automatically of their selves and their own situation and not how a nine-year-old person feels. You know there is a communication thing there that I think, ... If you happen to grasp it, it makes a world of difference.

A different expression of love came out as "caring" in several fathers' statements about what makes a good father. Joseph sees caring and teaching as going together. He said:

> I think having that teaching quality and a caring one, I mean you can't have a father without a caring father. But I think probably over and above anything else it would be probably be one that was of a type of teacher, one that could, you know, answer questions or point a kid in the right direction of whatever he'd want to know.

Several men emphasized the active nature of such care. It is not enough to have it; it must be demonstrated actively if it is to communicate engagement to children. Colin discussed the necessity for fathers to have a genuine interest in their children:

> What makes a good father? What makes a good father is somebody that's really interested in what the kid thinks and feels; that makes a good father.

Similarly, Jeff talked about the necessity for fathers to engage in their children's lives:

> Researcher: In everyday terms, what makes a good father?
>
> Jeff: A father who really is a part of the kids' lives, not just the guy who goes to work, comes home, eats dinner and watches TV. You have to interact, and it becomes a part of their lives. I think that's it.

In summary, a way for fathers to express love is through active, engaged caring, listening, and seeking understanding of their children. Not all men may be comfortable in demonstrating an abundance of physical affection, but their active interest and provision of an emotionally sensitive and caring environment are all part of father love. These aspects of fathering were sometimes difficult to separate from men expressing the need to "be there" for their children.

Being There

Another prevalent theme expressed by fathers in the sample when asked in open-ended ways about what the father's role is, or what makes a good father, was the idea that fathers need to "be there" for their children. Being there was a way of expressing care, investment, concern, availability, interest, emotional support, and love. Being there is a way for fathers to provide moral guidance, a listening ear, "moral support," and encouragement. It allowed them to monitor their children's progress, issues, concerns, successes, and areas that needed general attention.

The way that being there was used did not necessarily connote physical proximity or engagement. It could mean availability, monitoring, or just having the child know that the parent was available. The following exchange occurred with Neil as we talked through the fathering role:

> Researcher: In everyday terms, what makes a good father?
>
> Neil: A good father? Somebody that cares, that's committed.
>
> Researcher: Is that it?
>
> Neil: Well, that's not it. The brief answer, that would be it. Somebody that will be there when you need them or somebody that will, if they can't be there, that will do whatever they can do to meet your need, somebody that wants to meet your needs, yes.

Similarly, Alan spontaneously expounded on a sense of what it means to be there for your children. He has an ability to articulate this concept well, but he expressed a sense of gnawing doubt in the end of the quotation because he felt he had not had the benefit of a positive model from an involved father figure. Alan revealed:

> Someone who's there all the time to listen to the children's problems, and try and help them with what problems they have, to answer whatever questions that they might come up with no matter if they're stupid questions or crazy questions. To comfort them when they're hurting and be there to congratulate them when they do something right. Just to be there for them with whatever needs they need. Help them with whatever problems they have—I guess, is what it is, because I never had a real father, so I don't know.

Roger talked about evaluating his ability to be there for his son, and felt that he had come up short. He needed to make the difficult decision between working a shift that provided good income for his family and changing jobs to have more available time. He chose to invest the time in his relationship with his son. Roger explained:

> I want to be there for him, I want to be there at night times when he comes home from school and so that he can talk to dad. And if he has any problems, that we can go places together. And I didn't see myself that way. If I was working the three to eleven shift and he had an important ball game that night, or important anything, and dad couldn't make it, because dad had to work. And you know I never had that. My dad was always there for me. And I look at it as I always want to be there for him, and teach him the right values and stuff.

Roger had a positive fathering role model from his own father, who demonstrated the importance of being there by making it happen in their relationship. It was also clear that Roger felt that being there for important events and shared activities would facilitate his ability to influence his son's values in a direction that he considered to be positive. Being there got him some directional capital. Roger continued in his discussion. He talked a little about the fact that gender roles are not as neatly segregated as in the past, and how it is important for the whole family for him to spend time with them. The following shows that there is a blurring of fatherly roles with family roles, fathering, and husbanding:

> Well, like I said in today's society anymore, it's not being the father being the sole provider where it used to be years ago. Now his mother and I both work full time. And we both provide—a lot of times I've seen relationships where the father was always out and about. And I said that's why I always feel that when I'm out having a beer, and it's time to get home ... I don't want to be out until all hours of the night. Because I feel it's my responsibility to be there. If something ever happened and I wasn't there, I don't know how I would feel about that. And just feel like we should be, you know be a family instead of, you know, her going her way and my going—I would want to be there in a family. I really enjoy the family situation where it's, you know, my wife and I and him going out all the time. Instead of me going out and her taking him to the mall all the time, and I never get to see him here, and we go down to my sister's pool and I'm never there, you know. I always want to be there when he experiences all these new things.

In the end, what was important to Roger was that he would be there with his son as he experienced new things. Craig made a statement that nicely summarized many of the qualities expressed concerning the importance of being there:

> Researcher: What do you see as the father's main jobs or responsibilities with regard to his children?
>
> Craig: Just what I've said, that to be able to be there when they need you and to be able to take care of them, be able to be there, everything. When they need something you'll be able to take care of it.

Some observers would label Craig's statement as "instrumental," having a focus on getting a job done. Such characterizations of men's roles are often cast in a disparagement of traditionalism. However, another view of Craig's statement is that it reflects an active sharing of love. Whereas nurturance and caring are cast as traditionally feminine roles, Craig's expression of being able to "take care of it" may be viewed to be an active expression of nurturance.

When talking through the tough parts about being a father, several men brought up the time crunches they experienced in trying to fulfil multiple roles at once (Daly, 1996a). For Mark this translated into compromising his felt need to be there to experience the developmental milestones and new events of his children:

> Researcher: What's the toughest part of being a dad?
>
> Mark: Not having enough time to be there, not being able to be there all the time. You worry, well, not worry, but you're concerned about the first time he walks he'll be at day care and you won't see it. Or, you know, like the first time he does anything will be when you're gone or doing something else.

Mark's comments show that he defines the father's role as an involved man who shares in the development of new skills and abilities of his children. Implicit in his comments is the anxiety associated with missing important events or milestones in his children's lives. Although Mark focused on the development of motor skills (he had one infant), other fathers discussed the importance of helping their children through decisions and relationships. One way that these themes were expressed was to talk about fathers as teachers, models, or moral guides.

Model/Teacher/Moral Guide

When combining the related themes of teacher, model, and moral guide, exactly one half of the sample talked about this aspect of the paternal role. The idea of living by example was prominent. Some men were very planful in this regard. For instance, Leo said:

> The major role of a father is to be a role model and to be what you want your children to be. As they grow up not become so concerned on how they're acting or how they're behaving or the mistakes that they make, but just concerned about me as a father or any father living the life that he wants his kid to be.
>
> Researcher: What makes a good father?
>
> Leo: That's a tough question. I'll give it a shot. I think a good father would be an individual that would look ahead in 20 years and say to himself "What do I want my child to be 20 years from today?" and then begin at that moment living that goal.

Leo believed the main way to teach children is by living through example. Other fathers also expressed a keen awareness that their own behaviors would shape their children's lives through modeling. Mark said:

> So I guess the role is not only provider, but a role model or, you know, to help influence and shape his life, and instill ... values and the morals that my wife and I share into him.

It is interesting that Mark was focused on instilling values shared by he and his wife. Although he did not explicitly express this, perhaps he consciously avoided transferring unshared values. Robert talked about what makes a good father by focusing on a combination of the themes developed thus far:

> What makes a good father? Spending quality time with the children, showing them what love is, sharing love with them. Allowing his children to understand him, understanding that he's a role model, and he reflects on his children, whether he understands or not they perceive so much, and they're going to interpret his mannerisms, his ways of thinking, his talk. So he needs to understand that.

Bruce talked about serving as a guide as children grow into maturity, and the need for fathers to model positive values and lifestyles so that children will not be drawn into the dangers of drugs:

> Researcher: In everyday terms, what makes a good father?
>
> Bruce: That's a good question. I guess just to be their guide, to be, hopefully, your thinking is the right way to think and to guide them into maturity, hopefully have the values and not to grow up to be—you can't guarantee it—but not to be drug addicts.

For Scott, teaching, modeling, and guiding was a way to show caring or investment:

> Researcher: What makes a dad a good dad?
>
> Scott: Hum ... when he teaches his children what he thinks is right and wrong and ... the right discipline. Just the teaching, teaching them and caring for them. Not shucking them off. ... Let them know you care. That's most of it.

So, for Scott, responsible fathering means teaching children a sense of right and wrong and caring for them so as to demonstrate interest and involvement.

Role Sharing

Fathers in the sample were asked to address whether or not there were certain things that only a dad could do with their children, that is, things that a mother could not do, and vice versa. In response to this line of questioning, there was an even split. Some men maintained that aside from pregnancy, the physical delivery, childbirth, and nursing, there were no substantive differences between mothering and fathering. Roger responded:

> Like I said, my wife and I do everything the same with him. We both teach him, ... we both take him for a walk, we do this with him, we do that with him. We both provide for him since we both work and all that. I think it's more instead of just a fatherly responsibility and stuff, it's a parenting responsibility because my wife and I do the same things. I can't see any one thing that I do that she doesn't do, or that I do that she should do. I don't think—in that realm at all, it's I think, like I say in the years past, it used to be you taught it this, this and this, and I teach it this, this, and this because you're the male and I'm the female. But I don't see that anymore.

Tom responded to the question, "In everyday terms, what do you think makes a good father?", by stating:

> Basically would be the same thing in making a good parent, trying to be there when your kids need you, help them when they need help, praise them when they need help, pick them up when they fall down. Scold them or chastise them when they need that.

Tom's insights show an awareness of emotional needs, connection, correction, and the role-sharing nature of mothers and fathers in parenting. Craig saw essentially no difference. He wanted to see that the parents were interchangeable so that in the event of some unforseen crisis, they could replace one another:

> Researcher: Tell me what you think of when I say "Would you describe the father's role?
>
> Craig: The same as the mother's. You know, you teach them right from wrong, left from right, how to tie their shoes, everything. You're their reference point to a certain age. When they have a question they look at you and you give them the answer. That's your responsibility to give them the correct answer or to at least give them a multiple choice that they can choose the right answer. And if they choose the wrong one you find out why. I don't look at it as father's versus mother's role. I look at it as parents. For some reason if we were to be separated, divorced or one of us would die, you should be interchangeable. You know, if my wife were to pass away tomorrow or to leave for some reason, I should be able to change diapers and feed them and take care of them and give them baths just like she could. I don't look at it as a male versus female role.

Others stated that there were important differences—generally in regard to tenderness, emotionality, or gender-role socialization. Craig said that there were no differences in theory, but he acknowledged some in practice:

> Researcher: Are there any things that only a mom can do?

Craig: If for instance one of the kids stubbed a toe or cut a finger or some thing, they would run to her before me. So she can be more nurturing than I can, I guess, more outwardly showing a sign of caring than I could. Whereas if a kid was to walk up to me with a bloody finger, I would more attack the problem of, hey, let's fix the bloody finger so you stop bleeding, and saying, oh, and have a pouty face, and give them a big hug, and I'd be more concerned with, you're losing bodily fluid and we've got to stop it. And then after that it would be like, okay, get back to what you were doing. Outwardly, she shows more signs of emotion than I do.

Glen expressed considerable frustration over the fact that although there are no logical reasons why there should be gender-role differences between mothers and fathers, in reality the children behave as though there are significant differences. It is possible that his children may not be reacting to differences in roles as much as styles of interacting. Without further data, it is difficult to partial out. Glen said that he did not want to be the "second string" caregiver, and expressed frustration over the fact that his children treated him as such despite his efforts to be equally involved in their care:

Researcher: Tell me what is the father's role?

Glen: (pause) ... What I'd like to see the father's role is um ... be more than a contributor. More than a strong contributor, more than a strong contributor, more than a back up. That the father's role would be just as much responsibility and contribution as the mother's role. So the children would see that there's a parental unit that is raising them. As opposed to "Well this is what I go to mommy to and this is what I go to daddy to." Why do my children get upset when my wife drops them off at day care and they give me a big hug and kiss and say "By Daddy, have a nice day at work" when I drop them off? And that is, my belief is cause daddies are supposed to go to work every day. They have to. And mommies they are supposed raise children and my mommy's going off to work. So they resent her and accept the very same thing in me. So in some sense I don't see that as right and I see that as them viewing our roles different, and to try and answer your question on what do I see that role as. I'd want to see that role as um ... where our children would certainly see differences in the way we approach them, but that they would recognize that our roles are equal and contributing and I think they see is as contributing in very different ways. If they're sick and not feeling well, if daddy can't stay home that's OK, but if mommy can't stay home and we have to find a neighbor they resent mommy for it. And sometimes I wish they'd resent both of us for it. 'Cause it's both of our responsibilities.

In considering differences in maternal and paternal roles, Ned spoke from his experience as a single-parent father and used it as evidence that moms and dads can, and frequently do, cover for one another:

> Researcher: Are there some things that only a dad can do that a mom really can't?
>
> Ned: No. We would like to think that. We would like to think that the dad's the only guy who can do these things. But moms can do those things. There have been single moms forever and ever. You know, single parenthood, single fathers, that's a relatively new thing. Back when I did it about nine years ago or ten years ago it was really radical. But now it's more and more single dads are around. But you would like to tell yourself I can do these things and a mom couldn't do those things. But when we look at it realistically, we step back, you know, moms can do those things, too.

In discussing the convergence of men's and women's roles in today's society, several men discussed the fact that things were changing. Roles are in flux. This caused some concern, confusion, or discomfort. Nelson stated:

> It's a very fine line today to understand a father's role. I think he needs to be involved but by the same token don't take anything away from mom.

Nelson's comment shows that he is aware that crossing role boundaries can bring personal devaluation. There is a delicate balance to be maintained between being involved enough without making other parents or caregivers feel unnecessary. Steve offered his insights into the changing nature of parents' roles in society:

> Researcher: How would you describe the father's role?
>
> Steve: Well, we're at a turning point in our society here. Whereas, I was raised, my father was—my mother stayed home, ... my father went out and worked, his interaction with children was actually very limited and his job was bringing the bread home, okay. And after he'd work, fifty, sixty, seventy hours a week, he would spend a couple of weeks of vacation a year with us and some weekends doing some things with us, and other than that, his time was his time. Now we're at this turning point where dads are expected to be able to do mom things and moms are expected to be able to do dad things, you know. And so it's really difficult to explain that. But the role of a father is to be the bread winner, okay, to be the man there who's there anytime a child has any question at all. He should be able to answer it reasonably for that child. To provide love for the kids, moral support, as far as any of their little activities that I'm to take and say, do, and be there to play with. And all the other little things that go along with it, giving them baths, changing diapers, all the abilities of what was traditionally a woman's job, the tradition woman's job, being able to also be accomplished at that, too. A lot of dads don't know how to give a kid a bath, let alone change a diaper, etcetera.

Steve eloquently described many aspects of the modern androgynous parent. Prior to having children, Thomas had given a lot of forethought to the meaning of parenting roles and the implications of role sharing. He held frank discussions with his professionally accomplished wife concerning sharing the responsibilities of parenting. He described the father's role in the following manner:

> I think the father's role is to be responsible for what you have participated in creating. I think a child is a unique, completely unique person. And that for the first two decades of that child's life, you have to be there for them because they don't know anything about the world. But then, at the same time, you have to prepare them to make their own decisions, contradictory and probably impossible things, as it may be. I think the father's role is to bring up a child who will be able to function as a person in a dangerous world. And also, I think there are lots of things about fairness and justice that one institutes in a child about, as well. And the best way I think of teaching it is to live it. It's a real difficult charge, by any means. For my life I made that commitment, and we decided to have the child, to have Paul. Living up to that is something that I continually have to do. It's always difficult to do. But that's part of it, I guess.

Men in the sample were specifically asked whether they had special obligations toward their wives/partners as fathers in a manner that was different from before having children. In essence, this was an attempt to see if the addition of the fathering role made any tangible difference in the way in which they experienced and expressed the husband's role. Some men talked through increased commitment to marriage, the need to balance time and attention, or the willingness to be less the center of attention in terms of their wives' time. These are discussed in detail in the chapter on the effects of fathering on marriage (chap. 8, this vol.). Gilbert talked about the need to present a unified front in more than agreeing on decisions:

> You always try not to belittle or get mad at your partner. So you don't want your child to see that you're thinking negatively about them in any way. So you should always try to treat your partner with respect and dignity, if not love, at all times, but even more so if you have a child, I believe, so he feels the same way.

Gilbert's comment shows an implicit awareness that he is modeling appropriate love and respect between marriage partners, which is a form of training his children in attributes of a successful marriage relationship.

THE TOUGHEST PARTS OF BEING A DAD

In discussing the difficult parts of fathering, most frequently discussed things were *discipline* (saying no), *having time, launching children,* and *being helpless* when they are ill or incommunicative infants.

One of the more interesting responses came from Neil, who discussed the uncertainty of his own life, and the sense that as a father he was being called on to provide leadership despite not knowing where he was going himself:

> Researcher: What's the toughest part of being a dad?
>
> Neil: Probably not knowing where you're headed yourself and trying to guide the rest of the family, and not just not sure where you're standing and giving out edicts or mandates that have to be met, and saying, what the heck am I doing this for, I don't even know if it's right. The uncertainty of life, thinking that you're doing the right thing but just not being sure.

Similarly, some men discussed the fact that they were still learning the role of father, and they were learning by trial and error, from their children, or flying by the seat of their pants.

ASSUMING THE FATHER ROLE IS A LEARNING PROCESS

Several men spontaneously commented (before being asked how they had learned to be a father) that fathering roles are learned by process, through interaction with others. Sometimes it is other fathers or mothers who teach men how to father, but often, it is their children:

> Researcher: Let me ask you this: What's the father's role?
>
> Vicente: What's the father's role? I'm learning that. Outside of being a provider and a role model—which is actually a father's role and a mother's role—I guess you could say, more specifically with a father, I'm learning that kids are generally mother—I mean, they're just clung to their mothers anyway. I think dads have to put a little more time on the clock. And the growing and developmental stages of a child, definitely spending that time there, taking time out to play with them and talk with them. ... You're a provider, you're a teacher, you're a role model you're a leader. You have to be, I guess, later on as she gets older, learning how to be that best friend. Protector, you know, it's a lot of things, I think, a father becomes as the child gets older. Right now at this stage, I find myself as being a provider and a role model and a teacher. I'm sure that's, like I said, a change as she gets older. But that's what I see right now.

Whereas Vicente was able to elaborate on numerous aspects of the fathering role, and although he had insight that the role changes with the age and developmental abilities of the child, he knew that he needed to learn the role. He sounded as though he expected to keep learning the role as his children's developmental status and interests changed. Ned talked about the mutual learning that fathers and children engage in. He stated:

> We're teaching our kids to be good kids and they're teaching us to be good dads, sort of goes hand in hand. We learn from each other. But there's

> thousands of challenges, and thousands of tough parts. You know, you take that in stride.

A few fathers made comments indicating they were somewhat insecure, defensive, or confused about the father's role, but this was fairly unusual. Robert said in regard to the question of what the father's role is:

> I hope I answered that correctly anyway. It's really hard for me to understand exactly what my own role is ...

Each father was asked what makes a father a "good father." This question was asked far into the interview so that rapport was already established and various issues about fathering and life had already been discussed. Each father in the sample offered insight into the meaning of good fathering.

TOWARD AN UNDERSTANDING OF GOOD FATHERING

Some fathers state that good fathering is a difficult thing to describe, yet they go on to specify several characteristics of good fathering. Every man in the sample talked about several different components of good fathering, indicating an awareness that it is multifaceted and that contemporary fathers are well aware of the multidimensionality of involved fathering. The average father in the study listed 3 ($M = 3.29$) components of good fathering, and most often the different components listed represented different aspects of good fathering—they were not simply synonyms for other terms they had used. Some men in the sample indicated that good fathering may differ from situation to situation, showing a sensitivity to individual differences, different contexts, abilities, and personalities. Alternatively, they may have simply been sensitive to the need to embrace diversity and the need to shy away from being moralistic or prescriptive. Again, without exception, all fathers were able to describe characteristics of good fathers.

The most prevalent component of good fathering could be briefly stated as "being there" for your children. Being there captures the relational components of involved fathering. The fact that it was the most prevalent theme expressed by the fathers in the sample indicates that they, at some basic level, value the relational components of fathering above the role performance components. Sample fathers discussed relational aspects of good fathering more than three times as frequently as they did role components. Relationship themes were discussed 62 times, whereas role enactment components appeared 19 times. Role components were represented nearly twice as frequently as personal characteristics (personality traits/styles) of fathers (discussed by 11 fathers). Thus, in order of decreasing prevalence, when asked "what makes a good father?," fathers in the sample focused most heavily on relationship building and maintenance, followed by role enactment, and least on personal characteristics of men in fathering roles. In order to facilitate a presentation of the composite picture of good fathering, this section presents the summary statements of men's descriptions without inserting specific quotes from the interviews. In compiling the following statement, a composite description was constructed, blending the 40 fathers' narratives into one. I chose to do this because quotes concerning good fathering were interspersed throughout the other previous thematic discussions. By constructing a composite statement, different aspects of good fathering emphasized by different fathers can be elaborated. The composite statement uses specific terms and phrases from different fathers' responses. In the following paragraph, various components of being there were detailed.

A COMPOSITE STATEMENT OF GOOD FATHERING

Relational Components

A good father is someone who is there for his children. He is caring and loving. His children know that he is committed to them. He is available to them, and he spends quality time with them. His time with them shows that he is genuinely interested in them. He demonstrates enjoyment in relating to his children, it is not just a job. He has fun with his children and values the time that they can spend together. Time together with his children is given a high priority. In "being there," a good father creates an atmosphere of emotional closeness and safety—an atmosphere where his children are free to be open to him and free to turn to him in times of need. His children can trust that he will do what is in their best interest. His children know that he is invested in understanding them. His children know that no matter what they do, they will always be accepted and loved by their father. Good fathers show concern and will comfort their children when they are hurting. A father's behavior and attitudes unmistakably show that he is child centered and willing to sacrifice his own goals and career in order to actively do things for his children. A good father has a friendship with his children, values that friendship, and will invest in developing a growing, individualized relationship with them. Good fathers value and relate closely with their children emotionally, understanding wise, and through shared activity and fun.

Role Components

A good father is a provider. A good father recognizes that provision extends beyond economic responsibility. Beyond seeing what material resources his children need, he will create and provide opportunities for their fun, learning, growth, and development. He will create space for his children to make choices in a supportive environment and to become their own person. Although a good father has guidelines and sets appropriate boundaries for his children, he recognizes that they need to be given space to explore their own interests and styles of behavior and expression.

A good father is a teacher, a moral guide, and a role model. He will live what he wants his children to become. He understands that he is a leader, and lives in a manner that reflects responsible service-leadership. He understands that discipline is not just a matter of correction, but that it requires self-discipline to teach through modeling and showing commitment and responsibility. A good father will integrate his faith into his fathering and will act on fathering instincts. A good father will attempt to answer his children's questions and to foster their learning, broadly defined to include scholastic, athletic, moral, spiritual, and practical knowledge.

Personality Components

A good father is understanding, a good listener, and will talk honestly with his children. He will try to remember what it was like to be a child, and will honor those feelings in his children. He shows patience toward his children, who are not at the same place developmentally as he now is. He recognizes that children need time, as well as appropriate support, to develop into maturity.

A good father is someone who will set a vision of good fathering ahead of himself and will strive to achieve consistent performance at that level. He will set realistic fathering goals. He will invest in regular self-improvement, and admit his weaknesses. In seeing his shortcomings, he will not be overcome by failing to meet his own or others' standards of good fathering. He will target specific areas for performance improvement. He will also appropriately recognize his strengths and will not withhold what he can do for his children. He will invest himself in continual growth toward good fathering. He sees that part of good fathering is maintaining a good relationship to his partner and maintaining a good household.

When the relational, role, and personal characteristics of good fathering are viewed as a whole, most men will readily admit they have vast room for improvement. Yet, at the same time, involved fathers have made significant investments into their relationships with their children, regularly attempt to balance various components of role enactment, and invest in personal growth so that they have more to offer to their children. Involved fathers know what good fathering entails and are committed to engaging in it and to personal growth so that they can continue to build their relationships with their children.

PATTERNS OF REPORTED INVOLVEMENT

Interview participants were asked about three different categories of father involvement. They were first asked about the division of time invested in parenting tasks with their spouse/partner in the following manner: "This is a tough question. I want to try to get you to split things up in terms of rough percentages, how do you split things with your wife (girlfriend, partner, etc.) in terms of overall time spent in parenting, the amount of time you spend with your children, the time you spend doing things that are parent-related tasks? For instance is it twenty/eighty, fifty/fifty, sixty/forty? How do you split your time spent in parenting with your partner?" The average father in the interview sample claimed to invest around 40% of the overall time spent in parenting tasks (M = 44%). However, there was considerable variation in what men reported to be their share of the child-care involvement. The "least involved" father claimed 10% of the time invested as his own, and the most involved father, a single dad with custody of his children, claimed 100% (SD = 18%). Using a conventional manner of dividing the sample into segments, those men who were within one standard deviation of the mean were considered to have "average" levels of involvement, those one standard deviation or more below the mean were labeled "low involvement" fathers, and those one or more standard deviations above the mean were considered "highly involved" fathers. For the interview sample, those ranges worked out so that low involvement men contributed 25% or less of the parenting tasks, average fathers claimed responsibility for from 26% to 61% of the parenting tasks, and highly involved fathers contributed to 62% or more of the parenting tasks. It should be noted that this division is relative and arbitrary and represents a bias against men who have highly participative partners. For example, a highly involved father who does 25% of the parenting work in his family may engage in more *absolute* child care than another father who does 50% of the child care in his family (with a less involved spouse). Specifically, men who have partners who are highly participative in child care would have scores that represent a lower percentage of overall child care than men whose partners are relatively uninvolved in child care.

The second aspect of involvement that was explored had to do with the number of tasks. The issue was discussed in the following manner: "Now, in terms of the number of parenting tasks, you know, the time that might not be related directly to the number of things, some things you can do really quickly, some take a long time but it's only one job. How would you say you split up the number of parenting tasks? Out of the hundred percent of the tasks that have to be done what percentage do you do, what percentage does your partner do?" As in the previous case, there was considerable variability in answers received. Interestingly, the mean for this question was slightly higher than for the previous one. That is, although most men perceived that they did not spend as much time in parenting as did their wives or partners, they accomplished a greater proportion of the number of tasks relative to the time invested. One way to interpret this is that fathers view themselves to be more efficient in accomplishing parenting tasks than their wives/partners. The mean for this question was 46%, with a range from 10% to 100% (SD = 19%). As in the previous question, fathers were divided into low, average, and high involvement fathers, with cutoffs being up to 27%, from 28% to 65%, and 66% and up, respectively.

The final aspect of involvement discussed with the interview sample had to do with the division of parenting responsibilities. The question was phrased in the following manner: "Then there's one other subject I want to probe a little bit, and that would be the responsibilities of parenthood, things like making appointments for the doctor. Making sure that there are arrangements for child care, making sure the kids have what they need in terms of clothing and food, and supervision, and education, sort of the executive decision making? But beyond the decision actually taking responsibility and making the arrangements how do you split that?" As in other studies, this is the area where the sample fathers were least involved. They reported a mean of 39% of the responsibility, with a range of from 0% to 100% (*SD* = 22%). Thus, categories of low, average, and highly involved fathers were men sharing 17% or less, from 18% to 61%, or 62% or greater of the responsibility, respectively.

Whereas 5 of the 40 fathers were in hi or low groups for single aspects of involvement (time, tasks, or responsibility), 2 were in the same category for two classes of involvement, and 33 fathers were in the same category for all three classifications of involvement. No father was "hi" for one category and "low" for another. As such, there was consistency in the level of involvement fathers reported across categories. Averaging across time invested, tasks accomplished and responsibility assumed, overall, the average father in the sample claimed to do about 40% of the parenting required.

PROVISIONAL BALANCES IN FATHERING ROLES

There are many issues of balance that were expressed by men in the sample. They talked about the challenges of balancing the need to bring direction to their children's lives without being dictators, fostering independence without being neglectful, balancing being a friend versus being a father, balancing adequate provision without spoiling a child, and balancing a just division of child and home-related labor with their spouses/partners. There were also issues of balancing involvement in fathering with the demands of other roles, such as worker, spouse, friend, or community member. Thomas expressed the need to balance the child's dependency needs with fostering independence, and treating children with respect, helping them to achieve their potential without directing or pushing them:

> Researcher: In everyday terms, what makes a good dad?
>
> Thomas: I think it's someone who can live with their child as a person and deal with them as one would deal with other people. ... I think good dads recognize and accommodate a child's dependence and their independence. They help kids live and realize their lives while not actually directing them. I guess that's certainly a contradiction in my life that I'm aware of.

Colin focused on the difficulties of balancing the disciplinarian and friend roles of fatherhood:

> Researcher: What's the toughest part of being a dad?
>
> Colin: The toughest part of being a dad is trying to maintain a balance between being buddy and being the boss, you know, and trying to find some median there.
>
> Researcher: What happens if you get out of balance in either direction?
>
> Colin: Well, if I'm out of balance as far as being too much the buddy, he loses his—what's the word? Well, I lose my authority. And if I'm out of balance the other way I lose my buddy, you know. I like to have a friend relationship with my son, but somehow it would also be where he understands that I'm an authority, and when it's time to go to bed it's time to go to bed. We don't need to argue about it for a half hour. And stuff, that's just an example, stuff like that can, you know, it can be difficult when you're too much of one or the other.

Similarly, Ned talked about the challenges of being a single parent and head of household without being a dictator, how to provide enough structure without being too flexible. He elaborated:

> The father's role is to be head of the household. If I had a mate I would share those responsibilities. But I don't, so I'm the father of the house, and I set the rules with their help. You can't be a dictator, you have to sort of rule by consensus. But the father has the final say. I'm the head of the household. I guide the children from point A to point B, help them to reach adulthood and always be there for them, always be there for them. You have to be stern sometimes and real flexible at other times.

Peter talked about the need to achieve balance in role sharing with his wife:

> The toughest part of being a dad is probably being able to delegate responsibility between the wife and the father, as far as the child goes. And who's going to do what and what's—it's pretty much body language depending on how each other feels is who takes care of the baby. It's not really a spoken thing. So if both of you feel bad you end up in a predicament where it becomes a coin toss or whoever wears the pants in the family who makes a decision, and it's not always a father who makes that decision, I know it hasn't been with our family.

Donald talked about the struggle to balance quality time with quantity time with his children:

> Researcher: Before you said you can't work nine to nine and be a good father. What is a good father? What makes a man a good father?
>
> Donald: I think it's kind of a balance between quality time and quantity time at least in my opinion, I guess because I didn't have either of the two so I guess I

am lookin' for what I didn't get. ... I think it is somewhere in between the mix of quantity and quality time.

Also noticeable in the last passage is the need to balance what you never got with what you can give as a dad. A father can only address the perceived demands of his situation with available resources, and these are limited by his own developmental deficits.

CONCLUSIONS

Fathers talked about "changing times," including roles and trends in father involvement, usually citing their father's generation as a benchmark, but it is still not possible to chronicle the degree of change in fathering roles over the past 25 years—a period corresponding to an awakened interest in fatherhood by scholars and popular press writers. It is clear, however, that in concert with a changing culture of fatherhood that portrays fathers' roles as a blend of involved and loving nurturance that goes beyond economic provision, gender-role socialization and teacher/moral guide; contemporary fathers characterize fathering in a multifaceted manner that encompasses each of those elements. As such, the role of contemporary fathers can be seen to be in transition from the historical periods preceding, yet bringing to the prescription a balance of what had been predominant roles in each of the previous historical periods. Marked characteristics of contemporary fathers that may be a real difference from fathers of past eras are a focus on the role-sharing aspects of parenting, and the predominance of loving/caring elements of fathering in the multifaceted mix of roles. Again—calling to mind the initial caution regarding generalizations about fathers—in some ways, contemporary fathers appear to be different from fathers of past eras primarily by virtue of the fact that they manifest multiple aspects of fathering roles. Because contemporary men are aware of so many facets of fathering roles, they necessarily have a different blend than fathers of the past, who are characterized as specialists (e.g., the provider or the moral overseer). By recognizing the importance of each of these specialized roles and attempting to incorporate them into a multifaceted composite, today's fathers are challenged to balance their involvement with their children by adequately expressing each component of the role (Palkovitz, 1987). Because this is impossible at any given moment, balance comes over longer periods of time, and the role investments of any particular father at any given time are provisional. Balances remain in tact until new demands arise and are recognized (or are perceived, even if they do not exist). It is a constant struggle to maintain balance, because the systems involved are dynamic. Because conditions in family life and relationships constantly change, balance cannot remain static. Balance is only achieved in movement. As elements change force or position, the necessary balance changes. It is probably impossible to maintain balance in the short run. Many men are centered on work during some portion of the day and centered on fathering at other times. This may explain why fathers who are traditional dads find it necessary to be so exuberantly playful and unpredictable when they come home from work and become "the toy," or the "playmate." Their animated attempts to center attention on their child(ren) may be an effort to bring balance for their lengthy absence. Greater absence is balanced by greater presence. If time is not available as a resource, then enthusiasm is brought into the equation. Or, consider the example of the father who has been working overtime to provide for a perceived financial need. He sees that his investment of time and energy into his work is creating emotional distance or stress at home, so he cuts back at work to have more time with his family. In reestablishing contact with his family he may temporarily suppress the "boss" role to emphasize the "buddy" role with his children and find new ways to show love while being strong. Within a very short time, his redirected involvement will result in a new set of balances in the demands of the family system, which in turn he must appropriately read and respond to with a new set of role enactments.

This view of provisional balances helps to explain why sometimes holidays or family vacations bring stress and conflict instead of the desired positive outcomes. When people leave familiar roles and routines, if they are not skilled at reading the needs and resources of the family system, and if they are not in a system characterized by flexibility, then adjustments to role enactments bring stress and conflict. They simply are not able to bring their involvement or role investments into balance with the expected or real needs of the family system.

With a little extrapolation, such an understanding leads to the interesting speculation that shipwrecked fathering is really nothing more than the failure of a father to appropriately read and respond to the dynamic changes in the worlds of his family, work, and community involvements in a manner that maintains an appropriate balance. Without balance, you fall. Without balance, you cannot walk alongside another, or lead another, or care for another with skill. Men who fail to adaptively balance involvement in these spheres over time are labeled as negligent fathers, "bad" husbands, unreliable workers, drains on the community, or whatever label fits their particular imbalance. There is a corresponding developmental imbalance in their children (e.g., acting out, eating disorders, attention seeking, substance abuse, etc.), their marriages (e.g., extramarital affairs, abuse, divorce, incompatibility, etc.), their work trajectory (e.g., absenteeism, workaholism, revolving door phenomenon, etc.), or their community involvement (e.g., being one of the "boys," a coaching over-achiever, busybody, a civic activist, etc.).

The reality is that developmental outcomes are multiply determined, and it could be viewed as an oversimplification to present the consequences of father role balance (or imbalances) in this manner. However, it is equally true that in a multiply determined, dynamic system, changing levels of resources and investment of those resources will change later developmental outcomes. Similarly, resource deficits will influence developmental trajectories. As such, changing involvement in fathers' role enactments will have developmental consequences for fathers, mothers, children, and the larger family and community system. You do reap what you sow.

At a less dramatic level than shipwrecked fathering, if you talk with any man concerning mistakes he may have made as a father, or mistakes that his father made in his own upbringing, it is frequently the case that the terms "too much" or "not enough" (or their equivalents) are invoked to describe or explain the problems. People implicitly understand that good fathering is a matter of balance and there is a dynamic interaction between father involvement, balance, and developmental outcomes. In the multifaceted, ever-changing demands placed on fathers, provisional balances must be continually monitored, adjusted, and maintained.

Chapter **4**

Fathering and the Life Course

This chapter details men's perceptions that they are genuinely different people than they would have been if they had never had children. It reviews major themes in men's discussions of the effects of fathering on their development and shows how those themes tend to cluster into two distinctly different patterns of change attributable to fathering. Specifically, some men experience major changes in life course and personality and focus on the *jolt* that fatherhood exerts in their lives. Other men perceive that fathering has had less dramatic (but still significant) influences on their development, serving as a *gentle evoker* of tendencies they always had, although some needed the stimulation of active engagement in fathering to move from dormancy. Men in the former group were more likely to be early timing fathers (men having their first child before age 21), and those in the latter group tended to be late timing fathers (those 32 or older when having their first child). Theories and data are synthesized to show that life-course transitions and personality factors interact to determine life-span developmental outcomes.

This chapter limits analyses to open-ended questions raised near the beginning of the interview and the closing questions from each session. The responses of the 40 fathers to this series of four questions are summarized here. The questions were as follows:

1. Sometimes you hear men make statements like, "I'm a really different person than I would have otherwise been because I have children." Other men may feel that fatherhood has had little or no impact on who they are as people. Do you feel that fatherhood has played a major or a minor role in shaping who you are?
2. Aside from how you spend time and money, those are quantitative things, things you can stick a number on; "X hours here and X dollars there," do you feel that fatherhood has made you a qualitatively different person? Has it caused you to develop differently than you would have developed had you never been a father? Has

it significantly affected *who* you are, your skills, your personality, or the course of your life?

Intervening between Questions 2 and 3 was the remainder of a 60- to 90-minute interview examining perceived effects of fatherhood on specific areas or domains of men's development (please refer to the interview outline in Appendix 1). The final portion of the interview included the following series of questions:

3. We've looked at a lot of areas of your life, and in some of them you've said that, "Yeah, fathering has made a difference" in who you are as a person. What I want to know now is how can you be sure that it's fatherhood that has changed you? How do you know that it's not just maturity or aging or your job or your marriage or your education? How do you know that it's fathering that has changed you?
4. In terms of rough percentages, if we take a look at who you are today, as a person, as a man, what percentage of you is who you are because of being a dad?

The reader may question the inclusion of Question 4, a traditional quantative assessment, in this qualitatively based study. The question was crafted and included toward the end of the interview process in order to get a sense of men's perceptions regarding the magnitude of impact that engagement in fathering had on their development. I wanted to understand fathers' perceptions of the relative influence of fathering versus other formative factors in their lives.

For the most part, study participants experienced the changes associated with fatherhood to be extensive and profound. Some men were so invested in their roles as fathers that they could not articulate or even imagine what their lives would be like without children. Fatherhood had become a core construct in their identities (Minton & Pasley, 1996). Thinking from a perspective outside of fathering was a novel or foreign concept. Some men could not even imagine thinking in that manner. In response to Question 4, Glen stated:

> I'm not sure I could separate what percent of me is not because of fatherhood. I'm just so enamored with it that I don't ever look at what I might have been, what could I be doing instead, where would I be. I'm where I want to be, I'm happy with what I'm doing. I don't feel the ability to disassociate myself from fatherhood.

Glen's view of life was centered in his role as a father. His satisfaction with engagement in his life as father precluded consideration of alternate possibilities. He was so taken with fathering that he felt that he did not have the ability to think independently from his construction of life as a father. When asked to assess how much of who they had become could be attributed to fatherhood (see question 4), the mean response of sample fathers was 56.33% (range 20%–100%, *SD* = 27.52%). None of the study participants perceived that fatherhood had failed to exert an effect on their development, and in the smallest estimate, fathering was perceived to account for one fifth of his development as a person. Most fathers attributed approximately one half of who they had become to fathering. Needless to say, if this were a quantitative study where a single factor accounted for 50% of the variability in subjects' development, it would surely be the discovery of a powerful shaper of development! From involved fathers' vantage point, fathering is that powerful of a factor in determining who they are as a person. The mean percentage of life determination attributed to fathering by early timing fathers was 60%, in comparison to 46% for late timing fathers.

In one way or another, virtually all men expressed that fatherhood gave them purpose or further direction in life, an opportunity to reflect on who they were as persons, and provided a context within which to refine their personalities. These themes were voiced by Chris:

> You can learn a lot about yourself as far as the person, if you could handle the pressure or the stress or whatever of being a father. It's just opened up a whole lot of doors because then you can want to teach your child something that you know ... it's opened so many doors. You have a lot [more] places that you can go with this child, you know, than if you were just getting old or just getting mature, you're like, "well, my life is over, I don't have too much to do." But you got a child, it gives you a second wind in life.

While acknowledging that fathering introduces new levels of stress, Chris' view, embodied in his statements regarding opening doors and second wind, is that fathering creates potential and motivation to grasp the possible.

Active fathering is viewed as an opportunity to overcome developmental entropy and stagnation. It was common for men in the sample to express that fatherhood provided opportunities to enact changes that they had recognized as desirable or necessary for years. In a sense, they grasped fathering as a catalyst to embrace what they knew to be needed, but difficult, change. Assuming responsibility for a developing child imposed a sort of deadline on their developmental stasis. Nelson equated "real" fathering with change, implying that men who perceive themselves to be unaffected by fathering have not applied themselves to the role. By not changing, they had not done what their children needed. He said:

> The people who say they've changed are real fathers, I believe ... fathers who say they haven't changed are just as selfish as they were prior to being fathers.

The literature on parenting folklore and people who are child free by choice indicates that parents often characterize nonparents as being self-centered or selfish (Gillespie, 1999). Although this is often cast as a negative stereotype of childless individuals, it may also be the case that parents are accutely aware of the sacrifices they have been required to make in raising children. Parents tend to articulate those sacrifices frequently. Nonparents hear parents' discussion of sacrifices and often comment that they are not sure if they could "put up with" the continual demands of parenting. As such, parenting may serve as a catalyst for confronting the need to set aside "selfish" desires and tendencies to become more other centered. In reality, this is true of every caregiving situation, whether it is parenting or another caring relationship. Involvement in caregiving casts the caregiver into roles and situations that require putting aside your own desires for the good of the other. Child free by choice individuals can experience developmental pull through other caregiving relationships. Biological fathers who do not regularly engage in caregiving or other forms of involvement may not experience pulls toward other-centeredness to the extent that caring fathers do. There is something about the nonreciprocal nature of parenting, taking responsibility for a nonpeer who is dependent on you, that forges development in directions different from adult friendships or noncaregiving relationships. Nelson's comment indicates that men who father without changing have remained selfish, and are not "real" fathers. Fathers believe that fathering involvement brings change.

MAJOR THEMES

Five primary themes were depicted in the responses of fathers to the study questions. In decreasing order of prevalence, those themes were: (a) fatherhood stimulates a "*settling down*" process (45% of the sample), (b) fatherhood can motivate one to become more *giving* (35%), (c) accepting and engaging in a paternal role involves major *responsibility* (32%), (d) *generativity* themes (29%), and (e) that the effects of fatherhood may be experienced as a "*jolt*" (29%) to the lifestyle or life course to which a man is accustomed prior to having children. Each theme is discussed, and patterns of theme clustering are presented.

Settling Down

The most frequently expressed theme was that becoming actively engaged in fathering had stimulated men to settle down. Some men discussed the theme in terms of significantly reducing or eliminating "wildness" from their lives, whereas others focused more on needed direction, consistency in doing the right things, or becoming more focused. Differences in how strongly settling down was expressed was related to the consistency of responsibility and the relative degree of maturity the men had achieved prior to making the transition to fatherhood. Donald focused on putting rebellion to rest and the need to define a set direction in his life when he said:

> I think it [fathering] kind of settled me down a lot because I used to be like a real rebel. Then the kids kind of made my life a little bit more significant and my decisions more significant. It gave it more meaning. … I would have been on a course setting really for nowhere for no reason and now I have definite points for definite reasons.

Donald's comments show that his active engagement in fathering led to a self-reflection and self-evaluation of his life course that initiated changes in his behavior and lifestyle because he had adopted a sense of responsibility. Assuming responsibility for his children gave Donald a sense of significance that allowed him to put aside rebellion as a cause. This type of taking stock was not uncommon. Manuel stated:

> When you have a child, you've got to take a serious look at your life. You got to really say to yourself, "do you really want to keep going the way you're going?" I did still do a lot of things I was doing. I'm not going to say that I didn't. But I kind of cut back on a lot of them. I knew that I couldn't go to jail. Because I had a responsibility to a child. I knew that I had to be around in case that child needed me. And I always was.

Manuel, Donald, and many fathers in the sample took a serious look at the course their lives were on. They made conscious decisions about needed changes and applied themselves toward achieving the necessary transformations.

Even where there are not obvious characteristics that warrant change, fathering can motivate "settling down" in a direction that is significant, although more nuanced. An example of perceived changes being more subtle, but meaningful, was provided by Neil. Shifts in his self-perception were brought on by role engagement over time.

> I've become someone different actually than who I thought I was. I would have to say and put it that way. I thought I was a kid. I always saw myself as a kid. But when I have to be a dad, I can't be a kid, I have to be a dad. And so even though I may act like a kid and kind of want to be like that, I have to be a dad sometimes even when I don't want to be, and I have to make those decisions and I have to reason with my children. … So I guess that's helped me to grow up, become a lot more mature, slow down maybe.

Neil's statement shows that fathering roles place demands for adherance to mature behavior even when dads do not feel particularly adultlike. His characterization of the process reflects conscious decisions to set aside natural tendencies, inclinations, or desires to become more mature. The developmental draw of active fathering can require denial of familiar behavior patterns and a stretch to reach new ideals. The process described by Neil and others could be schematized in the following manner: A man makes a commitment to active fathering. In the process, he has multiple interactions with his children. The father assumes that his children need a particular level of functioning from him, and he strives to provide the support and modeling that they need, even if he does not feel that he has achieved the status that they think he has reached. By desiring to provide what he thinks his children need, he approaches a new level of maturity that would not be achieved without the motivation to be a "good dad." The desire to be a good father presents an ideal and a developmental draw toward which involved fathers aspire.

Becoming Less Self-Centered and More Giving

Another prevalent theme in the interviews centered around men stating that fatherhood had motivated them to become more other oriented. Specifically, many fathers had come to recognize that they were selfish and self-centered prior to having children. Interestingly enough, marriage did not seem to bring this realization, it was engagement in fathering that caused men to become more family oriented, even when it "cost" them their own plans. Neil elaborated this theme in the following passage:

> My life ... when I'm by myself, a lot of times is for me, what I want to do for me, where I want to be headed or what I want. Me, me, me, my, my, my, now, now, now stuff. When I'm with them I have to refocus and say what they need, what they want—not always what they *want,* what would be good for them and to try to find a direction for them, especially when I don't know what direction I want to go ... sometimes. ... I'd have to put what I want aside.

It was common for involved fathering to induce men to a recognition that they had to decenter from their own interests and pursuits to become more oriented toward what was best for the children. In the daily give and take of relating to children, personal desires and needs are measured against family needs countless times. Nelson's comments reflect a major reordering of priorities:

> You don't come first any longer. Once you have children they come first. ... They become number one in your life. Without children you can pursue any goal or anything in life that you want to provided that the money is there to do it. ... It's only you yourself that you have to worry about as opposed to when you have a child or children, you know, you have to worry about them as well. You can't be selfish when you have children.

Nelson's statement was one that was echoed by numerous fathers in the sample. They seemed to regard a higher sense of sacrifice for their children than for their spouse or partner. Prior to having children, men recounted that they had been self-centered. They viewed their spouses or partners to be mature individuals who could understand their motives and choices. Taking responsibility for children, however, places fathers into an imbalanced relationship, where fathers carry a greater degree of responsibility than do their children. Thus, for some men, having children and being involved with them was perceived to contribute to a heightened awareness of others' perspectives, needs, and a generally enhanced sensitivity to others' emotions. The resulting reorganization of priorities is not just theoretical, it has consequences in terms of decisions, time management, and relationships. Bruce said:

> Well, it's what I do with my activities, my spare time. There is no spare time. If there is any, it's spent with the children. I have absolutely no time for friends ... before I'd socialize more with friends. You know, it's just completely even changed the way you think.

Not all fathers experience a change in priorities as radically as in Nelson's or Bruce's cases, but the shift in priorities and attitudes is no less real. Regular involvement with children can facilitate an increased awareness of others' perspectives and needs. Jeff stated:

> I guess the joy of having them has made me more sensitive to things around me, especially as they pertain to the kids.

Other fathers discussed a sense of increased empathy and the ability to discern the importance of honoring others' feelings and perspectives (see chap. 5, this vol.). Ongoing interaction with children, who have different perspectives and priorities than adults do, can cause men to evaluate the validity of their own perspectives and to value others' viewpoints as genuine. The net result is that, in fathering and other relationships, involved dads tend to become more other centered, which is a hallmark of maturity (Heath, 1991).

Fathering Entails Major Responsibilities

Approximately one third of the sample spontaneously discussed the responsibilities of fatherhood. Accepting responsibility as an involved father relates to the previous theme in that once responsibility is "bought into," choices are made that are nonoptimal in regard to self-gratification or self-advancement. Men have many practical opportunities to practice putting the interests of others ahead of themselves. Clifford put it this way:

> I think I'm a more responsible person because I have children. I have to look out for them and not just me. I have to be more responsible to them. I have to worry about other people beside myself. If it wasn't for my children I would probably blow a lot of money I guess. It's a lot more responsibility, making me a more responsible person, I guess, basically.

Craig, an early timing father, felt that becoming an involved father had brought a major shift in his perspective as well. The perspective shift he describes reflects new understandings of responsibility to provide and care for others. He states that his new perspectives on responsibility prevented him from doing irresponsible things that he was prone to do before becoming an involved father:

> I don't know, it's just maybe looking at things differently in life. I have a different perspective. ... I guess sometimes I have thought about quitting work and irresponsible things like that. Things that I used to do all the time. I thought twice about because of my kids so I guess you could say it made me more responsible. ... You're responsible to three other lives that you brought into the world, so you have to look at taking care of those.

Steve's statement that shows that "buying in" to responsibility then triggers other nonoptional aspects of fathering. Active fathering does not only prescribe what should be done, it proscribes what should not be done. Steve's comment demonstrates that the decision to actively engage as a father brings other previously unquestioned components under a new level of scrutiny:

> With kids comes responsibility, you have a responsibility for another life and that changes your direction of what you want to do, what you can do or what you don't want to do. You don't have certain choices, you have to provide for these kids. If I was split-loose and fancy-free and say, if right now I'm unemployed and I figure if I probably was never married, and especially if I didn't have kids, I could probably just take off and go anywhere and do anything I want to do. And right now I can't do that. I have to pretty much consider other people's aspects, not only my spouse, or my partner as you put it, but my kids especially. They're in the area. I have to stay in the area, I got to support them. I like to be able to see them. And I think to move out of the area or do anything I want to do would be too complicated, much too difficult. I'm not saying it can't be done but it would be difficult.

Joseph noted a marked change in his appraisal of responsibility with the birth of his children. It caused him to reflect on and ultimately change his career track, the lifestyle he was leading, and the nature of his social networks. His paradigm shift, to emphasize his responsibility to his children radically transformed his life course. He said:

> See, I was a cop before. So I was like, I would be volunteering for anything. It's like anything. Before then [having kids], any kind of job they had, any kind of danger they had or something like that. I had no responsibilities or nothing so I would have kept on going as far as I could, looking for that ultimate rush somewhere. That's the way I looked at it. And then once they came in [the children], I started looking and seeing something called responsibility, like a lot of things slowed up after that. I couldn't work the way I wanted to, the company I was keeping, I don't know. Looking around, you just couldn't

> destroy as many people's lives as you wanted to, that's the way you look at it. It's like every day is a reckless one. Then all of a sudden you discover a new sense of being.

Joseph was not alone in changing career tracks when he viewed the responsibilities of fathering. Greg, a late timing father, changed other components of his lifestyle beyond career. He talked about the major shifts in responsibility and life course that fathering had initiated in his life:

> Interviewer: So ... [fathering has] been a major influence?
>
> Greg: For me it has because I know the lifestyle I had before kids when I was living in the midwest, I was working my first job after college and I did a lot of credit and collection work, you know, repossession-type stuff. And once I had a gun pulled on me in Rock Island, Illinois, repo'ing a car. I thought that was going to do it. At nights I'd have to work late, I'd drive three hours to play a baseball game at night and that was kind of like your lifestyle. And I was fortunate to be able to do all that stuff in my 20s and kind of get it out of your system, and it wasn't until at what age 32, that I had Heather. I'm very fortunate where I see a lot of people younger that have kids right away or they always feel like they're kind of limited, where I never felt that way, I was very fortunate. It just happened to work out that way but I feel very lucky on that.

Greg's comments reflect a feeling that being a late timing father has the advantage of giving men time to "get things out of their systems" before they become fathers. His statement reflects themes elaborated by others as well: Some men feel a need for a time of freedom to explore different lifestyles, careers, areas of the country, travel, and a period of relative freedom from major responsibilities. Paul sensed a major shift in his sense of responsibility since becoming a father. He responsded to Question 1:

> I think that maybe the way I feel responsibility, I mean, I really feel—when I was married before and I had no children, I mean, even though it was difficult getting a divorce, it was all right; there was nothing to worry about. But now, you know, I feel responsibility for a family now. So, I think in that respect, if you have an argument or whatever with your wife, you know, it's not like, well—I mean, I don't feel that way that you can just be a free person—that you have a responsibility to a family. So, yeah, in some respects I think that I'm more responsible in that way, or I feel more responsible.

There are times when the responsibilities of fathering loom large in men's minds. A significant factor in the developmental pull exerted by fathering is that men come to recognize that now others are dependent on them. There is a change of responsibility associated with moving from a consumer of care to a provider of care. Alan related the shift in the following manner:

> Now I have a major responsibility to make sure that there's a place for us to be at, and there's is a place for us—there's food on our table and everything. Before it was the responsibility for our mom or whoever. Now, I'm the one in the major role, I have to make sure that there's things there for the kids and my wife.

Fathering responsibilities can motivate men to confront their own limitations and inadequacies in new ways, and in a context of involvement that has salience in cognitive and emotional consequences. When men have embraced the responsibilities of fatherhood and yet see their inadequacies, a developmental pull is exerted—their relationships with their children draw men to make them someone who is more mature and responsible than who they think they are. Thus, when men embrace involved fatherhood as something worth investing in, it has developmental consequences. The multifaceted nature of fathering leads men into complex balancing acts, realizing that they hold authority and power in their children's lives. And yet, this elicits ambivalence because of concerns of abusing the authority and power they hold. Men engaged in involved fathering may confront their own shortcomings, yet see the need for growth, empowering, and transformation in order to give their children the best that they deserve. Neil elaborated on the responsibilities in the following manner when asked if fathering had changed his view of who he was (Question 2):

> Who I am. Yeah, it has affected who I am because when I come home through the door I'm not just Neil, the employee, Neil, the nice guy, Neil, the gospel singer, Neil, the whatever else I am. I'm *daddy* to them, and I've had to see that a lot of times. I have to force myself to see it sometimes because I come home thinking I'm somebody else, but they see me as somebody totally different. They see me as daddy, and so I want to be the person that they see. It doesn't really change me, but I have to change my thinking. And so it's quality-wise, it has helped me to be a dad and to try and fill that—that word "daddy" is just, to me it's like a huge gap that has to be filled in by an insignificant person, a person who's not sufficient to fill in that need. So I try to do that because I see that they need that. So it does change me and it transforms me from who I want to be outside of fatherhood to be a father. ... It turns this guy that still thinks he's a high-school teenager in some ways, maybe emotionally and financially, and other ways into somebody that holds great power and authority—even though I don't want those things, really I guess I do, part of me wants to. But I don't want to use them against the kids or anything. I have to hold that position.

Neil's comments suggest that he has the desire to provide his children with appropriate direction, leadership, and guidance and to fit his children's expectations of what a daddy is. His desire to grow personally to the place where he can be trusted with the "great power and authority" he holds in their lives exemplifies the draw or developmental pull that children can exert on their fathers. In the following exchange, John, another early timing father, described the demands for responsibility that children place on fathers:

> John: I'd say children have triggered [my] maturity to a greater extent. I'm probably more mature than I probably would ever have been by having kids, because of the things that they actually teach you, by the things they do.
>
> Interviewer: Do you think fatherhood affected the way you approach and view responsibility?
>
> John: Definitely. I think, like I said before, children just demand it, almost, for you to be responsible. That's like, if I—let's say one day I don't feel like getting up—it doesn't work, and immediately your responsibility is—they'll tell you. Basically I took an accountability of how things that I've learned ... before having children, how I was acting, how sort of the thought process I had. Having children awakened all the stuff it seemed that I needed, the responsibility part, forces you to open your eyes just a little bit wider, become open minded a little bit, and close-minded in some other areas. But basically the way I know it was children that changed [me] is because I couldn't see myself doing these things before I had children. It wouldn't be something I would have done .... Basically taking care of two other people requires change. Because basically I was geared towards, I was barely taking care of myself. I wasn't making enough money, this and that. But you know, I wasn't treating my body well .... I just didn't really think about what I was doing. I just did whatever I wanted to do. It was nothing bad, it was just I never had to force myself to do something. I just did whatever I wanted to. Now it's you have to do certain things if you want to or not.

John felt that there are specific, nonnegotiable demands for responsibility that must be heeded and acted on. This leads to a discussion of the reciprocal process, the sense of responsibility that fathers feel for bettering the next generation, or *generativity*.

Generativity Themes

Generativity can be simply defined as the developmental task of caring for the next generations (Erikson, 1968). It was common for men in the sample to express their aspiration to see their children do better than they had personally, to surmount obstacles, to circumvent mistakes, and to have greater opportunities than they themselves had experienced. Implicit in these desires was the realization that these outcomes would not just occur by happenstance; they required investment and attention by the fathers. James expressed generativity themes in this manner:

> The way I grew up, I grew up rough, and ... now I have children I have to worry about. I have to mold them to keep them from doing the things I done. I

> want them to do better than me and their kids to do better than them. That's why I keep after all my kids ...

The desire for children to supersede their own growth, achievements, or stature involved a sense of fathers transcending time and their own lives through the development of their children. Men spoke of having a stake in the success of the next generation by involved structuring, provision, guidance, and "push." Some fathers discussed the fact that their children were their legacy. Vicente said:

> I was pretty much content with just life going on day-by-day, and one day I'll leave from here. Whereas now, I don't just want to leave from here. When I go, I want to make sure that I leave something behind to be remembered, which would be my daughter. Whatever I put in comes out.

Some fathers were cognizant and appreciative of the personal development they had undergone by engaging in involved fathering. Although they were well aware of the personal investment and sacrifice that fathering "cost" them, they were able to explicate the mutually occurring development of their own character (for an expanded discussion of cost–benefits analyses, refer to chap. 12 in this vol.). Ken's generative investment was stated to bring him great satisfaction and fulfillment:

> I think the quality of my life has been greatly enriched by having kids. I couldn't imagine not having that relationship ... with kids.
>
> Researcher: So, when you say it's been enriched, in terms of what?
>
> Ken: A satisfaction out of being able to help another human being grow and develop their potential. And I think an enrichment in just being able to see life through their eyes ... that's enriching and uplifting and rewarding and all those sorts of words.

Fatherhood May Be Experienced as a Jolt

Many men in the sample stated beneficial consequences of involved fathering, but a substantial number discussed how fathering had brought a "shock to the system" under which they were adapted to living. Nearly one third of the sample expressed the theme that fatherhood can be experienced as a major changer of lifestyle or self-concept. Bruce said:

> It just seemed like ... you just get jolted into these things. And it wasn't a direction I was headed in being single without, [or being] married without children.

Bruce felt the direction of his life was radically altered from what he had anticipated prior to having children. From Bruce's comments, it is not clear whether it was the suddenness, the pervasiveness, the unexpectedness of fatherhood, or a combination of those factors that resulted in the jolt to his life course. In a similar manner, Chris indicated that becoming a father had been a central motivator to his implementation of major changes in his life trajectory. His relatives had speculated that he would be imprisoned prior to turning age 18:

> Researcher: Do you think they're right? Do you think you would have ended up [in jail]?
>
> Chris: Yeah. I know that for a fact, yeah.
>
> Researcher: What is it about having a kid that keeps you out of jail?
>
> Chris: Thinking that I wouldn't want my daughter to come see me through eight inches of glass. That's not a very proud thing to me for kids to be out playing and saying, well, your dad's in jail. That's not a very good thing to a kid. So I try to stay from that as far as giving her that image of her dad. Then again, you're not really there as a dad either if you're in jail.

Chris' ability to take the perspective of a child whose father was incarcerated served as a powerful motivator to him to change the trajectory he was on as a teen. Assuming an active and engaged role as an involved father can cause men to curtail or give up destructive behaviors, risk-taking behaviors, criminal activities, substance abuse (see chap. 7, this vol.) and relationships that are with people in "the wrong crowd" (see chap. 10, this vol.). In short, men who make commitments to involved fathering can be jolted out of negative behaviors.

On the other hand, at times, assuming the responsibility for children causes men to postpone, alter, or give up pursuit of a dream, goal, or interest that may have been a positive direction in their development. In a sense, this is a different type of jolt, but it nonetheless derails the previous life trajectory. Michael said:

> I think fatherhood has played a major role because I had my kids so early .... If I hadn't had my kids so early, if I hadn't had them at all, I probably would be ... Let's see. My plans were to go to college and get a good job and all that, but all that had to be curtailed. Instead of going to the school of my choice, I ended up going to a community college and putting my self through .... Yeah, things are different because I have kids. But it's a decision that I made. That's pretty much it.

The curtailment of educational pursuits is commonly acknowledged in adolescent mothers. However, the literature does not as fully document accounts of early timing men who assume responsibility for children and may need to quit school in order to work sufficient hours to provide the basic economic support for their child(ren). Perhaps the disproportionate numbers of single-parent adolescent mothers explain the differences in the number of references to the sacrifices of single-parent mothers versus early timing fathers in the professional literature. Women are more likely than men to curtail their education in order to care for children. Single-parent women are more likely than single men to have custody of children. Men are more likely to be biological fathers without engaging in social fathering. None the less, for those men who assume responsibility for their biological children, and make efforts to economically provide for their child(ren) and partners, it may require dropping out of school. This decision limits earning capabilities in the long run, as we have witnessed with teen mothers. The pressures are real. Steve, another early timing father, responded to Question 2 in this manner:

> As far as the life course, yeah, I think there's been some changes there. If I didn't have my daughter at, two weeks before my nineteenth birthday, I probably would have went off to college and that might have changed—well, that might enhance my skills. I've still tried to seek after the same skills here that I'm getting, I just have to go about it in a different way and a harder way about it. Still, I think going to college would have been an adventure and an experience that I've never had, that I just never will take. The kids are expensive. I can't afford college, time, money, got to support the kids. ... I had to go from being a kid to a father. Myself, I was only eighteen, I was a kid.

Steve had accepted the responsibilities of caring for his children, although it meant putting aside his desire for a college education. He also felt that although he was immature, he had to make a transition from being a kid himself to taking responsibility and becoming a father.

Fatherhood is Experienced in Divergent Pathways

Each of the five major themes described could stand independently. However, men in the sample often expressed the themes in clusters, suggesting that there are distinctly divergent experiences for early timing, on time, and late timing fathers. Different timing patterns were associated with different developmental consequences of having children and becoming involved fathers. Modes of perceived change, although typically pervasive and profound, varied along two divergent paths. In one pathway, major, catalytic changes were perceived to be ushered in. Men fitting this pattern tended to have significant personal characteristics or life circumstances that they saw as obstacles to effective fathering (e.g., gang involvement, substance abuse, or a "partying" lifestyle that was viewed by study participants to be inappropriate for involved fathers). This pathway was more often experienced by early timing fathers than men who made the transition to fatherhood on time or relatively late in the life course.

In this pattern, men tend to emphasize a cluster of themes including settling down, responsibility, and the jolt aspects of fatherhood. The jolt of fatherhood derails the path that men were on and brings a radical and deliberate change in lifestyle. As such, fathering is seen as catalytic in precipitating life-course alterations. Manuel went through a particularly profound transformation that he attributed to fatherhood. The following quote is lengthy, but it weaves in each of the central elements of this developmental pathway and provides a richness in description that is valuable in illustrating this more dramatic life-course change:

> I can even take this back to when my 17 year old was born. Before then I was really rough and tumble on the street. My reputation is still known on the Westside. When I got around her I would mellow. There's a lot of things I would have done if it wasn't for her. There's no doubt. I would've been in jail for murder, there's no doubt. I would have been dead, there's no doubt. The things, the reason that I wouldn't put in to effect the things I wanted to do was because I would think of her. When the rest came into play, I knew that I had an ability to see that they go to school. That they're clothed, that they're bathed, that they had the essentials of life. So there was a lot of things I cut out. Sure. I drank, I did my dirt out there, I still did my dirt, but when I was around them or when they needed me, I was there. Yeah they did turn my life around as far as I stopped carousing as much, I stopped raising as much hell as I did. I was more focused on them than I was on myself. I didn't take the drastic measures that I would have took before. I still would get somebody back. There was no way I could let go somebody doing something to me. But the ideas that I had in my head would not materialize .... When I was fourteen, I hung in gangs. I was known all over Wilmington. I was one of the few people that could go through everybody's territory, okay. I had an attitude that if you did something to me, I was quick to get you back. I was a loner as far as hanging around people were concerned. I fought and had my head busted. I have been to jail eight times. When I say change of attitude, as I got older I thought of different ways of retaliation. Shooting people was not far off the mind. But when you have children ... I tried to explain this to other people who talk about "well I'm going to kill so and so" and they got kids. When you have children, the thought might come to your mind, but you also think about what you're doing to the child. That's what I'm trying to say is that, yeah, the attitude has changed some, but as far as me going out here and shooting somebody or blowin' up somebody's house, throwing a Molotov cocktail, something like that which I was inclined to do in earlier years, after Dee was born and the rest, you know, I kind of let things slide now .... Yeah I would say they changed my attitude in that retrospect. There's no doubt I would have been in jail years ago for murder without question. So I would say yeah it changed my attitude toward, I guess towards, I guess what I'm trying to say is I would be taking something from them if I go to jail. I would be taking away the father image away that they need. It wasn't necessarily taking the life, at that time it didn't matter, but I would be taking from them. I couldn't live with that.

In a qualitatively divergent life path, other men felt their lives were not significantly different than they would have been otherwise, except that their children had somehow drawn out tendencies that had remained dormant until becoming involved as fathers. Vicente stated:

> Because of being a dad. Hum. I would say forty-five percent of me is who I am because of being a dad. Because all these things have always, has always been in me. There again, it just took the fatherhood to really bring them out. It caused me to stand still for a minute and just look at everything, put a stop on everything just for a minute to take a real good look at life, where we're going with this thing now.

Study participants who perceived fatherhood to be more of a gentle evoker of latent tendencies were men who were relatively mature or well adjusted prior to making the transition to fatherhood. Some had stated that they had "sewn their wild oats" earlier and had gotten such things "out of their systems" by the time they became fathers. Roger talked about this and the relation between life-course alterations and personality shifts in the following exchange:

> Roger: Well, I think since it was a late time in my lifetime when he was born, thirty-two-years old, it was basically, it was a minor change in my personality. It was a major change in my lifestyle, but it was a minor change. I don't think it changed me and my values, or anything like that. It was basically, you know, just a different perspective of life, I guess, the way I look at life now. So, it was just a little bit more free and easy back then before him, now, you know, he's the number one priority now .... I was thirty-two-years old before we had him, you know, I had all my fun back you been back then. Where I can, you know, not say, well, I never got to do this, well, I did it all. So now it's time for me to put all my resources towards him. And it's not a feeling—I thought it would be a feeling like, at first, this is going to be terrible, the guys are going on a golf trip for five days, and I can't go this time. But it's kind of like, well, I hope they have a good time. And I have him here, and that's all I really need.
>
> Interviewer [in a later follow-up question]: Earlier you said that I was thirty-two-years old before I had him, and I had all my fun back then. Are you having less fun now?
>
> Roger: No. It's just a different kind of fun. Like say it was more of a single life, and a young couple being married, and, you know, let's say a free lifestyle. And now it's kind of like you just change your perspective on fun. Fun now to me is taking him places, taking him to the store, and, you know, taking him to the park and swinging him on the swing, instead of me being on the golf course with my buddies. You know, or my wife and I going away for the weekend, or something like that. So, I'm still having fun, it's just now it's a different kind of fun.

Others felt that fatherhood had required relatively minor adjustments to their life course because they never had major lifestyle problems to begin with. Gilbert expressed this theme:

> I don't believe I had any, should I say like, anti-society behavior before I married. I mean, I never was, I never had any—I would consider that I never had any real bad habits, whereas, I got older and became a parent that I would have to change because of my responsibilities. That's just the way I feel.

Men who experienced fatherhood as a more subtle elicitor of latent tendencies stated the theme in a manner consistent with Vicente's observation:

> I never really gave it any thought until fatherhood came along .... I never really focused on ... thinking about some goals and achievements and accomplishments that you have to make in life now, until fatherhood came along .... It's not so much as a change as more a development of certain underlying traits.

Forty five percent of the sample expressed themes of "settling down," the most frequently expressed perceived effects. In addition, 29% of the sample expressed that fatherhood presented a major jolt to their systems. As such, the most dramatic path of development was perceived by the fathers to represent a radical life-course turn. Perhaps this came in the form of a substantially altered lifestyle or a delay or abandonment of plans and desires for personal fulfillment.

A differing experience of fatherhood suggests that, for some men, fathering "draws out latent tendencies" that always existed but lacked expression or development. Active participation in fathering provided a catalyst or context to develop these tendencies to a fuller extent. I have previously theorized that the level of involvement in fathering will directly influence developmental outcomes for men during young adulthood (Palkovitz, 1996a). Consistent with this type of development, subjects expressed the themes of becoming more giving, assuming greater degrees of responsibility, and generativity themes.

PERSONALITY AND LIFE-COURSE CONSIDERATIONS

Life circumstances and degree of maturity distinguished between the men representing these two different reactions to parenting. Specifically, the early timing fathers, those who accepted responsibility for fatherhood at young ages (approximately 18% of the sample), tended to express the most dramatic life-course alterations. In contrast, on time and late timing fathers, those who were already relatively mature or who delayed childrearing, tended to focus more on the gentle evoker mode. It should be noted that the categories of change are not mutually exclusive. That is, some men experienced a jolt to their life course and noted subtle personality changes that emerged over time as well. In response to Question 2, Donald, an early timing father, described how he viewed himself to have changed "personality-wise":

> Before I used to be somewhat withdrawn and the only way out was to be a rebel. Now I can show my pesonality how I want to. I can be a more outgoing person, a happier person, my self-esteem is a lot higher. My kids make me feel needed, important kind of like a reason to go on. There is a reason to grind at the grindstone. It helps me bring my personality out. I don't know how, it just makes me a happier person altogether, most of the time, except when they are in bad moods. But they make me feel good about myself. ... My kids have made the quality of my life better. ... [They have] made me mature a lot faster.

It should be noted that relative degree of maturity and not age was the most important determinant of transitional experience. This pattern supports the notion that both the initial transition to fatherhood and ongoing, involved fathering require an investment of personal resources. Early timing fathers, who generally were characterized by less developmental maturity and less balance in their resources and roles, perceived the transition to involved fatherhood to require major readjustments, thereby creating a jolt to their life course and developmental trajectories. In contrast, men with greater degrees of maturity, and a more stable balance of their personal resources and roles perceived the transition to fatherhood to require more subtle rebalancing of personal tendencies and roles.

CONFIDENCE THAT IT WAS FATHERING THAT BROUGHT CHANGE

Toward the end of the interview, a brief recap was given of the major areas or domains where fathers had expressed perceived changes in their lives or development. Each participant was then asked to describe how he knew that it was fathering that had initiated the perceived changes. Although the question was posed differently to each father, customized to reflect his individual pattern of response to the earlier sections of the interview, the following excerpt from the interview with Steve gives a general sense of phrasing used:

> Interviewer: All right. We've looked at a lot of areas of your life. You know, work, health, social relationships, emotions, morals, religion, everything. And in virtually all these areas you've said, yes, fathering has had an impact. And now I have to ask you what I think is a tough question. How can you be sure that it was fathering that made a differences and not just maturity or aging, not just life circumstances around your work or your marriage? Are you sure that it's fathering that's made a difference?

Steve's response showed careful reflection, and represents one mode of responding to this exit question:

> Steve: You can't be sure. See, I didn't live both lives.
>
> Interviewer: Right. That's what I'm really asking.

> Steve: Well, I can imagine what life would be like, see, without the kids. I probably, if I didn't have kids, probably wouldn't want much to do with kids. I don't want much to do with other people's kids. That's what I base that on, but they're my kids. I think back at that turning point there, eighteen. I had a scholarship to go to college, probably would have went to college, I probably would have been involved in wild sex and drugs, alcohol and rock and roll. Probably would have got caught up into materialistic things on how much more money I can make, nice fancy sports cars I can buy to impress women. I probably wouldn't have thought about kids much at all if I had taken that road down there, so how can I be sure? I can't be sure. I can guess.

As an early timing father, Steve based his response primarily on life-course transition issues, and speculated as to how his life may have been different if he had not become a father at an early age. Alan, another early timing dad, began his reply by centering on life-course issues as well, but ended by noting developmental changes that occurred as a result. He said:

> I don't know that it's fatherhood. I'm just thinking that it is because if I—if my wife hadn't gotten pregnant, then we would have gotten married later than we did. And how do I know that we would have gotten married? I don't know. It just took its path. We would argue all the time about different things, but nothing that really would cause any problems. And then when she told me she was pregnant, we didn't know if we should get married then or wait until the baby came. We didn't know if it would be the right thing for the baby. And we sat down and discussed it and talked about it. If we were going to do it a year from then, why not do it now? Why put it off any longer than that, and have to go through problems when the baby came along? So, different things that have happened, I think it's happened for the fact because of having a baby, you know, because I've matured and took on more responsibility and learned to do without so that they can have and everything. So, that's, I think—because of fatherhood, that all this has happened.

Late timing fathers tended to respond differently. Roger felt that his life-course alterations had occurred for reasons other than fathering, but that the developmental changes discussed during the interview had been a result of father involvement. He said:

> I think a lot of mine comes with age. And you know, thirty-two years old and I kind of knew exactly what kind of person I was. And you know, I can say that if I had him at twenty-one and I was just going through some changes in life, but I felt like I was, all through the changes in my life. And when I had him, it, you know, I definitely think it was parenting that did it, changed me around, not, okay, now you're getting older. I was older as far as I was concerned. I went through my twenties where I went through some huge changes from twenty to twenty-nine. But now, when I had him, everything, I'd experienced just about everything, at least I thought, and so the things that changed in my life over the last fourteen months was definitely, without a doubt, due to parenting.

Anthony, another late timing dad, expressed uncertainty regarding how much of his development he should attribute to fathering. Throughout the interview, he had conveyed that he had been a stable person for quite a few years, and he did not see fathering as changing his development monumentally. In response to this wrap-up question, he said:

> Well I told you that from the very beginning that I wasn't sure whether it wasn't a factor of maturity on some of the things you asked. It's hard to tell whether it would have come naturally or not.

Paul, another late timing father, expressed a different take on the question. He had perceived major changes in his lifestyle, but not in his personality. In the end, however, his confidence in assigning causality was low:

> It's changed my lifestyle a lot. But in terms of who I am as a person I don't think that it's changed me that much .... Some of that's hard to answer because you don't know who you would be hadn't the child come along.

It should be noted that virtually none of the men saw fatherhood as a negligible contributor to who they were, and by far, the majority of men perceived fatherhood to be the single greatest shaper of their current self. This perception is consistent with Cowan's (1991) definition of life-course transitions as "longterm processes that result in a qualitative reorganization of both inner life and external behavior" (p. 5). He specified that before an event can be considered to be transitional, it must involve inner qualitative shifts in understanding and perception as well as noticeable changes in external behaviors, role arrangements, or personal competencies: "In sum, from the inner perspective, transitions involve a qualitative shift in perceptions of oneself and the world, and an imbalance usually, but not always, followed by rebalance in our emotional equilibrium" (P. A. Cowan, 1991, p. 15).

This statement resonates with the process that every father in the interview sample reported in regard to becoming involved as a father. The degree of disequilibrium was inversely related to the degree of developmental maturity and balance, but every father experienced a reorganization of roles or personal characteristics that significantly altered their life course and development (Marsiglio, 1995).

In the discipline of life-span development, Erikson (1950, 1980) described disequilibrium associated with making the transition from one developmental stage to another. In fact, the reallocation of ego energies is so marked that he termed the turning points of development *crises* and discussed the relative balance of opposing forces or directions. Thus, both life-course and life-span approaches to development focus importance on transitional events, and recognize that development is the net result of altered balances in various aspects of the self in response to changing demands.

Fathers in the interview sample spoke of life-course alterations with a greater degree of elaboration and animation than they manifested in regard to life-span developmental issues. It may be that men are more aware of or more comfortable discussing life-course transitions in comparison to developmental changes in the self. Alternatively, these findings may be viewed through a different set of lenses. Specifically, it appears that men's personalities tend to remain relatively stable throughout young adulthood (Costa & McCrae, 1988). Virtually all the fathers in the sample experienced fatherhood as a context that honed already existing (although possibly dormant or latent) tendencies. However, they perceived their life course to be altered significantly. Again, all of this depended on a prerequisite maturity level and functionality.

Balance Issues

Each man in the study brought unique and individually creative balances to their fathering experiences. Each had a different set of resources and demands. Each had achieved a level of adaptation by balancing their resources and demands in individually unique ways. Men who experienced jolt aspects of fathering had greater shifts to make in role investments than those who saw fathering as a gentle evoker. Because fathers describing jolts in life course had to make greater adjustments, they experienced greater disequilibrium in existing role configurations. Conversely, men who emphasized gentle evoker aspects of fathering had already achieved relative balance in their roles that needed little adjustment after becoming fathers. As such, they experienced fathering to bring minor adjustments to already existing characteristics.

Thus, at any given time, a person's developmental status can be evaluated by examining the relative balance they exhibit in different domains of development and different areas within those domains. People who are less well adapted exhibit a lack of balance in personal resources and roles in comparison to those who are well adjusted. Because people exist in dynamic systems, demands are continually placed on individuals experiencing life events such as marriage, birth of children, or work changes. In order to respond to the demands of a dynamic system, people need to reallocate resources in order to bring a new balance. What may be an acceptable balance for a man focused on a partying lifestyle will require relatively major reallocation when he invests in the role demands of being a father. In comparison, men who had already attained adult balances in their role investments experienced less dramatic disequilibrium when investing in the role of father.

At the time of the interview, the fathering experiences of study participants defined a major part of who they were as people, even if they were currently nonresidential fathers. Men perceived the transformation of life course and development to happen through the occupation of thoughts, the modification of short-term and long-term goals and life choices, and by shaping experiences of discrete events. Simply stated, the everyday contexts and events of fathering result in changes in development and life course for involved fathers. It is noteworthy that the average father in this diverse sample perceived fathering to be the single greatest shaper of their current self. This perception stands in stark contrast to the absence of professional attention to the effects of parenting on adult development. In reviewing contemporary textbooks and trade books on adult development, the developmental aspects of parenthood are most frequently ignored, and in other instances given brief and shallow treatment in an otherwise rich coverage of factors influencing developmental status.

Developmentalists have recently acknowledged that young adulthood, frequently recognized to be from age 20 to 45, is the "frontier" for new scientific discovery because of the relative lack of theoretical and empirical work that has been devoted to this part of the life span. Within young adulthood, the developmental effects of parenting represent a truly promising and virtually uncharted area of inquiry. Over 90% of all people become parents, and every parent recognizes that they are significantly different people than they would been if they never had children. The next eight chapters of this book present analyses of the understandings of study participants in regard to the ways that engagement in fathering has shaped the development of their self, social, and work domains.

In conclusion, fathers are able to articulate significant life-course changes that they attribute to fathering to a much greater degree than they can life-span development changes. However, as discussed in subsequent chapters, when asked specific questions regarding how they perceive fathering to have effected various personal, interpersonal, and career domains, they can give detailed and varied examples.

It may be that men are better able to view their lives in a personal historical perspective rather than a developmental perspective. Perhaps it is easier for the average person to elaborate changes in lifestyle or career or living situations than to reflect on developmental transitions and changes in maturity. Life-course transitions frequently have associated marker events, whereas shifts in developmental functioning occur more gradually and may be less salient.

Life-cycle components are easy to identify for the fathers in the sample, as well as demographers. They know when they made the transition to fathering, and they know the ages and stages of their children. They are not so skilled in matching the life-cycle stages to developmental outcomes in their lives.

The intergeneratinal connections of involved fathering are what forge developmental change, but they are elusive both to fathers and to researchers. The remaining chapters attend to these issues.

II

The Self Domain

Chapter **5**

Navigating the Emotional Currents of Fathering

There is a discrepancy between the stereotype of men as emotionally inattentive and the folklore regarding the emotional joys of fathering. Specifically, stereotypical accounts portray men as insensitive to the feelings of others and themselves. Further, even those men who are sensitive to feelings are stereotypically characterized as being so dominated by their left brain that they have difficulty expressing or regulating emotions. Traditionally, masculine men are portrayed as having a focus on getting a job done as opposed to being sensitive to interpersonal relationships. In contrast, the folklore of parenting paints the picture of warm and sensitive fathers who read their children's affective cues and provide timely and consistent emotional support and security. The folklore characterizes the joy, pride, and satisfactions of parenting and the warm affective environment between fathers and children.

This chapter examines men's feelings about fathering, both positive and painful. By interviewing men concerning the emotional aspects of fathering, it is possible to bring balance to these discrepant portrayals. The findings from interviews with fathers stand in stark contrast to both the stereotypical view of dispassionate men and the uniformly positive folklore regarding fathers' feelings. Fathers in the sample described the uniqueness of feelings experienced in the context of fathering, and their awareness of and need for both expression and control of emotions. The interview data show that men perceive that fathering has facilitated their emotional sensitivity, expression, control, and lability. There is both positive and negative transfer to other relationships.

In this portion of the interview, fathers were asked a series of questions concerning the feelings of fathering. Whereas the precise manner of questioning varied slightly from one father to another, the general flow of questioning was similar to the following questions:

Question 1. I want to shift gears for a little while, and I'd like to talk about feelings. I want to know about both positive and negative, good and bad emotions, feelings that you think about when you think about fatherhood. Really, what I'd like is a list of both good and bad feelings that you have around fatherhood.

Question 2. These feelings, the [recap of feelings listed in response to Question 1], can you feel those feelings in exactly the same way in other situations, like with your wife (girlfriend), or at work, or with other friends? Or, are the feelings of fatherhood really different than feelings you have in other contexts?

Question 3. Do you believe that fathering has influenced the way that you experience, control and express emotions? For instance, are there things that you've had to put a lid on for the benefit of the kids? Or, are there things that you've had to be sure to get out in the open so that they know what's going on?

THE FEELINGS OF FATHERING

In response to the request to list both the positive and negative emotions of fathering, men in the sample listed an average of three or four emotions ($M = 3.67$). In all, fathers listed 77 positive emotions and 66 negative emotions. However, although the listing of positive emotions required no prompting, the discussion of negative emotions frequently resulted from my further probes. Specifically, it was common for fathers to list a few positive feelings and then to stop. I would talk through those responses, and then follow up with a statement or exchange similar to the following excerpt from the interview with Alan:

> Researcher: How about on the other side of the coin, what are some uncomfortable or negative feelings?
>
> Alan: I don't think I've had any. I don't. I might have, but I can't ever recall.
>
> Researcher: I'm not trying to put words in your mouth, but just for example, fears, frustration, anger?
>
> Alan: Okay—fears, I had a fear ...
>
> [after the description of the fearful situation] Interviewer: any feelings of frustration or anger?

Without the follow-up questioning, many fathers would not have expressed negative emotions, or the degree of negativity that they ultimately did. It is not clear whether the positive emotions of fatherhood so greatly overshadowed the negatives that men simply could not address bad feelings without prompts, or whether demand characteristics prevented them from discussing negative aspects of emotions of fathering until given structure and permission by the probes. It could be that the folklore of parenting had shaped fathers' perceptual lenses to the point where they focused on positive emotions and downplayed or disregarded negative emotions in their own minds. Perhaps the probes provided inertia to overcome the suppression of negative feelings. Such probes were neither necessary nor employed for the positive emotions.

Even after probing the negative emotions, fathers listed more good feelings than bad ones by a ratio of 77 to 66. However, these numbers do not give a clear picture, because a small minority of fathers were quite "fluent" in negative expressivity. When looking at the frequency of positive and negative emotions, 44% of the sample expressed more positive than negative feelings, 38% of the sample expressed an equal number of positive and negative feelings, and only 18% of the sample listed more negative than positive feelings. This is noteworthy, because the "more positive than negative" group is nearly two and a half times as large as the "more negative than positive" group, and the group of fathers who expressed an even balance (i.e., an equal frequency of positive and negative emotions) was more than twice as large as the "more negative than positive" fathers. In addition, the "more negative than positive" fathers tended to list a high frequency of negative emotions, dwelling on the bad feelings, and thereby inflating the overall expression of negativity in the overall sample.

All of these factors combine to indicate that, in terms of frequencies, most men expressed the emotions of fathering to be more positive than negative, and a small minority of fathers who viewed fathering in a negative light skewed the frequency of positive and negative emotions toward the negative in the overall sample. It should be noted that men in the sample were not asked to put intensity ratings on the lists of emotions, so it is not possible to move beyond simple analyses of frequencies. Because the data do not specifically address the intensities of the emotions, it is impossible to know whether or not the frequency of emotions on one side of the equation balance those on the other. However, analyses concerning the overall costs and benefits of involved fathering (see chap. 12, this vol.), indicate that fathers in this sample unanimously saw the benefits to outweigh the costs. Thus, although some men listed a higher frequency of negative emotions than positive ones, overall, they felt fathering was a rewarding and beneficial experience. Discussion of these issues happened after many topics had elapsed since the discussion of emotions. Because this was the one unanimous finding in the entire study, it gives credence to the interpretation of positive and negative emotional frequencies to indicate that, overall, most men experienced more good than bad feelings around fathering.

Positive Feelings

Expressed positive and negative emotions tended to cluster around a few issues. The most common positive feelings were in the category of *joy* (joy, happiness, pleasure; 67%), followed by *love* (love, caring, closeness, compassion; 33%), *pride* (pride, satisfaction, self worth, accomplishment; 33%), *fun* (fun, excitement, enthusiasm; 18%), and *friendship* (friendship, companionship, family, and completion; 13%). Interestingly, these categories closely parallel the folklore of parenting. It is unclear from the interviews whether the folklore shaped the expression of such themes or, alternatively, whether the folklore exists because it is an accurate representation of the positive side of parental experience. Other less frequently expressed positive emotions included being in *awe* of developmental progress (10%) and feeling *good* (7%). Positive emotions expressed by 5% or fewer of the sample included feelings of power, preciousness, naturalness, being needed, and hope.

Charles stated some of the positive feelings that were common to sample fathers. He talked about the enjoyment that came from just having kids, knowing that the children are yours, nurturing their development, helping them to grow into adulthood, and in sharing activities and time with them. The positive feelings give a sense of ease to the relationship, thus tempering other times or challenges that may make fathering feel more difficult. Charles said:

> Well, start with the positive. The positive is the joy of having kids, number one. Number two, the joy of seeing them develop be great young men and women in their young life and to nurture them to be strong in their adult life. There's good times being a father. You can do so many things with them. You can go to the mall, you can go to the movies, you can take rides, you can go to the restaurants ... you know you just can enjoy fatherhood from the positive stand point. You know when things are going well, its like "God this is great, this is a breeze, there's nothing to it."

By far, the most commonly expressed positive emotion was joy. Numerous fathers talked about the joy they felt as they returned home from work and could hear their children stampeding toward them to greet them. Some men discussed babies crawling excitedly toward them, and the way that this enthusiastic greeting and expression of love and joy washed away cares of the day. Glen was one of the several fathers who described this scenario as a source of joy and responded to Question 1 in the following manner:

> Overjoyed, it's better than I expected. It's ... great. Overjoyed is kind of how I feel about it. Like I said, when coming home and when I'm putting the key in to door and the kids are in the kitchen, you know. You hear the big foot steps coming cause she's faster than her brother and the little one. By the time I get

> the door open they just mob me. And that [happens] every single time. And for no reason, and I think I'm going to be very hurt when my 6 year old finally doesn't do it one day for some reason, you know. And she'll be off on her own, but that's just an overwhelming feeling. Because they just, just want to give me something so badly and I want to soak it all in.

Glen's comments are grounded in specific events and reflect the reciprocal nature of emotional flow in the family. Their joy is contagious to him. His overwhelming feeling of joy is the result of his children's expressions of joy on his arrival. He recognizes that this display of affection will change as his children develop, and he anticipates the hurt that may accompany changes in this mutually enjoyable emotional expression. Several men remarked that the daily greeting of their children helped them to feel important, needed, and to focus on things that really matter.

Alan expressed a range of positive emotions he associated with fathering. Part of the "good feeling" is excitement, unpredictability, and watching the children develop and use their newly emerging skills and abilities. This diverse list was typical of men's responses to questions regarding positive feelings associated with fathering. Alan said:

> I guess the good feelings are love, caring, I guess, joy, excitement, always wondering what they're going to do next or seeing what they're going to do next.

Similarly, Anthony talked about the joy of watching children accomplish something. As he was discussing that, however, he included the fact that children are a source of unconditional love:

> The positive emotion is the joy when you see in their face when they do accomplish something or when you know that they love you unconditionally.

Leo focused on the depth of love and caring as well. His enjoyment of fathering was enhanced by the fact that his relationships with his sons surpassed his expectations for fulfillment. He said:

> The relationship that I've gained as a father has been very fascinating to me. I don't think I ever understood or could imagine how close and beautiful the relationship would become, how the love would grow and develop and the respect would grow and develop between my kids and myself. It's been pretty incredible.

Jeff expressed pride in his son and his athletic accomplishments, but he also discussed the fact that the depth of love that he experienced as a father had taken him somewhat by surprise. He characterized it in a manner that made it clear that he viewed it to be qualitatively different from the love he shares with his wife. His statement also reflects the fact that his children were drawing the love out of him:

> Well, I don't think anything surpasses the joy that having the kids brings. The pride, it's hard to stop talking about them, and I'm sure that I've bored people by bragging about the kids. You know, when they do well in baseball, or something like that. So pride is the big thing. I mean love, I probably, I didn't realize how much I had in me until they came along. My wife started the ball rolling and then the kids just, it snowballed.

Vincente states that the intensity of joy that he experiences as a father is unparalleled by any other context. As a father, he has experienced a depth of emotion that has expanded the range of feelings he had known:

> I never in life have felt the joy that my daughter brings me when I wake up and see her. She wakes me up. That's all ... You might be able to understand what I'm saying. And, I mean, when you're laying there—it's my first child—so, when you're laying there and you're asleep, and you roll over and you're feeling this little hand tapping on your head. They can't talk yet, but they know how to communicate with you. And it's like you can almost understand what they would want to say, or what type of expressions they're giving off to you when they smile at you. And that has been the most joyful thing I've ever experienced in life, I would have to say. And I've never been able to get that type of joy anywhere else.

Vicente's experience of joy in his relationship with his daughter is unparalleled in any other realm of his experience. Not all of the emotional currents associated with fathering are positive, however.

Negative Feelings

Negative emotional categories were not as numerous as the positive. Again, this may be because of the effects of parenting folklore in shaping the perceptions of fathers, or alternatively, it may be that fathers really do express fewer negative than positive emotions. The most commonly expressed bad feelings were *anger* (anger, frustration, irritation, impatience; 62%), *fears* (fears, doubts, confusion, worried, feeling "lost"; 49%), *guilt* (10%) and *tiredness* (business, tiredness; 8%). Negative emotional categories mentioned by 5% or fewer of the sample included disappointment, failure, helplessness, hurt, sadness, stupidity, stress, a sense of being a substitute, having a ruined marriage, and a sense of missing kids when separated from them.

It is interesting that anger is the most frequently expressed negative emotion of fathering. Anger is an emotion that is attributed to traditional males in society. Masculinity gives permission for the expression of anger. However, fathers noted that whereas they frequently experienced anger, they were aware they needed to control their anger and it was not appropriate for anger to be expressed through aggression toward their children. Ned described some of the negative feelings of fathering:

> Well, the frustration part, like at work, for instance, when you're frustrated at work and then you become very angry, and you could be real aggressive. But with your children you can't be real angry and real aggressive, and you get mad, and you tell them you're mad. But it's a different kind of frustration you receive. And, for instance, at work, you know, if you get mad at somebody you have the urge to hit them. With children you can't have that urge, you have to—you could be frustrated and you can tell your kids, you're frustrated, why do you make me say these things to you? So, they're real different. ... The only part about kids is, the bad part about them is that they grow up. And then you can't pick them up and hug them and kiss any more. Because like my son, he's eleven, and he weighs a hundred and thirty pounds. It's hard for me to pick him up. But they're always there.

Even in the presence of Ned's anger, he discusses the desire to hug and hold his child, and anticipates the emotional struggles of watching his son grow up and become independent, another emotion that fathers expressed when asked about negative affect associated with fathering.

Gilbert expressed that there are some fears associated with fathering, but some of those fears are centered on self-appraisal and performance. He indicated that those fears are fairly universal to new fathers, but subside with time, saying:

> Well, there's fears at first. But you always have fears like, am I going to be a good father and what exactly is it. But I think that all men probably go through that during the pregnancy and the first couple of weeks or months, you know, when the baby is conceived. But after that, no, no negative feelings like that.

Sometimes the self-appraisals of fathers with older children are not positive, and negative affect accompanies them. Thomas expressed ongoing self-doubts and the sense that his fathering presented an ongoing sense of being on trial. He had fears of being exposed as a charlatan or as having serious problems that could result in divorce:

> I guess having a family has in some ways intensified the periodic doubts I have about my abilities and competence, and such. It's kind of like a crucible sort of thing.

James voiced that he gets upset with himself when he sees negative attitudes in his teenagers that he recognizes as having roots in his temperament and actions. He said:

> And them teenagers got them attitudes. That's what upset me, and then I see my attitude in some of my kids.
>
> Researcher: What does that do to you when you see it?

James: Oh that hurts, that hurts, and then I feel like smacking my own self.

James' response to the hurt he feels is to ineffectively and inappropriately express anger toward himself. It can be a challenge to come out of the emotional spiral of negative affect without doing further harm.

Roger described the feelings of fear and helplessness that fathers can experience when their children are ill. Fathers' empathy for their sick or hurting children can cause them to wish that they could bring about changes, yet they often feel helpless or powerless, and this may result in feelings of panic. In such circumstances, men are confronted with their humanity, their ineffectiveness, and the fact that they are really not in control, no matter how noble their intentions and how pure their motives to help. Although such realizations are humbling, they are realistic. Roger said:

> The only time I've ever felt negative was when he's been sick, and I've felt like I've been helpless. It's kind of like, you know, he's got a bad cold, and he's all plugged up. And my first experience was, I think, when he was three-months old, and he was laying on my chest, and he wakes up, and he can't hardly breathe, and I'm panicking, and I don't know how to get him to breathe right. And he's all clogged up, and he's wheezing, and just felt helpless then.

Virtually all fathers expressed both positive and negative emotions experienced in the context of involvement with their children. Several spontaneously discussed the intensity of those feelings.

THE UNIQUENESS OF FATHERS' FEELINGS

Fathers were asked whether they could experience the same feelings that they associate with fathering in other contexts, such as marriage, work, or other relationships. A striking majority (92%) of the men interviewed stated that the feelings of fatherhood are different than those experienced in other contexts. Some were emphatic, and said that feelings of fathering are unique, whereas others said that although similar to feelings of other contexts, there were important aspects that distinguish the feelings of fathering from those of other contexts. Only 8% of the sample felt the feelings of fathering were indistinguishable from the emotions associated with other contexts. Anthony said:

> Even when I was going with my wife and everything, and before we got married we fell in love and everything, to me that always felt like passion. Even though I did love her. You know, I was passionate about her, too, you know physically and everything. The kids you don't feel that way, you just love them totally differently.

Glen describes the unique emotional currents of fathering in the following way:

> They are very much unique. I don't think I could feel them in any other context. I'd say for certain now. ... One of the reasons might be that the emotions that flow between my children and me, they're innocent and pure they're not, they're not what I want to hear. They're freely given, they're not judgmental. ... They're there because they want to be there and I return them because I want to return them. And it doesn't matter that she's just been punished for something that she did. I always have the ability to hug her and look her straight in the eye and tell her I love her very much. And you know the punishment that she just received just kind of went away. She, she knows what she did wrong and at the same time, that the action was bad and she's not a bad person and she accepts that. So I, don't have that at work, I don't have that with my wife. There's to much politics influencing all of that.

Glen attributes the uniqueness of paternal emotions to the innocence, the purity, the lack of politics, and expectation. He feels that his relationship with his daughter is not encumbered by the clutter of politics and demand characteristics—it is free flowing and true. That allows him to experience emotions without questioning motives or underlying factors because in his mind, his relationship with his daughter is more "pure." Some may argue that the perceived purity can be accounted for by a greater degree of comfort in relationships with children, who are not really his peer, but Glen felt that there was a qualitative difference in the emotional currents he experienced with his children.

Other men had different reasons for experiencing the feelings of fatherhood as unique. Some men attributed the uniqueness to a greater intensity of feeling between fathers and children than in any other relationship. Colin described the relation between the uniqueness of fathers' feelings and intensity in this manner:

> I think the feelings are stronger. I may feel those same feelings in other types of relationships, but the feelings that I experience with my son are stronger. I don't know how in any other way to put it. But they're more intense, more from the gut kind of feeling.

Some overtly stated that they had more feelings toward their children than toward their spouse or girlfriend. Anthony said:

> Quite frankly now I feel that at least at their ages they have switched over and taken more of my emotional emotions with them than I really give my wife. We've been together 17 years so she doesn't really need a whole lot, I guess, but I look at them as being more important emotionally than I do my wife, at least for me.

Anthony distinguished between the emotional maturity of his spouse and the perceived need of his children. He felt that his wife did not need as much emotional support from him as his children did. Anthony, among others, cites the reason for emotional uniqueness between father and child as being related to the responsibility that fathers carry toward their children. Because of developmental differences and differences in resources and needs, fathers have a different type of relationship with their children than they do with anyone else. Tim eloquently analyzes these issues and also points out that the genetic connections between fathers and children contribute to the emotional currents.

> Researcher: Can you experience the same emotions in different contexts?
>
> Tim: No, no, absolutely not. I mean, if you have a partner for life that you care a great deal about you can experience similar things, but that partner for life is going to be, let's assume, let's hope, a mature adult who is able to take care of themselves, and hopefully has some sense of responsibility, and can survive in the world. This child can't, this child needs me or his mother or someone to take care of him. So, yeah, I think it is unique. Fatherhood is unique in that regard because it does differ from a relationship with a friend, or it does differ from a relationship with someone else. And even—I used the term, I guess I emphasized the helplessness or the fact that the child needs you. I suppose you could draw a parallel to a relationship where you had a partner for life or a spouse or someone you cared deeply about who was incapacitated in some way; that they had to be taken care of. But again, I think it's kind of different because if you have an adult who's permanently incapacitated you're not—if it's an adult, there isn't that biological connection that you have in your head. Maybe that's artificial, maybe not, but you consider it anyway, "so this is your stuff," as Carl Sagan would say, "your stuff going on for billions of years."

Clifford placed a great emphasis on feeling different toward his children because they were genetically linked to himself. His feelings toward his children were also different because of the permanence of parenting and the fact that he did not choose them. He said:

> Children are something that I've made. My job and my girlfriend that's something that I choose to be in, a relationship that I choose to be in. Uh, the children they're mine, they're going to be mine forever. That's something I can't change and I, they came from my loins, and its just totally different feeling than ... anything else that I have in the world I guess.

Numerous fathers talked about the uniqueness of their emotions regarding their children being connected to a sense that they were biologically connected. In a different approach, Peter confirmed the relations between responsibility and dependency in an analysis of the similarities and differences between the frustrations he has experienced as a father and as a military officer. A new aspect of emotional investment comes out in the following exchange; the fact that others may evaluate you based on the performance of those for whom you are responsible, thereby upping the emotional ante.

> Peter: I think the only time that I felt similar is ... in the Marine Corps ... being put in a position of leadership where you're in charge of some people. And depending on how they perform is how you perform or is what your evaluation is based on. So other than that there's no other context that I can think of where you have the same kind of feeling.
>
> Researcher: Was that the same or was it—
>
> Peter: Similar, but not exactly the same.
>
> Researcher: Can you tell me what the difference is?
>
> Peter: The difference is probably the fact that a lot more frustration is involved in leadership than is with the baby. With the baby this is taken for granted that they don't know what to do, they're maturing or they're doing whatever they need to do to become themselves. Whereas when you're leading people you already assume that they have some skills and that they should develop them as best they can to have a certain attitude. But if it doesn't happen, it doesn't happen and you get a lot more frustrated.

Anthony expressed the view that marriage is different because it is an arrangement that is voluntarily entered into by adults with the capacity to make responsible decisions (and to reverse them). In contrast, being someone's child is involuntary and is irreversible, thus bringing a higher degree of emotional responsibility to the parent than marriage. He says:

> I'll tell you, when my wife I were as I've described, single, and didn't have children I could feel a little bit guilty about some things. But she was an adult and she could take care of herself. If she didn't like it ... she married me for what I am and I married her for the same thing. Nobody put a gun to our heads. If she didn't like it or I didn't like it we could go our separate ways. But, they're my children. They're mine until they grow up and leave.

Donald felt closer to his children than he did to his wife, partly because he felt a degree of criticism from his wife and a freedom to be himself with his children that was unparalleled in other relationships. When asked about the uniqueness of his feelings toward his children, Donald replied:

> I imagine that it has something to do with the fact that ... it's like they are mine. They are close to me and I have lived with them for four years now and watched them grow up. So I suppose that they would have the most influence on me than just about anyone. They can get to me like that as opposed to

people at work who come and go and I only see eight hours five days a week. They don't really have as much influence on me or get to me the way my children do.

Researcher: You have been with your wife for longer than you have been with your kids.

Donald: I know. It seems as though my wife should have the same affect on me, but she does sometimes, but not really as much as my kids. I don't know why. I am closer to my kids than I am my wife in some senses.

Researcher: Can you talk about that a little bit?

Donald: Well, with my wife sometimes I feel a challenge. I feel like I am walking on egg shells with her because I don't want to upset her, don't want to make her mad. With my kids I can be myself more so than I can with my wife. I can be myself a little bit with my wife, but I still have that sense to where I have to have respect to her, act a specific way in public with her. With my kids, they don't care how I act. They don't care what I do. They are happy to have me around so I can feel a lot more loose with my kids than I do with my wife.

Peter's comments relate to the issue of controlling affect. His comments indicate that greater tolerance is needed in the context of being responsible for those who are developmentally immature. Thus, it may be necessary to control frustration and to express encouragement to a greater extent in fathering than in working with peers. Others attribute the differences in emotional intensity to the continual novelty of the father–child relationship as children undergo rapid developmental changes. Newly emerging skills and characteristics contribute a level of freshness and excitement to the relationship that may not exist in a long-standing relationship between peers. Paul talks about this aspect of emotional uniqueness and intensity as follows:

I mean, for me there is [a difference]. I just—my daughter to me is just lovely. I just think she's a wonderful human being. So, I mean, I don't know. It's kind of, like, being infatuated maybe when you first meet your spouse or fall in love or whatever. But children, they go through these different stages. And it's like being infatuated for years, I guess, because I just still feel that way ever since she's been a little child. You know, you always see something new and you can see the development—perhaps the initial stages of love or whatever. But I don't see that or see feeling that way, say, like going to work or in other relationships.

Other men were less able to attribute reasons for the differences in paternal emotions from other contexts, but the following quotes offer further insight into the types of differences they noted:

Researcher: Can you explain how it's different?

> Randy: Boy ... You know, when the baby comes up to me and hugs me, you know, I mean, it's like the love I feel for him it almost like hurts. You know, I've heard that expression and I could never understand it. But it makes you so happy, you know, it almost makes you feel, you know, like you were when you broke up with one of your girlfriends, you know, that same type of feelings. But it's just that much love. And I feel the same way about Carrie [his wife]. I mean, I love her but it's different, though. There's not much of a difference in the love, but there is a difference.

Although Randy was unable to articulate the differences in emotions toward his children and his wife, he was certain that such differences existed. Similarly, David expressed differences in intensity and expression, but was unable to articulate the reason for those differences.

> David: They are unique. I think they are totally unique. In comparison, I think that they stand alone. When Tracey and Jill [his daughters] received their awards for sports I get choked up, I'm an emotional person. I have to fight the tears. They always make fun of me, but I have to fight the tears on that. But there is a pride in that situation when somebody comes in and says the business looks great, or the building looks good. ... You're dealing with pride in both situations. They're totally different. I think the same thing would even be with Esther [his wife] and the girls. If Esther was to receive an award or somebody at church says she said she does a fantastic job at Sunday School, or something like that, there is pride, you know, it's like, "Yeah, it's my wife." It's not the same feeling as when Tracey or Jill or Sally get an award.
>
> Researcher: Why is that, do you think?
>
> David: I guess I would have to say I really don't know. I just know it's different. It's probably different even if you look at it through the love situation. My love for the girls is a lot different than my love for Esther which is a lot different than my love for my work.

Anthony was unable to even imagine any other context that could elicit the same degree of positive or negative emotionality as being a father:

> I can't imagine anything else in this world that would give you as much pleasure or guilt as being a parent.

The few men who saw no differences in their emotions toward their children and others did not differentiate in any regard. They simply said that they had been frustrated or experienced pride with kids, spouse, and work, and there was really no difference. However, they did not seem to consider or to be aware of the types of issues already discussed. Because I did not want to put words in their mouths, I did not probe further concerning intensity of feelings, sense of responsibility, or similar issues. The three men who expressed that there were no differences in the emotional currents of fathering and other contexts tended to be cognitively and logically oriented in their discussion of every aspect of fathering as opposed to experientially or emotionally oriented. It is possible that they were not at the same place of emotional integration and differentiation as the men who could articulate differences in the emotions of fathering and those associated with other contexts.

EMOTIONAL CURRENTS AND EMOTIONAL CURRENCY: THE GIVE AND TAKE OF EXPRESSIVITY

When fathers were asked if there were differences in the way that they experienced, expressed, or controlled emotions, the most common answer was that they needed to be careful about their anger. Craig remarked:

> Yeah, my anger is reactive. If I see something wrong I like to fix it or if I see something that needs to be done, I have to do it. Versus, you know, I'm a control freak, is a good word for it, in control. And you can't control three small children because they all have minds of their own. At that point where I'm not in control I start to get angry, and with anger you either repress it or you lash out, so you can't lash out at three kids. So I do have to control myself there. So, yeah, I find that to be a difference.

Similar statements were made by 54% of the sample. As such, suppression of anger was the most salient difference in emotional flow expressed by the sample. This fits with stereotypical characterizations and "licence" for men in American society to harbor and express anger. It is clearly recognized by fathers, however, that their anger is often unjustified and would bring negative results if given full vent. Therefore, they were aware of needing to exert emotional control over the expression of anger. Some fathers discussed mechanisms that they found to be helpful in maintaining control of their anger and frustrations. Leo realized that as a child, he had been much more of a problem to deal with than his own children were, so he felt that he should be encouraged by that and "take it easy" on them. He said:

> They're nowhere near as frustrating as I was and that's refreshing and comforting—and so I'm very sensitive when they make the mistakes or when they're doing wrong to try and settle down and communicate to them, you know, that I was not real pleased with their reaction or their response.

A few fathers talked about the need to mask fears or concerns from their children to keep them from becoming upset. Fears were most often discussed in terms of centering around serious illness or marital discord. Fathers stated that they thought that their children would not have understanding of the issues involved, and therefore, should not be apprised of the father's fears or concerns. In essence, they had to be strong or brave for the sake of their children. Again, this pattern of emotional regulation corresponds with traditional stereotypes of men in American society. Fathers who model such patterns are inadvertently socializing the next generation to invest in traditional gender roles as well.

In terms of emotional expressiveness, fathers talked about the need to be open with their children, to express love and approval, to show excitement about the things in which their children were interested, and to nurture and express their own childishness so that they could connect emotionally with their children. Craig provided the following example:

> The things that I wouldn't necessarily look at as being a big deal, you know, just to me, I find myself having to be expressive so the kids will take an interest in it. For example, I took the kids to Disney World in April, and you know, you see Mickey Mouse five-million times in the park and every time—"Hey, wow there's Mickey Mouse," and all the kids go, "Ooh," and they run over to him. Versus my wife, who has seen him about a billion times—[who says,] "Let's go do something else." So I find myself giving almost a phony expressionism to the kids which they don't pick up because they're kids, but I guess eventually they will. They'll be like, "Big deal, there's Mickey Mouse," too. But, yeah, I do right now, I do find it different than I would be reacting to.

Gilbert had made some conscious decisions to be more expressive than usual so that his son would understand his emotions and behaviors. He was interested in having open, clear communication with his son so that he would not need to assume that he knew what his father was thinking:

> I try to be more open so he can see who he is and who I am. And you try to explain certain things. Which normally you probably wouldn't because you want him to know what you're feeling inside when something good is happening or something bad in the family, like a sickness or, you know, just in debt; which we've had and things like that. I like to sit down and explain to him exactly what it is and get his feelings on it. Because I don't want him to just believe he knows what's going on because he's there, but not talking about it. Because since he's a child and he's seeing things differently from the way we see it, maybe he's interpreting this situation completely different.

Similarly, Glen knew that he needed to overcome his natural tendency to be quiet. Like Gilbert, he had decided that he needed to work at freely expressing emotions to his children. He wanted his emotions to be free flowing toward his children, but for some reason, he had not noticed changes in the way he expressed emotions to coworkers or his wife. His emotional expressiveness was greatest toward his children. He said:

> I've never been one to really outwardly express a lot of my emotions. If I have problems to deal with, I most comfortably deal with them kind of individually, just really kind of grinding at them myself and solving them. Um, not because I didn't want to share them or because I didn't feel others could help. But just my background and training as an engineer, I guess my nature is kind of to be analytical and linear and precise and that's just the way I tend to deal with my emotions. Um, I deal with children kind of not on that basis. But on the basis I described, free flowing, innocent and ... but I don't see that I deal with my emotions in terms of how I would share my feelings with my wife or things going on at the office any differently as a result of fatherhood. The way it would be different is, is how I would share them with my children.

Clifford related a similar pattern of greater expressiveness toward his children than toward others. His greater expressivity toward his children was seen as part of his responsibility to teach them:

> I try to be more verbal. Uh, I'm basically a quiet person. I try to be more verbal with them. Instead of holding things in, just keep them to myself. I try to explain to them. I guess, I'm trying to say. Where if I didn't have children I just, just ... let it go, you know. I know I have to teach them the right way. The right things to do I'm trying to say.

Mark made a similar decision, but for different reasons. He wanted to be involved with and expressive toward his son so that his son would not grow up having strong traditional stereotypes regarding masculine patterns of behavior. Mark wanted his son to experience him as an involved and sensitive man. Mark said:

> I try to work harder at showing my emotions with him so he doesn't grow up to be the typical male. I don't want him to grow up in a household, you know, where dad works all the time and when he comes home he eats dinner and goes to the bed and that's it. So I try to spend more time with him and play with him more, and cuddle him and get up with him in the middle of the night instead of leaving it to his mother, you know, that type of thing.

Only three men in the sample spontaneously talked through experiencing emotions differently due to fatherhood. They talked about having more fears than they would have otherwise experienced, becoming more childlike, and wanting to be more open-minded so that they could empathize with their children.

It is interesting to note that every man in the sample noted ways that their emotional currents had shifted since becoming fathers. Each father was able to cite specific feelings that they were working on expressing and or controlling because of being fathers.

BALANCE ISSUES

Men in the sample talked both positive and negative emotions associated with fathering. Their ability to express a greater range and frequency of positive affect indicates that although both positive and negative emotions abound in the context of fathering, the positive outweighed the negative. The balance of emotions was tipped toward the positive, at least for most men in this sample. Fathers also discussed the balances they must strive to achieve between expressiveness (for positive emotions) and suppression (of negative emotions).

Differentiation and integration of emotions had taken place for many of the sample fathers. Specifically, they could distinguish subtle differences between emotions felt toward their children and any other context. In addition, they had come to recognize that fathering entails many different emotions, integrating them into a whole. Because increased differentiation and integration are hallmarks of maturity (Allport, 1961), these data substantiate that involved fathers perceive that their relationships with their children were associated with emotional development. For these fathers, negotiating the emotional currents of involved fathering offered a rich context for men's emotional development.

Chapter **6**

Faith of Our Fathers: The Relationships Between Involved Fathering and Men's Faith, Morals, and Values

Does fatherhood as an experience lead to significant changes in mens' views about what is important, their moral beliefs, and their religiosity (religious beliefs and practices)? The specific focus of this chapter is on the perceived relation between men's active engagement in fatherhood and the development and expression of men's religious faith, morals, and values.

SOCIOHISTORICAL CONSIDERATIONS

Recent social movements including Promise Keepers and the Fatherhood Initiative (Promise Keepers, 1995; Blankenhorn, 1995) have begun to reemphasize the role of fathers in contributing moral leadership to families. The history of American fatherhood documents that men tended to exchange the role of "moral overseer" for the provider role during the 19th century (see chap. 3, Palkovitz, 1996b; Pleck, 1987, 1997; Rotundo, 1985). These roles are not mutually exclusive, but the assumption of a primary focus on providing relegates moral oversight to a secondary level. With the recent focus on "the new involved father" discussed in chapter 3, combined with the centrality of the provider role, father as moral guide is likely to be overshadowed by other aspects of paternal roles. Indeed, during the past 100 years, mothers have been more likely to hold primacy in supporting moral ideals within the family (Hoffman, 1981) and initiating church linkages for their family members (Bohannon, 1991).

The study of the impact of fatherhood on adult male development has been limited, particularly in regard to fathering's effect on men's moral and religious beliefs and behavior (P. Cowan, 1988; P. R. Newman & B. M.

Newman, 1988; Palkovitz, 1996; Palkovitz & Palm, 1998; Palm, 1993; Snarey, 1993). Whereas the influence of fathers on children's moral development has been studied (e.g., Hoffman, 1981) and the role of father as moral leader (e.g., Blankenhorn, 1995) has been a focus of discussion, the reciprocal effects of parenthood on fathers' moral behavior and religious beliefs and practices has not received the same attention. Although not directly related to faith, morals, and values, Griswold (1997) identified themes from the 19th century suggesting that parenthood makes men less selfish, more refined, and better disciplined. This chapter seeks to address whether contemporary fathers believe that fatherhood has changed them in relation to what their religious beliefs and practices are, how they view moral issues, and what they value.

LIFE-COURSE CONSIDERATIONS

It has been suggested in theoretical literature, and modestly supported in some empirical literature (Mueller & Cooper, 1986; Palkovitz & Palm, 1998), that many of the events of early adulthood cause men to focus on questions of religious faith, and to act on or operationalize faith in ways not previously required. Specifically, the life decisions and life-course transitions frequently associated with the transition to adulthood and differentiation from one's family of origin cause reflection and action on faith-based values. Among a broad array of issues linked to early adulthood are questions such as the following: Should couples engage in premarital sex? Should they cohabit? Should they use contraception? If they decide to marry, will the ceremony be civil or sacred? Who will officiate, and what texts or sacraments will be included in the ceremony? As couples conceive children they begin to consider what, if any, ceremonies or sacraments will be enacted on behalf of the child. Should the infant be baptized? Dedicated? Christened? Circumcised on the eighth day? What should religious education or training look like? When should it begin? Who is responsible for providing religious education? How do parents model and express their beliefs appropriately and to what extent should children be given choice in matters of faith?

The questions and issues noted here represent concrete operationalizations of underlying faith or values. Engaging in active fathering roles may also initiate a revisiting of core questions regarding the human situation (e.g., Where did I come from? Why am I here? What is the real meaning of life?). Fathers sometimes consider such issues in anticipation of (or in response to) children's questions. In doing so, men's beliefs and values may be clarified or called into question. Changes in beliefs, values, and morality would be expected. These changes may be paralleled by changes in religious faith and practice as well.

FORMAL FAITH COMMUNITIES AND MEN'S RELIGIOSITY

Faith communities generally have either formally or informally developed positions or statements in response to the types of questions represented earlier, and young adults evaluate the extent to which they subscribe to the positions, and ultimately, the faith associated with the positions. These evaluations may take place at the same time that identity issues are being consolidated. In essence, it is during young adulthood that the question "Is my parents' faith my faith?" gets revisited and operationalized numerous times.

During early adult development, decisions regarding faith and associated behaviors are accompanied by perceptions of a new level of accountability, responsibility, and imposing deadlines as men assume fathering roles. Such decisions carry a greater gravity and exert clear effects on children, spouse or partner, and grandparents, as well as effecting the texture of one's own life. Decisions regarding religious faith and its practice have implications for everyday activities and interactions between people in close relationships. Fathers who have reflected on their religious beliefs recognize that their conduct sends messages regarding the vitality of faith to family members who observe their daily behavior.

When making lifestyle or life direction decisions, thinking men question their alternatives and the underlying foundations for them. Some long-standing perspectives and underlying beliefs are confirmed, strengthened, anchored, and deepened. Others are weakened, revised, or reversed. Dissonance theory (Festinger, 1957) suggests that there should be a match between people's beliefs and their behaviors or discomfort from the discrepancy will motivate the discordant person to change either their belief or their behavior. As such, during early adulthood, the belief/behavior interface takes on a new level of importance in integrating the role of father into continuously developing (integrating and differentiating) levels of identity, intimacy, and generativity (Christiansen & Palkovitz, 1998). Fathering is "rubbed up against" faith identity, intimacy with God and spouse/partner, and ways to share faith with the next generation.

DEVELOPMENTAL PULLS OF FATHERING AND PROFESSIONAL PROVIDERS

In realms other than faith, involved fathers frequently describe an increased awareness of responsibility over and above what they had experienced as husbands (Palkovitz, 1994). The responsibilities of fathering are not symmetrical with those of being a husband. Fathers express that their spouses are self-responsible peers, but recognize that, as fathers, they hold a higher degree of responsibility toward their children. As elaborated in other chapters, engaged fathering fosters heightened awareness for a need to control and express emotions, model health, engage in provision and reduce risk taking, all for the sake of the children (Palkovitz, 1999). This is not to suggest that all fathers recognize or focus on these issues, nor should it be inferred that they fully and quickly comply with their consciences. However, incorporation of an active fathering role into a continuously evolving array of other roles (i.e., husband, worker, community member) causes reflection and reevaluation of behavioral choices and belief evaluation with a higher degree of gravity than previously realized. Simply stated, engaged fathering creates a developmental draw for men (Palkovitz, 1999). Involved fathers are motivated to make positive contributions to their families, which in turn require them to continue to grow and mature.

In all areas of active fathering, individual men feel more or less prepared to engage in the plethora of role nuances that exist. In places where they perceive that they already have maturity, expertise, needed support, confidence, and/or accomplished success, men engage and respond differently than they do in areas where they feel a gap between their abilities, resources, maturity levels, and the required skills or responses. Draw is exerted in areas where men are at or near a stage of "readiness" for continued development and where they have access to the resources needed to go to the next level. In contrast, where there is a perception of incompetence, inadequacy, limitation, or ignorance, men respond along a continuum of responses, ranging (on one end) from escapism through denial, avoidance, or withdrawal, to the other end of the spectrum, where they exert significant time and effort toward securing the needed training, experience, or knowledge. In short, the continuum ranges between "cut and run" tendencies and "be the best that you can be" tendencies. Men with different developmental histories, supports, and motivations are likely to select different positions along the continuum in regard to a particular perceived need.

These principles operate in every arena of father involvement: from caregiving to provision and play. Similar patterns should be expected and recognized in regard to the fathers' roles in facilitating the development of their children's religious faith, morality, and values. In the same way that some men defer "care and feeding" of their offspring to their spouse until they learn the requisite skills, or take on what could appropriately be labeled "assistant parent" roles, a significant proportion of men defer religious instruction and participation to their spouse, another relative or friend, or a clergy person because they view others to have greater qualifications than they do for training their child in religious faith.

Some fathers feel they are not adequately equipped to participate in the spiritual training of their children. In short, they believe that others can do a better job than they can in leading their children into maturity in matters of faith. This may well be the case, but children may perceive that their fathers' declinations on taking leading roles in their religious training means that, from their fathers' perspective, faith is not important. When men participate in activities and openly model and declare them to be important (as they often do with economic providing), then not doing so in other areas could be mistakenly interpreted to signify that the neglected area is not important.

On the other hand, an analysis of historical trends shows that other functions—such as formal education, medical care, and specialized training—have shifted from home-based enterprises to specialist delivered services. Part of the rationale for the shift from home to professional oversight of these areas has been that trained specialists are better equipped to handle these important functions. Thus, it is in the best interest of the child to send them to a professional for these services. Religious education may be viewed by some to fall into the same category.

It is common for families to view church programs (e.g., Sunday schools, youth groups, etc.) to hold significant responsibility for the training of their children in regard to matters of faith. Nock (1998) cited a Gallup poll, which found that 90% of American parents want some form of spiritual training for their children. When this is coupled with Snarey's (1993) finding that fathers sense that the largest gap is in their ability to provide moral training to their children, it is easier to understand fathers' reliance on others to provide significant spiritual and moral training for their children.

SPIRITUAL PRESCRIPTIONS FOR FATHERS

There are many stylistic differences in enactment and numerous ways to interpret daily operationalization, however, Judeo-Christian scriptures straightforwardly state that fathers are to know how to give good things to their children (Matthew 7:9–11), to discipline (train) their children (Deuteronomy 8:5, Proverbs 3:12, 13:24, 15:5, 19:18, 22:6, 23:13, 29:17, Ephesians 6:4, 1 Thessalonians 2:11–12, Hebrews 12:7–11), and to avoid exasperating and embittering their children in the training process (Ephesians 6:4, Colossians 3:21). In numerous passages in the Old Testament, it is clear that paternal modeling is important in the transmission of religious values (e.g., 1 and 2 Kings), and parents are commanded to teach the words of the Lord to their children, talking of His commands and words when sitting in the house and when walking along the road, when lying down and rising up (Deuteronomy 11:19).

There is modest empirical support that families who follow these scriptural prescriptions have children who are more positively oriented toward matters of faith, have more positive adjustments, and a closer concordance of values with their parents (Chartier & Geohner, 1976; Clark, Washington, & Danser, 1988; Francis & Gibson, 1993; Kieren & Munro, 1987). Some fathers may be unfamiliar with a scriptural emphasis on fathers' responsibilities toward their children in matters of faith. Alternatively, fathers may be too embarrassed to admit their perceived lack of preparation, or perhaps feel lost in their ability to tap appropriate sources to facilitate their own development as men of faith.

FATHERS AND FAITH COMMUNITIES IN FRICTION

Active members of faith communities have been quick to criticize men who abdicate their responsibilities to "train up their children" to others when it comes to matters of faith. This is especially true of members of denominations who take strong traditional (sometimes characterized as patriarchal) approaches to family life based on their interpretations of the scriptures. A common conservative perspective is that men are to be the spiritual heads of their households, and abandoning their primary roles in these matters is a serious breach of responsibility.

However, those who are quick to criticize fathers who arrange for others to provide their children with qualified religious instruction often applaud fathers who arrange for professional music instructors, language tutors, and skilled coaches, teachers, or physicians to provide care and training for their children where they would not be as qualified. Uneven metrics are applied.

Perhaps men who feel inadequate as spiritual mentors are engaging in the best alternative they know of—to be the broker/provider for securing appropriate instruction. This is a strategy they have effectively employed in other matters with positive and encouraging results.

Men who experience disapproval from religious leaders or members for using the same strategy in matters of faith are sometimes surprised by the negative reactions they perceive. The unexpected disapproval can be generalized to the point where this group of fathers, who are already feeling somewhat tentative or challenged in their faith to begin with, perceive the disapproval to be another indicator of a gap that exists between them and other "more spiritual" people, thereby placing yet another hurdle between fathers and the level of faith integration they need to achieve before they can positively contribute to their children's faith. A cycle of perceived inadequacy and disapproval can lead to further distancing between men who have been marginalized by organized religion. In some cases, men who feel disapproval and rejection from faith communities make explicit statements discounting the importance of active participation in faith-based communities and activities. Doing so while delegating their children's faith education to others sends a mixed message that undermines the process of faith integration in their children.

FAITH AS A GENDERED VENTURE

The demography of church attendance and membership reflects the fact that in comparison to men, there are disproportionate numbers of women who regularly attend services, join churches, and participate in the life of the church (Dalbey, 1988). This may be an indicator that contemporary men are challenged in regard to being well prepared to shepherd their children into a vital faith. Although I have not seen representative data, informal observation suggests that disproportionate numbers of women also serve as teachers in religious education programs. As inequalities in gender representation skew occupational and gender-role socialization, the demographics of church participation and religious education can transmit the message that faith is feminine.

FAITH AND GENERATIVITY

Simply stated, for fathers to have something meaningful to give, they must have a reasonable base of resources. In this case, religious identity, faith-based knowledge, intimacy with God, and generative tendencies would be prerequisite skills for men of faith engaging in a generative manner with their child as they coparticipate in the life of the church. Men who have a central, vital faith as an axis mundi (Latshaw, 1998) integrate fathering roles and challenges into their growing faith walk. As active fathers, such men tend to learn about God as Father, see the miraculous hand of God in conception, birth, and developmental milestones (Palkovitz & Palm, 1998), reflect on their own inadequacy to control all aspects of their child's life and health, talk about the centrality of prayer in shaping their fathering (Latshaw, 1998), and place a high priority on finding ways to be generative in their faith.

In comparison to atheists, agnostics, or undifferentiated people, persons of faith tend to hold different perspectives on the meaning of life, how to measure success, what is important and of lasting value, and appropriate responses to life's challenges. Followers of Christ are taught to place higher value on relationships than material goods and the eternal than the temporal, although they often fall short and readily admit that consistently walking in these virtues is a challenge. Men of faith are challenged to impart these values to their children through lifestyles that are consistent with their beliefs. Large individual differences exist between men who hold these values in terms of the centrality of the values, their ability to articulate the values, and the degree to which they are able to consistently model behavior appropriate to their stated values.

Whereas there are a range of events and issues in young adulthood that bring a focus to personal reflections on faith, clearly there are varied responses to the issues raised. The next section focuses on examining and describing different patterns of fathers' responses to the issues of faith, morals, and values that they confront in raising their children. Beyond describing a continuum of responses, data are summarized to bring understanding to the developmental path that brought men to the various places they occupy along the continuum of faith responsiveness. Implications for religious institutions and local congregations are discussed.

Pertinent Sample Characteristics and Interpretive Notes

Demographic data, collected prior to the interview, reflected moderate diversity in religious preference and identity. On a written personal information form, in response to an open-ended blank labeled "religious preference," 18 fathers listed various Protestant denominations, 8 wrote Catholic, 7 indicated Christian, 6 gave no preference, and 1 registered as Agnostic. Whereas this distribution reflects a range of religious preferences, it is nonrepresentative of faiths outside of the Christian tradition.

In addition to information presented in the preface of this book concerning factors that are likely to influence analyses of the data, further disclosure is appropriate in this chapter. I am a person who perceives faith to be my central value. Beyond labeling myself as a Christian in a cultural sense, I am a follower of Christ, and have served for over 12 years as an elder and youth group leader in a local, nondenominational Christian church. Aspects of faith are openly discussed and practiced on a daily basis in my home with my wife and four sons. As a family, we regularly participate in faith-based services and devote significant chunks of time and other resources to faith-centered volunteer work and short-term missions locally, regionally, and abroad. Undoubtedly, these contexts of active, ongoing involvement in a faith community, generative activity, spiritual leadership experiences, and faith development have exerted influence in the analytic process.

Interview Questions. In this chapter, analyses are limited to open-ended questions raised in the middle of the interview centered on fathering and faith, morals and values. The analysis focuses on the following questions and the rationales that fathers used to explain how or why they have or have not changed:

1. Has fatherhood influenced your participation in religious activities or resulted in shifts in the underlying beliefs or faith?
2. Has fatherhood influenced your views of moral issues?
3. Has fatherhood resulted in any shifts in your values?

Definitional Issues. Although study participants were not provided with operational definitions of terms central to this chapter, the following set of definitions are offered to clarify the major areas of study. They are based on the common (*American Heritage Dictionary*) understanding of the three important areas that were addressed in the study:

Religion—A set of beliefs, values and practices based on the teachings of a spiritual leader.

Moral Issues—Issues that are based on the judgment of goodness or correctness of character and behavior.

Values—Principles or standards considered worthwhile or desirable.

RESULTS

The analysis of each question is presented in the form of general patterns of change and more specific themes related to each area of change. The themes provide some insight into the meaning and motivation behind the general patterns of change.

Question 1: Has Fatherhood Influenced Your Commitment to Religion/Religious Beliefs?

The general pattern of responses to this question reveals that about one half of the men interviewed reported no change in their religiosity that was specifically stimulated by fatherhood. The other half reported changes of varying magnitudes, most often pertaining to practices. There were also some men who described changes in practice without accompanying changes in underlying beliefs.

The men who reported no change can be classified into three distinct groups, each having different reasons for no change. The first group has continued in strong positive religious beliefs established during childhood or early adulthood. A second group had distinct negative feelings regarding religion based on earlier negative experiences. A few men in a third group adopted stronger religious beliefs during early adulthood, but they were initiated by life experiences or circumstances other than fatherhood. The men who reported changes in religiosity could be differentiated into two subgroups. The first group had become more involved and increased participation in religious practices. The second subgroup was aware of the significance of religious commitment but was still seeking the best ways to express or enact their beliefs. Descriptions of each of these groups is presented with accompanying representative quotes.

No Change—Religion Always Central. One group of men had made decisions predating fatherhood that religious faith was integral and vital in their lives. For these men, although fatherhood was not seen as a fundamental force in forging their faith, they talked ardently about the relations between fathering and religious conviction. Because faith is essential to their personal identities, it informs fathering decisions and behaviors to a significant degree. Religious faith serves as an axis mundi for some of these men (Latshaw, 1998) and all other experiences are given meaning in regard to their operative construction of faith.

With some fathers, it was not apparent whether early religious beliefs were merely adopted in a manner of identity foreclosure or if religious identity achievement was established prior to fatherhood. What makes this group different from the negative experience group is that these men embraced a specific set of religious beliefs versus rejecting them.

No Change Group—Negative Experiences. A separate group of men declared that fathering had not influenced religious behavior or underlying beliefs. The issue of spirituality was settled prior to becoming a father, and was related to decidedly negative experiences. Men who had not changed their negative opinions of religion described some of the important reasons for this stance. Fatherhood was not seen as a major influence because these men had made a previous decision concerning the role of religion in their lives. Many of these fathers appeared to be in a state of *religious identity foreclosure.* A number of these men described early negative experiences that caused them to reject religion as a viable force in their lives. There were three distinct themes related to this group of men.

It was seldom the case that the fathers in the study had not been exposed to religious perspectives and activities, rather, a *need to avoid hypocrisy* led some men to withdraw from participation in organized religious activities. Craig wanted to have consistency between his behavior in the context of religious services and everyday life. He said:

> I feel that, you know, if you're going up to stand in church and in front of [a] hundred people that are also in there, and you're professing faith in God and how holy everything is, and then you turn around outside of church and not act that way, it's not really worth it. And if I'm standing up there in church with three kids sitting next to me on a Sunday, and on the way home I trip and fall and rip my Sunday clothes and, go "Goddammit", it's not reinforcing it. ... I'm a firm believer that if you say it then do it. If you're going to stand there and say it and not do it, then you're really wasting my time.

In fact, the most widespread and prominent theme expressed by this subgroup involved examples of hypocrisy that soured men's view that faith can be a meaningful anchor. Vicente expressed disgust at the level of hypocrisy that he had witnessed. He felt a need to see consistency between beliefs and behaviors. He said:

> Anybody can take and go to church on a Sunday, pick up the Bible for that one moment, and follow the preacher, and then do their jig the rest of the week.

Thomas summarized this general sentiment by saying, "You know, if you don't follow your own conscience in this, it's false." A second theme that emerged in this cluster was the experience of *personal loss or hardship* that caused a doubting or censuring of God (if He does exist, how can He allow this suffering?). These fathers recounted specific negatively interpreted incidents where they felt that their prayers were not answered and they could not understand or believe in a God who would allow evil to happen. At times the loss was coupled with interventions or explanations from representatives of faith communities that created negative evaluations about faith. Chris' mother died of complications from pneumonia when he was 9 years old. He recounted his experience:

> Well, my mother was taken away from me at a very young age. And the preachers and everyone tried to explain to me why she was taken away at a young age. But to me it wasn't a good enough reason to me. I mean, I can go to church or I can go and do whatever, but it still is going to be a part of me that's hurt, not disliking God or nothing like that, but it's just, you can't understand it. I mean, I have a preacher sit down and try to explain it to me, that you know, this is the reason why, or whatever. But to me, as a person, at seven-years old … but me as a person, no, I feel as though my Mom shouldn't have been taken away from me at an early age.

A third theme identified was that *the desperate and decaying state of "the world"* also caused men to doubt the existence or nature of God. Gilbert had ongoing doubts regarding the existence of God and the truth of the Bible:

> But just in life in general, it seems to me the more I live and the more you see that's around you it just puts, you have less confidence in religion and in faith … just by seeing the state of the world, I guess, and the moral aspects and the way people live and everything. I don't know, it's just, you know, defaces your trust in religion or in the Bible.
>
> Interviewer: Rather than defacing your trust in other people or their ability to live according to those principles?
>
> Gilbert: No. Well, I would say it's the same. But the point is—it's hard to explain. But I would say that, in other words, I'm not sure if there is a God or not. But even if there is, I don't believe that he has anything to do with what's going on in this planet. If there is an almighty, I'm not sure. There might or there might not be. But if there is, I don't think he has any guidance; it's what's happening. I mean, he is just an observer as far as I'm concerned. If he does exist he's just observing. And just because of the state of the world and all the illnesses and the disease and the hunger, and the famine, I mean, it's so simple to see, well, if there is a God, well, then why is all that going on? And I'm sure that nobody's prayers are really answered. I mean, when you think about all the starving children and all the bad things in the world.
>
> Interviewer: Okay. So those views really aren't linked to anything about fatherhood?
>
> Gilbert: No. Like I said, I don't believe so. They're just everyday living in life.

Gilbert described himself as a nonpracticing Catholic, stating that he did not "get into it too much" and indicating that he did not actively promote his son's participation in religious matters. Once again, this shows consistency between his level of belief and his behavior. He did not desire to encourage his son to invest in something to which he did not feel genuinely dedicated.

As a whole, the group of men who did not change and continued to hold negative views of religion talked about early negative experiences with people or institutions of faith. Some men described their early choices to steer away from organized religion, citing combinations of justifications delineated earlier.

Because of the manner in which these men had squared their own experiences with their beliefs about God, most fathers expressed a critical magnitude of ambivalence about religious faith. Many fathers who experienced ambivalence or foreclosure chose to defer religious upbringing of their children to the women in their families. Anthony referred to religious upbringing as his wife's "thing":

> Interviewer: Has fatherhood influenced in anyway your commitment to religion?
>
> Anthony: No. I don't have any commitment.
>
> Interviewer: So there hasn't been any change in terms of religious faith or behavior?
>
> Anthony: Me? No. The mother, that's her side, that's the job she does. She takes them to church every Sunday and ... Sunday school ... That's her thing, that's her side of the coin. I teach them how to do things, she's responsible for that.

Similarly, Chris had deferred religious training to female relatives. He said:

> Because I'm not in the more religious—well, I'm a religious person but I just don't go to church. It's not real important to me no more. When I was little, yeah, it was important. But now, no. It's up to the kids if they want to go, they feel free to go. If not, I don't holler at them or nothing about—
>
> Interviewer: Do you think that they look to you to see what's the right thing to do about religion?
>
> Chris: Not my crew. They know—I mean, if their mom wants to take them to church—well, their grandmother does go to church every Sunday. They feel welcome to go if they want. They know that it's not just me.

Chris did not seem to think that his modeled indifference toward organized religion detracted from his children's interest in pursuing things of faith.

Another important idea expressed by the group of men with consistently negative feelings about faith was that matters of faith were ultimately the *child's choice,* and that as long as their children were experiencing *exposure* to religious activity in some manner, they had the *opportunity* to choose for themselves. These fathers did not want to bias their children or "force things down their throat." Donald said:

> My mom always brought me up to go to church. By the time I was ten or twelve or something I always had to go to church and I hated it because I did not

> agree with anything. I just sat in church. I still don't agree with it, but sometimes I wonder whether I should bring my kids up religiously or try to at least give them the opportunity. I guess I am more prone to living the religious life now that I have kids even though I don't.

The distaste that Donald had developed for organized religion during his early years of forced attendance now prevented him from exploring it in any formal way. Yet, he wondered if he should provide opportunities for his children so that they could make up their own minds. He stated this question as a sign of his inclination toward living a religious life, although he had not followed through with it in any manner. Craig had a similar experience and had taken a parallel position:

> I went to church every Sunday for, I guess 18 years, and when I finally was able to have my own house and start dealing with my kids, I've taken the attitude of let them choose their own God. Because years of having God forced down my throat didn't change me as a person, in my opinion. And it's actually made my sister go the other way versus, you know, the church, I really don't need anything to do with … they even expressed interest in going to church on their own, you know, what is God, where did I come from and all that. But I'm not personally interested in going every Sunday to church. If they start bringing it up more and more frequently, I'll end up taking them until they say, well, enough is enough, I don't want to go any more and I'll back off if they don't want to go. I think my wife feels the same way. When she needs God, God will be around. Other than that you can take it or leave it, but I don't want to force values that I don't have a strong faith in on them.… If they want to go worship God, that's fine, we'll take them up there and if they get tired of it after a couple of Sundays they won't want to do it any more, but it's up to them. As they get older I believe that they'll form their own values. So if they want to be Buddhist they can be Buddhist or whatever they want to be, it doesn't matter.

Craig's ambivalence for faith comes through in his statement in a number of ways. First, he doubts that his children will maintain an interest in faith for long. Second, if they do express an interest later, it does not matter to him whether they select a major religion different from the faith in which he was brought up. These statements indicate that faith is not central to his value system.

No Change Attributable to Fathering—Other Life Experiences. Several fathers talked about reasons other than father involvement for changes in religious dedication, such as recovering from alcoholism and having prayers answered. Although this group described substantive changes in religiosity, they perceived that the increased commitment was not directly related to fatherhood. Adam's quote provides an example of both "other circumstances" and "answered prayer" as primary reasons for an increase in faith:

> No [fathering didn't change my beliefs], alcoholism did. ... I was arrested for DUI in Massachusetts, which required 30 days in jail, ... so it was going to ruin me. So I ... quit drinking and I started praying. ... I went back and the paperwork vanished.

Adam's experiential reality regarding faith did not depend on any fathering-related factors. Independent of fathering, he had experienced an increase in his religious faith.

Such cases were rare, with only one other father citing answered prayers as stimulating a greater sense of belief.

Change Groups-Introduction. The men who identified fatherhood as an instrumental influence on their own religiosity can be divided into three distinct subgroups. The first group described changes in religious beliefs and practices that were stimulated by fatherhood. The second group reported fatherhood as an influence in the deeper development of their religious beliefs. A third group was motivated to seek a place to express their religious beliefs and feelings and was somewhere in the process of this search.

Change Group—Fathering Initiated. The first group of men saw fatherhood as a catalyst for their own faith development. Fathers in this group expressed this in a variety of ways.

Although some men did not see a particularly faith-expanding effect of having children, they realized that becoming a father had modified the direction of their faith trajectory from erosion to stability. Glen had noted a sense of something missing in his life, and felt that his faith was eroding. He did not reengage in faith in significantly observable ways after becoming a father, but he noted a change in his faith trajectory, which he felt was significant. He described it in the following exchange:

> Interviewer: What did fatherhood have to do with you commitment to religion?
>
> Glen: A couple of things. One is I think, in a sense there was a gap there. That is going from a strong Catholic to a practicing Catholic, to a weekend Catholic, you know, or convenient type thing. And so a gap exists there and kind of knowing subconsciously that a gap was there but never doing anything about it. And fatherhood was, was an opportunity to do something about it. Because if I wanted to raise my children with a strong religious beliefs, then I should get back on track myself. So, it probably was just ... a point in time that was convenient to say, "Well, OK, you've known this gap has existed and you want to do something about it, now is as good a time as ever." So, the timing is one thing.
>
> Interviewer: The kids imposed a deadline in a sense.

> Craig: Yeah, but also in another sense it's a way to use that time. If you want your children baptized you have to attend classes. If you want your children to grow up with a good religious upbringing you should talk about God. You should read books, you should ... go out and buy a bible.... It was about time that I did.... My wife suggested that I teach CCD on Sundays to a sixth grade class at the parish that we belong to. Prior to fatherhood it would have been, "What do I want to do with kids and what do I know about religion anyways?" Other than what I've learned and not really practiced a whole lot. Then I saw that as a challenge. Well this is a way for me to uh, reinvest in my religion, get closer to God, learn some more.... Had fathering not come along this gap might have widened to the point were there wasn't any faith left. And that certainly is not the case now, so from that stand point its stronger in a relative scale. On an absolute scale it probably hasn't changed much. Stayed on the same, same continuing track ... yeah, the direction was kind of towards apathy, and it's no where near that now. And I can attribute [that to] fatherhood.

Craig's insights and expressivity capture one aspect of the developmental draw that fathers feel. If they want their children to have a strong and positive role model to follow, then a "tune up" is likely in order. Craig was only one of a significant subgroup of fathers in similar circumstances. Other fathers decided they needed to take responsibility for providing religious guidance for their children. It was partly their own sense of inadequacy as a moral or religious guide that motivated some fathers to invest in attending services. Steve elaborated this theme as well. He said:

> By the time like I was eighteen or nineteen, I considered myself an Atheist. Although, now I probably consider I was just Agnostic because I've taken a reversal from that. And I think the reason for, is raising kids you have to provide some sort of moral structure. And I think religion provides the institution for a moral structure, at least, an institution that can provide this, you know, in their teachings, in philosophy. Although I'm not particularly in agreement with the religious community, but I do agree with the philosophies. So I think that's affected my judgment as far as how to judge religion. I was rather against it. I'm not against it now.... How has that changed? I guess it's a fear of my children growing up without any kind of structure to fall back on. I always figured for myself, see, when I was younger I had all of the morals I needed. I didn't need to go to church to have somebody to impress it upon me to have morals, so I figured I had it on my own. Well, now I question, do I have the ability to teach that to my children? I don't know. When I was a kid, I went to church. So I'm not really sure of myself and I have a theory that, you know, well maybe not enough is being provided, not enough of the right guidance and insight. So that's where I started changing my own feelings on the matter. I altered it so perhaps I can bring the kids into it, at least they can go to church and have the same choices I had. I went to church and I made a conscious choice afterwards.

Vicente felt that he needed to learn more about faith so that he could teach his children appropriately. He talked about his lack of preparation and his decision to remedy it. Coming to an understanding of matters of faith and wanting to share his understanding with his daughter in an appropriate way and time served as a motivation for him to be more committed to religion:

> Interviewer: Has fatherhood influenced your commitment to religion?
>
> Vicente: Yes. I find myself now reading more of the Bible, going to church a little bit more. I'm trying to find out more about how to relay this to my daughter. Coming up as a kid, I didn't have a whole lot of, what you might call, religious background. I was familiar with—the most I was familiar with church was Easter Sunday ... and you go to church. But you never knew what anybody was talking about. You knew it was a God. You knew it was a devil and there was a heaven and a hell. But you never really understood it. From becoming older, and venturing into that myself, I pretty much understand what it's about now. The salvation and Christianity and things like that. So I think about how I'm going to break that to my daughter as far as teaching her what it's about. You know, where do you start that at?

Some fathers had made the decision that it was important to take their children to religious services, and were attracted to the activities, the relationships, and the messages that they experienced while taking their children. Some men were encouraged to engage in more significant levels of faith community activities. Ned exemplifies this pattern:

> Interviewer: Has fatherhood affected your commitment to religion?
>
> Ned: Very much so. I'm a Methodist, and up until the time I got out of the Navy, which was about seven or eight years ago, at that time my work was real, everything, everything, to me. But when I got out of the Navy, I got back into the community thing. And I used to take my kids up to church with my mother in Rockford Park. And while they would be in church I would jog around the park, you know, physical fitness, goofy stuff, or go home and work on the house for a while. But then I went into church a couple of times with them because they had a program for the kids, you know, and the people in the church made me feel real at home and real happy. And I found a real good feeling there. So, now I've gotten back into my spiritual part. Religion's real important for me and my children. We go to church every Sunday. I teach Sunday School, and my daughter's in my Sunday School class. So religion and family life in general with being a father I think are real important.
>
> Interviewer: So, there's been a change in terms of church attendance, how much you go to church, and you attribute that to having kids?
>
> Ned: If it wasn't for my children going to church I would not be in church today, no.

Change Group—Enhancement of Religious Faith. A second group of men who saw faith as central to their own identities cited the miracle of birth or child development as faith bolstering. Some of these fathers were men of faith prior to having children, others were stimulated to think more about faith as a result of their fathering experiences. Ken talked about it in this manner:

> Well, I guess that when I see my kids, what I see is a miracle. And I understand the biology of it but that just doesn't fully describe what I see when I see my kids. And I've got to believe from seeing them, I have to believe in God. And that's just not an evolutionary biological sort of thing. So I think it comes right down to the fundamentals of being able to affirm your faith.

Other men similarly talked about the fact that watching their children grow and develop is like witnessing a miracle every day, bolstering their belief in a higher power.

Fathers with relatively high degrees of dedication to Christianity discussed learning more about the nature of God as Father through nurturing their own children. David expressed this theme:

> Before the girls were born I had no idea what it was like to be a father. We always looked to God as being our father and if you haven't been a father, well, then, you're going to look at Him in a different way than if you have been a father. What I want and desire for my kids, I can identify a lot more with what the Lord wants me to do. I believe that ... my faith in Him has increased because I'm a father, yes. Because I have seen him intervene with the kids, you know.

Some men experienced a deeper faith due to increased commitment to programs related to children, most often Sunday school, or youth group involvement. As fathers of children in these programs, they were asked to teach or lead in some capacity, and involvement in religious activities lead to reflection and clarification on issues of faith, as in Craig's case (discussed previously).

Change Group—Seekers. A third group who reported changes in religious commitment were fathers who recognized that more was needed in their faith lives and were seeking a place to bring children to church but had not yet found one that consistently met their needs. Roger talked about an unacted upon desire to get back into a pattern of church attendance. He cited business as a deterrent to getting around to finding a church:

> We don't go to church on an every Sunday basis.... Hopefully, I'd like that to change, my wife would like that to change. We have very busy schedules. I still work weekends; she has weekends off. But I see us trying to get back

into—see, I was raised that way, we went to church every Sunday, and I kind of like when he's old enough to know, I'd kind of like to be able to have him go to church every Sunday, and let him make up his own mind but at least give him that opportunity to hear what I heard when I was a child and make up his own mind—and my wife also, she spent a lot of time in church, and kind of like to get him into the same situation we had when we were children.

Once again, the theme of opportunity and choice were expressed. Some fathers who encouraged church participation for their children did not necessarily align themselves with the teachings or practices of the church. Rather, they believed that the church could provide a socially supportive and positive environment for their child's development. Paul, who had voiced serious doubts about the existence of God, still felt that it was important for him to get his children to church:

Interviewer: Could I ask why you feel it's important to attend church?

Paul: Yeah, you can ask. At least where I go to church I think the people are very nice, I think it's a very good social connection. And I think with churches, even though I don't really agree with what all the things they say, I think they teach good morals and give you a good social network for kids. I mean, they just really, I think it's good for their development. And, you know, they can still struggle with all that religious stuff later too, you know.

Other men also talked about the importance of having supportive peer networks for their children and the social developmental benefits they perceived to exist in faith-based communities.

Summary. Overall, about 60% of the 40 fathers described some important changes in external behaviors/commitment to religion that they viewed to be directly related to active involvement in fathering. For some men, this meant returning to church after a time of being absent from organized religion. Others were searching for a faith community that would offer more positive experiences than their own experience as children or young men. These patterns represent a variety of potential paths related to religious practice and fatherhood. Personal interpretations of prior experience seem to play a principal role in defining and directing potential change.

The subissues of religious practice and religious belief were addressed. This distinction was important for some men who reported changes in their practices but not in their foundational beliefs. Fathers reported changes in practice about 60% of the time but only about one third reported changes in their actual underlying beliefs (i.e., belief in God) or faith. In contrast, prior to becoming fathers, almost two thirds of the men had made previous (disconfirming or affirming) decisions concerning the centrality of religious faith in their lives. As such, fatherhood rarely played the jolt role, as described by Palkovitz (1994, see chap. 4) in regard to religiosity (i.e., precipitating major changes in direction). And, when fathering was seen as an influence on faith, fatherhood most often functioned in the gentle evoker (Palkovitz, 1994, chap. 4) mode (i.e., bringing adjustments to preexisting trajectories).

The more differentiated analysis of the distinction between religious faith versus practice reveals how some of the fathers thought about changes in this area. The one third who reported changes in faith often described changes in very positive, spiritual terms where prayers had been answered. Randy described a crisis time during his fathering when he felt that God directly answered his prayers and gave him revelation of what was going to happen. He recounted a time when his infant daughter had been in the hospital:

> The first two nights we didn't know whether she was going to live or die … I prayed. I mean, I didn't know what else to do. And after I prayed I fell asleep. And I know it was God because He lifted that from me. I know God did that. And I woke up after that hour and a half because Carrie [his wife] had called. And she is just hysterical because they were transferring Robin [his daughter] from that hospital to the other one and they wouldn't let her go with her, you know. And I just—I told her, I said, "It'll be all right." And I *knew* that. So I know it's made my relationship with God better as far as becoming a parent.

Some of the changes that the fathers reported regarding religious practice were more peripheral, not affecting inner convictions at all. These tended to be factors such as attendance at church for the primary reason of modeling for the kids. Some fathers felt that although faith was not important for them, they needed to give the appearance of participation so that their children would be exposed to faith and consider it on their own. Paul was a father who fit into this category. He explained:

> I guess I'm committed to going to church and having her brought up in a certain way. But once she's grown-up I'm not sure that I won't … revert back to, you know, just doing what I want to do.

Some fathers stated that although their external expressions of faith may have become more deliberate and observable, they did not perceive their underlying belief structure to have changed significantly. Ned distinguished between differences in his behavior and stability in his underlying beliefs. His statement was typical of men who felt they had changed their overtly observable behavior without a corresponding shift in faith. He expressed that he had "renewed" himself and that there was a "big change," yet he stated that his faith had not changed because the change was more in degree of commitment than in direction:

> Interviewer: Has there been a change in your religious faith because of having kids?

Ned: Not in my faith. Well, there's been a—it's the same faith I've always, I've always been a Christian. But now that I'm a parent and I go to church with my children, I've renewed myself and got back into the, being a servant of God, which is real good for me, real good. I'm teaching my children religion and—been a big change, big change, big change. Religion is real important to me.

In some cases, although behavioral participation in faith activities had increased, the underlying beliefs did not support the behaviors. Specifically, some fathers appeared to be "going through the motions" to fulfill a perceived obligation to expose their children to faith, although they themselves did not hold faith to be a vital or central reality. Consider Scott's point of view:

Interviewer: Since you've had children do you think you've changed your commitment to religion?

Scott: Mmm ... probably a little more committed to getting them involved in the church and trying to understand what its all about. A little more so, yeah.

Interviewer: So has there been an increase in your own church attendance or?

Scott: Yeah a lot more.

Interviewer: OK that's kind of a behavioral expression of religion either you go to church or you don't—or you participate in a religious service. How about in terms of your own faith? That's something that may or may not be reflected in behavior. Do you think your faith has been changed in any way?

Scott: No. (PAUSE) I mean I've always believed in God so. It's not really changed, I'm just more attentive to the church ... more so than before. Because its a little harder to explain to them. You have to let them know who Jesus Christ is and you know try to learn a little bit more about the church.

Clifford constructed his experience in a similar way:

Interviewer: Ok, how about your commitment to religion? Has that changed because of fatherhood?

Clifford: It's probably intensified it more yes. ... I want my children to come up believing in God. Where before I wouldn't go to church. You couldn't drag me into a church, but now I, you know, I believe. How can I tell my children that there is a God in heaven if I, you know, if I don't believe in it. Don't participate and church and that kind of thing.

Interviewer: So has there really been a change in your own faith or just in what you try to show the kids?

Clifford: Hasn't changed my faith. I probably participate more in going to church. My faith hasn't changed I guess no. But I uh, I go more regularly than I used to church services, religious services. Because of [my kids] probably.

The interview data illustrate that fathers' magnitude of faith integration into their own lives portends how fathers perceive parenting to have effected their developing faith. Specifically, men with different degrees of faith identity and integration into their lives responded differently to queries concerning the effects of fathering on their faith trajectories.

Active engagement in fathering roles with developing children brings minimally reflective fathers to a position of recognizing their own strengths and weaknesses related to different areas of leadership, provision, wisdom, or support that they are being challenged to supply. Fathers evaluate their own maturity levels because they need to genuinely appraise what it is they have to offer their children regarding religious upbringing. Common realizations include the need to reduce or eliminate hypocricy from their own lives, the importance of providing consistent and positive training, degree of preparation needed to teach the knowledge base of a faith, and the central importance of the ability consistently to model the characteristics of a faithful disciple. Obviously, any realistic evaluation of these factors will reveal shortcomings and areas of need, as well as strengths and resources in every father, no matter how mature he may be in his faith. However, there are significant individual differences in how men respond to recognized shortcomings and how they utilize perceived strengths.

Toward a Continuum of Fathering and Faith Categories

In early work on fathering, and in pioneering work in grandparenting, it has been common to devise typologies of fathers (Robinson & Barret, 1986) or grandparents (Neugarten & Weinstein, 1964). Similarly, different parenting styles have been described by Baumrind (1975), among others, to provide a general picture of clusters of characteristics that tend to go together in parents' interactions with their children. It must be clearly stated that these are often initial efforts to describe common patterns of responses manifested as people assume roles. Later scholarship goes beyond description to identify factors that contribute to assuming different typologies or to the developmental outcomes of applying the typologies. It must be further stated that it is unlikely that any individual fully fits within any single typology. That is to say that there is no such thing as a "pure type" (e.g., even the most authoritative parent sometimes uses elements of an authoritarian style, even if infrequently). With these cautions voiced, it is possible to begin to outline different types of fathers in regard to fathering and faith.

The categories outlined here are best conceived as occurring along a continuum. An anchor on one end of the continuum would be actively discouraging fathers—those who ridicule, disparage, or discount things of faith. No men in the current sample voiced attitudes that are confirmatory of this extreme, but experience and anecdotal evidence support the existence of men who take such approaches toward matters of faith. At the other end of the continuum are men for whom faith is the central organizing theme in their lives. They are wholeheartedly committed to growing in and exercising their faith in every role and circumstance of life. They are highly invested in being generative in their faith, and view every interaction as an opportunity to model or to directly discuss faith. In between these anchors on the continuum are more moderate positions where men value things of faith but vary in their perceptions of their own commitment or ability to transmit substantive faith to their children. (Please refer to Figure 6.1.)

Whereas distinct categories of fathering styles can be described and located along the continuum, it is probably more realistic to view the styles as somewhat overlapping and dynamic as opposed to mutually exclusive and static. The categories of fathering styles in connection with fathering and faith are presented in increasing levels of commitment or centrality as they were represented in the interview data. As previously noted, no men in the current sample described themselves as actively discouraging faith, so the presentation begins with a consideration of the uninvolved/disinterested/detached father.

Uninvolved/Disinterested/Detached Fathers. Typical of this pattern, a man who does little or nothing to promote or facilitate the spiritual development of his children has likely decided that faith is not central to his own life. He typically has basic and significant questions concerning the existence or agency of God. Frequently, past experiences with organized or individual religion have left him with an emotional wound or a "sour taste." It is common for men in this category to have had the experience, as children, of being forced to attend religious services that they saw as

Discouraging	Disinterested	Provider	Generative
Negative Faith Identity Openly Disparaging	Negative Identity/ Identity Foreclosure Faith not Central Serious Doubts/Questions	Identity Issues Uncertainties Lacking Knowledge Inconsistent Modeling	Positive Identity Axis Mundi Firmly Grounded Living Faith
Discourage Faith Involvement	Child's Own Choice Expose to Various Faiths Minimal Encouragement	Faith Important Actively Encourage Find Appropriate Mentor	Faith Vital Generative Agent
Negative Experiences	Mostly Negative Experiences	Mixed Experiences	Mostly Positive Experiences
(The Path)	(The Rocky Soil)	(The Thorns)	(Good Soil)

FIG. 6.1. A continuum of fathering and faith.

irrelevant to life or hypocritical in regard to the lives of other participants. At the time of the interview, this group of fathers had little or no commitment to faith. They expressed past disappointment in clergy or members or institutions of faith. They had experienced that prayer was ineffective, and that God, if he exists, is disinterested or detached from the affairs of people. They tended to express a low tolerance for inconsistency/hypocrisy, both in identified followers of the faith and in themselves.

These fathers felt they had little reason to invest effort in training their children in matters of faith. Because they were minimally invested themselves, and had no desire to be hypocritical, they ignored or stayed out of any type of religious training. They did not actively engage in encouraging or directly discouraging their children in matters of faith, although modeling indifference sends a loud message to children.

In terms of religious identity status, they could be characterized as foreclosed. They generally cited singular events, instances, or experiences that had caused them to strongly adopt a disinterested posture. It is important to note that they felt they were being genuine to their beliefs and experiences. In fact, the need to avoid hypocrisy was so central to these men that they concluded it would be virtually impossible for them to encourage their children to explore faith. These are men of high integrity—they will not feign interest in or assign importance to faith in order to have their children positively disposed toward faith when they themselves do not hold those values.

Spiritual Providers/Encouragers. Men in this category tended to have some unresolved identity issues regarding their own faith, and needed support to succeed in encouraging their children to pursue things of faith. In general, men in this category had made preliminary or tentative commitments to faith themselves. The tentative nature of the commitment was unrelated to duration—some men had been in this state of faith development for quite some time. Persistent questions or ambivalence had characterized their own religious development. Paul was a prototypical provider/encourager. He encouraged his daughter to attend services, and reported increased participation in his wife's church, but he expressed ongoing doubts regarding the existence of God. When asked whether fatherhood had effected his faith, he responded:

> I wish I could say, yes, but I can't. Like I said, I just struggle with the existence of God and stuff. I just, I mean, I don't—and just our existence altogether—I mean, what is God?—you know, what are we doing here, people doing, how life can exist at all? I mean, it's just so hard for me to grasp. I just don't know. So, I'm no farther along, even though I think about it a lot, I'm no farther along in having any answers than before. You know, I kind of, like, try to pray as if there is a God, but I just—I'm unconvinced one way or the other.

Fathers such as Paul tended to view matters of faith in terms of knowledge or instruction *about* God rather than as a living relationship *with* God.

Faith was not a central organizing theme in their own lives, but they had respect for the value of faith matters. They desired to expose their children to faith (sometimes to a variety of faiths), and allowed their children to choose for themselves whether they wanted to follow in any particular faith tradition. In a sense, they were hoping that their children would experience a greater degree of commitment than they themselves had been able to achieve.

Provider/Encourager dads talked about the positive peer influences and the benefits of disciplinary structures of faith organizations, but questioned their own ability to impart knowledge or to model a consistently positive lifestyle to their children. In short, although they saw the value of religious structures and knowledge, they questioned their own abilities, qualifications, or preparation to impart things of value (religious knowledge and consistent modeling) regarding faith to their children. As such, they deferred generative functions to others—religious schools, Sunday schools, or youth group programs. In addition, they frequently pointed to another individual whom they viewed to be better qualified, either through knowledge or demonstrated consistency in faith walks. Often these other figures were female family members or long-term trusted and respected friends. Fathers in this group encouraged their children to explore faith issues under the guidance of these other persons or institutions whom they viewed to be more proficient, stable, or able than themselves. In essence, they valued generativity of faith, but felt unqualified or ill-prepared to provide the guidance, training, or example needed. They highly valued the free choice of children in deciding matters of faith. Thus, they engaged in a paternal role that is comfortable and positive in other arenas—the provider. They provided a trustworthy model/mentor to achieve what they felt incapable of doing themselves. However, these fathers seemed relatively unaware of the mixed messages they were sending. There is a marked discrepancy between stating that faith is of value and a father admitting that he has not valued it enough to be a primary provider of training.

Active Generative Agents. These men tended to hold a strong conviction that matters of faith are real. Spiritual considerations were also viewed to be vital or central to understanding and succeeding in the world and an afterlife. These men had strong personal identities as far as seeing themselves as men of faith. Although fathers who were acting as generative agents in the faith development of their own children were painfully aware that they had shortcomings and flaws, they also regarded training their children in matters of faith to be among their highest callings. They were frequently willing to admit their own flaws and shortcomings to their children and to the interviewer and to speak about ways of improving their positive influence.

Faith was the superordinate value or construct, whereas fathering, with its roles and issues, was subsumed by and integrated into faith. Clearly there was a reciprocal influence in the lives of these fathers between fathering and faith, and the roles and issues of fathering brought reflection, clarification, and refinement of faith. However, faith was the starting point and brought a significantly higher degree of shaping, informing, and purpose to fathering than fathering brought to faith.

These men were grounded and growing in their knowledge of the faith and the degree of consistency between their understanding and their daily lives. Faith seemed to be much less compartmentalized into something that is done on certain days or in particular contexts. Religious activities were not limited to participation in programs, but were central to the daily activities of the home, as reflected in scripture reading, family prayer, and the application of scriptural principles to everyday events and relationships. To fathers who are generative in their faith, "religion" is not just another demographic variable, it is the axis mundi (Latshaw, 1998), or permeating force. In a study on the transmission of religious beliefs and practices from parents to adolescent sons, Clark et al. (1988) found that men who fit the description of generative fathers are "especially important in transmitting their religious beliefs and religious experiences to their early adolescent sons" (p. 471). Note the similarity to both the scriptural prescriptions and the categorization of generative fathers in their statement that, "If fathers frequently attend church, discuss religion at home, and are committed to their religion, then their sons will attend church with similar frequencies to the fathers. If fathers do these religious activities infrequently, then the fathers and sons will not likely agree on church attendance" (Clark et al., 1988, p. 470).

These fathers frequently encouraged their children to participate in organized religious activities that were supplemental to their primary role as shepherd of their children's faith walk. These fathers viewed themselves to be a significant point person regarding religious training.

Once again, although it is true that no man is likely to be a "pure type" of one of these categories, it was not difficult to categorize each study participant as fitting into one of the groups. There may be long-term or short-term temporal fluctuation in the relative degree to which characteristics of other groupings apply to fathers in each of the categories, and differences were evident in the styles of faith generation that men had chosen to follow in their families.

Descriptions of these types are interesting and may afford value in terms of understanding and describing different faith trajectories of fathers and their children. However, the more interesting and important questions regard how the fathers got to be this way, and how to facilitate development at different junctures in their faith walks.

IMPLICATIONS FOR RELIGIOUS INSTITUTIONS AND LOCAL CONGREGATIONS

During early adult development, men come to recognize that if they are going to be an effective spiritual father, they need something substantive to pass along. As men recognize their own shortcomings in terms of biblical knowledge or consistent living, it is critical that church leadership recognize the importance of this being approached as a teachable moment as opposed to time to chastise men for their shortcomings. Times of men's reevaluation and questioning coincide with significant life-course transitions or changes in the functioning of their roles as fathers as a result of countertransitions in their families. Transitions—including becoming a parent, fathering a teen, midlife chanllenges, assumption of grandfathering roles, and changes surrounding or following any family crisis—are times of particular questioning and sensitivity for fathers.

One way to view the findings is that the lack of strong paternal investment in men training their own children is an indicator that there is a great need for effective men's ministry in the church directed toward discipling, training, and equipping men. Rather than criticizing fathers for engaging in a provider role, which we applaud in other domains, it would be more fruitful to design and offer men's ministries that will support men who desire to grow to be generative in their own developing faith. Perhaps men who are successfully mentoring their children in matters of faith could serve as leaders or mentors in such men's ministries. This suggestion parallels biblical criteria that qualifications for church leadership include an assessment of successful fathering (e.g., 1 Timothy 3:4–5, Titus 1:6).

It is important for churches to be in touch with men as they experience these transitions in their own self-understanding, and to have supports to offer men in a manner that they can engage in the support without condemnation, negative judgment, or ridicule. Men who have a positive commitment to active, engaged fatherhood are likely to do what is necessary to learn other kinds of new skills. However, if structural or emotional barriers to such resources are too great, then they may turn aside from the help that they need and desire. Men who recognize that they need support and training may not be comfortable admitting these needs, unless there is no condemnation or discounting as second-class citizens involved. When men come to recognize their own shortcomings, it is a different matter than being told by their spouse, partner, friends, parents, or clergy that they need help. Such a realization exerts a developmental "pull" rather than a "push."

Interestingly, the four categories of fathers developed in this article can be viewed to parallel types generated by Jesus in the parable of the seed and the sower (Matthew 13:3–23). Fathers who adopt a posture of actively discouraging faith in their children may be likened to the seed that fell on the path. They may have heard the message of the kingdom, but did not understand it, and what was sown in their hearts was, at least for the present, snatched away. Consequently, they have no room for faith in their lives, and actively discourage their children from pursuing faith as well. Uninvolved fathers may be likened to the seed that fell on rocky places. They have heard the message of faith, and received it to a degree. However, it appears that their faith has shallow roots, and they express doubts and ambivalence that is often linked to troubles in their lives. Their faith is unfruitful to the next generation. Spiritual provider fathers are represented by the seed that fell among the thorns. They have a measure of faith, but their lives and priorities reflect a higher value on things of this world: "The worries of this life and the deceitfulness of wealth choke it, making it unfruitful." (Luke 8:14, NIV, states that "the seed that fell among thorns stands for those who hear, but as they go on their way they are choked by life's worries, riches and pleasures, and they do not mature.") Fathers who are active generative agents in regard to their faith are represented by the seed that fell on good soil. They have heard the word and understand it and, through their generative fathering, they are producing a crop.

Because fathers have been scrutinized under deficit models for so long (Hawkins & Dollahite, 1997a), it is particularly important that this not be the case in the area of fathering and faith. Perhaps because of the highly personal nature of faith, and the profound implications of "correct" choices, it is a very sensitive and vulnerable move for men to admit the need for support or training. If men are going to increase their active involvement in faith generativity, it is essential that religious institutions take initiative in providing positive support to fathers growing in their own faith walks, no matter their level of maturity.

Question 2: Has Fatherhood Influenced Your View of Moral Issues?

A slight majority of men reported that fatherhood has influenced their view of moral issues. Those who reported no changes had clearly established and made some basic decisions about moral issues when they were younger. Anthony represented that group of men:

> I came to the realization of what they [my morals] were in my earlier 20s after I got out of my home ... and I've stuck with those all the way through. They're my core philosophies.

Some fathers spontaneously talked about important influences on moral issues other than fathering, such as jobs or religion. Other men had been exposed to different philosophies or values that brought a different balance in their views of morality. Tom was one of those men:

> I've always been pretty strong at what I felt and believed. If stuff has changed, it hasn't really changed because of kids. It's changed because of I've seen a different view on it, or heard different views or read a couple different, you know, someplace, and then sat back and looked at my view and maybe changed a little bit.

The fathers who did report changes in moral views due to parenthood explained the changes in a variety of ways. For one group, fatherhood was a time to be more thoughtful and reflective about moral beliefs. They noted the importance of being an appropriate teacher and model of morality.

Reflection and reevaluation of their own positions and behaviors had often resulted. Again, the need to avoid hypocrisy was strong. Manuel recognized the need to review his own ethics and to bring his behavior into conformity with what he wanted his children to do. He said:

> Considering back in the day I was very little on morals. I would say maybe the last year I've been took a different look at morals. I was more in the past of a um, skirt chaser, get it while you can. If I'm going to teach my child morals I've got to be following them myself. And that's something that I'm definitely working on now. I can't say to my child this is wrong if I'm doing it. When I was drinking I used to tell my kids I don't ever want to catch you ever with a beer near you. Now let's be honest, what good is me telling them not to do something that I'm doin' it? It, it's no good and I have to, I have to look at that. ... As far as morals right now I haven't given them the strictest moral code like I should and I can be frankly honest with that. ... But yeah I would have to say before I can really give them the morals I want them to have I got too really take a serious look at my morals. Because I want to pass on to them the same morals I'm carrying myself on.

Others reported moving beyond reflection to a more careful monitoring of their own behavior. Another subset talked about heightened awareness of some social evils (i.e., early sexual activity, drugs) and expressed concern that their children would not make the same mistakes that they may have made. Ned described how having children brought a new set of lenses for him to view the world through:

> Back in the old days you didn't think about pornography or liquor stores being open on Sunday or the drinking age of people. But now all these things come into play because you're thinking about your own kids. Do you want pornographic magazines coming into their hands? Do you want them drinking underage?

It was common for fathers to describe how they desired their children to "grow up better" than they had, despite the fact that "the world is becoming a worse place." Implicit in this view was the understanding that if fathers were to give their children this opportunity, they themselves would have to play an active and positive role in the process.

A significant proportion of the fathers indicated they had not had positive male role models in their lives. Chris stated it this way:

> I try to get my kids not to make the same mistakes that I did, as far as, well, I didn't have no real male role model there ... to point out the good and bad things to me.

Abortion was one of the specific moral issues that over one fourth of men mentioned. It appears that having children provided a new perspective on this particular issue for some of the men. Children took on a new value as fathers reflected on the possibility of their own children being taken away through abortion. Ken said:

> I probably didn't have a position on that [abortion]. And now, you know, [I'm] very much pro-life because of my kids.

Randy elaborated on changes in his perspective on abortion, children in poverty, and contraceptive availability. He said:

> Well, the abortion issue has got to be the—we watched a thing the other night on the Public Access channel, right? You want to talk about a biased program? I don't think I ever seen anything more biased for abortion than I have on this program. I mean, I couldn't believe it. Listening to the people that are for abortion saying that they're not a child because they're not breathing yet, well, that makes me mad and hurt sort of type of thing. Having the miscarriages, you know, I mean, I just can't believe in this day and age people as smart as they are supposed to be, I mean, they're just fooling themselves into thinking that that's not a person. You know, that's one thing that's, you know, poor kids, the other issue is there. But I really didn't pay that much attention to this type of thing. But now that I have kids, yeah, that's one of the things. The other thing is the passing out of the condoms in high school. You know, I just don't agree with that. They say safe sex, what happens, why not no sex? Never once has it been said, "Just don't do it." But no, "Here protect yourself, just do it this way." I mean, that's just morally wrong. And as I said, as a parent now, that's something I think about, whereas before, I knew it wouldn't—I wouldn't think about it as much or to the degree that I do now.

Glen noted that he felt that he had been challenged in areas of morality that he would not have considered before having children. He recognized that if he was going to have a firm foundation for providing moral education and guidance for his children, that he would have to make some changes. He said:

> Those type of things never were challenged before and never stood a chance of being challenged. Now um, I'm in the position of raising children with a certain moral belief so, I've got to do that and challenge myself.

James, too, reported that he had changed some of his moral perspectives since having children. He described the shift in a manner that suggests that his conscience had gained a new voice or authority in his life since becoming a father:

> In the back, a little voice in your head said "this has got to be done this way for these kids."

Joseph had gone beyond reflecting on issues of morality and modeling to making changes in his behavior for the sake of his children:

Interviewer: Have you changed what you think is right and wrong as a result of having kids?

Joseph: Uh-hum.

Interviewer: Do you have some specifics on that?

Joseph: Well, I stopped drinking, for instance. Stopped carousing with certain friends and clientele that I felt were doing wrong things. Like drugs, for instance ... to have a foundation to where you can know what's right and what's wrong for yourself first. And then your children can follow an example if they wish. As long as they're under your roof you really have more control about that. If they don't want to follow that example you have other ways of being able to tell about things, what happened when you don't follow such certain rules and regulations about society. I guess that's the way I look at it. I guess it scares them at first until they get older, and they start to get on their own. But then maybe they'll think about some of the things you told them in the past, and it might help them out.

In summary, slightly more that half of the group described some significant changes related to parenthood and their views on moral issues. These changes are related to new issues or perspectives that arise from the experience of fatherhood. A smaller proportion of the sample talked about specific changes they implemented in their behavior because of child-inspired shifts in thinking about morality.

Question 3: Has Fathering Resulted in Any Shifts in Your Values?

This question reveals the highest degree of articulation concerning the influence of fatherhood on the three different areas examined. Close to 80% of the fathers in both samples reported some changes or shifts in their basic values. In the interest of brevity, exemplary quotes will be kept to a sentence or two, and no attributions will be specified. This mode of presentation seems appropriate for the values section because many fathers expressed the same sorts of thoughts and insights, and the themes are general enough that individual attribution is not necessary. One of the primary values that emerges as a change is the shift from a selfish emphasis to a child and family-centeredness: "I am less selfish with my time more and more giving. ... I think giving more of your time, so we do pop those family [video] tapes in once in a while, and you look back at how time has passed so quickly. ... I think probably the biggest value is giving your time and caring." There were also a variety of other value issues that emerged in the descriptions of changes with more value placed on time, respect for parents, less emphasis on materialism, and more awareness of racism: "I value time and cash much more now than I did before having kids. ... I have a moral high value of life now. I have a higher value system on life and I also learned through the birth of a child how precious life is. ... I tried to teach my girlfriend's kids as far as respect for your mom and your dad, because you never know when they're not going to be here."

Once again an important rationale behind the changes in values was the need to change some of their own behaviors and begin to practice what they preach: "I'd say the value system has changed from the standpoint [that if] I expect to raise my children with certain values then I ought to practice those myself." Many of the men talked about being models for their children.

The small group of fathers who reported no changes generally felt they had a stable base of values and children had no real impact. There were a few fathers who stated that there were no child-catalyzed changes in their values, but then proceeded to talk about the importance of fathering: "No, I don't think so. I think it was all, it's all been there. It just takes the children to be walking around and your realization that this is what you're here for."

In summary, the majority of fathers has seen some major shifts in values and the way they approach the world. The primary changes cited were less selfishness and greater emphasis on the value of life, time, family, education, modeling, and the environment. As these values are integrated and operationalized, they tend to have positive effects not only for the sample fathers, but for their communities as well. Thus, support is offered for Erikson's assertion that parenting is a common pathway to generativity.

There are many ways to construct meaning around these findings. Erikson's theory of life-span development, and particularly the stage of generativity versus stagnation (Erikson, 1968; Snarey, 1993), provides a practical framework. The findings about changes in values that shift from an emphasis on self to an emphasis on others, particularly children and families, are in line with the development of parental generativity versus self-absorption. The results indicate that 80% of the fathers echoed this change in response to the open-ended question about shifts in values. If the question had been submitted in a more pointed manner, it is likely that an even greater percentage would have expressed "feelings of generativity." This internal alteration in what is most important expands opportunities for other changes. The primary question that streams from this change in basic values and orientation is "How do men as fathers express these feelings through behavior?" The distinction between the culture and conduct of fatherhood (LaRossa, 1988) and the nongenerative nature of culture (Deinhart & Daly, 1997) emerge here as relevant questions. Most men can identify the feeling of generativity, but it is not as clear how this generative attitude translates to parental behavior.

A primary focus of this chapter is on religiosity (religious faith and religious practices) and moral beliefs. These can be consolidated with generativity and generative fathering as one area of potential attitude and behavior change. For some men, the generative spark is linked with the actual birth of a child and serves as a "major change." The developmental pathways that this spark ignites may be governed by religious and moral beliefs that have unfolded through the identity stage of development. It appears that some of the men in the study adopted a positive set of religious beliefs and behavior that was solidly in place before fatherhood. Another subset of men had a negative attitude toward religious identity firmly set in place, that is "I am not a religious person." For both groups, fatherhood had little perceived impact on religious practice and commitment. A previous pathway was either firmly set or rejected.

The foreclosure on ideological issues that depicts negative attitudes toward religiosity is of greatest concern. It was apparent that the men in this group had often found no substitute for religious identity. They provided a number of grounds for their rejection of formal religion, but seemed unclear and ambivalent about their responsibility as moral guides for their children.

There was also an openness to define or discover new pathways for religious or moral development for about half of the fathers. This group appeared open to changes and some saw fatherhood as not only an "opportunity for change" but as an imperative to change for the children's' sake. Fathers in this group talked about returning to church or searching for a "community of faith" to provide an anchor or starting place for the promotion of their children's' moral development. Men also talked about changing some of their own behaviors (e.g., being a "skirt chaser") so that they would model positive moral behavior. They felt accountable for helping teach their children to circumvent mistakes they had made. Other men who had a unyielding set of religious beliefs or practices found that the experience of fatherhood helped them to transcend to a new profound level of appreciating the nature of God by viewing children as miracles and a new understanding of "God as Father."

Fatherhood clearly precipitated some degree of generativity in most of the men. Although the lowest proportion of men expressed generativity in regard to religious faith, when looking across all three associated areas of faith, morals, and values, an impressive majority of the fathers who participated in this study expressed feelings of generativity toward their children. How this feeling translates into generative behavior is not as clear from the interview data.

The role of fathers as moral leaders has shifted over the last 150 years in U.S. society as men have devoted more of their time and energy to the provider role (Christiansen & Palkovitz, 2001; Palkovitz, 1996; Pleck, 1987, 1997; Rotundo, 1985). Mothers became more responsible during this time for children's moral socialization. In this study, a number of men confirmed this separation of responsibility by describing wives, sisters, or grandmothers as the ones who brought children to church. Even some of the fathers who reported greater church attendance described their spouse or partner as the primary instigator. This is consistent with findings that in the United States, in comparison to men, women have higher religiosity scores (Chancey, 1996), more general belief in God (Schwab & Petersen, 1990), greater involvement in church activities (Argyle & Beit-Hallahmi, 1975; Bohannon, 1991), engage in more prayer, and maintain a greater degree of belief in the afterlife (Klenow & Bollin, 1989).

More importantly, there appears to be confusion among some fathers about their own religious identity and the related role and responsibilities of fathers as moral guides. Confusion and uncertainty in consideration of these matters were cited as components that kept men from more active participation in the nurturance of their children's religious and moral development.

The data also suggest some plausible barriers to fathers' generative behavior. The generativity spark from the transition to fatherhood seems to be nearly universal among the diverse group of fathers interviewed in this study. This spark creates an opportunity for change (a sensitive period) for fathers.

The first barrier is most evident in the younger fathers. From Erikson's (1968) theoretical perspective, it appears that many of these men have not fully resolved their identity crisis. They have not completely resolved or identified their ideological beliefs. Although they may be clear about what they have rejected (God and formal religion), they have not replaced these beliefs to know what to transmit to their children. Some men in this group suggested that their children should be exposed to religion and given the opportunity to make up their own minds. Because persons with strong religious convictions tend to believe that they have discovered an important truth, they are seldom ambivalent about decisions their children make in regard to religious faith. Most people with strong religious identities desire their children to follow their chosen faith. This position taken by many fathers in the sample, that they want their children to be exposed to different faiths so that they can decide for themselves, appears different than tolerance or respect of diversity. It seems to reflect fathers' own uncertainty and reluctance to take a position as a moral guide. This lack of resolution may limit their capability to be generative fathers (Dollahite, Hawkins, & Brotherson, 1997).

A second potential barrier for many men is the enduring primacy of the provider role (Christiansen & Palkovitz, 2001; Deinhart & Daly, 1997; Futris & Pasley, 1997; Palkovitz et al., 1998). From a social role theory perspective and a historical perspective, fathers still experience the provider role as their predominant identity and fundamental mode for generative behavior. Most men did express this sense of responsibility as providers in other parts of this study. The data reported here suggest there were a number of fathers who did not embrace or enact the role of a moral guide for their children. This belonged to the mother. Earlier in their lives, these men had sought out role models for spiritual and moral direction. Many were disillusioned by the models available to them, especially from their own fathers. Ironically, many appeared to be mirroring the hypocrisy, ambivalence, and confusion they had found so distasteful in the models available to them. Whereas some men saw a need to "clean up their act" and stop some of their "immoral behaviors," they did not clearly identify positive moral behavior beyond vague references to increased religious practice. This limited investment of time and energy in this role of moral guide could be detrimental to the moral maturation of their children as well as to the father's own moral development.

A third barrier to generative fathering may come from male socialization toward independence (Bergman, 1991). This theme emerges in some of the interviews with the fathers who wanted their children to make their own choices about religion and religious beliefs. This was most often stated as a reaction to having religion "shoved down my throat." Fathers' wisdom seemed flawed when they decided not to take responsibility for the religious beliefs and practices their children are exposed to on the grounds that they want to respect children's freedom of choice. This view ignores accountability and the legitimate control parents maintain over a young child's life. Fathers' own modeling of independence and distance also provides a powerful reinforcement of independent aloofness that may push children away from formal religious practices, community involvement, and commitment to a specific set of beliefs. Social learning theory would suggest that this would have the strongest impact on boys. Some fathers seemed to be unaware that deferring religious initiative to mothers or other female relatives sends a strongly gendered message concerning the significance of religious beliefs in contemporary culture.

A final barrier to generative fathering that is addressed in data from this study is the lack of regular contact that some fathers have with their children. Erratic contact limits the father's influence on the child's moral development—or as previous researchers (Hoffman, 1981; Lamb, 1981) document, father absence exerts a negative bearing on moral development. In addition, lack of contact for fathers may also truncate possibilities for fathers' own generative growth. This is an issue for a growing number of fathers who do not live with children (Blankenhorn, 1995; Popenoe, 1996). If these men are not living in households with children present, they are not experiencing the same incentives and motivation for growth in their own moral, religious, and values realms.

Limitations of the Data. There are a number of limitations of the study in trying to describe men's changes in values, morality, and commitment to religion. There were many men who did not clearly differentiate the three areas that the questions probed. This may reflect imprecise wording or my lack of communication skills as an interviewer. Alternatively, it may be reflective of a lack of integration and differentiation of these distinct areas by the fathers (Allport, 1961). As such, inability to articulate the differences in each of these areas may be reflective of a lack of maturity in the moral, religious, and value realms of men's development. If this is the case, then there are significant implications in regard to fathers' ability to be generative in these domains. This emphasizes the need for positive male models in Sunday school, youth groups, and community organizations that foster moral development.

Another important limitation may be the use of the narrow term, *religion*. In retrospect, greater articulation or different results may have been obtained if the interviews had employed the broader term *spirituality* (Catalfo, 1997). Discussions of spirituality might open the door to other dimensions of fathers as spiritual and moral models that were not tapped in the present data. Future research in this area should consider the use of the broader term.

Implications for Practitioners. These data provide some important insights for addressing some of the social concerns about fatherlessness and the impact of father absence on children, specifically in regard to the concern for children's stunted moral development. The following are some specific areas that should be addressed in fathering programs:

1. The baby boom cohort of fathers, which includes the majority of men in the study, may have some unique patterns that interface with the role of fathers as moral/spiritual guides (Catalfo, 1997). The stage of generative parenthood (Snarey, 1993) may be a time for members of this cohort to reexamine their own spiritual and moral beliefs and how these are passed down to their children. Snarey (1993) reported that religious affiliation does not contribute to the child's and father's outcomes in his study. The present study suggests that the quest for spiritual identity may have some significant links to fatherhood and thus to father and child outcomes. Religious affiliation (Roof, 1993) may not be the issue. Rather, father's interest and ability to serve as moral and spiritual guides may be the more important issue for both children and fathers.
2. The author was impressed by the power of early perceptions, experiences, and relationships in shaping men's views, especially in regard to religious faith and practice. The qualitative data summarized here send a loud and clear message that children observe the consistency, or the lack thereof, between fathers' "talk" and "walk." Both fathers and children stand to benefit from increased investment of fathers in generative fathering (Hawkins & Dollahite, 1997a), positive father involvement (Pleck, 1997), or good fathering as described in this book (see chap. 3).

BALANCE ISSUES IN FAITH, MORALS, AND VALUES

Numerous balance issues were apparent in regard to fathering, faith, morals, and values. Perhaps the most pervasive was the need for fathers to avoid hypocricy in faith, morals, values, and their behavior. In short, they needed to find consistency between their "talk" and their "walk." Fathers talked about decisions they had made to bring their preaching and their practice into balance. Some fathers had chosen not to voice strong opinions or positions regarding faith, morals, or values because they could not support them in behavior. Others had chosen to work toward bringing their behavior into line with what they viewed to be appropriate faith, morals, and values. In reality, it is probably the case that all fathers do some of both, and the balance depends on their stability and maturity. A subtheme of balancing the walk and the talk was that fathers found it challenging to balance their own levels of faith with what they viewed to be necessary supportive role modeling. That is, some fathers seemed to struggle with showing what they viewed to be appropriate levels of participation and commitment to organized religion when their own beliefs were not consistent with those of the faith community. A related balance issue was that of providing enough instruction in regard to faith versus relying on other instructors. Fathers also expressed concern regarding providing balance between appropriate modeling and guidance and allowing children choice. One area where this balance is pointed is in the delicate differences between generativity of faith and proselytizing. Those fathers who had adopted positions far on the child choice end of the continuum tended to have ambivalence or doubts regarding the correctness, importance, or vitality of their own faith, morality, or values. Fathers who were highly tilted toward generativity had a high degree of confidence, and perceived these issues to be central in defining success as a father. Specifically, they tended to believe that transferring their faith, morals, and values to their children was among the most important aspects of fathering.

One thing that was obvious from the interview transcripts was that the balances between behaviors and beliefs in the areas of faith, morals, and values are constantly in flux, even if core principles did not change significantly. The fact that fathers are involved with developing children who experience different issues and pose different questions depending on their changing developmental status guarantees continual rebalancing.

Chapter **7**

Fathering and Perceived Changes in Health

This chapter looks at the thoughts of fathers concerning the relationships between fathering and perceived changes in health over time. No father perceived that his health was unchanged, and although most men associated perceived changes in health to be associated with various aspects of fathering, a small minority of men felt that changes in their health were attributable to aging, but not fathering. Most changes in health associated with fathering were positively regarded by fathers. Many fathers discussed improvements in their diets, reduction of harmful habits, increased access and use of health services, and reductions in risk-taking behavior. On the other hand, fathers attributed decreased exercise, lack of sleep, and increased stress to fathering. A significant finding is that, for the sake of their children, fatherhood was perceived to motivate men to reduce or eliminate detrimental behaviors that they had been unmotivated to change prior to fathering. Sample fathers discussed reduction of health risk-taking behaviors, and greater desire to care for their health for their children's sake.

DIET, EXERCISE, AND LONGEVITY

Some fathers express that they have a desire to take care of their health so that they can enhance the probability that they will enjoy longevity and to be in good health to enjoy time with their children and grandchildren. They also recognize that time in physically active engagement with their children is time well spent. Physically active times provide both exercise and a context for building relationships. Health and fitness also includes the avoidance of harmful substances and practices. Healthy lifestyles involve the modeling of positive choices regarding nutrition and habits. Ken, who played team sports through college, represented this broad array of themes in a singular response to the general question of how fathering had influenced his health. Each of these themes is considered in this chapter. Ken said:

> Well, you know, I think there's a feeling that I'd like to be around for a while for my kids. And so I work, try hard to keep myself somewhat fit even though that's a struggle. And then beyond that, if you consider exercise to be good for you, I like to go out and exercise with the kids. And so beyond the health benefits of that is the enjoyment of being with them and doing things with them. And so that's been really, really good over time. I think some things that are unhealthy—I don't know that I would have gotten into much—but certainly having kids and having to set an example for them keeps me away from maybe indulging in drinking or, you know, other things that if the kids aren't there, seeing how you really act, you might slip into. And I have fundamental beliefs in taking care of your body and being healthy that I think comes from athletics. And I wanted my kids to pick that up and feel similarly so that they have a nice, long life. I can contribute to that.

Ken's quote shows the importance of modeling healthy lifestyles, working at maintaining fitness, and avoidance of harmful substances or practices. Ken's statement was fairly characteristic of the types of themes that most fathers in the sample discussed, but a small segment of the sample felt that fathering had little impact on their health and fitness. Rather, increasing age was perceived to be the key factor associated with primarily negative changes in health. Glen's comments demonstrate this pattern of reflection and expression that is characteristic of men as they mature through the decades of the twenties through fourties. At the same time that fathers are involved with their children, they are aging, and are aware of changes in physical ability and health. Many men in middle age recognize that they are fighting a losing battle. They struggle with fitness, weight control, being in condition, and modeling appropriate eating and healthy lifestyles for their children to follow. Glen revealed:

> From age 20 to now there has been a change in diet, exercise and the way I view health. But don't attribute any of that to fatherhood at all. Just kind of the natural progression from the 20's of invincible, jump off a cliff and not get hurt, to the 30's "Well I'm not invincible," to the 40's "Well cancer could be around the corner." So I think its an age type of thing more than fatherhood.

Recognizing that they are models for their children makes engagement in "fighting the loosing battle" more pointed and more worthwhile, because the stakes are higher. The outcomes of their efforts are not limited to themselves, because there are recognizable consequences for their children as well. Fathers recognize that the daily decisions they make will affect not only their own health, their longevity, and their ability to actively interact with their children and grandchildren, but also the choices their children make. In short, in regard to men's health, children provide a source of motivation that appears to be unparalleled. Most fathers perceive that because they are fathers, they change their behavior more radically and with greater persistence and gravity than they did for themselves or for their partners. Perhaps, in this regard, children provide motivation that surpasses self-motivation and encouragements for health that can be received and responded to in a manner that prompts from a partner cannot. It is seen as a genuine concern when children express concern for fathers' health and fitness. When spouses do the same thing, it is more likely to be seen as nagging.

In addition to motivating men to make choices that are toward positive health and fitness practices, children serve as active agents in encouraging fathers to care for themselves. This happens through two distinct kinds of pressures. The first is pressure to quit harmful practices, such as smoking. The second is through encouragement to engage in health promoting practices, such as positive diets and regular exercise. In both instances, children can be powerful motivators in encouraging men to take better care of themselves. Jeff recognized that his children were the primary "driving force" behind his newly renewed efforts to be healthier:

> One of the reasons I have started up again, with trying to get back starting on a jogging program, is to improve my health. I hurt my arm over the winter, and I went to the doctor and he told me to lose some weight. ... I said, "Well, he's right." I really want to be around for as long as I can, and so I have to take care of myself. And there have been a couple of other areas that I finally realized, a couple of areas that I was fighting with, and I was just having no luck fighting them. And a combination of just knowing that these things had to be stopped or just for the general physical well-being, and the kids are the driving force.

Jeff's desire to "be around" for his children, and to be in good health so that he can enjoy them motivated his resumption of a fitness program. David talked about his children's concern for his weight. His awareness of their concern had effected his desire to lose weight. He did not want to be a source of concern for his children, and once again, he expressed the desire to have time to spend with them once they had grown and left home:

> Because I'm overweight and because the kids have shown concern of my being overweight and I think that that is probably the only time that it has really had an effect. I have always been bigger than them. I have always been able to keep up with them and there has never been any reason for them to doubt my capabilities. They have only become health conscious in me being overweight like I am and them showing concern and talking to me, letting me know that they want me to be around after they've left the nest for a while. Yeah, that has created concerns.

John had been encouraged by his children to get regular checkups and to alter his diet. His children motivated him to get medical help, to learn healthy behaviors, and to practice them regularly, although he admitted less than perfect compliance. John enlisted his children's help in initiating positive changes and relied on them for motivation and support in improving his health. John explained that

> this past year where they actually noticed where they had started feeling, I guess concerned of, you know, my health, and made me actually go to the doctors and say, well, what's wrong with me? Is there something wrong? Is it just me? And ever since then, the kids will say, well, you can't eat that, you can't eat this. I try to educate them so they can actually help me keep myself healthy. You know, they want to eat coffee, sugar, they want to eat coffee. They want to drink sodas all day, and eat potato chips all day. And I've sort of learned a lot about nutrition because of them. I've gone to the doctor a lot. I'm seeing a dietician, I take medication.

John had learned more positive health and nutrition practices because of the prompting of his children. He was motivated to take better care of himself because of his children's encouragement, and because he wanted to help them to grow up in healthy ways. He recognized that he needed to improve his nutrition if he was to expect them to eat healthily. John also knew that by educating his children in regard to healthy nutrition, they would help to hold him accountable to a healthy diet. Similarly, Leo recognized that there was a mismatch between what he encouraged his children to do for their health and what he modeled to them. In an interesting twist, he stated that he encourages his children to encourage him to care for himself better. He recognized that he did not get enough rest, and that kept him from hypocritically encouraging them to get proper rest. Leo revealed:

> Eating properly, making sure I exercise well so I can keep up with my kids. It's a battle and struggle. I wish I could say resting properly. I try to encourage them to do that, but I know I don't do that. But I'm aware [that] I don't do that and they're aware that I don't do that and they're aware that I know it's a problem and I encourage them to encourage me to take care of myself.

Fathers recognize that they need to have their lives in line with what they can require of their children in regard to modeling appropriate health practices. They know that though there are struggles and inconsistencies, they need to improve their own health both for the sake of longevity and for the sake of modeling positive health practices to their children. As such, fathers' active involvement with their children motivates them to engage in more positive health practices. Some changes that are initiated by having children have major positive consequences. The use of harmful substances is one area where major changes can be initiated by involved fathering.

SMOKING

The most frequently expressed change in health habits had to do with smoking. Men who smoked heavily before having children either seriously curtailed levels of tobacco use, stopped smoking in cars or other enclosed spaces while with others, or quit altogether. Again, they recognized that smoking has serious deleterious consequences for their own health, but they seemed to be relatively unconcerned for their own well-being until they became active in father involvement. Engagement in fathering motivated them to take better care of themselves for longevity, for health, and for improved social relationships. Further, they recognized that they were models for their children, and that secondhand smoke has negative effects on others as well. It is noteworthy that men were relatively unconcerned with their own health until they had children. Some had smoked heavily (consuming firsthand smoke) for years. When their partners became pregnant or their children were delivered, they became sensitive to the effects of secondhand smoke, and were thus motivated to reduce or quit smoking altogether. They would do for their children what they viewed to be unnecessary for themselves or their partners.

Ned talked about changes in his smoking and drinking behavior and related the changes directly to fathering experiences and roles:

> I used to smoke a lot of cigarettes. I'd smoke a pack a day, plus. But it's real funny because I would sit on the couch with my two children who are—let's see, I guess I quit smoking about five years ago—and I would sit on the couch with them and one on either side of me, and we'd be watching TV together. And I noticed that they would slide away from me, mostly during the winter time because that's when the windows were all shut. And I'd say, "Come on back over here, get close to me, let me hug you, I love you." And they would say, "Daddy, we love you, but the cigarette smoke burns our eyes and makes us cough." So, a little light when on in my head, bing, you know, I said, "Well, I'm affecting my children." And this was before ... everybody was real worried about the secondhand smoke and all. So, when the Great American Smokeout came right about that time, I quit smoking. And I was real surprised that I got through the day. And then I said, "Well, I'll try to make it till tomorrow morning," and I did that. Then I tried it for a week. And so, I don't drink or smoke at all now. And also the drinking part, I used to get drunk, I used to work in a state of—because you get a certain tolerance built up to alcohol, you can perform really when you're drinking. And I used to stay drunk, go to work drunk. And people would say, How can you be so happy after all the beer we drank last night? I just stayed drunk, that's what it was. So, I haven't had a drink in about twelve years, I guess, and no cigarettes in five years. And the drinking and the smoking is directly—I don't do those because of my children anymore. And I really stress that to my children. And I use other people, relatives and friends who I see drinking and smoking, and I use them as training aides for my kids so that they won't smoke. I point them out and say, "Look at Uncle Rodney throwing up over there, you don't want to do that." So, hopefully my kids won't grow up and be smokers or drinkers.

Ned's comments make clear references to the social aspects of smoking: The smoke caused his children to move away from him because it burned his children's eyes and made them cough. His desire for physical closeness with his children motivated him to stop smoking. Although he had worked for years under the influence of alcohol, he stopped drinking before his third child was born. He had not only changed his own behavior, he was openly critical of others who abused substances in the presence of his children. His belief was that his positive modeling, coupled with his negative statements regarding substance abuse, could help to prevent his children from starting unhealthy behaviors.

Steve had not entirely quit smoking, but he had stopped smoking in the presence of his children. He was aware of both the effects of secondhand smoke and the amount of concern that his smoking caused his children. So, whereas he was cutting back significantly, he was not yet at the place where he was able to stop smoking altogether. Steve's comments came in response to generalized question regarding health:

> Researcher: Do you think that fatherhood has had any affect on your health habits?
>
> Steve: Yeah. I smoke. And they're constantly on me about smoking. So, for example, today, after I have my morning coffee it's hard to give up that one morning cigarette. So that's why I'm sitting here going [Steve takes deep breath.] Yeah, so the kids are after me about smoking. I don't smoke around them. They know I smoke, but I don't smoke around them. I don't smoke in the house, and I don't smoke in the car with them or anything like that. I go outside and smoke. That's another thing. I do that for them, I'd breathe it as a kid, it was terrible. So I don't subject them to it.

Scott reported that although he had never been a smoker, prior to his son's birth, his in-laws quit smoking for the sake of his child. This case shows that involvement with and commitment to the welfare of children can bring intergenerational motivation to change long-established habits. Scott reflected on the situation:

> Scott: I never smoked so we never had to worry about that. It did help my in-laws. My in-laws gave up smoking because of him.
>
> Researcher: He's their first grandchild?
>
> Scott: Right. I ... told them when they came down, "Well, you know, you guys smoke." We spend a lot of time out on their deck. I said, "There'll be no smoking in the house." And they were like, "Well, we want to give up smoking before he was born," because I told them I don't know how much I could bring him up with to their house with a smoke-filled house all the time. Both of them give up smoking before was he born.
>
> Researcher: Wow!
>
> Scott: So it turned out to be a plus.

> Researcher: How did they respond when you said that?
>
> Scott: They said they were, they were looking at that, as soon as my wife got pregnant, they didn't even want to smoke in the house when she was pregnant when we were up there. They would go outside and there was like, yeah, that would be terrible to come up here and we have to take him out to a hotel to spend time up here, and they're like, no, we're going to give it up before he was even born. And they did. And I told both of them I'm very proud of them. I thought it was a great thing to do for a grandson. So I said we'll have more kids if you do that. I think that was a promise that we'd have a grandchild if they gave up smoking.

DRINKING

A large proportion of fathers in the sample talked about their decisions to stop or reduce drinking alcoholic beverages, especially in the presence of their children. Whereas most men felt that responsible consumption of alcohol is not a health risk or a morally compromising behavior, they had become sensitized to issues regarding drinking around their children. For some men, long-established patterns of alcohol abuse had to be confronted when they became fathers. Robert described a dramatic event with his son that motivated him to lead a sober life:

> I am an alcoholic. I gave up the drinking and have spent the last nine years sober. My son was very influential in that ... I recall awaking, turning over in bed, reaching for the nightstand, and him holding a bottle and saying, "Here, this is what you want. You don't want me." I can't say that I stopped drinking on the spot, but that little boy saying that to me was the major cause for me setting the bottle down completely.

Robert's son was 5 years old at the time of that pivotal interaction. The transition to parenthood did not trigger a desire for sobriety in Robert, but his young son's direct and powerful statement served as a primary motivator to alter a long-standing pattern of alcohol abuse. Similarly, Manuel recognized that drinking interfered with his fulfillment of fathering roles in the way that he desired to carry them out. Namely, his involvement with alcohol prevented him from investing time and involvement with his children in ways that he felt were appropriate. Manuel, who had limited material resources, also recognized that his drinking used money that could provide basic material needs for his children. Years later, Manuel still felt disappointment and remorse at the missed opportunities he let slip away with his oldest daughter. He viewed his involvement with his younger children as a new chance at fatherhood without the negative influence of alcohol abuse. Manuel said:

> Actually, I wouldn't say that fathering had an affect on my drinking. I would say drinking had an affect on my fathering. There's no doubt even with my

> oldest daughter I made it a point I would never come around when I was drinking. Not one beer, any time I was around her, I was straight. I might not held around her that long. But I would never come around her drunk. I would say my drinking had affected on my fatherhood, my parenting, because it, I would sometimes take money that I would want to give the kids and I'd drink it. And then I'd go over there and see them a couple of days later. I ain't got no money, I'm broke and I'm crying the blues. Um, so it made me less of a father than I could have been even with my oldest. Less than what I would have been. And like I said I know she has no complaints about what I did for her. But me, I know, that I could have done more ... but I still have a chance with the younger ones, but not her. I kind of, well I didn't lose her. But I didn't do everything that I could have did. ... I have thought about that even in the past few months.

Manuel stated that fathering did not effect his drinking, but his realization that drinking diminished his effectiveness as a father served as a motivation to change his drinking behavior. In short, Manuel's motivation to be a better father gave him a new focus, direction, and ability to control his drinking so that he would not repeat negative patterns with his younger children. Clifford cited his involvement with his children as the reason that he had curtailed his drinking as well. He expressed that he had significantly reduced serious risk-taking behaviors—drinking and driving while under the influence—because he did not want to be hurt or to have to explain an arrest to his children. Again, it is interesting that men's close friendships or relationships with a partner did not trigger the same motivation to reduce or eliminate risky behaviors. Clifford explained:

> I don't want the children to see the daddy coming in pissy pissy drunk, uh, falling down, that kind of thing and uh. Before ... maybe I would have driven while I was intoxicated, but now, you know, uh. I have to worry about getting hurt and how do explain to your child why you got arrested, you know, if you get stopped for drinking and driving, so. I've, I've, cut down a lot on the drinking problem.

ABUSE OF ILLICIT DRUGS

Very few fathers in the sample talked about involvement with illicit drugs. Those who did discussed drug usage as a past practice. Fathers who talked about their decisions to become drug free made comments similar to those made by James. James talked about his children's role in motivating him to make a decision to give up illicit drugs:

> James: One time my son was little he saw me roll one of them joints up and I said, "I'll never do this again, not in front of him." But any of my kids seen me actually get high or anything, that's one thing I didn't, wouldn't let them see me like that.

Researcher: Why is that?

James: Respect for my children.

Researcher: More respect for them than for yourself?

James: Uh-hum.

Researcher: You felt like what you were doing was wrong?

James: Yup.

Researcher: You were going to do it but you didn't want them to?

James: That's right.

Researcher: How do you explain that?

James: I don't know. It's like you don't want nobody doing bad because you're doing bad. And I felt bad about it because I couldn't quit at first, I just couldn't quit and I didn't want them to see me getting high like that.

DIETARY CHANGES

In response to a general question regarding the effects of fathering on health, Scott immediately noted changes in his diet. He recognized the importance of modeling healthy food selection and dental care:

Researcher: Lets turn attention to health for a little while now. Do you think fathering has had any effect on your health habits?

Scott: Yeah, to want them to eat better, you have to do it yourself, so. It makes you more conscious of what your eating and, you know, brushing your teeth every night, you know, every morning. So they will do it and they go by example, so.

Similarly, Craig realized that modeling health to his children required a healthy lifestyle from him. So, even without direct comments or specific health issues that are at the forefront of father–child relationships, there is a pressure exerted for men to model positive health, diet, fitness, and grooming. Craig reflected:

I realize that I got to keep healthy to keep them healthy, I got to set a decent example for them because it's all imprinted in them now.

Roger noted the change in his diet since his wife's first pregnancy. Again, this indicates that either Roger, his wife, or both were aware that their behavior was not the most positive health promoting behavior that they could have chosen. It took the pregnancy and parenting to motivate them to eat better for the sake of their child(ren):

Our eating habits have definitely increased on the better half. I mean, we're more apt to eat healthier now because he's around. We don't want all the chocolate chip cookies and stuff. You know, you bring a little of that into him and he's got to have treats and stuff. When he was—this all stemmed from the time my wife got pregnant. You know, we wanted to eat more healthy. We wanted to eat more vegetables, eat more fruit. Fruit was more available than cookies were in the house. Before that, we were, you know, get a pizza every night and a cheese steak the other night. So we were—it definitely changed our eating habits and that's continued right on through, you know, once she was pregnant right on through now, he's fourteen months. We ... have changed those eating habits. We try to sit down and have a meal, a healthy meal and all that. It's not a, you know, a Burger King night and a McDonald's night the next night, so it's definitely changed for the better for us.

Roger was motivated away from "junk foods" and fast food toward a more healthy food selection. Similarly, Clifford noted a positive change in his diet. He recognized that he needed to eat more healthily if he was going to model and instruct his children in positive nutrition:

It's definitely probably uh, changed my diet habits. I probably eat a little bit more healthy because of them. Before I didn't like eating a lot of vegetables. That sort of thing, but um ... how can you tell your child to eat their spinach if you don't eat it I guess.

Alan had diversified his diet to include more fruit and vegetables as well. In addition to noting the positive change in diet, he also commented on the fact that he was now constantly eating because his children wanted him to taste everything. This was presented in a manner that made it seem as though he was eating more now that he had children:

Researcher: Change in diet?

Alan: Always eating all the time, whatever they're eating, I'm eating, too. They want me to taste everything.

Researcher: Has it affected the varieties of foods that you have or the quantities of food?

Alan: The variety I don't think—well, it has because there's things I never tasted before that I taste now. I never tasted squash before, but I know what it tastes like now. And the quantities, I'm always eating all the time.

Researcher: When you talk about the squash, have you tried to get more vegetables and fruits in, or not really?

Alan: Yeah. Because before, I usually never ate fruits, or I would eat them, but it wasn't nothing big on my list to have to go get it. But now, there's fruits out there I never knew that they were out there until now. My wife goes grocery shopping; she's always bringing something home I never

> heard of before. So, we're buying more fruits and more vegetables. So, try different things.

CHANGES IN EXERCISE

Because time is seen as more valuable after having children, things that are "more optional" or self-absorbed often are reduced in frequency and duration. Exercise is often one of those things. Roger talks through the conflict of knowing that the exercise and time invested in his own health and fitness is worthwhile, yet knowing that routines are difficult to establish and that time at the health club takes away from time with the children/family. Roger recognizes the benefits of exercise, but he has decided to invest instead in time with his son. He is so captivated by the rapid developmental changes that his son is going through that he fears missing something by taking time for his personal fitness program. Aside from the pull his son places on his time, practical concerns of time, energy, and transportation provide additional challenges for his fitness routine. Roger said:

> Because of the responsibility of him. I'd say I'd cut down on a lot where I just leave here and go to the Y[MCA] health spa three days out of the week and come home after that and my wife and I would have dinner. Now it's almost a feeling of I don't want to go—I want to go but I don't want to go. I know I feel much better when I go and I work out for a couple of hours and I come home. But I'm afraid I can't I can't get into a routine with it because my wife's schedule and my schedule. Now it's kind of like I don't want to pull myself away from him. Because at this age he's fourteen months old. He's doing something new every day. He's saying a new word every day and he's doing all these different changes. At this time frame I don't want to pull away from that.

Tom reported that his participation in organized team sports had dropped off since having children who participated in sports. Because there were limits on time and transportation, he felt that it was more important for the children to learn cooperation and to experience team sports than for him to continue in his participation. Because, practically speaking, something had to go, he decided to set aside his own participation for the benefit of the children's involvement in team sports. Tom said:

> Before I got married I was always, whatever the sport happened to be that they were doing like this dorm against that dorm, or the dental clinic against the hospital or something, you know, I was always participating in those things after work. But when the kids started participating in sports, my wife and kids pretty much always come and watch the games and stuff, but when they started having their practices and their games, we have one vehicle and no

way to get both places at the same time, then that's where I'd say, "Well, I'll drop out of my sports." It's more important that they are into sports and learn values of team participation and stuff like that. So that's where some of mine dropped off.

Steve had shifted his participation in sports from playing in adult leagues to playing with his children in backyard activities. He still considered that to be some exercise, but he still felt that both the quality and the amount of exercise was diminished in comparison to his previous participation in sports with adults:

I'm too tired to go out and exercise. If I run around with all these kids, I got to play with these kids, that's exercise too, you know. Even though I don't play team sports—like you indicated team sports—like say, I used to play baseball. Well, I play baseball with the kids but I'm playing whiffle ball with them, I'm showing them how to play baseball. I'm not actually out there with adults running around. It's not quite the same amount of exercise or the same quality of exercise, but I'm still getting exercise. But it's geared toward the kids, running after them, and doing a lot of exercising my vocals here in the field.

In response to a general question concerning the effects of fathering on his health, Nelson indicated that he had significantly cut back on his regular exercise program. Again, lack of time was cited as a primary factor:

Researcher: What impact, if any, has fathering had on your health habits?

Nelson: Cut into them. You can't, you don't have the time to invest in health care. Like jogging, I like to run every day, you don't run as much. You don't exercise as much, you just, I mean it's a time-consuming task that could be spent, done, you know, time spent with the children. I mean, it's just that.

When asked whether he had experienced any changes in exercise since becoming a father, Alan indicated that he had. Some types of exercise had increased and others had decreased. Again, the quality and quantity was viewed to be different. Alan elaborated:

I'm more running and walking now, have to chase after Rachel all the time. But I think some things have been limited and some things have gotten more. I do more running, as I said, and more walking now—always outside with Rachel wanting to walk and see different things.

INCREASES IN HEALTH RISKS

Perceived increases in health risks were infrequently noted by sample fathers, but some men stated that they had experienced an increase in the overall level of anxiety, worry, stress, or responsibility. Being a dad can bring on worries that effect health and feelings of well-being, although there is no empirical data that fathering per se brings on any significant changes in health (e.g., increased blood pressure) that are directly tied to parenting stress. However, subjective well-being is an important measure of health, and some fathers report increased stress and anxiety that translate into lower assessments of subjective well-being. When asked about changes in health related to fathering, Clifford, who did not get much physical exercise and who was significantly overweight, said:

> I probably worry more. Probably has my blood pressure up, uh ... um ... I don't exercise as much as I used to cause uh. I, I do now that I've been divorced I guess before that were I gained a lot of the weight because my wife didn't want me to go out because she wanted me to help with the children. So I know its not healthy picking up the weight. So that's affected me that way.

He attributed his weight gain to changes in time associated with family commitments and dynamics. He perceived that his cutting back in exercise led to his weight gain and increased worries were adversely affecting his blood pressure. Mark reported that worries regarding his children had contributed to insomnia and associated physical discomfort:

> Well, because I'm more worried about things, I don't sleep as well. So like I said earlier, I've been having some medical problems. They thought at first it was Lyme's disease, but it tested out to be nothing of that sort. They think it's because of the stress level of being a new father and that that's causing me not to sleep as well, to have some pains in my joints.

In a pattern that diverged from all other men in the sample, Nelson reported that he had begun smoking since becoming a father. He attributed this to be a result of divorce and child-related stress:

> Researcher: You smoke moderately now and you didn't before. What made that difference?
>
> Nelson: Divorce. I think that combined with the extra added stress of the children's demands and not knowing what course of action to take a lot of times.
>
> Researcher: Do you smoke in front of the children?
>
> Nelson: Unfortunately, yes. It's mostly done like in the car where I can hang the cigarette out the window. But in the house, not really, it's pretty much isolated to the car.

Nelson was aware that his smoking was not providing positive role modeling for his children, but he was taking measures to limit their exposure to his smoking.

The previous quotes show that father involvement is not uniformly associated with improved health. Most men experienced the strain of time and energy, and decreased their individual work-out time and organized sports time. They tended to remain active through playing with their children, but that was seen as a lower quality and quantity of exercise than personal training or team sports.

ACCESS TO HEALTH CARE

Another health-related issue that changes in importance as men become fathers is health care coverage. The availability of and the quality of benefits packages takes on new importance in selecting and holding jobs. The benefits package takes on new levels of importance because there are implications not only for self and spouse, but for children as well. Consider Donald's response:

> Researcher: Any change in terms of access to medical care, how important benefits package might be to you in terms of work?
>
> Donald: It is important now. Before, I would'nt even of considered it. It didn't matter to me. I never went to see the doctor and now it is important to me because I know things like my son going into the hospital. That would cost me $3,000 because I didn't have insurance. My wife having children. If we didn't have insurance it would have been unreal now if we had to pay. I look for a benefits package when I am working or when I choose my job.

Similarly, Roger indicated the central importance of health care coverage in the benefits package and its role in his decision making regarding work:

> I probably would have made a career change from this hospital if wasn't for the benefits package because I get free service from working here for me and my family as long we come to this hospital. I probably would have quit a couple of years ago. There was a point where I just am bored with the medical field. It's driving me up the wall. I'm tired of it.

Benefits packages can affect retention rates for employers, particularly in the case of employees with children. People with medical benefits are more likely to make use of preventative health services such as regular checkups. The increased access to health care coupled with children's expressed concerns about fathers' health may motivate fathers to utilize health services to a greater extent than men who are not fathers. This is a question that could be easily answered through future research at health care facilities.

BALANCE ISSUES IN FATHERS' HEALTH

Themes reflecting balance issues were not as prevalent or as pointed in this chapter as they are in others. Most men recognized the value of positive health practices and there was more for them to do to improve their diet and exercise programs. Balance issues were reflected in subtle ways in regard to perceived relations between fathering and health. Balance was an issue as men discussed the struggles of finding time to engage in regular exercise programs. They were attempting to get enough exercise while having enough time with their families. A balance issue is also implicit in the practical limitation on transportation. Some men stated they could not regularly get to the gym because they only had one car and their families needed it when they were free to exercise. They were voicing the tensions of balancing their own needs versus those of their families. Similarly, when fathers talked about giving up team sports so they could spend more time with their families or so their children could experience team sports, they were balancing the benefits to self versus other. In talking through nutritional changes, fathers indicated they could control their impulses to eat junk food, but they needed to purge it from the house because their young children could not resist it and they would spoil their appetites before getting a healthy meal. Fathers were balancing their own food preferences and developmental abilities with those of their children.

Perhaps the area where most striking effects were realized was in fathers' reported willingness to change health practices for the sake of their children. Fathers discussed giving up harmful habits and engaging in more healthful practices for the sake of their children, to enhance longevity, and to model healthy behavior to their children. In short, fathers frequently found new balances in health practices as a result of wanting to change for the sake of their children.

Longevity data indicate that divorced men predecease married men by 4 or more years on the average (Santrock, 1997). Although much of this effect has been explained by increased stress and conflict and loss of affiliative support from the spouse, it is often the case that fathers have minimal contact with noncustodial children within a year of the divorce (Seltzer, 1991). Perhaps the lack of ongoing paternal involvement with children contributes to shorter life expectancies by eliminating the ongoing benefits of modeling positive health and nutrition.

III

The Social Domain

Chapter **8**

Being a Father and Being a Husband: The Effects of Fathering on Intimate Relationships

The relations between parenting and marriage is the one area in the professional literature where there is an abundance of empirical work and where, until recently, there has been a fair consensus in the resulting data. Predominant trends in the data indicate a developmental pattern in marital satisfaction reflecting steady decline from the birth of the first child through the child(ren)'s teen years and marked improvement during the launching and empty nest phases of the family life cycle. This is the prevalent pattern, although there are considerable variations. The men in the survey indicated that, in many ways, these trends do describe their experiences. Interview data elucidate subtle patterns in the trends. The role of individual maturity and the convergence of the couples' perceptions emerged as key factors in understanding the relations between fathering and marriage.

INTRODUCTION

From men's perspectives, fathering brings a complex mix of influences into intimate relationships. None of the men interviewed perceived their relationships with girlfriends, fiances, spouses, former spouses, or significant others to be unaffected by the presence of children. There was unanimous agreement that children change relationships. Exactly how the relationship is changed is somewhat specific to the context of the overall relationship, but in virtually all cases, a complex blend of influences was realized.

Most challenging was the need for men to balance the demands of being an involved father and a husband or partner at the same time. Most men recognized that their relationships with their partners were characterized by a blend of positive and negative functioning before having children, and the presence of children was not the determining issue in the quality of their marriages. For virtually all couples, parental status ushered in greater stress, less time alone with partners, more daily hassles, and a greater degree of perceived fatigue. The combination of these factors presented challenges to couples desiring to maintain or increase levels of intimacy in their relationships with their significant others. For most, the challenging aspects of fathering were counterbalanced, at least to a degree, by initiating a significant joint focus and a new arena where men could share commitment and communication with their partners. However, having children in and of itself neither increases nor decreases marital intimacy, although it introduces a whole host of changes in how time and energy is spent in relationships. Interview themes revealed that, overall, the most important factor in influencing men's perceptions of the influence of fathering on marital quality was the way that the time spent with spouses and children was perceived. Men's characterizations of their family relationships provide an indication of their developmental maturity. Men who are other centered, focusing on the ways that they can facilitate their children's development and their partners' lives, expressed mature ways to experience intimacy and generativity.

Simply stated, men who perceive time, communication, and energy invested toward their children as an appropriate part of commitment relationships expressed greater adjustment in their family lives. They were less likely to discuss fathering's negative influences on marriage, and when they did, they were much more muted in the terms they used. Men who were self-focused, expressing concern or frustration over what fathering "cost" them in terms of their relationships with their partners, tended to view fathering and marriage to be in an antagonistic relationship. Every father simultaneously experiences some measure of joy and fulfillment from investing time and energy into the next generation and some measure of "loss" in focused time and attention from and toward their partner, but the degree of focus in these opposing directions reflected differences in maturity and a sense of fulfillment in fathering roles.

This study purposely does not focus on the effects of children on marital satisfaction, because there is a plethora of data and interpretive literature in that area. Instead it focuses attention on a few specific, but open-ended questions regarding men's perceived effects of fathering on their relationships with their wives (girlfriends, fiances, cohabitors, etc.).

Those questions took the general form:

1. How do you think fathering has impacted your relationship with your wife (girlfriend/fiancé/partner)?
2. Has fathering had any influence on your feelings of closeness with your wife?
3. Do you feel that having children has affected your level of commitment to your wife or marriage?

4. Do you have any conflict over how to raise the kids—like one of you being more lenient and one of you being more strict? What happens when you disagree about things like that?
5. Do you think that having children has had any influence on your sexuality in terms of how frequently you make love or the quality of your lovemaking with your partner (wife/fiancé ...)?

From the transcripts of the interviews focused on this area, there was a significant amount of text produced. Men were very articulate when discussing the perceived effects of fathering on marriage or like relationships.

OVERVIEW OF PERVASIVE THEMES

The pervasive themes expressed by study fathers were that:

- Marriage (or a similar relationship) was radically transformed by the presence of children.
- There were both positive and negative effects attributed to the addition of children to the dyad.
- The presence of children tended to increase the commitment fathers felt toward their partners.
- The overall amount of time couples spend together is not much different from before having children, though time alone or time focused on the marital dyad is perceived to be significantly less.
- Frequency and quality of sexual relationships are significantly altered by the presence of children.

The major conclusion from the data regarding fathering and marriage is that homogamy in partners' views regarding balancing child and couple time and energies was the most significant factor effecting perceived adjustment in marriage and parenting. When couples were similar in the ways they viewed family time and commitments relative to couple investments, fathering did not represent a significant detriment to marital development and could, in fact, enhance marital closeness and commitment. However, where fathers expressed significant differences between their own versus their partner's views of appropriate use of time and energy in relation to fathering, couple relationships were perceived to suffer.

THE EFFECTS OF FATHERING ON TIME TOGETHER

Having children brings both a competition for time (alone or other-focused) and a context for shared time (family time and shared activities; Daly, 1996a, 1996b; Dienhart, 1998). Provided that both persons in a relationship can agree to view the overall allotment of shared time as appropriate shared time, the presence of children can be seen to contribute to the quality of the marital (or significant other) bond. To the extent that it is viewed as a competition, a distraction, or a detractor—by either partner—it can lead to significant discontentment and frustration.

Changes in time spent together were primarily in time spent alone as a couple. Whereas some fathers perceived that they spent significantly more time focused on family events than before having children, other dads stated they spent much less time with the family since having children because their share of family providing required them to invest longer hours at work, or in multiple jobs (see chap. 11, this vol.).

Most fathers perceived no change in the overall amount of time spent together with their partners. It was very clear that the nature of that time changed radically, and the time was perceived to be qualitatively different. Most men discussed significant decreases in the amount of time they spent alone with their partners. After having children, couples' conversation was not perceived to be as personally focused, intimate, or relationship oriented. Much of the conversation centered around childrearing issues, milestones, or just catching up on what was happening in various aspects of children's lives. Attempts to have dyadically focused conversations were often abbreviated by interruptions from children. To have extended periods of time to converse alone, child care or the ability to stay up past children's bedtimes was required. However, financial and energy resources challenged the frequency of both, limiting couple-focused time and conversation in most dyads.

Interestingly, at the same time that there was a perceived drop in other-focused conversation, sharing, and discussion, there was a sense of increased focus on a common goal, interest, and commitment: raising the children successfully and enjoying children's development and family relationships. Although this resulted in a degree of couple cohesion, it also represented a significant shift away from a focus on the couple and onto the family as a whole. Men who were neither allocentric nor otherwise mature enough to make this shift (or those who simply did not desire to), found fathering to be a detriment to their relationship with their partners.

In contrast, Roger perceived that the couple focus on raising their infant son had brought a forum for greater communication and a positive reorientation of how he and his wife spent their evenings:

> Oh, [there is] definitely more [communication], yeah. Like I said when you sit on the couch at the end of the night after he goes to bed, and you start talking. And then it used to be where we'd sit there and watch television, and she'd get tired, she'd say, "Okay, I'm going to bed," she'd go up and I'd be sitting there watching a movie for another hour, go up, come upstairs, she'd be asleep. Well, now we sit, talk, and then say, "Hey, do you want to go upstairs and go to bed;" we'll go upstairs and go to bed together. And you get in bed and you start talking a little more. So, it brought us even closer together. Where

sometimes it would be just like I said. It definitely changed us around in how we spent the nighttimes.

Not all changes are viewed so positively. Some things that change after having children are missed. Thomas noted the shift from adult-oriented activities alone with his spouse toward more family time. He also noted a change in overall energy level, which he hesitated to attribute to parenting:

We spend less time going to movies and doing cultural things. But we spend more time as a unit. We also spend a lot of time tired. But that's a—I'm not sure if that would have been a whole lot different without a child, because of our work.

PERCEPTIONS OF CLOSENESS TO PARTNERS

It was the perception of most men that children complicate relationships, but they do not make or break them. Men's perceptions of closeness with their partners varied considerably. Fathers who focused attention on shared activities experienced a sense of increased closeness, whereas those who focused on sharing feelings and thoughts of a highly personal nature experienced declines in closeness.

Craig felt the degree of closeness his wife expressed toward him was somewhat dependent on how things were going with the children at the time. His wife was a stay-at-home mother, and he worked long hours to be the sole provider for the family. Craig elaborated:

Interviewer: Any change in emotional closeness or distance with your wife?

Craig: It changes day to day. If she has a good day then everything's great. If she has a bad day, it's my fault. ... It was a mutual decision that she stayed home when it's a good day, and it was my decision that she got stuck in the house with them when it was a bad day. So it's just the way it goes. You either let it build up and blow up between the two of you, or you let it roll off. So we just take it one day at a time.

Those men who expected to continue to have large segments of time with their partners, similar to the time before becoming parents, expressed significant disappointment and competition with their children for their wives' attention. They perceived their marriages to be less close and expressed frustration with the quality of their marriages.

Steve voiced some strong negative effects of having children and then tempered the statement with a recognition that children provide a shared focus and bond, although the way time is spent is radically altered:

Before my wife and I were married, you know, we dated, we went everywhere, we did everything. First it was sex all the time, everywhere. Baby comes along, well that's all stopped. You don't go out no more and when you do go out it's been after a long time and you're just about going stir crazy and you get a grandmom over to watch the kid and you go out. Sex is shot to hell, you just forget about that. Having kids plays a major, major role. You can go on, I can almost go on forever with negatives as far as what happens. There are some positives, you know. When you have a child with a woman that brings you and that woman a little bit closer, you have something that's the same between you. Like I said before, there's really no genetic link between the two of you except for the kid now. So that creates an emotional bond, too.

Steve elaborated on the fact that there was less time to talk about work and to express physical intimacy without interruption. Since becoming a father, he had lost a source of instrumental and emotional support. His sense of loss is expressed in the following quotation:

For one thing it's like we come in from work at the end of the day and we're trading off war stories from work. It used to be like a traditional thing just to vent the pressures from work and we'd sit there, oh this person did this and that person did that. My girlfriend and I used to work in the same sites. We knew a lot of the same people so we'd gab about everybody. Then we'd talk about maybe if there was a problem within the work or something like that, we could talk it out with each other. Your partner might not have the answer but it helps to talk about it. Now it's, kids run in and it's "mommy, mommy," or the baby walks in and he's going to be two tomorrow so he's walking around, he's not quite talking yet, but he's very jealous if daddy spends a little time with mommy. Even if we're talking or sitting next to each other or want to give each other a hug and he's, "Uh-uh, that's my mommy, only me hugs mommy." Like I say, by the time you put the kids in bed and you think you're going to have some time together you're pretty well exhausted.

Some men just simply missed the way things had been with their partners prior to having children. Some of it was based on shared activities, and some was based on time to share. Some men saw the transformation to be pervasive:

Interviewer: How do you feel that parenthood has impacted your relationship with your wife?

Bruce: That's almost like you're in a totally completely different relationship now. It's nowhere near what it was when we were dating and got married. It's put a tremendous strain on our relationship.

Interviewer: How?

Bruce: Well, everything is, revolves again around the children, and we have less energy for extracurricular activities. We never go out, that's like once every two months when you get a chance to go out to dinner without the kids. And it's just totally different. It's not even close to what it was before.

Bruce seemed to be feeling displaced. He was not able to reconcile his feelings of displacement in what he perceived as a child-centered marriage. Some men miss the feelings of focused attention and companionship that they had previously experienced with their partners. Even when time is set aside for focused attention, it is perceived differently. Some "displaced" men may have difficulty suppressing feelings of resentment toward their children.

John had clearly reflected on the effects of fatherhood on his relationship with his previous girlfriend. Their cohabiting relationship had dissolved after the birth of their two children, who now lived with John and a new girlfriend. John recognized that fathering was not the root cause of the relationship's failure, but, in his view, it did contribute:

> [Kids require] a lot of team work. I was a—it should have brought us closer, but it didn't. I don't want to blame the failure of the relationship on the kids, because it probably wasn't. But it helped, I guess, because of the stress. And we were both young.

Of all men in the sample, Will expressed the greatest sense of displacement in his relationship with his wife. His two teen age children were highly involved in competitive sports. His daughter was approaching Olympic class gymnastics, and his son toured extensively playing competitive tennis. Will's current family situation represented a significant departure from where he thought he would be. When asked how fatherhood had effected his closeness with his wife, he responded:

> Well, I'm now somewhere down behind a dog. I think it's my wife, the son, the daughter, then the dog, then me. So I'm kind of like last in the pecking order in terms of wife's priorities. So yeah, a dramatic effect. I count the least.

Although Will expressed this with humorous inflection and affect, he was experiencing emotional pain at the sense of distance he felt from his spouse.

It was relatively rare for men to report that they felt closer to their partners after having children, and those who did came from two distinctly different categories. The first were characterized by relatively shallow concepts of relationships. This group of men, who talked about parenting as improving their marriages, tended to have surface conceptualizations of intimacy. They said that doing more things together, like taking their children to the mall, had brought them closer to their partners. Such descriptions of increased closeness parallel school-age children's focus on shared activity as a basis for friendship as opposed to more mature constructions of intimacy as shared thoughts, feelings, and internal characteristics. The second, more mature, category reflected a perspective that allowed fathers to interpret the decreased personal time and decreased sexuality as appropriate. Some men reported increased communication around childrearing issues, and related gaining a new respect or understanding for their partners. For these men, fathering may have facilitated the development of marital intimacy. These men were developmentally more mature, and focused on other-oriented aspects of the relationship as opposed to a "what's in it for me" attitude. Both groups of men, those who were developmentally immature and those who were altruistically oriented, were able to perceive fathering as enhancing their relationships.

Donald perceived that he and his wife had a more enjoyable relationship now that they had children. This perception was based on the notion that the children provided an excuse for them to engage in fun activities they enjoyed together that they would not have shared without the kids. Here, the focus is on the external components of shared activities leading to greater closeness:

> Donald: There are those times when we really have a good time as a family. Then its really nice. Things that me and her could not have done by ourselves like go to Sesame Place or Dutch Wonderland [local amusement parks for children].
>
> Interviewer: Why couldn't you do that?
>
> Donald: Well, I guess we could have, but we would feel a little funny about it, but now that we have kids we kind of have an excuse to have fun. I say it was all [about] having fun in our relationship.
>
> Interviewer: Those fun times have brought more closeness between you and your wife?
>
> Donald: I think before the kids, we had a hard time finding stuff that we liked to do together. I like to go to the movies, but she doesn't like to spend that much money. She likes to go out to eat, but it doesn't really matter to me if we go out to eat or not. I think she likes to go to clubs, but I hate clubs. There is not really much that we agree on as far as activities, except the kids and trips.

Gilbert was one of the fathers who expressed an increase in closeness that he attributed to shared commitment and responsibility. The shared focus on their son caused a realization that the marriage was important to save, increasing commitment as well as closeness:

> Well, like I say, I think it's brought us closer together knowing that we have something that we both love so much and are responsible for. And we do love our son and we do enjoy him. And I think it's brought us closer together. Like I said, in a way it could have saved the marriage because of the entanglement of separation—not necessarily divorce probably but just separation and not wanting him to go through this, and knowing that he wants to be with both of us and not a broken home. So I would say it's helped the marriage.

Roger felt that he and his wife shared more feelings and more conversation since having a daughter. They were less likely to rent movies and more likely to spend time talking. Roger perceived that the birth of their daughter had changed what would be a fairly quiet relationship into one that focused on one another to a greater degree:

> We share our feelings a little bit more. You know, you sit down you say, well after he goes to bed at night, and that's our basically our time together. Spend about an hour and just watching television, talk. And it's kind of a feeling where before, you get into a rut where, you know, you do this, do that. And then the next thing you know you'd be going to bed, and you wouldn't really sit around and talk. And now we make it a special time where after he does go to bed, we say, "Well, what did you do today?, ... What did he do today?"

Fathering, and joint parenting with partners, brought meaning to otherwise tumultuous and difficult relationships for some men. Manuel, who had fathered children with three different partners, talked about how his children brought a sense of closeness and meaning to his relationship, even after the passage of time, with his first partner:

> [Manuel talked through the fact that his first partner and he had been separated for quite some time] ... Um we went up to dinner last year and we talked. And I said, "You know what?" I said, "We've been through hell and high water together. We done fought. Separately we done both went down both the roads, whatever." I said, "But there's one thing that we did. We done raised some hell of a good kids." She said, "You know what baby? You're right." And that's the first time in a long time that we held each other. First time in a long time.

Although Manuel and his former partner did not have many positive memories of their relationship, focusing on their partnership in raising children provided a framework for closeness and meaning.

FATHERHOOD AND COMMITMENT TO MARRIAGE

None of the fathers stated that parenting decreased their commitment to their wives. Those who said that fathering had little or no impact on their commitment indicated they were very committed to marriage before having children.

In response to a question that asked if fathering has had any impact on his relationship with his wife, Donald described a stabilizing influence:

> Well, I think before we were pretty rocky. We always had this certain attraction to each other, but there were times when it just didn't matter and before our kids, we tried to break up several times. Two or three times in a couple years. Now I think after the kids there have only been two times when we almost

broke up over major issues, and we just went to see a marriage counselor and dealt with it and put it behind us. I think it makes me and my wife think twice before we think about giving it all up.

Similarly, Neil described an increased commitment to marriage. He noted that even in relationships where the partners are relatively "cemented" prior to having children, there is an added commitment realized after the birth of children:

We are cemented by them. I shouldn't say that. We were cemented before that, but there is some extra glue in having kids because we're both committed to them and to each other, so I guess they helped us grow some extra muscle there that holds things together, or tissue, I guess I'm not sure whatever part of the body that is that keeps things together.

Thomas talked about how having children had caused him and his wife to recognize that they really did need one another, although they tended to be independent and demanding people in general:

Interviewer: In terms of your relationship with your wife, do you feel that parenthood has had an effect on that in any way?

Thomas: Yeah, it's saved my marriage. I don't know how rational this is, but I am aware that Diana doesn't need me, or doesn't need to be married. There are some things that she wants out of a relationship, and if I were not able to provide that, our relationship would be much more conflicted and probably would not have lasted as long as it has. She'll probably—if you were to ask her the same question—she'd probably say pretty much the same thing. We're both very similar personalities and we both demand a lot of the people that we're around.

A degree of increased commitment results from the realization that each parent plays a central role, not only in the lives of the child, but in supporting one another in parental roles. Partners come to realize that they need one another, not only for one another, but to do what they need to do for the sake of the children. As such, engagement in parental roles brings an increased sense of appreciation for and commitment to partners for their role as parent and spouse. David expressed this clearly:

I think the need for each other has really increased with the children. And maybe it's because the responsibility has become so much more immense than just taking care of yourself. I'm sure that's the reason, or one of the reasons.

John discussed the perception that children need two parents to be raised in a healthy manner. Reflecting on his own experiences with divorce as a young child, he was able to focus on wanting to be in his marriage for the sake of his children:

Interviewer: How do you think having kids affected your commitment toward marriage?

John: It increased it a lot. To me it seemed beneficial for both children to have both parents. My parents divorced when I was four, right after kindergarten, or around first grade, five or six. Then I remember I used to cry for my dad when he used to come over and visit. You know, I got raised by my mom, and there's a lot of things I didn't get to know, or do, or stuff like that. I didn't want ... [my children] to go through the same thing. I wanted them to have the advantage of having a mother and a father to get the aspect of both parents.

Similarly, Mark was able to talk through how the commitment to marriage is increased by the added responsibility of parenting:

Interviewer: Do you think it has affected your commitment to each other in any way?

Mark: It's probably increased it.

Interviewer: How or why?

Mark: Because again we have someone else who we're responsible for, someone whose dependent on us. So to make it best for them, or this person we have to be committed to each other and committed to the responsibility we've taken on.

Whereas men may feel more or less close to their partner, they recognize the need to be there for their children and to support their partner in their parenting roles. As such, while commitment is often influenced by, but not driven by, closeness. In the end, commitment yields a sense of closeness.

Colin stated a keen insight regarding the distribution of focused attention leading to perceptions of greater distance. He shows a developmental progression, where he adjusted his expectations to focus on the "common bond" represented in his child as opposed to the marriage. His quote shows the difference between retrospective views of relationship development and momentary perceptions of how things feel at the time:

Actually at first we became more distant from each other, I guess, because our attention, our attention and affection was focused on the child. I guess I didn't know how to give what [I] needed to two human beings at the same time. I can't really explain why that it first made us more distant. But I think now we're closer than ever because of it, because we have, we have a common bond and through some of the rough times, that probably kept us together when otherwise we might not have stayed together. And now after this amount of time we're glad that we did stay together. And I feel that we're closer than we've ever been.

Colin perceived the relationship to have evolved through different phases of closeness and strain, to which he was able to adjust. In the final analysis, he felt closer to his wife than he had ever been. Not all couples fare so well from the challenges of sharing and redistributing attention and affection.

PARENTING AND SPOUSAL CONFLICT

Disagreements with partners over discipline, strictness, parenting style, or division of child-care tasks played a very minor role in most men's view of marital quality. In some cases, dads felt they were more strict (or said their partner spoiled the kids), and in nearly an equal number of cases men felt their wives were more strict. The remainder of the sample talked through "areas" where one was more lenient and the other was more strict, and other areas where strictness standards were reversed. As such, there were no clear patterns in parental permissiveness by gender.

Although a high percentage of couples reported differences in ideas regarding what was appropriately lenient or restrictive for their children, these disagreements were almost universally characterized as minor. They did not appear to present major challenges to most couples.

Anthony was able to see that his disagreements with his wife regarding strictness and leniency were really just another avenue for interacting around different values. It was not the presence or absence of children that lead to disagreements with his spouse, it was just the focus of ongoing disagreements that preexisted children. It is the case, however, that children provide a richer, more complex context for such disagreements and negotiations:

> Anthony: We both have two different philosophies in raising the children.
>
> Interviewer: Does that cause conflict at all?
>
> Anthony: A little bit yeah. My wife is pretty permissive with them. I have to clean up the consequences of her permissiveness. That bugs me because it takes away from my time. I don't like that, you know ... I don't have much patience for that.
>
> Interviewer: Your differing views of what's appropriate with the kids, has that led to any conflict between you and your wife?
>
> Anthony: Serious, like I'm going to walk out if you don't do this kind of thing?
>
> Interviewer: No. I was wondering if it has led to a change in your relationship with her because of children?
>
> Anthony: No. Because, it's the same fight we've been having for seventeen years. It's just a different day.

Steve reflected on the fact that he and his wife took turns expressing more strict views with the children. However, the disagreements were characterized as both relatively frequent and minor:

Interviewer: Are the kids ever a source of disagreements about what's too lenient, what's too strict?

Steve: All the time, yeah. How we handle that is always open for debate. You know, "Well, you're being too mean right now, you're being too strict, you're overdoing it" and "Well, you're not being strict enough."

Interviewer: Who usually takes which position in your relationship?

Steve: Actually we switch back and forth on that. We both have pretty much domineering attitudes. I'm stubborn and bull-headed and so is she. I'm just about ten years older than her and I've learned just to keep my mouth shut and let her have her way. Still, as far as like being too lenient or too strong or whatever and how we discipline the children, what we do is, we've come up with a system. For example, we use certain buzz words if one thinks the other's overdoing it. We have a buzz word that we use. So in the heat of anger, if you're really angered and the kids really got you mad or something like that and you hear this word and it's like, oh, yeah, yeah, I must be going over the edge and we both do it, and we both look after each other to make sure we don't overdo it.

Steve and his wife had seen the need to work on this area of tension in their relationship and had come up with an effective technique. Their "buzz word" system did not eliminate their differences in perception regarding what was too strict or too lenient, but it did serve as an effective deterrent to letting disagreements go too far before they could be addressed.

Jeff felt the biggest disagreement in his relationship with his wife resulted from the fact that he was significantly more lenient than his wife, which displeased her. Again, however, this was not perceived as a major source of marital stress:

Jeff: My wife's the disciplinarian and I'm the pushover. And that's probably our biggest area of disagreement, no question about it.

Interviewer: What happens when there is a disagreement? Do you guys work it out in front of the kids? Ignore it? Maybe it will go away? Work through it?

Jeff: A combination of the three. We don't usually settle things in front of the kids. We'll do that away from them. Work through it, sometimes. And there are times that I'll go along with whatever my wife will say, because more than likely she's right. But then there are times when I feel right and I'll override her, not in front of the kids, but not—we'll go away, and I'll tell her what I think, and then, okay, well, this is what's going to happen to the kids. So I guess it really is a combination of the three.

Interviewer: I also sense that this hasn't been like a major problem in your relationship. I mean, that disagreements or controversies are somewhat minor?

Jeff: Oh, yeah. And we do joke about it. I don't hesitate to tell people that my wife is the disciplinarian. And she'll half-jokingly and half with a little dig say, well, you know, when I tell them no, they'll come to you. But I can't think of any time when it's turned into any kind of problem or major disagreement.

Fathers in the sample were able to cite examples of child-centered disagreement and needed negotiation in their couple relationships, but there was also ample evidence that the nature of the coparental relationship was affected by the couple's maturity level and the achievement of intimacy prior to having children.

ISSUES OF INTIMACY AND GENERATIVITY

The interviews with fathers provided support for the Eriksonian concept that sufficient resolution of intimacy issues must be accomplished before generativity can develop. Men who were engaged in dysfunctional or negative relationships prior to having children saw their kids as competing with them for time and attention with their partners, and focused on the hassles and conflict initiated by parenting. A high proportion of those with negative relationships had extremely dysfunctional patterns of relating with their partner prior to having children. Their relationships were characterized by high frequencies of substance abuse, physical and verbal abusiveness, and low commitment to their partners. For a few of those extremely dysfunctional couples, assuming responsibility for parenting provided a "jolt" that some men characterized as catalytically triggering positive changes in their relationships. Other couples claimed they were "blown apart" because they could not or would not meet the additional demands of parenting.

A small subsample of fathers said their partners could not handle it when the fathers gave their affection to their children. Perhaps they had not met their wives' intimacy needs (whether or not they were legitimate). Similarly, men who felt displaced by or in competition with their children had not had their intimacy needs met. When parents engage in intimacy with their children before their partner's needs are met, the resulting experience is often one of distance, resentment, and rejection. These patterns of emotions may indicate that the adult engaging with the child is not mature enough or ready to enter a mature intimate relationship. Relationships with children are not reciprocal to the same degree as adult peer relationships, thus making them "safe" for a person with trust issues to engage in. Alternatively, these patterns may simply indicate that the disgruntled parent (whether they be the one engaged with or "displaced" by the child) is not mature in intimacy. Jealousy toward children who take time and attention from the self may be an indication that, for various reasons, couple intimacy has not been achieved at an adequate level. If it had been previously achieved, disgruntled parents perceive that it is now diminished below adequate levels or absent altogether.

Most fathers could describe both ways that fathering had enhanced and detracted from their relationships with their partners. It was clear that some degree of focused attention was redistributed from the couple to the family. Yet, if this was viewed to be appropriate or desirable, then it enhanced the couple's relationship.

Clifford expressed both an awareness of shifting relationship focus and a greater family closeness:

> Clifford: It kind of took away from each others, you know, instead of the relationship centering on us. It centered more on them, I guess.
>
> Interviewer: Do you think it affected your commitment to each other in any way?
>
> Clifford: It probably did.
>
> Interviewer: For better or for worse?
>
> Clifford: It probably, a little bit of both maybe. It probably brought us closer together but then things got stale I guess. It wasn't time for each other, and we kind of grew apart maybe.
>
> Interviewer: How would parenting bring you together?
>
> Clifford: Just the love of child. Watching him and she and he grow. Uh experience in different things they may do everyday, uh ... you know, you come home from work and look what junior did today. It is probably a little bit of a brought us together and took us apart.

For some men, fathering caused them to realize that their marriages required more attention than they had devoted to them prior to fathering. Glen was one such dad, who determined to invest greater effort on working through marital issues after having a child:

> I'd tried to describe it as best as possible by saying well ... um ... you could no longer survive on auto pilot. Um ... what I mean by that is during the normal course of being married you get bumps along the ways, hills and valleys. If you didn't pay to much attention to some of those, you still manage to do okay, in my view. Some of the deep valleys, some of the crises that went on obviously I had to pay a lot of attention to. But you could still manage to move along at a positive direction without putting a whole lot of effort into it. And uh, quickly found out after fatherhood that just the time constraint as well as the additional responsibility type feelings. Um, that, couldn't, that our marriage couldn't survive with that. That we had to make time for each other. We had to talk about things that normally may have worked themselves out over a period of months. And um, I think from that stand point things have changed in our relationship, where we've had some a crisis that needed to be dealt with up front and we managed to do that. But no longer just kind of cruisin' along and enjoying things. I think we both felt that, that um, really if we had tried to do that our marriage might not survive it.

Not all men viewed the challenges associated with parenting to be responsible for the state of their relationships with their significant others. Ken was a dad who could reflect on his first marriage and recognize that there were inherent difficulties prior to the additional strains introduced through parenting. He also recognized his own immaturity contributed to the eventual failure of the relationship:

> I think in the first marriage, we're talking really a short period of time. So as I said, my first wife left with my first biological child at age one. So we had about a year of difficult marriage situation going into the birth of the first child. And the child was, had, was a difficult baby, colic, didn't sleep well, cried a lot. And so the stresses on the marriage, instead of what my first wife thought of bringing us together, it didn't. It made things more difficult. So, you know, I think, if anything, there was, you know, it's just too little a time to make any impact beyond the difficulties of raising a baby. So the parenting didn't, I don't think, change the underlying problems of the first marriage. It didn't get resolved. So we split.

The recognition that love now has to be shared across more relationships than in the couple pair brings a transition point to marriages that some men negotiate with relative ease. Fathers who have made the cognitive and emotional shift from couple-centered to family-centered relationships may express a degree of loss, but, overall, they view the change as appropriate, positive, or normative. David explained:

> Instead of channeling our love to just towards each other, we've been able to channel our love, or we have channeled our love together towards them. It changes—I think it changes your lifestyle. Before kids there was seemingly a lot more intimate times, a lot more romantic times. A lot more times just talking with one another. Again, along with kids there is—again, there is the work load and that I think that does get involved which starts to rob time from the intimate times where we talk.

One of the things that allowed David to accept the decreased couple intimacy was the "channeling" of the marital couple's love "together towards" the children. David's view of channeling love together toward the children reflects both an activity in a partnership and a decision to invest couple love into the family. Whereas he was able to express the sense of loss that comes when intimate couple time is diminished by workload and time together as a family, a sense of value and satisfaction was expressed in partnering together with his wife to love their daughters in a way that they needed to be loved.

Not all couples are able to positively adapt to reduced patterns of couple-centered intimacy and affection. Nelson had divorced his wife shortly after the birth of his second child. Nelson stated that his wife had become overtly jealous and aggressive toward him as he expressed affection toward his children, particularly his daughter. He stated that he came to care more for his children than he did for his wife, and after their divorce, he maintained custody of the children:

> Interviewer: How do you think having children affected your relationship with your previous wife?
>
> Nelson: She got jealous. She was jealous of her children. She's very violent. I thought it was cool because she's a very passionate Hispanic. But the love that I've had for her started flowing to the children, especially Jenna. And it wasn't hard to do, I guess I should have been more aware of what was occurring but she became jealous of the love that I had for Jenna, I mean Jenna elevated way beyond her as far as my love, my shared love was concerned. I just, you know, it just eventually faded our marriage.

Beyond a sense that he should have been more aware of what was happening, Nelson did not express any question as to whether it was appropriate for him to "elevate" his love for his daughter "way beyond" that for his wife. However, in Nelson's view, the shift in affection was responsible for fading the marriage. It would be interesting if there were data concerning Nelson's former wife's view of the relationship dynamics. It is clear, however, that Nelson believed jealousy and eventual relationship failure resulted from lack of agreement on how family affection should be distributed.

FATHERING AND SEXUALITY

One of the most common perceptions was that the frequency and spontaneity of sexual intimacy declined markedly after accepting responsibility for children. Reasons for changes in sexuality varied with the age of the fathers and their families. With young children, there were unpredictability and privacy issues. With older children, energy was a major factor: Teens tend to stay up late, and when parents want to go to bed after their teens, they are often fatigued. This is coupled with the perception of less other-focused conversation, so the overall effect is that it moves the physical relationship out of the realm of intimate sharing—an expression of love with energy—and tends to reduce it more toward a sexual act (if there is enough energy).

In regard to reported changes in sexuality, those who indicated that there had been a decrease in the quality of sexuality tended to focus on issues of frequency, spontaneity, creativity, and energy. Some men, who reported perceived increases in sexual quality, focused on more mature intimacy issues—the shared feelings, commitment, and closeness, independent of frequency and other "surface" indicators. Decreased frequency was coupled with increased anticipation. When these were linked with a perception of increased intimacy, then sexual quality was perceived to be enhanced. Donald expressed the pattern of both decreased frequency and increased quality in the following exchange:

Interviewer: In terms of your sexual relationship with your wife, do you feel that having kids has influenced the frequency, the numbers of times that you guys have relationships?

Donald: It has decreased it. Half the time we actually can't get started because of the kids. It probably used to be three or four times a week before the kids or if not every day before the kids. After the kids it just rapidly went down to once a week, once every other week. We usually don't have that much time alone, especially with both of us working because I work evenings and she works day. We are not really together a lot, except for the weekends. We sleep together at night, but that's it.

Interviewer: In terms of number, lovemaking is much decreased. How about the quality of your sexual relationship?

Donald: Sometimes it seems better. I really think it depends on both of our moods. If we both really want to do it, it usually turns out better than what it used to be. It used to be just sex. Plain and simple sex, you know, just for the sake of sex. Now I think we both really miss each other, and we both want to. It makes for a better time.

Some men saw rapid changes in their sex lives right after the birth of their first children due to privacy, fatigue, and partners' anxiety over how the baby was doing. If these were overcome, things frequently returned to normal:

Roger: Well, yeah, in the beginning it definitely did, you know, because you're like so scared you're going to wake him up. For the first, about, two-and-a-half months he spent in our room, in the crib, you know, in the cradle. It basically did then. Now it's, I don't know, it's even brought out our sex life even better.

Interviewer: How so?

Roger: I don't know, we're more at ease. I think, like we discussed before, our emotions, we opened up our emotions a little more than we did before. Because, you know, there's so many emotions when he comes. There's like, say the frustration of not knowing what to do, the happiness of when he walks, or gets up and crawls for the first time. And you talk about that. It brings out, it opens, I know it opened up me a lot. And just talking to my wife about different things and about him. So it made, I don't know, it just made our relationship that much stronger.

For Roger, the perceived increase in sharing of feelings and communication carried over into perception of an enhanced sex life. However, some men's sexual relationships with their partners never saw a recovery in terms of frequency or quality. Joseph talked through how this happened in his relationship, and his own role in it:

> Once we had them then we didn't—after we had the two, then we like, I don't know, like after a while you lose like a spark in there somewhere, like the romance or something is like gone out the window. And then you got to try to rebuild it up and you don't have no answers on how to get it back, even though the answers might have been there, you're not really looking for them as hard as you should. I wasn't the greatest individual in the world to try to come up with some kind of solution like that. I'm still lost now, to some degree.

As described earlier, Will had an unusually complicated lifestyle centered around taking his two children to competitive athletic events, often while his wife was traveling to events with the other child. He described their lives as somewhat separate: They just seemed to alternate which child they were focused on. Although expressing their low degree of sexuality in a humorous manner, clearly, Will perceived a significant change in sexuality and attributed it almost completely to having children:

> Interviewer: Do you think that having children has had an influence on your sexuality in terms of—
>
> Will: We don't have sex any more, we're married, for Christ's sake. I have been married eighteen years. My wife tells me I'm happily married. Yeah, it has a dramatic effect.
>
> Interviewer: in terms of frequency?
>
> Will: Yeah—little or none, can I say it that way? And then when I ask for it then I get these looks, you know, "Is that all you think about?" But yeah, it's dramatically affected our sexual life. We don't have any.
>
> Interviewer: And you attribute that to the children?
>
> Will: Yes, ninety-five percent of it.

It is seldom acknowledged that sexual relationships go through developmental phases related to transitions and countertransitions in the lives of families. Fathers in the sample noted marked changes in the frequency and quality of their sexual relationships. Changes were often perceived by fathers to be related to different phases in the lives of their partners as coparents. There was considerable variability in the range and duration of perceived effects of parenting on sexual relationships between the coparents.

BALANCE ISSUES AND THE PROVISIONS MADE

In regard to marriage, the balance issues appeared to be few, but significant. Specifically, men talked about balancing time as fathers and husbands. In regard to marriage, all other balance issues were subsumed under this issue. Related to this was the idea of balancing a flow of couple-directed intimacy, time, conversation, affection, and energy versus family-related intimacy, time, conversation, affection, and energy. In regard to agreement with their partners, men also discussed the need to balance strictness and permissiveness regarding child control with views of their partners.

Joseph focused on the difficulties in trying to satisfy the needs of both partner and children at the same time:

> Then you've got to try to find time for her and the children, and sometimes you just have to find time for the children, and then she's, like, has to wait until her time comes. Sometimes she's satisfied and sometimes she's not. Just inopportune times to try to be a father and a husband both at the same time.

Joseph's comment implies that neither role, husband or father, in and of itself is difficult. The challenge comes in trying to do all that each entails at the same time. Joseph's comments further imply that he feels that he and his partner have not been able to work out the needed balance. This may be partially due to the self-focused perspective reflected in the way that he referred to his partner needing to "wait until her time comes." It can be difficult when couples require a significant perception of couple exclusive activity or time. A different perspective is offered by Robert, who expressed a mature and satisfying adjustment to balancing fathering and marriage. His response reflects the developmental process of partnering together to parent in a mutually agreeable child-centered family. Robert indicated that things are not always easy, smooth, or agreeable to both partners, but that with effort and perseverance, mature love will bring a satisfying solution:

> Interviewer: How would you say that having children has affected your relationship with your wife?"
>
> Robert: We have had conflicts over the way we both felt about certain areas or certain things that they have done. We have both matured. We are both in total agreement that our children come first. We have learned to become less selfish due to the children. It has in most ways brought us closer together."

CONCLUSIONS

It is easy to understand why the typical patterns of change in marital satisfaction are reported in the professional literature. People experience changes in other-focused time from the delivery of their first child (or the entry into stepparent roles) on through the teen years. The nature of the time and energy necessary to raise children fluctuates over the developmental path of the children, and by the time children are teens, there has been a cumulative effect of couple-focused time deprivation. When this is coupled with changes in energy and the issues that teens go through in discovering their own sense of identity and individuating themselves from their families, it is not surprising that marital satisfaction frequently ebbs at this point. It is also predictable that marital satisfaction increases beyond the children's teen years. As children move out of the family home and become more independent, parental energies, although still considerable, are directed in different ways. As each child is launched, more or less successfully, couples have more discretionary time to invest in interests other than parenting. If they invest that time in relationship building once again, then there is likely to be an increase in marital satisfaction. Sometimes couples report a second honeymoon when they reach the empty nest phase.

For couple relationships to continue to grow and prosper, both partners must be content with the flow of love, attention, and conversation being directed toward the family instead of the couple. When this is not the case, the result is discord, frustration, and potentially fractured relationships. Where there is couple agreement on the direction and flow of communication and love, fathers experience enhanced closeness and commitment with their partner. Whereas sexuality is likely to decrease in frequency after having children, the quality is viewed as enhanced if the father is family focused versus couple focused.

This chapter closes with the reminder that, ultimately, children do not make or break relationships. Steve said it well:

> I think there are a lot of problems in a lot of relationships, and a lot of them are within my relationships. Children complicate it but I don't think ... they're the cause, they're not the roots of it. They just complicate it.

Chapter **9**

Fathers in Families: The Effects of Engaged Fatherhood on Relationships With Relatives

As noted in other chapters, becoming a father serves as an important marker event in the lives of men and significantly affects the developmental trajectories of men who choose to engage in fathering. Assuming the role of father necessarily brings changes to family positions, other family roles, and relationships in extended families.

When a man becomes a father, he expands his existing cast of roles. Roles he had already filled continue to exist, but they get altered by the addition of a fathering role, which changes the distribution of his energies, time, and priorities, and expands his skills and awareness of deficits. In addition to becoming a father, he typically continues to engage in a husband (or partner) role (see chap. 8, this vol.). Similarly, becoming a father does not erase the new father's role as a son or son-in-law, but being a son with a son or daughter of your own changes relationships with parents and parents-in-law, who are now grandparents as well. New fathers are still brothers, but they are brothers with children. As fathers, they gain new insights into their role as uncles. Seldom discussed in the professional literature is the fact that becoming a father casts one into a role as a model for other family members to observe how to father (Daly, 1995). Brothers, brothers-in-law, cousins, and nephews watch and evaluate the strengths and deficits as someone in their family, and perhaps in their generation, enacts the fathering role.

As men become fathers, their transition to fatherhood creates countertransitions in other family members. In a manner that is parallel to fathers assuming an expanding array of roles, other family members have new responsibilities to assume while continuing to engage in preexisting roles. A fathers' parents may become grandparents for the first time. Grandparents may become great-grandparents. Siblings may be aunts or uncles for the first time. In more subtle ways, having children signals some measure of maturity that can cause the father's parents, grandparents, aunts and uncles, and siblings to reflect differently on their own maturity and generational position.

As family members enact roles in relation to fathers and their children, embracing or rejecting various aspects of the roles, it creates another dimension for relating—either building on or challenging the relationship. The birth and growth of a child in the family likely does both, but at the very least, it causes a change in the preexisting relationship between family members. The addition of new roles and generations creates new patterns of interacting and alters established patterns. Stated more technically, any life-course transition creates functional relationships that did not exist prior to the transition and unhooks some relationships that did exist before the transition. The creation of new roles and relationships in the family causes a new way to evaluate, understand, appreciate, and criticize relationships, both past and present.

In his four-decade study of fathering across generations, Snarey (1993) found that successful fathering followed two primary patterns: modeling and reworking. In modeling, fathers attempt to replicate the positive characteristics of fathering they received from their dads. In reworking, men strive to rectify the limitations of the fathering they received.

In the sample of fathers who participated in this study, it is remarkable how few men spontaneously talked about the positive things they learned from their own fathers. Only 2 of the 40 men spontaneously discussed modeling positive things after their own dads. In contrast, a full 50% of the sample talked through things that they tried not to model, places where they felt the need to rework their relationships with their fathers, and to create roles that went in opposition to the direction with which they had been parented. Some of the most emotionally laden statements of the interview emerged as men talked through the hurts they were reworking in relationships with their fathers as a result of being fathers themselves. It was also noteworthy how many of the men in the sample discussed the desire for greater male contact/approval in their lives as they grew up. Their engagement in fathering roles gave articulation to the lack that they had felt in their childhood or youth. Some fathers, perceiving they were doing a better job than their dads had done, felt empowered to decry the lack that they had experienced. Some men had experienced the physical loss of their fathers, either through death or separation/divorce. Many more, however, talked about their fathers' emotional absence due to other priorities (e.g., work). In many families where the fathers were residing in the home, they were perceived to be either physically or emotionally absent a significant portion of the time. Another significant portion of the sample talked about physical and/or verbal abusiveness that they had experienced from their fathers. A few men talked through resentment over feelings that they were little more than their dad's trophies.

Overall, the picture was remarkably bleak. The degree of negativity in the father–son relationships in this generation of fathers was particularly striking in that the sample in this study was skewed toward men who had made commitments to be involved fathers for their children. Presumably, the picture would be even more bleak for men who had cut and run in the face of paternal responsibility. Alternatively, a total abandonment brings a total lack of expectation for ongoing support and relationship. When fathers are physically present but emotionally distant, the cumulative hurt may be greater. This requires focused research in order to be addressed with authority. At any rate, the current generation of fathers is working through many issues of perceived paternal lack. Fathers of the past generation may have been known for their engagement in provider roles, but the current generation finds many facets of fathering to criticize and to change in their engagement with their own children. In the face of all of the talk of "new involved fathers," hopefully the next generation of fathers will have a significantly higher proportion of men who are modeling positive fathering examples imparted by their own fathers and a lower proportion of fathers who are so focused on reworking.

On a more positive note, engagement in fathering roles often facilitated men's greater understanding toward their own parents. Issues and positions that had seemed unrealistic or unreasonable to them as children or teens looked different from their vantage point as fathers. As fathers, they could more easily empathize with their own parents and the positions they had taken on issues. By "walking a mile in the shoes" of a parent, fathers came to appreciate the difficulties they had caused for their own parents, again recognizing that their parents had not been "so horrible" after all.

When men become fathers, it can create new links with siblings, allowing them to "fit in" with brothers or sisters who had children prior to their own transition to fatherhood. Men in this category appreciated the ability to join in family conversations that are often dominated by discussion of the children's newly developing skills, the challenges they are presenting, or their accomplishments. It can also elevate the new fathers to be regarded as men of responsibility. They comment on how they are no longer viewed as "punk kids" or other equivalent terms. In addition, if the father's siblings live in close proximity, it allows opportunities to get the kids (cousins) together to play, thus increasing contact between siblings (aunts and uncles). They also tend to engage in mutual support groups, exchanging advice, baby sitting, and passing along hand-me-downs from their children to nieces and nephews. Expanding the family by one generation creates multiple and significant opportunities for increased interaction and support.

Not all of these, of course, are positive. Sometimes siblings or parents make hurtful comments, or there are disagreements over limits set and appropriate actions. Fathers are sensitive to the comments and feedback (or lack thereof) they receive from their parents, in-laws, and siblings. Sometimes childrearing is an arena that highlights shared values and practice. At other times, it brings magnification to differences in values, practice, and judgment.

In the long run, it seems that the general tenor of extended family relationships is not altered that drastically. Specifically, where things were fairly positive to begin with, having children provides another set of avenues for generally positive relationships to continue to develop (not withstanding occasional problems). In contrast, where relationships were relatively strained or negative, having children tends to provide numerous opportunities for continued friction, disagreement, and hurtful exchanges. An exception to this generality appears to be that the quality of the relationship between the father and his own parents, particularly his mother, shows positive development more often than not. Sample fathers talked through many ways that they were more critical of their own fathers and mothers, but they also talked about greater degrees of understanding and appreciation. Given the high degree of reworking that was taking place in this sample of fathers, the increased levels of understanding and appreciation brought balance and provided a positive context for ongoing interaction between a father and his relatives.

SOME FATHERS FEEL CLOSER TO PARENTS

Since becoming a father, Donald indicated that he had experienced increased closeness with his mother, although he spent less time with her now that he and his wife had children. The perceived closeness was facilitated by Donald's sense of having more in common with his mother now that he was a parent:

> Interviewer: Even though you see her less and spend less time with her you are closer?
>
> Donald: Yes. When we are together, we have more to talk about than what we used to. I could not relate to her as a parent because I wasn't a parent myself. It was a parent–child relationship and now it is a parent–parent relationship.

Jeff indicated that he sensed that his wife was closer to her parents as a result of having children. That increased sense of closeness figured into his planning for the future regarding residential location. The intergenerational closeness caused him to think in terms of staying in the immediate area. Jeff explained:

> Well, I think, you know, again, it's drawn us—my wife's always been able to be close to my parents. I'm sure that, again, that there's that closeness is probably, you know, been increased because of the kids. One of the reasons I couldn't move away, I couldn't take the kids away from their grandparents.

Many quotes have not been included in this section, but many men did discuss the fact that they had greater understanding, appreciation, or closeness to their mothers as a result of having their own children. Many had thought through what their fathers' presence or absence in family life contributed to their mother's experiences. By becoming fathers, they gained new appreciation for the effects that fathers have on family life, and the way that fathers' engagement in family life effects maternal well-being.

CLOSER TO SIBLINGS, FAMILY IN GENERAL

Becoming a father offered men new ways to relate to their siblings, particularly if they already had children. This was true even if the family had been close growing up. The presence of children in your own family can bring close families even closer together. Roger felt that he had more connection to his family because of the increased attention and common ground of having children:

> We were all close as kids, and we always had a close family, but I always felt like, not an outsider, but I was never in the clique because they all had kids. It was kind of like, we'd get together and everybody would be talking about their kids, and I'd be sitting there, like, yeah, I'd play with the kids and all, but I didn't have a kid. I didn't have somebody that everybody could make a fuss over. And now that I do, and we go, we spend a lot more time together. And I told my parents that. I said I feel like when I had Matthew that my wife and I got even closer to the family.

Tim elaborated the same theme. Instead of focusing on attention and a sense of belonging, he emphasized the consensus building aspects of family get-togethers. These feelings had built over time. Being a younger sibling, he was "behind" his siblings in terms of making the transition to marriage and parenthood. By having children while his siblings' children were still young, he felt that he had "caught up" with them from a family life-cycle perspective:

> And with my siblings, all of us have kids so it's been good. I have three sisters and all of us have kids, it's nice, it's another way of drawing consensus. For a number of years, they were—either they had kids or they were married, and I wasn't. Or then I was married but they all had kids and I didn't. And now I've caught up with the three older siblings, and having kids. So it's been good, it's a way to share, it's just another thing we can build consensus on siblings, you know, what do you think of this, what do you think of that? We can—oh, actually it's been—you know, it's really been good for my wife, my siblings and my wife. All my sisters and my wife have really become a lot closer since she's had Andrew because they have been able to help her with, you know, tips and ideas, do this, the baby will like this, do that, and that sort of thing, and it's been really a positive thing for her.

Some men reported that they had less time to spend with their siblings because of their responsibilities with their own families. Yet others reported spending increased time or communication with their siblings. Much of this was perceived to be triggered by having children. Peter, who had enlisted in the air force, sensed that having children had increased his overall level of communication with his family:

> [There has been] a lot more like writing and sending pictures back and forth. ... Before, I was kind of anonymous out here, you know, I'd drop them a line every now and then. They couldn't contact me when I was in the barracks anyway, it was just too difficult. So anytime they heard from me is when I sought them out, and now that they can get a hold of me and they've got a lot more to talk about than just miscellaneous stuff, they contacted me more often.

As in the previous quote, not all increased closeness with siblings was attributed to having children. There are maturational and circumstantial factors that can contribute to sibling closeness as well. Glen expressed this well:

> I can tell you that my relationship with my siblings has greatly intensified over the past few years, maybe three to five years. I don't associate at all with fatherhood. I associate it with growing older and having a parent die and not having grandparents left. And um, living away from all siblings and my father, just a general desire to spend more time and get to know my, my siblings better. So, I don't know why, I don't, but I don't associate that with fatherhood at all. Its just kind of where I am in life.

RESPONSIBLE ADULT STATUS GRANTED

Some men talked about how they were viewed to be irresponsible or immature before having children. Becoming fathers launched them into a new status in the eyes of their parents or siblings. Fatherhood served as an indelible marker that indicated maturity and responsibility. Peter sensed a shift in the way his family perceived him since he had a baby. The tone and topics of conversation had shifted with his family members now that he had a child. Peter elaborated:

> I think my family out on the west coast might feel differently about me that I'm not so much of a punk kid now that I've got a family, and that I've got responsibilities and that they understand I've got to take care of him. And when I talk to them they ask me about those issues instead of other things that they might ask like, got any friends or anything like that, they ask how the baby is.

Alan sensed an increased sense of respect from his family as well. He felt that his parents had not believed that he and his wife were ready to handle the responsibilities of parenthood, but their success had garnered them a new level of respect and reciprocity in advice giving and receiving. In essence, now that they were successfully parenting their children, Alan and his wife were granted mature adult status by other family members:

> Researcher: How has parenthood affected your relationships to other relatives: your parents, brothers and sisters?
>
> Alan: They see us as, I guess, they see us as different people, they see us more matured, more responsible than we were before we had children. Before, they considered us, I guess, they considered us children ourselves, because, I guess we didn't go through the same, I guess, we didn't have the same responsibilities, or we see now what they had to go through. My mom has always told me from day one, when I was old enough to understand that some day you'll see what it's like to be a parent, you'll find out what heartaches you go through and everything, and you'll see the advantages and disadvantages of being a parent. And I see what she means now. There's a lot of problems that goes along with being a parent. The advantages outrun the disadvantages, I see. They see us as more responsible. They, when we first had my daughter, the first daughter, Rachel, they said that they would help us the best that they could, that we would need all the help, that we would need all the help that we could get. Where from day one, well, we found out that my wife was pregnant, we planned it, and we done everything together. We've amazed them because they didn't think we could do it. They see us as responsible adults now. And they come to us sometimes for problems they have—which is hard to believe—because I always thought me going to them—they come to me with their problems.

In extreme cases, having a child was an undeniable marker of heterosexual normalcy, and an indicator, therefore, of parents' success in raising "normal" offspring. Thomas reported that his parents were concerned about his ability to assume responsibility and his sexuality prior to his fathering of his first son. He was obviously repulsed by his father's attitudes and comments, but there was an apparent shift in the way that Thomas' parents viewed him. Thomas said:

> My parents were very worried about my being homosexual. They were very worried about whether or not I could take on responsibilities. And now, you know, Paul is like a trophy to them. It's kind of a marker that they had—the way that my dad put it. Once, [my father] said, "Now I have at least one son who's a success." That's a big disgusting caldron of problems. But that's kind of the way that he sees it.

Whereas Thomas' father had viewed Thomas' transition to parenthood as a positive achievement, Thomas resented his father's positive evaluation of the situation because he had required an overt sign of "success." Several fathers talked about differences in opinion or perspective with their fathers, but Thomas' statement of negative feelings toward his father were the strongest voiced in the sample. In fact, most fathers in the sample talked about ways that assuming fathering roles brought heightened levels of understanding between them and their fathers.

FATHERING FACILITATES UNDERSTANDING, VALUING, APPRECIATION OF RELATIVES

By far, the most common theme expressed by sample fathers was that they had gained a new level of understanding and appreciation for their parents, and they had placed a new value on what their parents had provided for them. Although this was far from universal, and it also was far from unidirectionally positive, it was prevalent. Even men who had new insights into their parents' behavior in a manner that made them more critical tended to have greater understanding and appreciation at the same time. Part of this appreciation comes purely from maturation. However, a greater degree results from the perspective shift of being a father. Roger stated it in this way:

> Like I said, the only I can think of is it's a different perspective now. When you're a kid, and you think you're father's telling you things, you always know more than your father does, until you're in your father's shoes. And it's kind of like, gosh, when I was a kid maybe I should have listened a little more, maybe took his advice a little more. A lot of things my father told me that I did do, I'd say probably ninety-nine point nine percent of them turned out right. There wasn't too many times he was wrong. But when you're a kid and you're, like, you know, I know more than that.

Manuel had experienced an increase in his understanding of his parents and their perspectives as well:

> Definitely more understanding. ... And um, I understand, I sit back some nights, now I understand why you did this. And now I also understand why they said, "You're going to get yours. Wait 'til you have kids some day." I used to, I never understood that until I had them. Now I see why they say, "Wait 'til you have kids." And I understand now.

Glen came to the realization that his parent's lack of involvement in attending athletic events and in being busy was not because they did not have interest. He came to realize that his parents had adopted their pattern of involvement due to time constraints. Although Glen seemed to be happy that his father was involved with his children, there is a hint of surprise and perhaps jealousy mixed in with his newfound understanding. In talking about his father, Glen said:

> He spends time with his grandchildren. Not only, our children, and he enjoys them. And uh, when we were growing up he had his own business and, and mom was the bookkeeper and so he worked very hard and she worked very

> hard. There was less time for us and I not really sure that I thought that … I don't want to say that he didn't enjoy us, but I mean, I grew up I don't remember him attending a swim meet or a baseball game or anything that I did. And he does that with his grandchildren now. So, I'm surprised by that, I just kind of thought that he was that way, and I find that maybe that it was the time and the financial constraints of the business that made him that way when we were growing up.

Glen elaborated further. He stated that he was purposely doing some things differently than his father had. This is a classic case of reworking:

> Yeah, it has and it partially answers you previous question on um, um, maybe more understanding of my father or my parents during my childhood. Yeah it does, I think sometimes I'm trying to um, say well these are parts of my childhood that I wish I had. I wish I had more time with my father, I wish I had more time with my parents. Going on vacations, I wish they just made me feel special, as opposed to the four of us. And, and so in some sense I try and do that with our children. Just take my daughter out, or just take my son out. Or go to school events because I want to. Not because my wife isn't there or not because, "Gee, I went to one last week, do I have to go again this week, but just cause I want to. So in some sense I think I'm trying to a say "Well, gee my parents didn't have any time for that cause they were busy with the business. So there's some hard feelings about that in some sense I think I recognize what they were going through and what they were doing the best they could as well. So I'm more appreciative or understanding.

Ken, a successful executive, reflected on his own decisions regarding parenting and how he had purposely planned to do some things differently than his father had. The challenges of succeeding at work and being as available to his family as he desired proved to be a challenge to Ken. In retrospect, he felt that his pattern of involvement had not been much different than his father's. Disappointed in his own parenting performance, Ken realized the difficulties of achieving balance in all that is needed, which brought him a heightened appreciation for his father's efforts and a measure of healing to the relationship:

> I think when I first had kids my objective was to be a super parent, was to be a lot better parent than my parents were to me. So there—well, actually maybe on the critical side, I saw the flaws coming out of teenagehood into young adult. You know, you kind of get to the point where you think your parents don't know anything and have made a lot of mistakes. And the piece that I disliked the most was that my father spent all his time working, day and night, owned his own business. And my mother was pretty, had low self-esteem, and so was not very actively involved with us either. So I was determined that my kids would see a lot of me, and that I would be involved in as much as I could be with them. What I saw in looking back over the time period now that I've

spent raising my kids is that I haven't spent a huge amount of time with them either. There's been a lot of time working. And I've been away, times when I would have rather been home. Certainly my oldest son, I think, would say that I probably didn't spend enough time with him. So, you know, I can appreciate now the difficulties that my father had in trying to balance work and family, and how he was trying to provide for his family. So probably there's been even some healing done there in our relationships. But that didn't occur until recently. And I'm getting to where I'm the parent of adults or young adults. So it's been a number of years to be able to look back on. So I think there's benefit. But I think there's some criticality there, too, that you'd like to be different.

Some men were able to articulate understanding beyond that gained in regard to their own parents' emotions, decisions, or behaviors. They expressed a new appreciation for intergenerational relationships and the continuity of generations. Ken expressed it this way:

I think that there's a, certainly the understanding your parents better after being a parent, you know, that certainly happens. But I think it's even more than that. I think it's just continuity of kind of generational life, and a stream of life that you start to see.

Becoming a father also helps men to regard their parents from the perspective of their parents' peers. Several men talked through the perceptual switch that occurred when they came to the realization that their parents were people too. Such a realization is hindered by the child's magical perspective that their parents are all-knowing and perfect. Steve talked about his parents from his new perspective in this manner:

When you're growing up as a child, I was under the impression my parents were super people, you know, superman, superwoman, my mother had X-ray eyes, ultrasonic hearing. My father was perfect, not an error in him, or at least that was what I thought. Then also, by the same token, it was almost, you know, it's like, well, I wouldn't do that if I was a parent. And when I grow up and I'm going to be a mom and dad, I'll always let them have ice cream anytime they want or anything like this, you know. And then you have kids and then you realize that when you have those children and you're taking care of them, everything you have done to your parents is coming back to you now. Every single thing, every worry, every restless minute they had worrying about you, everything is coming back to you. So it goes back down to the cliche what goes around comes around. It's like I'm going through the thing with my sixteen-year-old daughter, she's at that independence age. I remember when I was sixteen and it's like I must have been like holy hell and a terror to my parents, because my older brother moved out. I was there all alone with my parents. And I was the youngest, the most irresponsible, the most immature, but the most head-strong; I can do it myself. I'm going through that now with

> my sixteen-year old. I can see this. I can see exactly what my parents went through and who they are as people, and actually it took a long time. I was actually in my late twenties before I realized who my parents are as people and what their social standing is, or how they compare or are seen in the eyes of their peers, you know.

Now that Steve had children of his own, he understood the challenges that he had presented to his parents. He was now also able to think of them as people with peers. Each of the previous quotes indicates a greater degree of understanding.

SOME FATHERS BECOME MORE CRITICAL

Greater understanding does not always lead to greater appreciation or valuing. Sometimes it allows greater criticism. Some are reluctant to evaluate what it is like to fill a role until they have been there themselves. Once they experience it, however, they may find that it is considerably more enjoyable or easier than they had ever imagined. This can lead to devaluation of previously held judgments regarding how well their parents had done. Tim had that experience:

> I think [fatherhood] it's affected my relationship with my dad a bit. ... I guess I've got a lot of emotional baggage with my dad for the most part. ... He'd always say things like, "Wait until you have kids then you'll see what it's like." And I'm having kids, and I'm going, "Yeah, I see what it's like, it's great. So what was the big problem, you know, why was having kids such a chore for you?"
>
> Researcher: Has it made you more critical then?
>
> Tim: Yeah, I think so, which perhaps maybe isn't fair because he had four and I only have one right now. Maybe down the line it will even itself out. But yeah, that's made me feel a little more critical, I think.

Tim was enjoying fathering much more than he anticipated, and it made his father's lack of enjoyment all the more striking and disappointing. It caused guarded criticism, because Tim recognized that, by comparison, his father had more responsibility in regard to the number and age of children. Still, it seemed clear that Tim perceived himself to be in a very different place than his father. Consistent with his earlier expression of family friction, Thomas did not qualify his criticism:

> It's caused me to be more critical of my parents, especially my father's activities. My dad was a bastard. He worked all the time—and I guess I give him his due for his economic successes. But he was abusive, verbally abusive, and completely out of touch until all of us started having successes. And then he was there to take the credit for it. And several times, when I was in graduate school and

> visiting, he paraded me around. You know, I really hate him for that. You know, because it was really taking what was my achievement and making it his, or attempting to make it his. And my own activity, my own actions, instead of telling him to go fuck himself was, you know, to sit by and act like a trophy. You know, not say anything, just kind of be quiet and shake hands with all these friends that were my dad's friends and being introduced to. And then on the one particular trip, I spent half of it at the beach in a hotel by myself because I needed to get away from that. In my own activity, actions, I'm trying very hard not to do those things because it's given me nothing but grief.

Thomas had made a conscious decision to behave differently in regard to claiming success for his children's activities. Most men in the sample experienced blends of understanding, criticism, and appreciation. Their enhanced understanding may have increased both criticism and appreciation. One way to view this is that greater cognitive complexity is achieved through fathering—there is greater integration and differentiation at the same time—and this is mirrored in greater understanding leading to both greater criticism and greater appreciation. Of course, there are blends across areas (e.g., a father may come to appreciate the physical provision of his father to a greater extent than he ever had, and yet to criticize the amount of time he spent away from home).

MODELING FATHERS

As stated earlier, few men spontaneously discussed the positive things they desired to model from their fathers. Those who did recognized limitations and shortcomings as well. Neil reflected on his desire and tendency to model his parents, and the tensions created in trying to meet their standards while being his own person:

> Somewhere along the line I got the idea that I was to emulate my parents. So that's what I did, I tried to do whatever I thought they wanted me to do and yet still do my own, what I wanted to do, … so I was trapped between deciding what I wanted to do or what they wanted to do. So I recognize that, fortunately, and I try not to do that to my kids. So I try to say to them, if I have a specific desire for them I'll spell that out and tell them, that's what I want you to you do, and here's why. And if not, as long as what they want to do falls within the dictates of my moral reasoning, I'll let them do it.

Tom admired his father's ability to deal with crises and difficult situations in a calm manner. He recognized that it made his father more approachable than his mother, and he desired to operate in a calm manner so that he would be approachable to his children as well. Tom said:

> The way that my father always tried to be temperate—we could tell when he'd lose his temper and stuff. He tried to be real fair about stuff. Like the first time

> I got a speeding ticket, you know, I went and told dad. Dad said, okay, how fast were you doing? Where was it? When do you have to go see the judge type thing. And at the same time my mother's flying off the handle—well, you went and told your father about that but you couldn't tell me. Well, yeah, right, ma, because you're blowing off the handle. My mother always did tend to blow off the handle over things real easy. I've tried to remember that and tried to do stuff in my father's way as best I could. But every once in awhile he'd lose it, and blow off the handle. But then afterwards sit down and talk, and try to talk to me and explain what he was feeling, [and understand] what I felt, you know, after both of us settled down.

This quote gives an example of learning to control emotions (see chap. 5, this vol.) through modeling. Tim's statement captures the truth that even "good" fathers, usually worthy of modeling, have flaws and weaknesses that result in occasional lapses of positive fathering behavior. The quote also demonstrates, however, that fathers who motivate their sons to model them have ways to bring healing and understanding when they do not conduct themselves in positive ways.

REWORKING FATHERS

It was quite common for men in the sample to discuss the need to rework things that they had learned from their fathers growing up. Most common was the perception that fathers of the past generation were too invested in career or providing to give the time and attention needed at home. Although they may have been perceived as adequate or excellent providers, they were still not viewed to be family men in the contemporary sense. Most of the reworking included an element of wanting to compensate for perceived lack in their own lives. They wanted to "be there" for their children in a manner that superseded what their fathers were able or willing to invest in them. Gilbert recognized that there were both positive and negative elements to the way he was raised. Over time, some of the values that Gilbert had placed on different aspects of his childhood experiences had shifted:

> It's funny because a lot of the things that you thought were bad about your childhood, when you stop and reflect, you realize it wasn't that bad. And then some of the things that you thought was good, you realize that it could have been better.

Leo observed his parents in order to learn some positive parenting techniques, as well as some tendencies to avoid in his own parenting. His reflective observations had brought him to some conscious decisions about how he wanted to raise his own children:

> Observing the way my parents raised me has made me very aware of how I want to raise my children. I feel my parents have made some mistakes in the

> way they raised not only me but my four brothers and my sister. … My dad was always in business and my dad was always an employer and it didn't matter who was working for him, whether it was one of his own sons or daughter or someone that came off the street. He was the employer. Unfortunately, he was not only the employer at work, he was the employer at home. And there are only two times a year through the years that I have grown up with my father that I the felt like I had a father and that was Christmas day, it was always a very special time and then once a year we would take a trip to Canada fishing for a week. So two times a year and I had father and the rest of my life I had an employer that I worked with and lived with. He taught me to work. I appreciate that and he was also a very godly man. He taught me to love and respect the Lord, the importance and the value of church. So I respect the heritage and the relationship that I have with the Lord, because of my dad and I think he really taught me how to work, but I think I lost a dad. So having kids kind of made me aware of those things, gave me the desire to change them.

Alan was raised by a stepfather and did not want to participate in activities that he perceived to require a "real father." He made some decisions about availability to his children and involvement in their lives, rearranging his schedule and making a point to be involved with them. He said:

> Like … going on camping trips with different relatives where fathers and their sons went out. I couldn't go because I didn't have—my real father wasn't with me. And I wasn't going to go with a stepfather because he wasn't my father. So, there was just things that you needed a father for that I couldn't do. But now I'm being more of a father to my children than I ever had. So, I'm trying to make up for what I didn't get when I was a kid, for them, so that they can never say that they never had, you know, whatever it is. My daughter's getting ready to start dance class. I've let work know that I want to rearrange my schedule a little bit so that I can go with her to her dance classes. I want to spend as much time with her as I can so that she can never say daddy was never there. Because I'm always there—when she was in the hospital. My wife said, No, you don't have to get off work, I can stay there. But nope, I want to stay with her. Because there was times when I was younger that I had medical problems with my ears, my father was never there with me when I needed him there. So, now when my daughter went into the hospital, when she was sick, I wanted to stay there with her. And I feel my daughter and I have gotten closer because, when my daughter first was born it was just, my wife was the one that stayed home with them all the time, and I was always working. So, I never saw them—saw my daughter. And now that we're on our own and everything, I feel that I'm spending more time with her. And when I went to the hospital, she didn't want my wife to stay with her, she kept asking for me. So, I thought that was good. So, from the time she was born until, I guess, she was a year-and-a-half, she was always with my wife, my mom or whatever. And she always went with mom-mom and mom all time. But now she's asking for me, and I thought that was good. Because I see that we're getting closer and that she sees me as daddy that she knows that I'm there for her.

Among the most distressing realizations a father can have is that he is following in the footsteps of his own father in ways that he perceives to be inadequate. Men will exert significant effort to be different along the dimensions that they found to be most lacking in their own lives. Steve talked about this issue:

> I realized some years ago, though, I'm becoming my parents, my father. I was becoming my father and it wasn't, I didn't want to become my father. Especially when I was a kid, ... like this is the impression that he gave me, he was perfect. It doesn't necessarily mean I believed everything about it. There were certain things he did that I didn't want to do, and I retained that. When I seen a few years back that I was starting to become my father I took a backtrack, and really got in touch with myself as a child.

Steve made some decisions to change his current fathering behavior by recalling his feelings as a child. By getting in touch with these feelings, he was motivated to bring changes that he perceived to be needed. He wanted things to be better for his children.

BECOMING MORE SELF-CRITICAL

As men become fathers, they do not just become more critical of their own fathers. They also engage in a fair amount of introspection and evaluate themselves by whatever yardsticks they view as appropriate. Virtually every father I have ever met has a true desire to provide positive and developmentally facilitative atmospheres for their children. Some are painfully aware of their own flaws and shortcomings as they desire to do better for their children. Ken perceptively talked about the Law of Flaws:

> It made me examine my childhood, and tried to come to grips with how I was parented, and how that shaped who I am. And seeing my kids developed made me raise up questions about well, gee, they do things this way and I do things a little differently, and why is that? Especially in areas that I think are flaws or faults in myself. ... But it's kind of a law in yourself to have some flaws, seeing that doing the best you can, your kids are going to have them, too. And that's a very frustrating difficult realization because you don't want that for your kids. But it's the case anyways, no perfect parenting.

The overall picture that emerges is that when men assume active fathering roles, most experience positive changes in their families. Active engagement in fathering serves as a turning point that brings perceptions of more time spent with extended family and more communication. Becoming a father tends to engender greater degrees of closeness between men and their own fathers, mothers, sisters, and brothers. It opens a realm of communication, gathering, and mutual support that did not previously exist. Active engagement in the fathering role triggers reflection that fosters greater empathy between a father and his parents, greater understanding, and greater appreciation. It can bring healing through understanding. It can also bring a perception of a new level of responsibility and peer status.

In contrast, some men find that they have less time to invest in extended family relationships. As they engage in fathering roles, they become more critical of their own parents, especially their fathers. Clashes in values or relational styles leads to more friction, conflict, and distance.

RELATIVE BALANCES

The reality is that becoming an involved father brings a blend of positive and negative experiences to families. More time spent together in new arenas of interacting can be a stimulus for new ways to bond or new areas of conflict to arise (or both). Fathers work through shifting balances between increased understanding and criticism of their own parents, modeling and reworking, closeness versus the need to establish independence, and being an adult parent and an adult child. These balances are interdependent and overlapping as men mature as fathers, sons, and siblings. The manner in which these balances are experienced, negotiated, and expressed affect the perceived quality of intergenerational relationships within families. The emotional climate of a family where a father is centered in more modeling than reworking, more understanding than criticism of his parents, and more closeness than independence is different than families where the opposite valences are operative. Of course, the way that a father's parents and other relatives perceive and expect family relationships to develop is pivotal in effecting the emotional warmth and openness of communication that takes place around these issues. The conduct of much of this content is private and personal. Few families have intergenerational discussions regarding the relations between fathering and family relationships. Understanding the primary issues and typical ways of approaching them may facilitate intergenerational communication and adaptation as sons become fathers and parents become grandparents.

Chapter **10**

The Social World of Fathers: Friends and Community Involvement

As in other areas of development described so far, men felt their involvement as fathers had changed their social relationships to a significant degree. Virtually all fathers noted changes in frequencies of social activities. Some men felt that, overall, their social level was diminished or hindered by fathering, whereas others perceived enhanced social worlds. Having children can lead to a broader social network that is based around similar interests or activities, but those relationships tend to be relatively short lived, less intimate, and more surface. The focus on shared activity at the expense of the opportunity to explore shared ideals limits the developmental complexity of friendships during adulthood.

A new view of developmental maturity supported by these data, proposes that it regresses in many men during adulthood—at least when relationships are child centered or child initiated. Meaningful social relationships that persisted over time tended to have their origins before the transition to fatherhood and continued to have significant meaning and closeness for men. However, even long-standing friendships are perceived to change due to children.

The years of active engagement in their children's lives can be perceived to be a time of relative isolation for fathers. On the other hand, social relationships can be enhanced: more network, more diversity (in some ways), more communication, more positive behaviors, and greater responsibility.

EXPERIENCES OF DIMINISHED SOCIAL LIFE

Men who focused on the losses that they experienced in terms of time and closeness with friends felt that fathering had negatively influenced their friendship patterns. This was the most common pattern displayed by men in the sample. Quite a large group of fathers felt their social lives had been seriously compromised or given up. The reasons they cited varied considerably, and ranged across a number of categories. Some reasons were practical, and others were philosophical. Practically speaking, they cited lack of time, financial limitations (e.g., the cost of getting sitters or the need to curtail "extra" expenses that previously would have funded social activities), practical concerns with finding appropriate sitting or child care, the prevalence of child-exclusive activities, and a decrease in the frequency of spontaneous events. Philosophically, they discussed having previously been involved with people who had held the "wrong focus" (e.g., partying lifestyles or gambling or substance abuse), shifting priorities, and the shallow nature of prior social relationships.

Anthony felt his social life had changed dramatically since becoming a father. He indicated that he and his wife spent available time alone together as opposed to with groups of friends. He stated:

> I don't think we have much of a social life now with the kids, we just don't have time for it. The only time we want is to spend it with each other when we go out, we go out to see a movie or something. We need that. ... Overall, we had some social friends before we started having children, but all that is history. Gone. They're all gone. We don't maintain them.

Anthony's comments reflect a shift in priorities. Since having children, he and his spouse preferred to spend time alone focusing on their relationship, as opposed to investing in and maintaining other friendships. Similarly, Steve's comments show that active fathering was associated with shifts in time spent with friends as well as the value placed on friendships:

> I used to place a whole lot of value on my social life and friendships. Then as I started having kids, and getting busier and busier and having to work more, and I'd spend less time with my friends, they would be like, "you know, you must not like us any more, you don't come around that much any more, you know, you're snobbing us," or something like that. I used to be concerned about it, and now I'm not. I could care less what they feel and what they think. If I got kids and I've got to be home and I'm coming over and I can only spend an hour, and you get upset because I left after an hour and you want me to stay and have that beer and everything, well, I'm going out that door, and you can't stop me. And before I had kids, if I went somewhere and I really didn't want to stay somewhere, I probably stayed. It's affected me in a way that I probably place less values on my friendships and social life.

Steve's comments show that having children provided the impetus necessary to work through situations that he previously found to be uncomfortable. In the past, he had stayed in social settings longer than he was comfortable, but since having children, he left similar settings using time with his children as justification. Craig attributed the change in his friendship patterns to shifts in demands on his time as a father as well. Because there are a limited number of hours in the day, time must be spent on important things. Craig's comments make it clear that he had assigned involved fathering a higher priority in his use of time than friendship:

> It's time management. There are some people without kids who have extra time and some people with kids who don't. Instead of hanging out with friends and talking about cars or talking about sports or anything, you're home putting kids to bed or giving them baths or cleaning the house, making lunches. It's time management. You don't have any time, so you ration it out to the more important things.

Similarly, Vincente attributed changes in time socializing to adjusted priorities. He perceived that he spent more time at home since having children. He felt he had little time for anything beyond work and spending time with his daughter. However, he did manage to squeeze in time at the gym. He admitted:

> My life used to be nothing but a social life. I stay in the house a lot now. Maybe twice out of the month, I may go to the local bar and sit and have a beer, you know. And that might be for about an hour. And then I'm back home, you know, or I'm spending time with my daughter. It goes back to working and spending time with my daughter at home. That's basically all I do outside of going to the gym.

Active engagement in fathering can bring significant shifts in the basic texture of social time. Bruce's reflections show that network size is not the only factor effected by active fathering. Types of activities engaged in change as well. A significant proportion of the sample voiced parallel shifts from male-only sports centered and leisure-time activities toward child- or family-centered activities. Bruce voiced it this way:

> I hardly ever see friends.
>
> Researcher: So there's a big contrast to before kids?
>
> Bruce: Yes.
>
> Researcher: Is there a contrast in comparison to when you were married but without children?
>
> Bruce: Yeah. I still played racquetball and saw my friends, and we played basketball.
>
> Researcher: So you feel it's affected the number of people you interact with?
>
> Bruce: Yeah, sure.
>
> Researcher: Can you make a comparison, say, before kids I had a network of X number of friends and now I have so many?
>
> Bruce: You know, I had at least five good friends that I would see almost once a week, probably more than that.

> Researcher: And now?
>
> Bruce: I haven't seen them in years.
>
> Researcher: Has there been a change in the types of people you spend time with?
>
> Bruce: Well, yeah, now everything's all kid-related.

Many men perceived that engagement in fathering activities changed the nature, frequency, and duration of social interactions. Most men felt that fathering had brought accompanying decreases in friendship.

ENHANCED SOCIAL LIFE

In contrast, other fathers experienced increased or enhanced social lives. These tended to be fathers who had made a conscious decision and held to the perceptual frame that this was the "time of life" for centering on children and if that shift transformed friendships, then they would make the best of it. Men in this group of fathers stated that they now had more to talk about with others (kids and their interests and development), and they attended more child-centered or child-initiated activities, which placed interactions in an informal and relaxed setting. They were engaged in more home-based or home-centered activities, had experienced more social contacts, and were challenged to juggle all of their social calendars. Greg is a good example:

> Researcher: Do you think there's been an overall change in the number of people you interact with?
>
> Greg: Oh, yeah. I'd say just by becoming involved in the YMCA program and the dads and the Indian Princess thing, you're meeting other people that normally you'd never meet on the face of the earth and they don't care where you work or what you do. You get together once a month and you go on different outings.

Greg's comments reflect that child-centered social encounters have different qualities than other types of adult social relationships. Specifically, the people met through child-centered activities are from different social circles than he would have ordinarily encountered. Further, the common focus on child-centered activities and childrearing serves as a social filter that brings a homogamy along a different dimension that can supersede other filters such as occupational status or social class. Active engagement with children creates a different set of parameters and interactive contexts than occupational or educational filters. Some men experience enhanced social relationships by framing this phase of their lives as the time to focus on children and their interests, and may genuinely connect with the parents of other children. Leo had made a conscious decision to have his home be his children's social epicenter and had made a choice to establish relationships with the parents of the children who were spending time at his home. He explained:

> Because I want my kids and all of their friends involved in our home, I have to discipline myself to make my home interesting to them and I want to know what they're doing and so I want to be involved with them all the time. I don't think that I would normally do that if I was not so interested in the future of my kids and the way I was brought up. So I really strive to get involved in the things that they do, the friends that they have and even try to get to know the parents of the kids that are involved. So I find myself disciplining myself to communicate to those people and get involved in their lives.

Leo's comments indicate that he had decided to invest the effort to get involved in the lives of his children's friends and their parents. Whereas Leo used his home as a center for building child-initiated relationships, other men talked about changes in social relationships with other children and parents outside of home-based contexts. Consider Ken's situation:

> Researcher: Any effect on the types of people you spend time with?
>
> Ken: Like I said, I think you spend more time with other parents. But I'm finding that I have also spent more time with other kids, friends of the family—which is also really rewarding. I'm sure I wouldn't have done that without my kids. No way I would have tied into those other neat kids.

Ken, whose children were between age 16 and 22 at the time of the interview, focused on his extended social network with friends of his children. Those relationships may be gratifying and may provide a new perspective, however, they are seldom truly peer relationships. Although social networks may expand numerically and include greater age diversity than the networks of nonparents, fathers may not have as much time to invest in truly reciprocal peer relationships. John felt his social network had decreased in size since having his children. He had recently come to the realization that his children could create a context for meeting people and had decided to apply himself toward increased interaction. John said:

> I guess I was sheltering myself with my kids for a long time. But in the past year I've switched that around. I've tried to use them to my advantage to meet people, talk to people, get them to actually meet other little kids.

Paul noted that involvement with his children provided topics of conversation that facilitated interaction with other parents. Besides providing a common ground for discussion, his desire to model involvement in a faith community brought Paul into an expanded social network because he had begun to attend the same church as his wife since having children. Paul explained the situation:

> When you run into other parents, it just seems a lot easier to talk to them. I mean, you can discuss childhood and what the kids are doing and that kind of thing or some of the stages that they go through. So, I think that's helped me with, just in communicating with other people.
>
> Researcher: How about in terms of the number of people you interact with, your network size, do you think it's bigger, smaller, the same?
>
> Paul: I think it's bigger now. See, before I had a child, my wife—we went to church, so, our lives are kind of involved with church, too. And she went to Methodist church. And I would go with her sometimes but I kind of, I went to a Quaker meeting a lot of times by myself. But then after we had Bridget, I thought it was important just for the family to go. And since then, I've become more involved in the church, and I'm just more involved with a greater network of people now than I was before. And I know that is a consequence of having her.

PRACTICAL FACTORS

In discussing the relationships between fathering and friendships, it becomes apparent that many of the moderators of social lives are practical. When children are welcome at social events, they tend to be events that are child centered, or events where families are present. The nature of interactions, conversations, and activities are different there than in adult exclusive contexts. Further, when fathers attend child-centered events, these tend to take place in mixed gender as opposed to male-exclusive settings. When time is invested in these contexts, because time is a limited resource, fathers curtail the overall amount of time spent "with the fellas." Many couples lament the fact that these family-related gatherings frequently yield gender segregated subgroupings of adults, which may be a way to compensate for the lower overall amount of time spent in gender exclusive groupings of friends. Chris talked about changes in spontaneity and flexible, open-ended time to spend with his friends since becoming a father. He had experienced a decline in time with his friends and explained the change:

> I can't hang out all the time with my friends like I did before … the phone could ring and I could just pick up and instantly change and go on out with the fellas; not no more. I still—more financially I might not have the money to go out with them, or the timing might be bad, as far as a baby-sitter or whatever. My friends, we still hang out maybe, not as much or as many hours as we used to, but we still might hang out a little bit. Might go out and maybe have a beer or whatever, but it's like maybe have to rush home or whatever for the kids' sake, or something like that.

Craig noted a significant decrease in time spent with friends as well. The practical constraints of time, money, and the availability of a babysitter changed his friendship patterns. Use of extended family supports made some social interaction with friends possible, but more limited than the past:

> Researcher: Has fatherhood affected your social life or friendships any?
>
> Craig: Yeah. My social life has almost completely diminished. As far as, you know, going out after work or going out on weekends, it's a hassle just to find a sitter for three kids, it's kind of tough. The oldest one may go to an aunt's house or may go to her grandmother's house, but the other two are tougher to get a sitter for. As far as money being tight, once you do find a sitter and you pay them, then where are you going to go on a limited amount of cash?

Child-friendly contexts result in a different flow of conversation. Because the setting is more likely to be mixed gender, much of the focus is the kids, and conversations are frequently punctuated by interruptions from children, there is not the opportunity to get into "deep" subjects, or to work through issues that require intimacy. There is less likely to be alcohol involved, and even less likelihood of excessive consumption, so conversational flow is different. Randy addressed the changes in venue, activity, and conversation since having children.

> Well, before we had kids and it's even true with who we used to go out with. They didn't have kids, either, so we used to go out to a bar and we'd be there till two [a.m.], you know, if we had four drinks a night it would be a lot. But it was just someplace that we went.

Leo indicated that he is careful about the character of the people who become his friends because he recognizes that they will influence his children. He expressed that their moral character is more important than social status:

> I'm very careful on the type of people that I associate with. I want them to be clean and wholesome. I'm not too concerned about their social status or their financial status, but I want them more or less to be in agreement with me because the friends that I have ... become a part of my life and they also become a part of my kids' life and so I want my friends to have pretty excellent moral standards.

Joseph has made a similar change in friendships and kinds of activities. These changes have enhanced his self-concept:

> Researcher: Has it changed the types of people you spend time with?
>
> Joseph: Yeah. Like it's changed your company. You judge your company a lot better. Or just friends that you'd be around, if your friends were around that

> used to drink or smoke or whatever, maybe I might change them. Me personally, I did. And to me it's a better feeling because I feel better, to a degree, about myself. It's not that I dislike them or hate them or nothing, it's just that isn't the kind of life that I want to choose for my kids to be around, in that type of environment. Because it's like, it's like a disease and once you see something and you start picking it up, it's like a vice, it's a bad habit, hard to drop.

If children are not welcome at events, then a sitter is required, or fathers must decide whether they want to leave their families behind to attend. Because of availability of sitters, the financial constraints, the time limits imposed even when sitters are available, and feelings of guilt, fathers' social relationships in the absence of children tend to be limited. When they do occur, they are often with spouse alone, because time with others can be spent with kids too. This means that, overall, the amount of time men have to invest in male-centered or male-focused relationships is significantly different after having children. Adult-centered relationships diminish across time and the overall amount of intimacy declines. Glen revealed that he was looking forward to Monday night football because it provided a context and an opportunity for regular interaction with other men:

> I can't wait for Monday night football to start, cause that's kind of time for me to get together with the guys on a regular basis. Before children there was never any need for that, because if you wanted to you did it. If you didn't want to you didn't. ... Those things were satisfied just by default, they were all along. And now I find that well all the these other interactions and you know, the kids and the parents and the couples. Its just nice to be able to get a group of guys together and just watch football. And so we started out Monday night session and you know, that falls into the category of increased social interaction, because it's a regular thing set aside just to meet some other need, and that is "no women or children."

Glen's enthusiasm for get togethers with only men to meet a "need" would seem selfish and exclusionary to some. Some men feel that, philosophically, it is wrong to have events that preclude the participation of either females or children. Their partners and kids are part of the family, and they will not go if other family members are not welcome. Ned made the choice to stay home instead of attending events where his children were not welcome:

> Fatherhood has affected my social life and my friendships because a lot of times you'll—some people will have parties and they'll say, "No kids, we're not bringing kids today." So, I just don't go to those parties. I feel that unless it's a party where there's going to be a lot of drinking, stuff like that—which I don't drink at all. But if I'm going to somebody's house and they say, "No kids," well then, I just don't go. I think they're part of my family. They are my family, my unit. So it's affected a whole bunch.

LONGEVITY OF FRIENDSHIPS

In regard to longevity of social relationships, the nature or style of the fathers' friendships and relationships mattered immensely. If they were "old time" friends (those preceding the transition to parenthood), who changed in synchrony with men as they became engaged fathers, then the relationships were maintained despite less shared time and spontaneity. This was particularly true if both men in the relationship had children, or if those without children were "child friendly." When men get together with friends who do not have children, they are very conscious of the effects of their children on the relationship (when kids are present). They often feel that friends do not understand what it is like to have kids, or that the children bring obstacles into the relationship. Steve felt that his social network had decreased in size and his social contact frequency had diminished since having children:

> I interact with a lot less people. I used to have a clique of probably twenty or thirty people, regular basis of seeing these people twice weekly, or at least weekly. It's now four or five people that I interact with. These are close old friends of mine that I've known for a long time. And I value their friendships because of the longevity of the friendship. And I have so few friends, I only want to keep up with close knit of friends. That's all I have time for.

In a different pattern, Roger had a close friend who was able to understand his need to spend time with his son. His friend adapted to changes in Roger's time commitments and had developed a relationship with Roger's son. His friend's adaptability and child-friendly demeanor allowed their ongoing friendship to continue. At the same time, his other friends were making the transition to parenthood as well, and their foci had changed in a manner that paralleled his own changes. Roger elaborated:

> It hasn't really changed my friendships at all. My best friend is single, he's not married, doesn't have any kids, and hasn't changed my relationship with him. We still spend time to go out and have a beer once in a while. He comes over a lot to see Matthew; he really likes kids. So, it's not like one of those situations where, "I'm not coming over there, you got a kid, and he's going to drive me crazy." And he's probably the guy I spend the most time with, so it's a lot easier that he likes kids and Matthew likes him, likes doing things with him and stuff. So, it hasn't really changed—like I say, last year we used to go play, the year before, when Matthew was born, we used to go play softball. You know, take my wife, we'd go play softball, and we'd go out, and we'd all go to Gallucio's [a local tavern/restaurant] and have a couple beers and pizza. Now, it's stay out to till twelve, twelve-thirty. Now, it seems like that crowd we were hanging out with is all having kids now. So, now we go play softball. We go to a family place, have pizza, or we go to Charcoal Pit [a local family restaurant], or something like that, everybody grab something to eat, and then we'll be home by nine

clock. So it's, my friends almost have changed the way I've changed. They're all starting to have kids, and starting to build families. So, it hasn't been a point where I look back and go, gosh, I wish I could be back where I was because all my friends are doing this. No, they've kind of basically changed with me.

Roger had stopped going on an annual weeklong golfing outing with his friends. I wanted to know if that was an indication that he had made a conscious decision to invest more time and energy into his family and to distance himself from his male friends. He felt that his decision to curtail the annual golfing pilgrimage had not really detracted from his friendships. He then elaborated on the reason for his decision to stay home from the trip:

Researcher: So, one way to interpret what you said earlier about being less likely to take off with the guys for a few days, or go on a trip or something, would be that you have, in a sense, distanced yourself from your friends to invest more time in your family. And I guess what I want to know is, overall, has that affected your closeness to your friends?

Roger: No. Like I said the trip, the go away for the weekend, when I used to go to Myrtle Beach in September for a week every year, and we'd go play golf and have a good time down there for a week. And, you know, I'd be leaving my wife behind. You know, well she can get along by herself. And now it's kind of like, I don't think I could leave him for a week. I don't think I could risk, you know, me missing something that he does in a whole week's time. You tell yourself, oh, it would be easy to do that; no way, not when you're actually with him, you know, I can't leave him for a week. And now it's kind of like my friends realize that. Like I say, I thought I'd be able to go for week and all that. But like I said, I don't think that I can, and I don't really want to. It's kind of like, you guys have a good time, and let me know how it is when you get back. And like I say I still spend time golfing during the week with them, on the weekends. And it's not like I'm missing out on something. Down the road he gets a little older, maybe I'll go back, maybe I won't, but not at this age. There's too much going on right now.

Roger felt that the annual trips may resume when his son gets older. It is interesting that he expressed that his wife could get along without him for a week. Assuming that she was a competent caregiver, his son could get along without him as well. However, the pull of his son's relationship became obvious in his statement. Roger did not want to miss his son's attainment of a developmental milestone. His involvement with his son kept him from wanting to go away for a few days.

Some of the effects of changes in social relationships were very much influenced by temporal issues directly linked to child development. Social relationships change as the age and developmental capabilities of children change. During infancy, fathers and mothers may experience a greater degree of exhaustion and more emotional and cognitive energy drain to make satisfactory adjustments to parenting. While children are infants, however, there are usually fewer issues of whether the children's social networks are positive and fewer child control issues.

These realizations were more common to older fathers, and changes in socializing were seen as temporary. However, it can be discouraging to young fathers to think their social lives are severely suppressed or "ruined," and things will never change. Young fathers need to hear the message of men with older children—the transformation of friendship patterns can be relatively short lived. This set of findings has implications for social support programs for fathers: There is a critical need for support regarding friendship patterns early in the transition to parenthood.

Older children frequently play the role of social "matchmaker" by initiating relationships through shared activities such as sports, school, or community events. However, the typical resulting adult friendships tend to be short lived relative to previous or long-standing relationships. This is because the interests, groupings, and development of children change quite rapidly. The "soccer dads" who were friends this season through joint participation in their kids' practices or attending team games or picnics may be involved in two separate activities (e.g., one goes into scouting or plays football instead of soccer) next season or year, so fathers never have a child-initiated context in which to see one another again. Thus, although child-centered activities may be gateways to relationship formation, the relationships are typically not as long lived or intimate as other relationships. They are characterized by less intensity, less disclosure, and less listening. As such, child-initiated friendships tend to be developmentally less mature than adult-initiated relationships. When social capital is continually invested in these contexts, the personal nature of friendships suffers. Ongoing friendships are more rare, and when they persist over time in the context of child-centered settings, they tend to be less mature. Men who withdrawl from more permanent and developed relationships for a season of child-centered relationships may be contributing to a sense of isolation and shallow, serial relationships that prohibit meaningful social support. By investing their time and energy into participation in child-centered events, men lay down time and energy that could be invested in mature reciprocal social relationships.

As children change activities (by season or by changes of interest), relationships with other parents must evolve if they are not to dissolve. Friendships forged around children's activities are characterized by the same tempo and developmental depth as children's activities. The size and nature of the social network changes, but depth and longevity tend to suffer. Tom has experienced this pattern of adult friendships forged in child activities. Although he had enjoyed the exchange of information and experienced a different mix of friends than he would have prior to having children, he recognized that long-term close relationships had not resulted. Tom disclosed:

> Over the years I have come up with friends that I probably wouldn't have had, but not bosom buddies—let's-go-out-fishing-and-drinking and stuff. I've come up with friends like through scouting and stuff, exchange of ideas between adults and different things. Like I've learned different things on how to cook quick for kids, you know, like how they can fix their own meals and things.

In a different pattern, Glen noted that he and his wife had formed friendships centered around their daughters' interests and activities that had lasted over the years. By comparison, when they attempted to build relationships with couples who did not have children, they were not as satisfying or as long lasting. Thus, Glen felt his daughters had brought a clarification of his values and foci that helped to serve as a selection filter for social relationships with other couples:

> Researcher: Do you think that since having children the number of people you interact with has changed, either increased or decreased?
>
> Glen: I'd say the number has increased and there's a turn over there. It's kind of something you see evolves too. That is, you kind of migrate to the people similar interests. Um so, where its increased it tends to be through people we've met because they have children or classmates of our daughters, that sort of thing. I find that it's ... what I would describe as difficult, having a, a meaningful friendship or relationship with another couple who does not have children. I found that its migrated to that, that, that those relationships lasted three, six months maybe a year. But not the not the years and years. And I've asked kind of "Why? Why is that?" ... I don't know ... it's not like there's not enough to talk about or enough common interests. Somehow there's just not as good a fit. ... I've found that we don't have um, any close relationships with couples who don't have children.

Some fathers suggested that friendships suffered because all their social capital was invested in children or work relationships. Others indicated that learning to communicate with their children and to consider their interests and viewpoints had helped them to develop more sensitive and responsive relationships as work. In addition, some men related that their relationships at work had improved as they began to discuss coworkers' children and families. The overall result was that they began to see one another as people with similar interests, common issues, and shared values instead of undefined workers. Talking more personally with coworkers regarding family life as opposed to only work-related topics brought a depth, common focus, and a sense of community and friendship that enriched relationships.

Clearly, the texture, the timing, and the flow of social events change after having children. Events tend to be more family centered, more likely to be based in a faith community, and less "party scene" oriented. Get togethers are of shorter duration (kids need naps, meals, and have shorter attention spans—they become bored or mischievous at places when they stay too long), less spontaneous, and less likely to entail "all weekend." In and of themselves, these changes are neither inherently more conducive nor prohibitive to developing socially meaningful relationships. However, many fathers indicate that although their social networks may be more extensive and more diverse since having children, they are also of shorter duration and less developed. Collin indicated that he had changed the types of people with whom he associated. Specifically, he pointed out that he and his wife spent less and less time with people who did not have children:

> When we became parents, what happened is that little by little, the friends we had who didn't have kids, we didn't see as often, and the friends who had kids, we saw more of. So that affected who our circle of friends were, who our primary associations were.

Similarly, Vincente changed his social networks after becoming a father:

> Before, most of the people that I hung around were usually single people, people who really didn't have the responsibilities of up-raising a family or anything like that. Whereas, now I find myself interacting with people who want a little more out of life, whose priorities are in a different perspective. Generally those people are usually family. And I'm finding myself being more interactive with them in being a social act and actually going outside of the family, having a social life.

Will stated the same theme:

> Mostly the people we interact with are those with children with compatible interests. In other words, we—especially my wife more so than me—we socialize with people that their children—or like go for gymnastics with my daughter or on the tennis circuit with my son. And just by coincidence my wife's running a tennis tournament this weekend; she was volunteered for it. So obviously, the children's activities affect our social activities. So we socialize with those with compatible interests.

The next quote shows that Jeff seemed willing to maintain friendship with his previous best friend, but the fact that his friend had six children prevented him from investing any significant time with Jeff. This brings out the point that fatherhood does not only change men who are fathers, but their age-mates who are having children. Because men respond differently to the pressures and demands of fatherhood (provision, time, etc.), different men engage in different patterns of social relationships. Thus, whereas a particular man may be adapting positively to fathering and may wish to invest in maintaining or building social relationships with other men, if they are fathers who do not perceive that they have the time or priority on friendship, then it can isolate men who are otherwise interested in investing in relationships. Another point that comes out in Jeff's statement is that the children's ages act as a filter of ongoing social relationships with other adults. If your children are not developmentally compatible, do not have the same interests, or are not of the same gender, then it may constrain ongoing relationships. Thus, as parents have children, invest time and energy into raising them, and look for others who have similar family configurations and interests, the pool of possible friends becomes narrowed quickly. As fathers struggle to balance all of the demands on their schedules and resources, the ability to coordinate schedules with others is compromised. It is no wonder that many men who are involved with their children have a sense of isolation from meaningful friendships. Consider the following exchange:

> Researcher: Do you think that fatherhood has affected your social life or friendships in any way?
>
> Jeff: Yeah. Actually, my best friend's fatherhood has—my best friend in high school's fatherhood has probably affected that more, because he has six kids and we never see him. Well, my wife's friends tended to fall—their kids tend to be the same age as ours, so we're pretty close with a couple of them. You know, I guess you tend to have more in common with people who do have kids, as opposed to, you know, singles. We have in the past had, say, some single people or some unmarried couples, or some married couples without, who don't have children over. And, you know, sometimes you wonder, how are they handling this. And they're not used to being around kids, especially our kids. So yeah, I think we tend to hang out with people who are like us, and with the kids.

Peter's comments indicate that friendships during the period of heavy parent involvement may rely on more than the ability to coordinate schedules. He has experienced a change in priorities and interests that he likes to see reflected in friendships:

> The types of people that I've hung around with recently have been either fathers or mothers themselves, and there's just a little more rapport there and something more in common with someone whose got kids than doesn't. I've had friends that haven't had kids, and I look back and think how I was before I had kids, and it's the same kind of thing, there's definitely like—I don't know if you could call it a maturity change or just a different viewpoint. Instead of having a viewpoint where things can be less planned or more planned.

Although active father involvement can be costly to men's social relationships in many regards, community involvement tends to increase as fathers are actively involved with their children.

COMMUNITY INVOLVEMENT

Community involvement tends to be enhanced, both on formal and informal levels. Men become more aware of, more vocal in, and more vigilant regarding community issues. They tend to volunteer to be scout leaders, active church members who are engaged in children's programming, community organization members, and so forth. Even those men who do not engage directly in formal community activity tend to become more aware and engage in informal support structures: They are protective of kids on the street, they want to inform parents of unsafe or questionable behavior, and they try to engage kids in things that will keep them from drugs and violence. Men become more community centered when they have children growing up in a community, not only for the interest of their own children, but for the good of the children of the community. Men who never took an active interest in speed bumps, parks, school issues, or religious education are more likely to become engaged when their children participate. Ken reflected on changes in his community involvement in the following manner:

> It's hard to project, again, without kids, what you might have done. But a lot of what I do, have done, I was—let's see—little-league coach, Y basketball coach, high school J.V. basketball coach, soccer assistant coach, I ran for the school board, I helped build the school. Yeah, there's been an awful lot of activities that have revolved around the kids. And that's been great.

Ned recognized that as his children changed and matured, his involvement in different community organizations paralleled their changes:

> Researcher: Do you think that being a father has had any effect on your involvement in the community or in organizations?
>
> Ned: Big effect, big effect. Being a father and maturing as I go along, I do a lot. I'm into work with the Boy Scouts, and with my church. And I was a Cub Scout leader for a while when my son was a Cub Scout. Now he's a Boy Scout, I don't do that. But now I still help with the Boy Scouts. So it's affected me a lot, yeah.

Similarly, Roger noted a change in interest in neighborhood association discussions that would affect his children's safety and development. He was engaging in community decision making with a new focus, interest, and energy. Roger's comments show how things that seemed inconsequential or irrelevant in the past now took on new levels of meaning and importance when considering the implications for his children:

> Well, we have the civic association over in our development. And it's kind of got, you know, they're starting to talk about playgrounds and stuff like that. And before when it was just my wife and I, you really didn't care about a playground, you really didn't care what was happening with the speed bumps in the roads, because you didn't have any kids possibly running out in the roads. And now you get a little bit more involved when you know it's going to affect your family a little more. So, I know with our civic association we make sure that we're there at the meetings, and we participate, and we have a say in

what's going on in our community. Before it would be kind of like, well, if we're off that night, we'll go. If not, we'll see. But now there could be something that affects him, because we plan on living there for another two or three years. So, he's going to be able to reap in the benefits if there's a playground, or something like that. So, definitely more involvement in that kind of deal.

In terms of community involvement, two separate spheres must be distinguished—the formal and the informal. Formal involvements included civic associations (building ball fields, playgrounds, putting in speed bumps, joining community watch, YMCA involvement, coaching, scouting, 4-H, Indian guides, school board involvement, PTA participation, and church involvement and oversight of programming like Sunday school classes or youth group leadership). Informal community involvement was represented by more awareness and outgoingness within neighborhoods, encouraging kids to come in off of the streets into gyms, and so forth. Chris pinpointed some concerns:

Researcher: Do you think fatherhood's had any affect on how involved you are in your community?

Chris: Yeah. Because if they're out there playing around or whatever, I'm more out there being aware of it. And I try to keep the drug dealers from around there and the alcohol and all that stuff around in the neighborhood and keeping it clean or whatever, so, yeah.

At the very least, fathers relate a greater awareness and perspective on community events, and frequently discuss a greater involvement in community affairs—a form of generativity. A few fathers cut back on their community involvement to have more time with their families and children, but they were already unusually committed men.

FACTORS FACILITATING SOCIAL DEVELOPMENT OF FATHERS

The perceptual framework that fathers employed made a difference in their adjustment to changes in friendship patterns. This is well illustrated by Glen's comments:

Researcher: Another area, your social life. What do you think fatherhood has done in terms of social life or friendships?

Glen: It's um, been good, its been enhanced, its been different, sometimes I miss um, what it used to BK, before kids. We are very good friends with a couple that, that a I started work with in Richmond, so we've known them for 13 years. ... Its kind of the next phase in life that excepted and understood and kind of gone along with. Um you know, the times we get together tend to

> be shorter, no weekend trips with the kids. But we still get together and its around the children. Go to a park or cook-out or um, something like that.

SUMMARY

Father involvement and responsibility for children provides a developmental draw on men that causes them to tend to decrease their "party behavior," to spend more time in family and community settings, to take active roles in nurturing the well-being of their communities, and to invest in the next generation. Men who were never so inclined in the past are recruited to active engagement through the development and interests of their children. Thus, the ways that men engage In their neighborhoods changes after making a commitment to involvement with children.

From the transition to parenthood on, having children exerts an influence on our social networks. Parents are more likely to socialize with other parents. Parents make friends with other parents through meeting them at activities in which their children are mutually involved. However, it is also the case that relationships with other parents dissolve as children change activities (by season or by changes of interest). Friendships forged around children's activities are characterized by the same tempo and developmental depth as children's activities. The size and nature of the social network changes, but depth and longevity tend to suffer. Looking in your own community, it is likely the case that it is parents who are involved in the school board, athletic leagues, scouting, 4-H, religious youth groups, and other community organizations dealing with children. When fathers carry a part of the responsibility for organizing, supervising, and providing community resources for their own children, generative and altruistic investments in the community are fostered. Men in the study sample talked through their motivation to invest in the next generation by community involvement generated by their child's own needs. In a sense, children serve as matchmakers and position brokers in their fathers' lives, bringing shifts in men's friendship patterns and community involvement.

BALANCE ISSUES

Many of the balance issues faced by fathers in the sample could be characterized as having to do with keeping both their children and themselves happy and engaged in social relationships. Fathers often needed to consider what was good for their children and to attempt to balance that with what was good for their own relationships. Fathers balanced ways to develop their children's interests and abilities while cultivating their own relationships. Some fathers struggled with balancing larger social network involvement versus time with the family. This was related to keeping an appropriate balance in maintaining the family boundaries. Some fathers were faced with balancing a "single lifestyle" characterized by spontaneity and flexibility of time in gender-segregated groups and family or mixed gender activities. There were differences in the degree to which men found a sense of connection or belonging in family versus constructing meaning from friendships or community involvement. Sometimes, involvement in relationships with friends and other families or volunteer work caused men to confront issues of how to balance caring for the best interest of their own versus others' children. Once they became fathers, some men gave increased attention to the trade-offs between the depth and the breadth of friendship networks and the number versus the intensity of friendships.

Balance issues in social relationships and community involvement were extensive for fathers as they engaged in fathering their children. This is not surprising, given the reminder in chapter 1 that fathers are only fathers because of relationships. Choosing to invest time, attention, and energy into any given relationship requires reallocations of social capital from other relationships. As fathers experience and facilitate the development of their children, they experience developmental shifts in their own social maturity.

IV

The Work Domain

Chapter **11**

Provisional Balances: The Effects of Fathering on Work and Career Development

Professional literature has emphasized the new "culture of fatherhood" (LaRossa, 1988), highlighting caregiving and nurturant associations between fathers and their children (Robinson & Barret, 1986; Rotundo, 1985). Because work and family compete for a father's time and attention (Christiansen & Palkovitz, 2001; Cohen, 1993; Hood, 1986; Lamb et al., 1987; Levine & Pittinsky, 1997), a father's involvement in paid employment can be characterized as an excuse for "buy out," or an avoidance from involvement at home (Hochschild, 1997). This perspective may hold validity in some families, but this view does not represent the complex interactions between the numerous roles that fathers perform as they care for the needs of their families or the conflicts men face in balancing occupational development and involvement as fathers (Hood, 1986).

This chapter examines the balances fathers achieve between paternal involvement in childrearing, commitment to work, career trajectories, company policies toward father involvement in family matters, and men's perceptions of supports and barriers to involvement represented in the interface between the home and the workplace. Of particular interest are fathers' perceptions of the dialectics of involvement in family and workplace.

Questions concerning work occurred approximately 15 to 20 minutes into the interview. The first work-related questions were open ended, with more focused follow-up questions coming later. Although the interviewer used an adaptable interview schedule, the general flow of questions was as follows:

1. In terms of your work history or career, what impact, if any, has fathering had on your work?

2. Have there been occasions where you have had to call in or take time off of work because of the children? Have there been consequences for that?
3. Do you feel that if you had never had children that your career would be further along, just as far along as it is now, or not as advanced as it is now? Why do you say this?
4. Do you have any other thoughts on how work and fathering interact?

FINDINGS

Analyses indicate that there are diverse paths in experiencing and balancing strains arising from simultaneously occupying husband-father, provider, and worker roles (Cazenave, 1979; Christiansen & Palkovitz, 2001; Cohen & Durst, 1996; Palkovitz, 1994; Palkovitz et al., 1998). There are numerous ways in which fathers achieved "provisional balances" in their efforts to juggle responsibilities at work and at home. The provisional balances accounted for both the long-term stability and the short-term fluctuations noted earlier. Occupational trajectories did reflect relative stability, still there was substantial short-term variability in patterns of involvement at work and at home, reflecting vacillations in immediate needs or deadlines. A notable exception to long-term stability, discussed later, occurred in some men who experienced a fatherhood "snap" (Daniels & Weingarten, 1982) resulting in distinctive priority shifts in the prominence of providing relative to other roles.

In listening to men's statements about interfaces between home and work, it became evident that both work and family could "feed" or detract from one another. Simply stated, fathers perceived both positive and negative effects of work on families and of families on work. The nature of the current balance and the perceived dialectics between home and occupational settings significantly affected men's satisfaction in the provisional balances they had attained. In some ways, family experiences were perceived to support work. Specifically, men discussed how skills gained through fatherhood experiences could be seen as supporting their career development. There was also a clear recognition that components of work enhanced family life. Material provisions, job security, benefits packages, job prestige, and flexible schedules at the workplace contributed positively to family functioning. On the negative side, family afflictions could be a distraction at work and "bringing work home" (physically, mentally or emotionally), working extended hours, and lack of flexibility in the workplace brought strain to men while they were focused on carrying out their fathering roles (Bolger, DeLongis, Kessler, & Wethington, 1989; Hall & Richter, 1988).

The prevalence of the provider role (Christiansen & Palkovitz, 2001) was the primary theme that came through in men's statements about fatherhood and working. They regularly talked about the need to be working, and the need to be working in a job that provided a living wage, job security, and necessary benefits. In comparison to pre-fathering experiences, work took on greater meaning and held a place of elevated importance in men's thinking after having children. Chris spoke about how having a family motivates one to work more consistently:

> Well, if you have family, you do have to work. If I didn't have a family, I wouldn't have to work. You could lounge around ... really wasn't no push to work. If you got family, you got to provide for that family. So you definitely work more hours, work harder and be loyal to the company, I guess. ... But before, you could be—"I don't feel like going to work," and you didn't have to get up and go to work since you had no kids, no family. Now that you got kids or whatever, even if you don't feel like it, you got to still get up and go.

Chris' reflections emphasize the central and compelling nature of provision for fathers, the pull toward working longer hours, and the recognition that job performance (consistency, loyalty) could effect job security. Similarly, Alan, a full-time bank clerk, discussed how becoming a father had given more meaning to his work and guided decisions he had made regarding job selection and commitment:

> It's [fatherhood] had a great impact because, before I had children the jobs that I had were jobs that had no meaning. They were just, I guess, to get along so that I'd have things to do. Since I've had children I've had to, I guess, plant my feet and try ... [to] get a job where I know that I want to move along and make it into a career, knowing that I just can't work, I guess, say, work for three weeks and then decide I'm not going to go work anymore, or work maybe a day and decide that's not for me. I have to take a job where—I'm in a job now that has advancements. I'm putting my mind to it stating that I'm going to stay with it and move on, and it's what I'm going to do. It's what I want to do for the rest of my life, you know, to move up. It's a career move that I've made.

Both of the aforementioned quotes reflect the importance of providing, and the ability to stay with a job over time. The idea of career advancement and job stability take on greater importance in men's thinking once they become fathers. Although the previous quotes place positive emphases on increased commitment to working, at other times, providing is portrayed as a necessary evil: It is needed for economic sake, but it is viewed as antagonistic toward father involvement because it prohibits or constrains fathers from spending more time at home. As such, waged work away from home can be viewed as a barrier to being unrestrainedly involved in the emerging culture of the new "nurturant" father (Palkovitz, 1997; Robinson & Barret, 1986; Stearns, 1991).

Recently, Dienhart and Daly (1997) persuasively argued that the "culture of work" is one of a number of "informal and formal mechanisms that usurp the primacy of fathering in men's lives" (p. 149). When couples first become parents, many mothers restrict work involvement or totally terminate their employment. The associated decrease in income is accompanied by increased living expenses. To offset the loss of the mother's income and the new costs of parenthood, many fathers increase their commitment to work. Often, a salient component of fathers' increased commitment gets played out in more time at work and less time at home (Belsky & Kelley, 1994). Some fathers work multiple jobs in order to compensate for loss of the mother's income, or to offset increased expenses of raising children.

In regard to the perceived effect of fathering on work history and occupational advancements, three distinct pathways were observed in this sample of fathers. Since becoming fathers, some men experienced heightened dedication to and increased involvement in work because of their concern with responsibility for provision and modeling a good work ethic. In contrast, a second group of men had come to the realization that work was not as important to them as the time they could spend with their developing children, and as a consequence, reported decreased commitment to work in terms of time and energy invested. A third group asserted that fatherhood had no observable effect on their work histories.

SHIFTS IN PRIORITIES

All men who reported that fathering had precipitated either an increase or a decrease in occupational advancement or work trajectory described shifts in priorities. Those who observed greater commitment to work mentioned the need for steady income, job security, and the prevalence of the provider role in fatherhood as influencing their change in work patterns. Their children provided a "push," "drive," or commitment to work that these men had, for differing reasons, failed to acquire before becoming fathers. Bruce, a full-time office manager with two preschool-age children and a full-time employed wife, addressed the increased importance of work and greater motivation to perform well on the job after having children:

> You try harder at work because with the kids it's like that responsibility ... that everything matters more now. If you fail, then you know that it counts more. I mean, that's a lot more responsibility on your shoulders or whatever.

Bruce's statement reflects the commonly held belief that though lack of employment is serious for all men, the consequences of unemployment are more serious for fathers with families than for single men. As a father, "if you fail ... it counts more." John, a former corrections officer who was working part time in distributions at the time of the interview, remarked that having children provided a purpose for working. His construction of providing entails a sense of involvement (Christiansen & Palkovitz, 2001; Palkovitz, 1997) and extends beyond self-advancement and beyond basic providing to the ability to be generous in gift giving. He explained:

> I think it [fathering] made me want to work. When I was working it made me want to work ... for them, really. Not so much just when you're paying support or something, but for things that they need, and you want to support your family, so you do it for that purpose. That's your major goal once you get married, not so much for your self advancement. ... And now that they're there ... you want to get extra things, especially during the holiday seasons and things like Christmas. ... So it did have an effect that way, me working extra for them.

Other men talked about creating opportunities for their children to experience things like travel or going to events that require the availability of funds beyond basic economic provision.

Those fathers who reported less advancement or commitment to work had also experienced priority shifts—they aspired to spend more time with their families. Some men described deliberate decisions to enter the "daddy track" and a reluctance to "sacrifice" their families for the sake of furthering their status at work. The following quote is from Anthony, a union auto worker with three preschool children:

> Well, I just place the children before it [work]. If they're sick and they need to go some where, well then I won't go [to work], I don't care. ... Before I used to show up everyday ... because that's what they pay me to do. I used to have a pretty strong loyalty to [the company] until I got a little bit older and realized what it was all about. That you're just a head as they call you. That's all you are they don't really care. Since I became a father, as I said many times, the kids come first. If something happens and I have to leave the job, I leave the job and go, I don't care.

Anthony had experienced a reordering of priorities (kids come first), coupled with the realization that his personal fulfillment was not his employer's focus—recognizing that he was just a "head" to them, but he was "daddy" to his children—brought him to reprioritize the way his loyalties got worked out in terms of daily responsibilities.

Acknowledging providing as an important form of involvement in satisfying the needs of the family (Christiansen & Palkovitz, 2001) may help fathers find a balance between the two extremes of provider "role rejecters" and provider "role over performers" (Bernard, 1981). Provider role rejecters either abandon or discount the significance of the provider role. Provider role underperformers need to be stimulated to view economic providing as a legitimate and important way to be involved as fathers (Christiansen & Palkovitz, 2001). In contrast, provider role overperformers may behave in a manner that reflects "intoxication" with work at the expense of their family lives and describe economic providing as their principal or singular way of being involved in their families. Provider role overperformers need to recognize that monetary provisions are one out of an array of essential resources and must come to embrace the importance of other methods of providing in the home—cognitively, affectively, and behaviorally (Palkovitz, 1997).

If economic providing can be viewed as one component in a broad array of ways to be involved as a father, then men can be encouraged to ask "What is most needed or what is necessary?" (Bernard, 1981). In some cases, or at some times, the appropriate answer may require greater involvement at home, and in other cases, or at other times, increased dedication to work is needed. Balances between family and work involvement are truly provisional, shifting as needs at home and in the workplace fluctuate. Provisional balances are easier to achieve when increased demands for direct involvement at home are yoked with lower demands and/or greater flexibility at work. In contrast, when economic demands of family life are greatest, fathers find it easier to provide adequately when there are increased demands for waged work, such as the need for overtime. Salaried workers sometimes consider moonlighting as a means of increasing their earnings, because greater commitment in regard to time on the job does not yield short-term gains in compensation.

Jeff, a refinery operator with children ages 8 and 10, explicitly addressed the tensions between involvement in providing versus home and placed a higher priority on fathering than on career advancement:

> Well, it's made me not willing to sacrifice my family for my work. I've had opportunities for promotions and transfers that I've turned down because it would have adversely affected the family. And in a way, I paid for it in one area, because I could be making a lot more money than I am now in another job, but it wasn't worth it. And so I've probably stunted myself a little bit in that regard in going up the corporate ladder. Because I'm just not willing to take the time away from my family that is required to do that. So it's had a pretty big impact.

One of the more enlightening reflections was provided by Glen, a marketing executive with some graduate education. He was aware of career advancing opportunities that he had foregone in order to be more involved at home. Glen's engineering background was utilized and reflected in the benchmarking procedures he employed to calibrate his career advancement in comparison to a cohort of peers. He responded to the open-ended question of how fathering affected his work in the following manner:

> I'm on the daddy track. There's a mommy track and there's a daddy track too. ... I've been working for [the company] for 13 years and, I know the people that started at the same time and within a year of me, with the same background, that is, four year engineering degree. ... Now 13 years later I'm able to see probably still 25% of those people, so its maybe 4 to 6 people that I still see on a, couple times a year basis. And I see where they are and where I am. And I attribute that, in part to my conviction and this overwhelming feeling of fatherhood. ... Somewhere along the line when fatherhood came

> along, the family priority just went to the top. There's, there's, nothing that's going to displace that. And so, now that I've been in the work place for 6 years since having Kelsey [his oldest daughter] and I've been able so successfully do that and keep myself at peace. But I also see that I'm at least a half level and in some cases a full level and a half behind those people that I was talking about. And the reason is because, in my view, I go to the kids doctors appointments during the day and I'm talking about routine check-ups. ... I try and see them occasionally for lunch when they're at the sitters or my wife's got 'em and we go out to lunch. So, I think I take time away from the normal work place environment to make sure that I go out of my way and spend a lot of time with them, just for routine things. I've scheduled trips around family events. I've canceled trips or refused to go around family events. And I think in the work place sometimes that can be misinterpreted as a lack of commitment to work and so I think in some sense, kind of how I'm describing the daddy track. I think I do an outstanding job and I have no doubt that I could be that level in a half higher if I was classified as a workaholic. But I've got a commitment to the family number one and work will follow. I've been kind of put on a medium track, that says, there's still progress, there's still room to move. But you're not going to be a corporate officer at that rate.

The conscious decisions that Glen had made regarding appropriate levels of involvement at home, while still doing an adequate job at work, had played out pretty much the way he had anticipated. His account reflected that he was satisfied with the way the overall mix had worked out. His statement did not reflect resentment toward the company, coworkers who had advanced at a rate ahead of his own, or toward his family for deterring his advancement. He had made choices that worked out to yield adequate provision and a life of involvement with his children.

Neil, a trucking contractor, who engaged in considerable volunteer work while raising three young children with his part-time employed wife, had experienced a particularly jarring shift in focus as well. His shift in priorities motivated him to change careers so that he could invest greater amounts of time in his family. This occurred as he reflected on the meaning of success. In Neil's thinking, success shifted from economic advancement and having occupational prestige to being a good dad and "patching up" his marriage. He reflected:

> I came to a point less than 6 years ago, I guess, just a little less than 6 years ago where I had to make that decision. I was working too much. I was trying to please my own father in our own business and was coming to a point of becoming quite successful, or the potential for good success financially and business-wise, and all ... but I was still struggling, struggling at home with my wife because I wasn't meeting her needs and I wasn't meeting the girls' needs and I was having a hard time. And it came right down to it and she said, "I'm leaving," and I said, "Go ahead and go" because I had my goals. And as I sat there ... I thought, this is not what I want to do. I have two children that mean more to me than this business does, maybe mean more to me than my wife

> does, to be quite honest, and if I lose this opportunity to be their dad—even though I may get all the things I wanted, I failed. I felt that inside. … It was mostly my kids that I thought about. I thought, I don't want to do this to my kids. My kids need a dad and they need a good dad, so what do I do? So I had to make a choice. And my choice was to leave the business and patch things up with my wife who I really did love … and to commit myself to being a good dad to my kids.

It was evident to men in the sample that they had to make determinations about how to invest their time and energy in order to counteract the need for providing adequately for the material needs of their families while investing enough involvement at home. The questions of how much is enough provision and how much is enough involvement have different answers depending on the perceived material, emotional, and relational needs of family members at different times and stages of their lives.

Fathers with children of diverse ages have a different set of considerations and contingencies than those with only children or children spaced closely by age. Common times for increased awareness regarding economic factors are associated with different life-course transitions or developmental stages.

When new infants are in the family, especially firstborn children, parents become aware of medical bills for prenatal care and delivery, the loss of income from mothers' curtailed or lost employment, and the high cost of diapers, formula, medical care, and often day care for the infant. Another set of factors has economic impact on families with young children. The timing of the transition to parenthood typically occurs prior to or during career establishment phases of the adult's life, unless they are late timing parents. As such, children become economic dependents well before parents' earning power peaks, and perhaps during a phase when parents are paying off education loans, household establishment costs, and car loans. Unless "hand-me-downs" are available from relatives or friends, procuring equipment for first children (i.e., a crib, car seat, stroller, and clothing) may entail greater expense than those associated with later children, who would have used equipment available.

The teen years are another phase of life associated with increased expenses for parents. Besides the growth spurts and associated food intake, in comparison to younger children, teens tend to have greater awareness and preference for fashionable clothing, increased social activity with associated entertainment (and food) costs. Many teens begin driving, which has associated insurance, gasoline and maintenance costs, and possibly expenses associated with purchasing another vehicle. Parents tend to encourage teens' participation in educational advancements such as tutoring, private schooling, music, art or dance lessons, and college attendance, all of which can be quite expensive. Although different families adopt different policies regarding how much growing teens need to contribute toward their own support, few teens are responsible for providing all of their economic needs.

Families with different numbers of children of varying ages have different economic considerations than those with only children or with children who are close in age. Close spacing of children is efficient in terms of developmental progress and providing for the emotional and supervisory needs of children, but it can be more taxing in regard to economic providing. When two children are attending college at the same time, it is a different scenario than having two children attend, but only one at a time. Having two or more teens on an automotive insurance policy is different than having one at a time, and having one teen in their growth spurt has different economic consequences for food and clothing budgets than having multiple teens in this phase of development. Similarly, having children of the same gender versus having both sons and daughters has different economic consequences—some associated with greater efficiency and some with greater expense. The important point is not to focus on all of the possible combinations and permutations of age and gender in children, but to recognize that these factors exert real economic pressures in different directions with different combinations.

ROLE OVERLOAD AND BALANCING ACT COMPLEXITIES

Of particular interest for this chapter was the finding that men are inclined to represent the work of fathering in terms of the overall set of tasks required—that is, they regard providing to be one component of the total package of parenting, which also entails housework and child care (Christiansen & Palkovitz, 2001; Palkovitz, 1996a). When fathers consider their involvement in childrearing, they regard paid work to be a part of the total picture (Christiansen & Palkovitz, 2001). Interestingly enough, it is clear that for many fathers, these assumptions are implicit as opposed to explicit. That is, most fathers had not directly discussed these issues with their wives because assumptions were made regarding the division of providing and household labor. In contemporary American society, one of the most prevalent expectations is that men are to be gainfully employed.

Balancing the full responsibilities of provider, worker, and involved father is difficult and costly in terms of time, energy, and personal choice. As discussed in chapter 3, contemporary fathers view their roles as more multifaceted than fathers of a generation ago (Christiansen & Palkovitz, 2001; LaRossa, 1988; Palkovitz, 1997). Glen, the marketing executive who described the "daddy track," expressed frustration at the fact that although he had made concessions at work to be more involved at home, he was still the "second team" in terms of providing nurturance:

> And I'd say that's one of the frustrating aspects for me is no matter how I want to be an equal in that sense, I'm only the best back up I can possibly be. Kind of a reverse of the financial situation although she works part-time and contributes to the income. We'd never be able to afford the house, the cars, the college on her salary. So at best she's good strong contributor, but a back up

> from the financial stand point. And, I guess, I'm frustrated that I don't ever see any way to be that strong equal contributor. There's just not a possible way.

Glen desired to have a more meaningful role in his home, but he felt his role as primary provider had precluded the possibility of having a position of equal importance to his wife when it came to providing nurturance. His absence from the home in terms of "face time" relegated him to the second string. There is a certain awareness of some of the issues faced by stay-at-home mothers, but there is no comparable representation of or sensitivity to the ways that sole-provider fathers face limitations in meeting their desires for fulfillment in families or on the job. This is an area that could yield fruitful advancement with future research.

Financial investors can testify that diversification is a principle that minimizes risk of loss. However, diversification also distributes investments into sectors that may not yield maximally fruitful gains when conditions are moving rapidly in some market sectors but not in others. Similarly, diversification of role investments can "cost" a person the specialization that brings recognized expertise either at home or at work. From one perspective, this is the "worst of both worlds"; Glen discussed taking the "daddy track" and yet being the second string at home, failing to see any way to get beyond that status. Diversification had kept him from being totally invested in either work or home. So, in a sense, he sacrificed career success in terms of advancement for the less than satisfying experience of being a good backup at home. A different perspective of Glen's situation is much more positive. It could be argued that he had the best of both worlds. While having a career that provides for more than his family's basic material needs, he experiences moderate job success (and reduced job stress from not taking on unnecessary responsibilities) and still has the opportunity to experience involved fatherhood. He did not specialize in either work or family involvement, thus limiting his achievement, still he was able to experience moderately high gratification in the roles of provider and nurturer.

A particularly perceptive analysis of the conflicts experienced in balancing work and family commitments was provided by Bill, a full-time lab technician with two children, ages 10 and 15, and a full-time employed wife. Consider the following example:

> Bill: There's some conflicts, like the hours. When I am at work it's this, the kid school hours, and if something takes place, well, I've gotta leave work to go. I feel obligated to stay, but then I feel obligated that I have to go too, you know. 'Course I want to go. I like to see the kids in their activities, but ... I sort of feel a lot of responsibility toward my work too. I don't like to leave things hanging.
>
> Interviewer: So there is a tension there?
>
> Bill: Yes. It's like a double-edged sword. If you give up one, you are going to burn on the other, you know. So it's a no win situation so I kind of play happy medium between both. You know ...

Men felt the squeeze of both work and family and needed to appraise the relative importance of the countless demands and balance their commitments to work and family based on their appraisal of the situation. As fathers experienced conflicting pulls from both home and work, it was obvious that there was an array of contextual issues influencing the decisions they implemented to achieve the needed balance.

THE ROLE OF "MICROPOLICIES" IN PROVISIONAL BALANCES

Although explicit national or corporate policy may be characterized as "family friendly," there are provisos in the corporate culture, or unwritten rules, that convey to men not to take paternity leave or to be "too involved" with their families, or they will be viewed as uncommitted to their jobs and perceived as unmasculine (Hwang, 1987; Lawton, 1991; Pleck, 1993). A 1996 report of the Ford Foundation addressed the need to change not only corporate policies, but attitudes, reducing "dissonance between policy and practice" (p. 21). Whereas work/family policies have traditionally been viewed as "women's issues," the following quotes illustrate that men invested in balancing work and family involvements have as much to gain from changes in corporate culture as do women. Work policy has addressed the fact that women have dual roles and responsibilities (Cohen, 1993), partly because women have traditionally been labeled as caregivers and fathers have not (Piotrkowsky, R. N. Rapoport & R. Rapoport, 1987). Formal work policies often do not address the fact that fathers also have multiple roles and responsibilities (Cohen, 1993; Grimm-Thomas & Perry-Jenkins, 1994; Hall & Richter, 1988). As Bronstein (1988) noted, "The workplace is less tolerant of men than women taking time off from work for child care, and ... society still does not sanction men's putting their family equal to or ahead of their career" (p. 5). Given contemporary patterns of dual career families, work/family issues are no longer strictly "women's" issues or "men's" issues. They are central to the everyday functioning of men, women, and children.

Will, an upper-middle-class father with two teenaged children, explained how a difference of values on the local level could create complications at the workplace. Wilson's comments, along with those of several other men in the sample, made it clear that policies on the "local" level were more significant than corporate or national policies when it came to expediting or obstructing men's attempts to carry out responsibilities in the interface between home and the workplace. Wilson offered:

> Before I had children I'd work long hours, but now, sometimes I'd have to get home to take one of the kids to something after school. So that had an impact on my work. And actually I got into a problem at work one time because I worked for a lady who didn't understand that I had to get home sometimes, you know. So that was a conflict. Sometimes people that don't have children or their children are grown-up, they don't understand. ... So yeah, it did

> obviously affect my work environment. Well, because I spent a lot of time with my children that I normally otherwise would be at work, you know what I'm saying. I was a workaholic before we had children, so my expectations changed. I like to spend time with my children.

Will's experience with a coworker who was unsympathetic to his need to have a flexible schedule at times brought perceived misunderstanding and discomfort in the workplace.

Men who were employed in settings where there was a mismatch between their own and their employer's views concerning the importance of father involvement expressed the greatest ambivalence about work. Although they recognized the necessity of steady income, they lamented working for an employer who did not share their values concerning parental investment. Means of coping with the perceived mismatch varied considerably from father to father. What became clear was that *micropolicies* (implementation of policies on the local level, i.e., immediate supervisor and coworkers, spouse, and personal levels) were more important than governmental or corporate policies in affecting men's perceived achievement.

Some fathers felt they needed to make clear choices between career advancement and family involvement. Robert, a father with two teenage children and a young infant, made the decision to leave a demanding managerial position to become a truck driver so that he could have more time with his developing children. He noted that there are both costs and benefits to such decisions:

> I spent maybe twelve to fifteen years in the retail management world. During that time, I was working 8 o'clock in the morning till 9 or 10, 11 o'clock at night. Five, six, and sometimes seven days a week. About five to six years ago, I gave this up. The reason I gave it up, it was excellent money, but the reason that I gave it up was, my children were growing up overnight, and I wasn't really getting to spend a lot of time with them. So I gave this up, took a lesser paying job, which did not help us. I mean, it worked out in both ways. It was a negative by the fact that it was a lesser paying job, but it was a positive in the fact that I was spending more time with my children. So its kind of leveled and equaled itself out since then.

Some viewed the pressures caused by aspiring to balance work and family commitments to be unfortunate but necessary (and temporary) conditions. Others distanced themselves from their employer or, at times, from their families in order to lessen the tensions. Greatest satisfaction was expressed by men who perceived that they had the freedom to exert significant control of their decisions concerning how to balance work and family commitments. Least friction was perceived in cases where persons both at home and at work showed flexibility in scheduling matters. Pressure was also perceived to be low as long as there was flexibility on at least one front. In cases where fathers perceived incompatibility and inflexible or nonsympathetic positions both at home and at work, they expressed the greatest frustration.

MACRO ISSUES

There was a contrast in the mean demographics of groups of fathers who felt greater commitment to work versus those who had cut back to spend more time with their families. Fathers who expressed greater commitment to work tended to be less well educated and to have correspondingly lower gross annual incomes than men reporting less commitment to work (Cazenave, 1979; Cohen, 1993). On the average, men reporting greater commitment to work since having children were 2 years of education and $10,000 per year "behind" men reporting decreased commitment to work. As such, those reporting less commitment to work were likely to be men who had met the basic level of provisional needs of the family and were now focused on investing time and energy into building relationships with their families. Caution needs to be exercised in stating and interpreting this finding, because the sample in this study is small, and although diverse, it is not representative of the larger populations. Nonetheless, the trend in the data is consistent with research by Zussman (1987), who studied middle-class fathers in New England working as engineers. He discovered that these men did not cite work as a source of identity; rather, they saw work as a way to support their families.

Clearly, education serves as a significant mediator in the previous findings. Specifically, it is often believed or asserted that involved fathering is a phenomenon of men who hold middle-class or higher status. Education is postulated to be a key because of greater gender equity awareness or enlightenment of the middle-class fathers. However, education is often confounded with income, and the primacy of the provider role for fathers may keep working-class men from having the option of greater "face time" involvement with their children. In order to provide a living wage, they need to invest more time at work than fathers who are better off economically. As such, working-class men may be more focused on immediate material needs of their families and not merely oblivious to ideological issues regarding gender equity.

In analyzing these data, it became apparent that men who had perceived that they had "enough" money to meet the realistic material needs of their families tended toward making decisions about how to invest more time and energy in their families and less in their work. On the contrary, those who were not satisfying the basic material needs of their families were focused on ways to invest extra time and effort at the workplace to get "enough" money. These trends further indicate that education may not have as much to do with "enlightenment" as it does with practical reality. Some men had made the "choice" of investing in their children at the cost of "self-advancement" years before, when they had decided to curtail their schooling in order to provide financially for their children. The consequences of such choices were often long term, as related by Steve, a computer operator and early timing father who had his first of four children when he was 19 years old:

> I think I would have been further along. And the reason for—and of course that's a big if—if I had completed college, and gotten at least a four-year degree ... even though I probably would have been suffering with immaturity for a longer period of time ... I think I probably could have started off at a position probably in any company that I would like to work up to right now. ... I think it's more difficult because I limited myself in education before starting to work. ... I blame myself for letting myself get into a situation where I couldn't go to college and probably some people would consider that a poor excuse, "well, yeah, you could have still gone to school," hard as hell, sure, some people can do it but I don't think I could have.

Steve reached a place where he felt that it was necessary for him to decide between furthering his education and providing for his children. He made the commitment to be an involved father, providing materially and otherwise for his family. Working-class fathers are sometimes criticized for their "traditional" values, their focus on the provider role, and their relative lack of focus on nurturance. Perhaps, in contrast, they should be commended for the commitment with which they pursue providing (Christiansen & Palkovitz, 2001), even if it means they must work multiple jobs or longer hours to provide a living wage.

PERSONAL COST–BENEFITS ANALYSES

Fathers spontaneously discussed the developmental benefits of fatherhood, and the relative contributions of fathering versus work, in moving them along their own maturational paths (see chap. 12, this vol., for expanded cost–benefits analyses). Whereas fathers recognized that their commitment to their families may have "cost" them in terms of job advancement, they recognized gains in personal development (Hawkins et al., 1993; Palkovitz, 1996a, 2000) that were perceived as more than off setting these. Ned elaborated:

> If I'd never had children I would be much further along, and I'd be much higher, and I'd have more money and all that. But I wouldn't be as happy. I wouldn't change anything, really.

Ned felt that the sacrifices made in regard to career advancement had paid off in regard to happiness. Similarly, Nelson, a single dad with two children ages 5 and 7, provided a cost–benefits analysis in favor of investing in children versus career:

> Oh, I'd be way beyond this as far as career was concerned. As personal growth is concerned, I couldn't touch it without the children. I've grown personally

> more than I could ever expect to have grown with the children than without. But career-wise, I could have excelled way beyond where I'm at now.

IMPLICATIONS

The themes expressed by the men in this study raise important issues that call into question an existing set of assumptions. Those assumptions can be briefly stated in the following manner:

Myth 1: Men Are as Involved in the Home as They Want to Be

Some men may be motivated to engage in greater degrees of direct involvement with their children but may not see clear to do so in terms of limited time, money, and energy. There are pragmatic limitations to involvement. Some of the limits are heavily influenced by institutional factors such as wage inequity, corporate policy, the culture of the provider role, and educational limitations. Other limits may be more personally constructed or derived (perceived needs, pace of work, energy levels, priority setting, lifestyle choices). However, the statements of sample fathers seriously challenge the assertion that men are as involved in their families as they want to be.

Myth 2: Men Use Employment as an Excuse to "Buy Out" of Caregiving or Housework Responsibilities (Hochschild, 1997)

Although there are marked gaps between men's and women's involvement in housework and child care that are not fully explained by hours of waged work (Pleck, 1997), in contrast to this being solely a gender issue, there are other practical considerations as well. Some men discussed the fact that they were the "on call" or more primary parent because their working wives had jobs that had less flexible schedules or more demanding supervisors. When the mother's job accounted for the primary source of income, where a female spouse or partner provided the majority of the family income, or where women's waged work represented a vital portion of family provision that could not be relinquished, this was particularly pronounced. Again, a complex array of factors was involved. If the mother's supervisors or coworkers were relatively inflexible regarding micropolicies, then fathers were more likely to express greater responsibility in child care. In this context, it is important to note that wage inequity puts men and women on unequal ground in their abilities to balance nurturer and worker roles. Whereas men are more often characterized as being "guilty" of less flexibility, there may be structural barriers that explain at least part of the difference. Simply based on proportions of men and women who are employed, and the continued existence of some sectors of the work world that are relatively gender segregated, more working men than women may have to deal with work-based micropolicies that are difficult or inflexible.

Myth 3: Policy Alone Will "Fix Things"

The less than overwhelming response to Sweden's family leave policies (Haas, 1993) is disheartening. The Swedish data suggest that policies may be accompanied by gradual change over time. Major transformations in role expectations and revising the conduct of acceptable or expected behaviors requires time. However, this study indicates that, in comparison to national or corporate policies, "policies" on the local level may exert a greater influence on men's perceptions of the relative harmony or disharmony of work–family interfaces. Specifically, the attitudes and behaviors of "local" supervisors are more important in affecting men's family–work interfaces than are corporate policies. Similarly, their spouse/partner's "policies" (role expectations, etc.) are more important than governmental ones in the daily experience of friction or support. As such, it may be instructive to view fathers', mothers', and coworkers' roles and values as micropolicies requiring interpretation and procedural implementation just as government or corporate policies do.

CONCLUSION

Both fathering and work are multifaced. Both consist of multiple roles, frequently changing demands and micropolicies that require implementation. Thus, the intersections between fathering and work are numerous, complex, and dynamic. Some functions of both fathering and of working are overlapping. Some functions of fathering and working are simultaneously synergistic and antagonistic. It is naive to believe that a comprehensive family leave policy or the elimination of wage inequity will quickly solve all of the obstacles and barriers that men face in attempting to simultaneously fulfill their obligations in the work and family domains. Such policies may be just, and would allow families greater freedom of choice in negotiating chosen role balances, but the implication from this study is that the ultimate interface is in the implementation of micropolicies on the local level, independent of corporate or national policy.

V

Summary, Evaluations, and Applications

Chapter **12**

Cost–Benefits Analyses

Toward the end of the interview session, each participant in the study was asked about the relative costs and benefits of fathering (Sagi & Sharon, 1983; Snarey, 1993). They were directly asked if they had experienced benefits from involvement with their children and, beyond finances, what the related costs may have been. Finally, they were asked if they felt the benefits of fathering outweighed the costs, or vice versa.

In the context of this series of questions, some men seemed to recap what they had discussed earlier in the interview process. Others brought out elements of their relationships with their children that had not been discussed up to that point. Most engaged in a combination of both of these styles of responding. The fathers' responses were interesting. Although they could easily articulate costs, they could also enumerate multiple benefits, many of which they declared to have intangible or inestimable value. After stating a benefit of involved fathering, they spontaneously said things like, "How can you put a value on that?" Table 12.1 represents the primary themes expressed when participants discussed the primary costs and benefits of involved fathering.

BENEFITS OF INVOLVED FATHERING

Satisfaction of Watching the Children Grow

The most prevalent theme in terms of frequency of expression, emotional energy, and number of words allotted to answering it, is amazement that fathers experience as they watch their children grow, develop, and achieve, knowing they are a big part of shaping their lives. Men in the sample elaborated on this theme in different ways.

Overall, the theme could be expressed as fathers' satisfaction with watching their children grow, develop, and accomplish things. Subthemes were expressed in slightly different terms. These included seeing that their teaching made a difference in their children's lives, and seeing that they guided, shaped, or molded their children's development and that as fa-

TABLE 12.1

Primary Costs and Benefits of Involved Fathering

Benefits	*Costs*
Satisfaction of watching the children grow	Time
A sense of pride	Sacrifice
Love received	Finances
Personal growth	Marital closeness
Perceptual shift/expanded self	Energy
Extending the family line	Potential
Fun	Kids grow up and don't need you as much anymore
Continued learning	You get spread out
Fathering gives life meaning	There are no "real" costs
Enhanced marriage	

thers they had done the best that they could do. This was closely related to fathers seeing their efforts "pay off" as they witnessed a life grow firsthand, that is, seeing the fruits of their labors. Fathers expressed a sense of taking joy in their children's accomplishments and their sense of achievement.

Manuel, who had completed high school but had not gotten any college education, expressed a sense of pride in knowing that he helped his daughter to get accepted into a good college. His quote reflects both the joy of observing children's achievements and the joy of hands-on shaping of their development:

> I get out of it the joy of seeing. I hate to make this sound like its a piece of clay. But actually it is a piece of clay. I'm molding something in my own image and I'm watching it grow day by day, step by step, and being all that it can be. And knowing that I had a lot to do with that. That is a feeling that no money or nothing can replace. Can you imagine the feeling I had knowing that my daughter graduates and is going to one of the top colleges and going for pre med? And knowing that I, little things that I did helped mold her into that person. ... I think all fathers get more joy out of that than being the richest parents in the world.

Similarly, Roger discussed his role of teacher for his infant son as one of the benefits of involved fathering. His statement shows that he attempts to "enter" his son's world seeking understanding of what his son understands and communicating in a manner that his son can grasp. This role taking has likely sharpened Roger's interpersonal skills in other relationships as well. In helping his son to learn, Roger perceives himself as a teacher, a role that he seems to esteem. He gains an increased sense of importance by recognizing the primary role that he plays in his son's instruction. Roger related:

> How you communicate with him, and for him to understand you and stuff. It's a real perspective that I get when I'm sitting there, and I'm trying to tell him something, I'm trying to read him a book and get him to understand. And when he does understand, it's like a great feeling, it's like, gosh, you know, I'm a teacher, you know, I'm instructor now. And I'm his sole person that's going to try to teach him to do this right now.

The previous quote was Roger's response to the question, "What are the benefits of fatherhood?" He did not explicitly state, "I gain a sense of importance as a teacher by being involved in my son's life," but that is what his response implies.

When reviewing the full record of fathers' responses to this question, the combined sense of responsibility and awe was striking. Men knew that they were ultimately not responsible for the "amazing" changes and accomplishments their children manifested, yet they had an overwhelming sense that their responses made a difference in shaping their child's personality and abilities. The primary emphasis was on seeing the rapid rate of growth, development, and accomplishments of the children. Yet, at another level, this is an expression of the fathers' generativity (Erikson, 1950; Hawkins & Dollahite, 1997b; Snarey, 1993). It was clear that involved fathers saw that they were investing in the next generation.

A Sense of Pride

Fathers expressed a sense of pride about their fathering. They listed pride as a benefit of involved fathering whether or not they were receiving compliments from others about their children or their fathering. They also expressed a sense of pride independent of the feedback they received, because of their kids' accomplishments, knowing they had played a role in them. In some ways, this was closely related to the first theme of having a sense of enjoyment of watching the children grow and develop. Pride came through having a sense that what they were doing was right. Sometimes they got praise from their children or compliments from others about themselves as dads or commendations about the behavior or accomplishments of their kids. Each of these contexts helped fathers to feel they had achieved something meaningful by investing in their children's development. Neil talked about the pride he experiences, and tied it to generativity themes as well:

> The pride from seeing your kids do something that you didn't ... know how to do or just thought they couldn't do or would never attempt to do yourself. And

> having other people praise your kids. It's neat to me. I can be proud sometimes. I guess that's a positive pride. Knowing that you're raising a family that will go on after you're gone, and hopefully that you've impacted them and they'll have some sort of impact on the future generations that filters down.

Because of his generative investment, Neil is actually expressing pride not only in his children's accomplishments, but in his investment in shaping the future through them, another expression of parental generativity (Kotre, 1984).

Love Received

Because investment in the next generation takes place in the context of intergenerational relationships, there is often a direct return for generative behavior (Palm, 1997). Dads also talked about the love they experienced in return for their involvement. They discussed it in different ways: love, friendship, or somebody who cares about you. They expressed enjoying the affection they received from their children and the greetings and excitement that their children expressed when they came home from work or being away. Although there was a clear sense of enjoyment in the affection they received, it was also an expression of the interactive, reciprocal aspects of generativity. These men liked the feeling of being needed, appreciated, and loved. To be desired as a special companion or playmate and to be loved by their children brought a sense of importance, meaningfulness, and worth to their lives that gave it purpose and value beyond what was experienced in spouse/partner, worker, or community member roles.

As Tim described his relationship with his infant son, he expressed the following:

> Well, you got a new best friend. That's one of the primary things. You get somebody who's just really, really interested in you and really, really wants to see you, wants to be around you, and that's a real high. You know, little somebody who, like when he gets scared and he yells. Then you come over and pick him up and he stops yelling and he smiles. Yeah, you can't put a tag on that, a value, it's hard to put a value on it. You get a new best friend who thinks very highly of you. I think that's how I would sum it up.

Personal Growth

A significant proportion of the sample talked about the maturation process that they experienced since becoming fathers. Many of the men talked about lifestyles or habits they needed to change—even if they were things that had been "good enough" for themselves or their partners. For the sake of the children, undesirable or negative things that they had allowed to persist for years needed to be addressed with a new sense of urgency. As a result, they had become "better men." It became evident that a high percentage of the men in the sample felt they had significant issues that needed to be addressed in their lives and maturity levels. Fathers saw their children as providing a catalytic motivation or drive, imposing a deadline of sorts, for the imposition of standards that either they had created, or had internalized from some unspecified source. These were standards they felt they had to address in order to be responsible, mature, well-functioning fathers.

It would be fruitful in further investigations to explore the source of these prescriptions for what is needed for good fathering. It is clear from these data, that no matter their limitations, men had a clear sense of a standard to which they did not compare favorably. They were clearly motivated to increase their level of functioning to that level for the sake of their children. They may have been satisfied with or resigned to their level of functioning before having children, but it was clear that many fathers in the sample knew they needed to address certain issues. Some knew they were not living in particularly fruitful, healthy, or positive role-modeling ways, but before the children it was good enough for them and for their spouses. Something about assuming the role of father motivated them to bring the needed change.

The general statement of this theme took the form of "being an involved father has made me a better person." Fathers in the sample clearly recognized their involvement with their children as a force that brought out the best in them, helped them to reach a higher potential, or a "land of opportunity" for continued personal growth and maturation. Involved fathering was seen as developmentally facilitative and generally stretching.

Some fathers noted they had not yet implemented or achieved the full degree of change or maturity they felt would be ideal for their children. However, they were making progress and were motivated to continue in growth and development for the sake of their children. This theme closely relates to the settling down theme and the gentle evoker pattern described earlier in chapter 4. Although the theme was stated in the general way, "being an involved father contributes to my personal growth," there were multiple subthemes that brought out different aspects of this overall sense. Involved fathers recognized that through taking responsibility for their children and in wanting to model appropriate things for their children, they had "settled down," given up harmful or risky lifestyles or activities, and generally stayed out of trouble. Some men talked in terms of an increase in general maturity, more discipline, or more goal direction. Other men sensed a change in overall perspective or a major adjustment of viewpoint or outlook on life, saying things such as, "Fathering made me stop and smell the roses, it made me less purposeful, goal directed, and task oriented." Another group of fathers, paralleling the gentle evoker pattern described in chapter 4, talked about developing a different blend of response tendencies than they were previously used to. Again, these took different forms. Some fathers discussed the sense that interactions with their children brought out more emotions than they had previously experienced or expressed (see chap. 5, this vol.), or made them more understanding or caring.

Chris was one of the fathers who viewed taking responsibility for his children as a major shaper of his life: It literally changed the direction of his life course. He cited fathering as a deterrent to a life of crime, promiscuity, and risk-taking behavior with friends and siblings. He talked about his children:

> Before I had kids or whatever, I might have been on the street of crime, or just messing with a lot of females, or whatever. So I would say having kids kind of settled me down to just one female; if you're listening. And, you know, keep me out of running and doing crazy things I used to do with my boys or my brothers.

Clifford perceived that involved fatherhood had yielded a greater degree of maturity, discipline, and responsibility in his life as well. Although not as dramatic as the previous quote, the sense of being responsible for others stimulated him from apathy toward activity:

> Well, one thing it's made me mature, grow up faster. Uh, more understanding. I've always been patient, but I probably am more patient now because of my children I guess. More discipline. It's, that's a big one there. I'm definitely more disciplined now. I know I know how to do certain things and I just can't keep putting them off. You don't feel like shopping for food one day, you know you have to do it, so ...

Perceptual Shift/Expanded Self

Glen talked about how spending time with his children had transformed his view of time and activities from one of goal-oriented, purposeful, task performance to a more relational style. He felt that, overall, he was less driven, and the change was needed. He explained:

> If I'd go to a funny movie, then I'd go with a purpose of it being funny and I'd have a good time. But I've not had the ability to do that otherwise cause it didn't seem to have a purpose. Fatherhood's ... made me a less purposeful person, made me a person to really stop and smell the roses along the way.

Glen's statement reflected a perceptual shift that he welcomed. Similarly, Peter talked of a shift in his viewpoint. Although he did not articulate the particular value of his changed perspective, he offered the following when asked about the benefits of fathering:

> Most of the reason is just having a different viewpoint. It's kind of like being at the bottom of a hill or something like that and really not knowing the experience of climbing it, and then when you actually do climb it or you're on

> your way up and you really look down you have a totally different perspective, and you already remember the perspective you had when you were down at the foot of the mountain, but now you have a totally different one when you're up going towards the summit.

Roger characterized involved fathering as leading to an expanded sense of self that combines pride and variety of activities and experiences. He viewed fathering as a "land of opportunity." When asked what he got out of fathering, he replied:

> Well, the old sense of pride. A sense of expanding myself. Like I say, it was on one track basically when my wife and I, it was like okay, we did this that and the other, now it's kind of like we—wide variety. ... It's kind of, you know just expanded, you know, the land of opportunity so to speak.

Extending the Family Line

Some men talked through the passing on of the family name, line, or legacy as a benefit of fathering. They expressed different aspects of what has otherwise been called *biological generativity* (Kotre, 1984). Not all of the discourse regarding "passing along" the family line was biologically oriented; some of this came out in a more social regard. Joseph reflected the "belonging" aspects of leaving a legacy:

> Just, I guess, the overall enjoyment of having them with you when you're doing certain events that you're at, a picnic or family reunion or something. And then you just realize all of a sudden, well, I got kids here, and you feel a part of that now. Before it was just you, and you have no legacy or anything and you feel kind of empty, everybody else running around ... and you're sitting there.

Fun

Several men talked about the sheer fun of fathering. Their kids gave them excuses or opportunities to express exuberance, experience child- centered settings with childlike joy, to play, and to do things that they would not otherwise do. Fathers talked about the fun they had at zoos, parks, and engaging in activities or developing hobbies they would not feel free to do without the "excuse" of doing it with their children. They also had things to focus on now with their spouses or partners that gave them enjoyable things to do as a couple. Some men felt they were happier since having children, or there was always some excitement or an increased activity level with something to do. Scott said:

> You get to have fun with your kids, I mean, its just seems like constant play time, you know. I have, I might have as much fun as they do, you know, things they do. Play ball or reading a book.

Continued Learning

Fathers spontaneously talked about their continued learning. Their children had provided a rich and varied context for them to learn many different things—about child development, about relationships, about themselves, and about specific skills and abilities.

Alan talked about learning responsibility from assuming his role as a father. He gained a greater sense of self-esteem and of being shaped in positive ways through teaching his children:

> It's positive because, I guess, because every day that I'm teaching them I'm learning more and more responsibility, and more—I'm getting more self-esteem from learning and seeing what other people are doing. And I'm trying to teach, I'm teaching them what I'm seeing and trying to teach them better than what somebody else might be teaching. So, it's shaping me up more because it's helping me to grow and to learn, I guess, is how I want to put it.

The fathers who talked about continued learning saw that their children were stretching them into places where they were unlikely to go without having ongoing, involved relationships with them. Adam recognized that there is a two-way street in the teaching/learning process. Some of the learning has to do with interpersonal relationship skills like reading signals, communicating in a way that is understood by your audience, turn-taking, and so forth. Other types of learning are more focused on the attainment of specific information or skill areas. Adam explained:

> They teach you as you teach them; you can learn a lot from children.

Some fathers talked about specific skills and interests they had developed through continued interactions with their children. For example, some men, who had previously not known much about soccer, learned the rules and strategies and some basic skills as their children participated in soccer leagues. They learned a new sport by attending their children's practices or games and through involvement with their kids at home (i.e., practicing or "fooling around" with the ball in the front yard). Other men talked about learning things about subjects such as model rocketry or scouting. As children get older and acquire interests and expertise that fathers have not developed themselves, it becomes clear to men that learning subject matter from children can reverse the teacher–student or master teacher–trainee relationship that fathers experience in many other contexts with their children. Watching your children achieve things that you have not attained brings a respect, awe, and sense of openness to learning from your children that is different than learning from other teachers. Some fathers view this as a benefit of involved fathering.

James focused on the continued learning of fathering in the following manner:

> It's like gong back to school ... you learn everything all over again. ... Yeah, it keeps you learning. ... Gives you a different outlook on life.

Some of the learning that comes from interacting with children entails learning an expanded array of interpersonal skills. You learn to take on other viewpoints and perspectives, taking that different outlook on life. That outlook, however, is not limited to role taking; that outlook provides men with a sense that there is more to life than the next paycheck or the meaningless repetition of daily tasks. Involved fathers come to see that they have a purpose that transcends their own life span.

Fathering Gives Life Meaning

Other men felt that having children gave meaning to an otherwise meaningless existence (i.e., the everyday humdrum of work and menial tasks now seemed to have a purpose) to provide for their child(ren). Fathers expressed joy in focusing on their kids. The other-oriented focus made life seem fuller and more worthwhile to some fathers. Neil felt he had become more other centered, although not completely, and his new allocentrism was accompanied by increased enjoyment compared to his more selfish orientation:

> I have somebody to impart my life to, what I'm about. And they, being the little people that they are, have given me a different focus to be about. I was about me, and I still am to some extent, but I'm more about them than others. There's more fun in it.

Donald straightforwardly stated that he felt that children give life meaning:

> I think my primary benefit of being a dad ... is just that they give my life meaning. They make me feel needed. My decisions are significant ... I think, generally, they make me a happier person. ... My self-esteem is a lot higher. My kids make me feel needed, important kind of like a reason to go on. There is a reason to grind at the grindstone.

Similarly, Roger talked about his relationship with his children as bringing more meaning or value to everyday life. He described a scene that many fathers in the sample talked about: the unique feelings that fathers have when they are warmly and enthusiastically greeted by their children when they return home from work. Roger described it this way:

> It's just brought out more of me. ... It gives me a, it's more of a value of life too. Where, you know, before you'd get off work and you'd come home, and you'd

> be, okay, I come home and read the paper, watch the news. Now it's like the first thing you think about when you get in that car is I want to come home and see him. And he's going to run to the door and yell "Daddy!" And that's going to be the greatest feeling in the world.

Enhanced Marriage

Although relatively rare, as discussed extensively in chapter 8, some men felt their children had enhanced their marriage by giving them and their spouse or partner a shared focus or things to do. These perceptions can be explained by Heider's (1958) social balance theory, where a premise is "any friend of yours is a friend of mine." So, when partners both point their hearts toward facilitating the development of their children, they align their hearts in the same direction. An increased sense of closeness can result from jointly sharing the goals and tasks of parenting, as well as jointly recognizing the accomplishments of children and sharing the satisfaction of seeing children's development. Roger stated it succinctly:

> Like I said, it's brought out more between my wife and I. It's just built our relationship even more.

THE COSTS OF INVOLVED FATHERING

Men in the sample were able to articulate the costs of involved fathering. When asked about the costs of fathering, men frequently asked for clarification—was the question about the financial costs, or personal, interpersonal, or other costs? I told them to focus on the costs other than finances.

Time

By far, the most frequently discussed cost involved time (Daly, 1995; Schor, 1992). Men discussed the need to invest both quantity and quality time with their children. Most fathers talked about the costs of time, and some seemed to use time as a proxy for freedom, spontaneity, or self-focused energies. When they said they did not have time to themselves any more, they really meant they had to curtail some of the past activities that had brought them personal pleasure. Craig stated that you are not only giving up some of your time, you are giving up all of your time. He indicated that even when he was away from his children, his thoughts and worries were focused on them, thus occupying the time spent away from them:

> You're giving up your time. You're giving up time, all of your time. When I do have the opportunity to have a sitter, I'm still thinking about the kids, is the sitter mistreating them, are they mistreating the sitter, is the house blowing up because they're tearing it apart? It's just constant. ... So it's just time, they take up a lot of time.

Closely related to the theme that you give up a lot of your time was the sense that involved fathering often required an other-oriented focus that caused men to sacrifice things of personal value to them.

Sacrifice

Some men articulated the need to lay aside their own goals and to defer or lay down dreams. Specifically, they talked about the need to put off education, career attainments, and other types of goals or dreams in order to fulfill the provider role and to have the time to invest in active involvement with their children. This type of sacrifice was more prevalent in early timing fathers than in on time or late timing fathers. I asked Donald about the costs of father involvement in the following exchange:

> Interviewer: How about the costs? Not just in terms of finances, but are there costs to being a father?
>
> Donald: Yeah. I think it takes a sacrifice because you've got to ... be kid oriented to be a father. To be a good father, you have got to be kid oriented in that your decisions that you make and stuff have to be oriented towards your family or your children. You can't always be out there for yourself, you know. Sometimes you got to say, "I'll do it for the kids. I'll do it for the kids." ... You know you have to sacrifice some time [pause] and some of your own goals. I guess in some instances you might have to put off some of your goals. If you are going to school, you'll have to put off school or at least slow it down; only go part-time or something depending on the financial situation which you could afford to do, but uh, and usually with career, you know, I think if you want to be a ... a great father or good father, you know, I think you are going to have to sacrifice somewhat of your career, not totally, you would be able to go to work nine to five and somedays work some overtime, but you are not going to be able to work nine to nine and be a good father, so you can be really impressive in that career. So basically, you have to sacrifice whatever you are working on in your life, some of it at least.

Donald focused on time, and personal and educational goals. Similarly, Joseph talked about involved fathering costing some men their dreams. I asked him:

> What are the costs of fatherhood? What do you give up or sacrifice?
>
> Joseph: I guess maybe higher income. That may be one thing. Some dream that you had, maybe wanted to be—I don't know—world traveler or something like that. Maybe you might give up something like that perspective.

Finances

The men were steered away from discussing finances if they questioned the manner in which costs was meant, but nonetheless, many fathers launched into discussions of the financial obligations of fatherhood. This fact speaks to the centrality and primacy of the provider role in contemporary fathering. Men said things like, fathering will cost you a "pretty penny," citing things like infant formula, diapers, and day-care costs. Interestingly, it was primarily fathers of young children who focused on financial aspects of fathering, although statistics reveal that covering the expenses of teenage children may be more demanding. There is no data to articulate this finding with specificity, but the costs of caring for young children appear to be viewed more as "add ons" to family budgets because the items are more likely to be separate from other family members (e.g., diapers, infant formula, and baby foods), and because the costs are newly assumed ones. By the time children reach older ages, although the costs are considerable, the idea of financial responsibility is not nearly so novel, fathers tend to have greater income generating capacity because of their location in their career trajectory, and the items purchased for older children are less distinct from those of older family members (e.g., foods are similar, clothing may be worn by different family members).

Men do focus on the expenses of teen children, such as the high rates for automotive insurance or college tuition. Although anticipated for some time before these costs are levied, they too can be viewed as "add ons" to budgets that had not covered them until the child's transition (e.g., getting a driver's liscence, acceptance into college) moves the added financial responsibility from a "planning stage" into an "implementation stage." These expenses are similar to costs focused on during infancy because they are easily distinguished from other ongoing family expenses. Billing statements for insurance and tuition clearly itemize expenses attributable to an individual child's support, just as infant formula or a new car seat are seen as an expense for an individual family member. Infancy, adolescence, and the launching phase of the child's life cycle have more individually attributable expenses than middle childhood, and these phases of childrearing get more focus from fathers in their discussions of financial costs of fathering.

Although the costs of infancy and adolescence are similar in sharing characteristics of "newly assumed" and "individually attributable" expenses, there is at least one significant difference between the expenses associated with the different developmental phases. Responsibility to cover increased costs associated with older children may be partially or wholly shifted to the child—"If he's gonna drive, he's got to get a job to help pay for insurance."

Marital Closeness

A large proportion of the men in the sample talked about marital changes as "costs" of involved fatherhood (discussed in greater detail in chap. 8, this vol.). Specifically, they cited less time with spouse/partner or decreased ability to talk through issues in privacy. This was expressed as both decreased sharing and decreased time and privacy for physical affection.

Energy

Fathers also talked through the energy, anxiety, and stress associated with involved fathering as a cost. Some men talked about the anxiety that their children had created for them, the stress created, or the sleep lost. Some sleep deprivation was due to nighttime caregiving while children were young. Some was attributed to increased demands on fathers' time as children age, so they spent time after children have gone to bed to catch up on work that was brought home from the office, or to complete household tasks (finances, maintenance). Some loss of sleep was due to concerns that fathers have regarding the safety, whereabouts, peer relationships, or behavior of their teenage children. Ken discussed some of these "energy" issues in the following quote. He also started with a focus on time, but articulated that it was not the time that fathering costs you, it is more energy or "self" cost:

> Well, you give up time. You have to spend much more time doing those family things. You have to give up energy. It's not just the putting in of the time, you've got to really put it in a way that's—the energy of being with them or the energy of solving the problems or dealing with the frustrations. So it can drain you. It can sap you at times. You might have to give up some of yourself. You might have to—you may be, for that specific point in time, you'd want to do something different that you can't do.

Potential

Although explicitly expressed by just one particularly insightful father, an interesting concept was that involved fathering cost you potential. That is, basically, anything invested in fathering took away from what could be invested in other pursuits or endeavors, but it was impossible to know with certainty what the actual versus the perceived costs were. Thomas said:

> I think they're costs in potential. It's an event that changes your life completely. This is really hard to say where you would be or what would be in a life without it. I guess potentially I could have written a book and had a completely different world where—and be enmeshed in a completely different social realm than I am now. But because of experiencing this event, I don't know anything about the potential of the other world.

Kids Grow Up and Don't Need You as Much Anymore

The implication of this theme is that men invest themselves in a relationship with their children, part of the meaning of their lives is created and fostered in the ongoing relationship. Part of their identity as a man is forged and extended (Minton & Pasley, 1996). A closeness is created that is positive, motivating, and self-defining. As children become more independent, less needful, and spend more time away from home, it creates a destabilization of each of these "positive" components of fathering. When your children do not need you as much as they used to, it is perceived as a "cost" because of the loss of closeness and the diminished sense of being needed and important. As the "involved father" portion of a man's identity shrinks, it is a cost to invest in creating other aspects that fill the void left by the diminished fathering role. Ned talked about the tensions of watching his children grow and change in regard to how much they need and appreciate him in different stages of development:

> And the only bad part about it is that they grow up, and then they start making their own little units, their own little families as they experiment because they're between childhood and adulthood. Especially my fourteen-year old—at this time, I've lost her, she no longer needs me, she needs me. She needs me to give her hugs and kisses and reassurance. But when they're fourteen, they're not children, and they're not adults and they're adolescents, and they're reaching and they're looking for friendships. So, they're trying to form their own little groups. And it kind of hurts you because at that stage, you know, they think that you're the dumbest person in the world. You have to remind yourself that when they go over to their girlfriend's house, they think that their girlfriend's father or mother are the best people in the world; that's only temporary. And all I have to do is look at my twenty-two-year old who's moved away, calls me every week and tells me how great I am, you know.

Ned's experience represents a fairly common trajectory. As children feel the need to establish independence and their own identity, they increase physical and/or psychological distance from their family of origin. Once independence is reasonably established, they begin to value and appreciate their familial relationships again. Fathers' adjustments to the distancing phases of the teen years may be facilitated if they recognize that it is a normative "phase" or "stage" that is likely to pass, with a potential for a later period of increased closeness and appreciation relative to the distancing phase.

You Get Spread Out

Perhaps more than any other single "cost," this theme represents the overall theme of this book. Men experience the diverse and sometimes conflicting demands of involved fathering to clash at times with demands placed by husband/partner, worker, or community member roles. They continually struggle to engage successfully in all that is required in each role. When asked about the costs of fathering, Peter said:

> Primary costs I think would be [that you're] just not as flexible to do an array of things, and things have to be kind of spread out as far as tackling one objective from another. That's probably about it. The only thing, probably

> the main drawback is just being inflexible to do a whole bunch of different things at one time.

Steve discussed the role strain in terms of costs in regard to time for self and spouse, but it is clear that time was being used as a proxy for energy, focus, and dedicated attention. He said:

> Sure, cost is everything. Everything costs money and everything costs, time, effort, whatever. Less time to yourself, less time to explore things you want to do, or less time to share with your partner. The biggest killer is time, I guess. And through this interview you've probably noticed that all the way through, is time.

Time or energy to invest in the diverse array of perceived needs requires continual monitoring and frequent rebalancing.

THERE ARE NO "REAL" COSTS

A significant, articulate, and impassioned group of fathers in the sample insisted there were no real costs associated with involved fathering. They had shifted their expectations and perceptions to the point where they had come to the conclusion that there were no real costs. In essence, they had already implicitly or explicitly done a cost–benefits analysis and determined that the benefits outweighed the costs. In essence that represents a net gain. In the same way that finances need to be invested in a security or another investment in order to get a potential return, the initial investment is not viewed as a cost when a return comes. Similarly, a large portion of men in the sample disregarded any costs associated with involved fathering because they perceived the benefits to outweigh the costs, thus a net gain meant there were no "real" costs. In this portion of the interview, Randy replied that there were no costs (beyond finances) to fathering. I pressed him a bit by saying:

> Interviewer: I've heard dads who have said stuff like, "Gee, it's cost an awful lot of time, it's cost an awful lot of privacy, it's cost an awful lot of stuff you'd like to pursue. You know, you can't go out and hang out with the fellas. You don't really have any of that?
>
> Randy: But that's the responsibility of being a parent. That all comes with being a parent.
>
> Interviewer: So you don't consider it being—[he cut me off quickly]
>
> Randy: No. Because I accepted that. That goes along with it. That's just—you know, it would be like going to work for somebody all week, and you expect a paycheck at the end of the week. No, I've never considered it to be anything negative.

Randy expected costs to be associated with involved fathering. He had made the assessment of what it would cost and had decided to assume the responsibility. Because he had anticipated and accepted the costs, he did not any longer regard them as costs. Robert could not conceive of involvement with his children as a cost. He viewed the overall benefits to so far outweigh the costs that he was unable to construct any aspect of his engagement as a father as a loss. He offered:

> I can't see how it would cost. That is what we are saying isn't it? What does it cost me personally kind of thing?" It's done so much for me as a person that I really can't say that it would have that kind of effect. You know, I don't see any of that in effect at all. I was on a one-way street headed no where fast and ... they, just through the fact this tiny being came into the world, changed my entire perspective of life itself so I can't see where I can go back and, you know, you would think that ... that may have cost.

Tim expressed a similar position. A distinction, however, is Tim's assessment that anything he had lost is negligible compared to the benefits he receives from involvement with his son. He felt that the pleasures that he had "sacrificed" were not really pleasures at all. Tim related:

> I feel the same way with Andrew. Anything I've lost from having him, anything that's been changed, any pleasure I may have lost was not a real pleasure anyways compared to the pleasure that he gives me, and I hopefully return to him.

In talking through the costs of involved fathering, Chris was in the process of telling me how much thinking fathering can require. He finished a long statement about this by stating, "... so it takes a lot of time and mind, straight mind." I was attempting to reflect his statement of effort invested and responded to his lengthy comment by saying, "It's work, isn't it?" Chris quickly discounted my recap by countering, "It's not a job, it's an adventure." Chris viewed father involvement in the same way that a backpacker views the "work" of hiking long distances over rough terrain under a heavy pack. To focus on the work is completely missing the essence of the experience—it is the adventure that counts. In a similar manner, Craig felt that failure to invest all of your time is less than optimal for both fathers and children. He said:

> Craig: If you don't give them all your time I think you're shortchanging both them and yourself.
>
> Interviewer: How do you mean shortchanging yourself?
>
> Craig: You're shortchanging the benefit of raising them, you know, taking an active part in it.
>
> Interviewer: So even though it costs you time, you get the benefit of seeing them grow?

Craig: You get a lot back. You're giving up something that's meaningful to you as a single person or as the person without kids. But you're getting that much more back, it equals itself.

Neil saw the equation even more positively for fathers. He felt that, for him, not to change his course of behavior would be more costly than to engage fully with his children and family. He experienced true happiness in being other centered instead of applying himself to pursuing empty goals and "success" as defined by traditional measures:

Neil: I would say would it cost me more to keep on doing what I want to do than to change my attitude and to change my motives, probably.

Interviewer: How do you mean that?

Neil: Well, even though I was pursuing financial gain for me and under the guise of doing it for my family, sometimes and doing what I wanted to do, I wasn't happy anyway. But I find a real contentment in trying to meet the needs of my family and I don't know if I can explain that, but it brings me more joy to do [for them] than it does to do something for me.

Vicente recognized the emptiness and the deceptiveness of the things he had given up for involved fatherhood as well. He felt the things that had appeared to be attractive were really destructive and better abandoned. Vicente had reached the point where, looking back, he wondered why some of the things he "gave up" for fatherhood had ever attracted him to begin with:

The costs of fatherhood. You know, I would have to say, for me, the cost of fatherhood isn't really something that I was too sorry about paying a price for. Just different things in life that you put down so that you could be a better father, which actually is making you a better person. I wouldn't say those things were really a cost. I would have to say they were pretty much something that I needed to let go of anyhow. Not that it was a bad environment or anything like that but, you know, just not being in the party crowd anymore, or hanging out at the clubs. All that kind of stuff really takes a toll on you. When you let it go, it's, you don't miss it. I mean, if you're really sincere about what you're trying to do and accomplish, you don't miss it. You can look back on that and sometimes ask yourself, why was you ever there? Fatherhood has just made me that type of skeptic where I look at things like that now—what did you ever do that for?

From his vantage point as an involved father, Vicente had difficulty even remembering the draw of past activities. Adam similarly felt the things that he had "given up" were trivial in reality. Again, the things left behind were viewed to be more than compensated for by the benefits of involved fathering. Adam explained:

> I guess you have to give up I want to say, trivial things. Things that were important, but actually weren't. So you're not giving up that much. I think you're not really giving things up, you're trading things off more or less. You know, you give something up, but you get something, I think a lot better in return. It's like a barter system.

Donald had questioned the value of the things that he may have had to abandon for involved fatherhood, and came to the conclusion that he would be better off in the long run by investing in his family and children. Again, he focused on the fact that true meaning comes from investing in your children and in viewing your everyday commitments and activities through that lens. Donald revealed:

> It's like you could be doing all that stuff, whatever you may be doing, going to school or working real hard in your career, but why? So you can retire and go to Jamaica by yourself? [laugh] You know? No, because you want to work hard so you can send your kids to school or help them buy their first house with their family, you know, or whatever. There is a meaning to it. There is a reason for it.

COST–BENEFITS ANALYSES

If one engages in a cost–benefits analysis of involved fathering, it is clear that there are significant contributors to positive and negative columns on the balance sheet. In Lamb et al.'s (1987) words:

> Increased paternal involvement promises both advantages and disadvantages to fathers themselves. Among the costs are the likelihood of diminished earnings and career prospects as well as retarded promotion, marital friction, dissatisfaction with the boring tedium of day-to-day parenthood, and social isolation from disapproving friends, relatives and colleagues. Among the advantages or benefits are the potential for personal fulfillment through closer, richer relationships to one's children, along with the opportunity to witness and influence their development more thoroughly. As in the case of mothers, the relative evaluation of the costs and benefits must depend on the individual's values and aspirations as well as both economic and social circumstances. (pp. 121–122)

Based on considerations such as those just described, Lamb et al. concluded that "The fact that increased paternal involvement may have both beneficial and detrimental consequences for mothers and fathers precludes us from concluding that changes in paternal involvement would necessarily be *either* 'good' or 'bad' in themselves" (p. 123).

In presenting the perspectives of the 40 men who represent a diverse group of fathers, we have marshaled the evidence to demonstrate that involved fathers encounter multiple developmental contexts across personal, social, and work domains and experience a wide variety of costs and benefits. Each father had unique developmental and family histories characterized by different patterns of father involvement, and each felt the costs of involved fathering were not as substantial as the benefits they had experienced.

Chapter 13

Provisional Balances Revisited

In fathers' own constructions, their relationships and activities with their children significantly contributed to who they were as developing people. Men saw fathering as a foundational force in shaping their own development. Fathering defined much of their identity (Minton & Pasley, 1996), took much of their time and energy (Daly & Dienhart, 1997), and shaped their daily schedules (Daly, 1996a, 1996b) and developmental outcomes (Palkovitz, 1996a). Beyond that, fathering gave meaning (Palkovitz, 2000) to an otherwise meaningless routine. Fathering anchored men's mental, physical, and relational life. Fathering changed men's foci, their lifestyles, their family relationships, their work lives, their community involvements, their health habits, their morals and values, their emotional lives, and their marriages. The transformations perceived to be brought about by actively engaging in fathering children had many positive demand characteristics as well as some significant challenges, hassles, energy demands, resource drains, unmet needs, and fears.

In the sense of crisis being an opportunity for growth as well as for risk, men in this sample had various ways to engage in their fathering roles to meet the challenges in the most positive ways that they could, given their resources. They worked to bring balance to their lives in conjunction with the needs of their families. They felt the need to balance provision and time with the family, discipline with building relationship, and time for the marriage with time for the family as a whole. Fathers found ways to balance investment in the community with time and energy for their families. The balances that sample fathers reached were provisional—they changed constantly as demands constantly changed. In looking for balance in these areas, men were drawn into greater levels of integration and differentiation than they had experienced previously. In essence, they had matured (Allport, 1961). Some maturation was manifested in virtually every realm of development. This is not to suggest that all changes associated with fathering children are perceived by men to be pleasant or positive. However, in the overall balance, they viewed fathering to be a valuable shaper of their lives for the better.

It is important to note, however, that it was not just that the men in the sample were fathers. They were involved fathers and they desired to be good fathers, even if they voiced some uncertainty about their ability to articulate the elements of good fathering. Essentially, to be a good father, you have to be a good person, which requires growth, change, maturation, and development for virtually all men. Thus, fathering, or more accurately, good fathering, exerts a developmental pull on men to become better people.

In short, when a man sees that fathering is a call in his life, when he desires to do well in the role, when he applies himself to fostering the development of his children, he sees the need to do well himself. Involved fathers attempt to rise to the challenge to become better than they are and to persevere through difficulties and struggles, because they perceive that it is worth it. This brings change for the better.

Although there are "costs" to laying down your life for the sake of others, there is a gain that transcends the self. It passes into the next generation, and beyond the family into the community and society at large. This is the hallmark of generativity (Christiansen & Palkovitz, 1998; McAdams & de St. Albin, 1998), a hallmark of midlife adjustment.

Because they viewed their engagement in fathering as a calling and a high priority, men in the sample applied themselves to overcome habits, tendencies, and circumstances they felt were not positive or developmentally facilitative for their children. Not all men made the same range and degree of commitment, but all men applied themselves to some changes that brought good. To varying degrees, fathers worked at making themselves better models, more understanding, more available, better teachers, adequate providers, and encouragers. Some men committed to improving family relationships, to engagement in the community through volunteerism, toward participation in a faith community, and involvement in children's friendships, schools, athletic leagues, churches, and scouting programs. Fathers in the sample thought through the importance of improving their communities and the world. Their commitment to their children led them to view the future differently. They were more likely to invest in it in a way that fostered enhanced quality and improved conditions. Committed fathers are not just committed to their children, they recognize the need to make themselves better, their families stronger, their communities better, and thus, the world a better place. Men who are committed to their children are likely to show commitment to family and community values and standards that improve society for everybody. Although social scientists may find these statements to be simplistic and maudlin, they would not be characterized as such by the men in the sample.

In recognizing their responsibility, the commitment, and the sheer scope of the tasks of fathering, men in the sample tended to see that they had room for improvement, a need to grow, and a need to put off some patterns and characteristics and to develop some greater capacities, new traits, and characteristics. Some fathers (see chap. 4, this vol.) viewed the transition to fatherhood as a jolt that brought significant, life altering consequences to them. Others felt their involvement with their children had merely nuanced the mix of characteristics and maturity levels. None, however, felt unchanged by fatherhood. Most men, in fact, felt fathering was the single greatest shaper of their lives—more so than marriage, education, family of origin, work history, or beliefs, morals, or values. In short, for this diverse sample of fathers, involved fathering was perceived to be the primary shaper of who they had become as men.

In reading the interview transcripts searching for unifying themes, "balance" emerged as the central, overarching theme. It permeated every domain, every area of inquiry within every domain, and was expressed in some manner by every participant. The idea that balance was required in different elements of the complex, shifting, and multifaceted role of fathering quickly lead to an expansion of the theme from "balance" to "balances." Seeing the diversity of creative ways that different men had worked to bring a sense of balance to their lives also supported the plural form, balances. Because of the centrality of the provider role (discussed in chaps. 3 and 11), I also began to reflect about the salience of themes of providing.

Because qualitative analysis has much to do with meaning making (Dienhart, 1998), I decided to explore various meanings of the emergent themes in dictionaries. The following is a series of pertinent composite definitions, edited from a number of dictionaries:

> **Provisional: serving for the time being;** temporary
>
> Provide 1: to take precautionary measures 2: to make a proviso or stipulation 3: to make preparation to meet a need, especially to supply something for sustenance or support.
>
> **Provider: one that provides; especially breadwinner.**
>
> Provision 1 a: the act or process of providing b: the fact or state of being prepared beforehand c: a measure taken beforehand to deal with a need or contingency: preparation 2: a stock of needed materials or supplies, especially a stock of food 3: proviso, stipulation.
>
> **Balance** 1: an instrument for weighing: as a: a beam that is supported freely in the center and has two pans of equal weights suspended from its ends b: a device that uses the elasticity of a spiral spring for measuring weight or force 2: a means of judging or deciding 3: **a counterbalancing weight, force, or influence** 4 a: stability produced by even distribution of weight on each side of a vertical axis b: **equipose between contrasting, opposite, or interacting elements** c: **equality between the totals of the two sides of an account** 5 a: **an aesthetically pleasing integration of elements** 6: **mental and emotional steadiness** Verb 1: **to compute difference between the debits and credits of (an account) 2: to pay the amount due on: settle 3: to bring into harmony or proportion.**

The word "provisional" connotes temporary, tentative arrangements that depend on conditions being met or maintained. Being well provided for means stability and foresight that yields preparedness to cope. Being a provider is a position that means that one has the means to care for others, beyond self-preservation.

The word "balance" itself holds multiple meanings, an intricacy that defies reductionism. Balance is complex to define, and even more difficult to maintain. Changing positions and conditions exert pulls and forces on elements to sway in different directions and to change in relationship to an equilibrium previously achieved. To shift to the plural, "balances," makes things even more precarious, demanding, and enigmatic.

Placing *provisional balances* together brings a juxtaposition of hope and despair, achievement and impending crisis, foresight and foreboding, a sense of tenuous solutions, subject to change without notice, or unknown periods of stability, with unexpected shuffling of elements expected. Provisional balances connote the shifting and temporary nature of maintaining equilibrium under dynamic conditions.

The prevalent theme in the transcripts is that in every domain of development (e.g., self, social, and work), men who are fathers construct provisional balances on a continual basis. In their own words, participants in this study of the effects of fathering on men's adult development discussed shifting balances between their need to be their children's "buddy" and "boss"; providing discipline without being dictator; providing enough material necessities and extras without spoiling; being involved in daily caregiving and activities without dominating; dividing time between work, family, and community involvement; sharing roles with wives; treating each of their children equally; simultaneously being strong and loving; preparing their children for launching without thrusting them away; fostering independence in their dependents; having time for themselves and being involved with their families; modeling faith without proselytizing; expressing emotions and regulating mood swings; being a mentor who is learning to lead; balancing the way things were in the past and the way they are now; being a son at the same time as being a father; and covering the costs and reaping the benefits of involved fatherhood. In each of these issues, provisional balances had been reached, but were susceptible to the dynamics of an unstable system of many factors.

In many ways, it is comfortable and fitting to frame men's adult development as provisional balances: The fathers in the study themselves acknowledge the provider role as central to fatherhood and manhood in contemporary America. They insightfully discuss their struggles to achieve balance in economic providing and involved fatherhood. They can easily recount how their schedules change over both short and long periods of time, and how seasonal or work cycle variations in demands result in different involvement patterns at work, or how events at home alter work availability. Even the balances they have achieved as providers are provisional.

Each man in the study brought unique and individually creative balances to their fathering experiences. Each had a different set of resources and demands. Each had achieved a level of adaptation by balancing their resources and demands in individually unique ways.

The emergence of provisional balances as the central, unifying theme offers a new set of lenses for understanding men's midlife development and life-course analysis. It is also essential to acknowledge that virtually all people experience provisional balances; they are not unique to fathers. An understanding of women's development may be enhanced from considering the balances that they have achieved and the roles and pressures they have juggled to do so as well. Similarly, nonparents and children and adolescents, as well as adults, have to continually negotiate balances that yield developmental consequences. For example, the developmental gains associated with participation in an extracurricular activity needs to be balanced against the time invested in it and the need to perform academically.

During adulthood, the maintenance of developmentally maturing provisional balances experienced in the contexts of fathering, marriage, social relationships, and work affords a different level of analysis for Freud's (1933/1964) markers of functional maturity in adulthood, "to love and to work," and to Erikson's construct (1950) of generativity. Without balance, a person falls. Without balance, it is difficult to walk alongside another, to lead another, to care for another with skill, or to accomplish meaningful work.

In two-parent households, mothers and fathers have the potential to provide a greater balance than what is typically available in a one-parent household. This is not to imply that two-parent households are always better, they simply represent a different set of balances. More often than not, two-parent households represent a more diverse blend of strengths and resources (as well as weaknesses or deficits) that are absent from single-parent households, regardless of gender of parent. However, two-parent families have the challenge of adjusting the balances they share with another adult.

The phenomenon of reworking (Snarey, 1993), discussed in chapter 9, also can be understood as a manifestation of working through of provisional balances. Most of what people model or rework is a balance of what they have seen to be appropriate or inappropriate balances in others' lives. The very process of modeling and reworking is a balancing act.

People have the mistaken impression that balance is static, that movement brings instability. That is true in some models. Any toddler can attest that trying to stack building blocks is an entirely different enterprise on a solid floor than it is in the back seat of a moving vehicle. Other balances, however, are more easily achieved and maintained with movement. Remaining motionless on a "parked" bicycle is impossible unless the bike is firmly anchored. Riding at a reasonable speed is easier than either remaining motionless, going too fast, or going too slow. (I have learned this practical lesson mountain biking with my sons.) As individuals' lives and relationships traverse time, changes are introduced that require rebalancing. Changes accompany time. To remain balanced, it is necessary for them to move. Individuals develop in the process, because they redistribute the way that they respond to the various factors pushing and pulling them in different directions. This is true whether they look at developmental characteristics of maturity, such as changes in integration and differentiation, or whether they focus more on contextual changes brought on by changes in health, economics, relationships, roles, and countless other variables that can be viewed as requiring adjustments in the balances people have temporarily achieved.

One way to view "good fathering" is that it provides a healthy, developmentally faciliative and supportive balance of attributes. On the contrary, shipwrecked fathering can be understood to be a lack of balance. It results from investing too heavily in one or more domains that leaves one unbalanced overall, and thus not well adapted. It is a misinvestment of resources that leads to unbalanced participation, and eventually, a fall. The fall could come in one or more domains (self, social, or work), but prolonged lack of balance will eventually result in succumbing to changing demands of movement working in conjunction with gravity. If one waits too long to adjust to an impending fall, if enough counterforce is not applied, then the fall will happen. Keeping something balanced is easier than righting a falling object, particularly if the falling object is comprised of many interdependently balanced components.

If one looks at fathers' interview transcripts through those lenses, then men who are attempting to be good fathers are constantly responding to movement (changes in contingencies, developmental capacities of their children, partners and themselves) and gravity (importance or priority, assuming responsibility for various areas of care). Balance would be a simple matter if there were neither movement nor gravity. However, relationships, being comprised of combinations of developing people, constantly change. Movement is a given of developing relationships. Because people invest emotional energy, personal commitment, hope, love, and other "intangibles" into relationships, there is an importance or gravity associated. The centrality of interpersonal relationships in human existence has been one of the best documented phenomena of social science. Involved fathers must continuously negotiate provisional balances because of the dynamic nature of developing and intergenerational relationships that are valued.

As documented in chapter 3, fathering roles are multidimensional. It is a constant challenge to maintain balance, because the systems involved are dynamic. As elements change force or position, the necessary balance changes. It is probably impossible to maintain balance in the short run.

True balance in roles is really achieved across substantial periods of time—perhaps days, weeks, months, seasons, or eras. In the short run, things appear awfully unbalanced (e.g., Thursdays may be a long day in someone's work schedule, but the "compensate" for it by greater involvement on other days). So, balance comes across longer periods of time and across a variety of contexts, but balance always requires active involvement.

There is a dynamic relation between involvement, balance, and development. The balances are provisional, but they affect development based on a history of involvement. When you invest in fathering, it yields a return, some of which is quite tangible. There is generativity, pride in seeing the growth of your kids and the value of the contributions they make to others, emotionally, relationally, and in other ways. Similar to financial investment, involvement yields a return. The return may be in self, social, or work realms (or an interaction of all of these), but there is a return. The return may be realized in a greater capacity for empathy, a more mature conceptualization of social relationships, a greater range and depth of emotion, or just plain "fun." As in financial investments, the returns can be reinvested (with the potential for even greater gains or loss of what was gained in the first place) or they can be withdrawn from the account to "live on." It is really no different with father involvement. Some developmental dividends are reinvested and some are needed for sustenance.

Where fathers invest, their dividends will be more likely to build. Is it in their career? their marriage? their kids? or is it a "balanced" investment into these different areas? One should maintain a diversified portfolio in sound financial investments in rapidly changing economic conditions, and the same is true in fathering. If a father does not invest enough time, effort, emotion, and involvement with his spouse, then he is likely to realize marital problems in the future. Many of society's problems with at-risk youth can be understood as misappropriations of resources leading to an imbalance in their families of origin.

Balance has been an issue at the forefront of discourse concerning men's and women's roles in contributing to economic and caring work in families. There are acknowledgments made that there are trade-offs between economic providing and other forms of providing (caring). Yet, no serious discussion has centered on the balance within individuals; the focus has been on equity across family members. That literature documents that when one attempts to invest too much in too many areas at once, role strain is realized, and the investments are seen as inadequate. Attempting to spread investable resources too thin is what is referred to as *role strain* (Marks, 1977).

Discussions with men concerning the effects of fathering on various aspects of their development (e.g., work, marriage, health, relationships, etc.) has caused me to see that current developmental status is really a composite picture of current balance of resources and investments in each of numerous realms. Future development is dependent on investment of resources into various realms now (you will reap what you sow), interacting with events and chance.

In "archaic" explanations of personality, balances of body humors were thought to determine characteristics. Although there are many factors that contribute to personality, only some of which are biochemical, people seem to have abandoned the concept of balance as too simplistic. Applying Occam's Razor to the concept of development, developmental status simply may be considered the result of the provisional balances of resources invested over time.

Textbooks on adult development have little to say about the effects of parenting on adult development, and even less to say, at least explicitly, about balance. As children grow and develop, parenting roles change. The balances between children's needs and parental resources shift, and new balances are established. As children become more independent (which is to say that they have achieved a new balance in their resources), parents need to invest their resources in other directions, or they become developmentally stagnant. If parents cannot relinquish some of their involvement with children as they approach the launching phase, their marriages may be at risk. Some parents choose to redistribute their energies by going back to work, others report a new honeymoon period with their spouse, whereas others get involved in volunteer work. But, virtually all balanced people reinvest their no longer needed energies into something other than their maturing children at that point.

Different individuals achieve different balances because they experience a different set of demands and resources. Some have an inheritance of high IQ, emotional stability, economic resources, and social position. They have a different set of resources to invest, and others have relatively few resources to invest in their children, marriages, or careers. Yet, each strives to achieve a balanced "budget" of resources and demands. It should be pointed out that a balanced budget of $10,000 per year and a balanced budget of $100,000 per year are both balanced, but the associated lifestyles are strikingly different. Similarly, a balanced budget of $10,000 may not be very glamorous, but it has different implications that a budget of $100,000 that is overspent by $10,000 every year. Continued deficits lead to bankruptcy. So again, the importance of achieving balance over the long term is highlighted.

The primary areas of controversy in life-span development, the perennial debates regarding continuity versus discontinuity, nature versus nurture, and universality versus context specific development can each be recast and understood in terms of provisional balances. This suggestion is not meant to recommend that developmentalists adopt some form of balance theory as a superordinate theory to explain all phenemona. Rather, it suggests that viewing developmental phenomena through an interpretive lens of provisional balances affords a different vista for understanding the issues and contributing to the development of emergent theory and research. In short, balance as a construct has little potential to be developed into a fully elaborated theory. However, balance is a useful lens for refining an understanding and a discourse concerning developmental phenomena.

By explicitly asking, "In any situation, what are the different factors that are exerting significant influence, and what are their relative contributions?" (a balance question), it is possible to come to a position of clearly examining the underlying issues, recognizing the state of our knowledge—the ability (or lack of ability) for disciplines to address the questions, and the complex array and interdependence of factors influencing developmental outcomes at any given time. Also, viewing development through the lens of provisional balances fosters an appreciation for both the resilience and fragility of people, relationships, and families. It has been stated that change is the only constant. With time comes change. There are temporal fluctuations in the push/pull/importance/salience/significance/priority/centrality given to any particular factor influencing development.

IMPLICATIONS FOR FUTURE RESEARCH

The current study provides empirical support to the notion that fathering changes men's life course and development. In order to make assessments of causal direction and to rule out other explanations for change over time (e.g., aging, maturation, education, other life experiences), it is necessary to collect data from fathers and nonfathers, or to track a sample of men prospectively, with several data collection points before and after the transition to fatherhood. It would also be instructive to monitor developmental change in men in a manner that could compare the effects of differing levels and meanings of father involvement over time with other life circumstances. Traditional funding sources have been reticent to sponsor such research, but some of the most perplexing questions concerning the nature of development and their causes await exploration in the everyday contexts of fathering.

CONCLUSIONS

As men apply themselves to active engagement in fathering, they immerse themselves into a rapidly changing and complex array of shifting conditions. Viewing good fathering as an ideal to subscribe to brings a different set of circumstances and therefore different developmental outcomes than deciding not to engage in fathering. Involved fathers develop differently than men who do not engage in fathering. Recalling that fathering is not the only pathway to generativity and there are fallacies in universally adopting the "more is better" approaches to father involvement, it should be recognized that good fathering is good for everyone.

This is a story that needs to be told in today's culture where too often the focus is on the breakdown of the family, and the "not worth it" aspects of family life. Forty diverse men who had made 40 different commitments to involved fathering (in 40 different patterns) recounted how they believed that fathering had changed them—mostly for the better. For some years now, it has been surmised that good fathering is good for child development outcomes, good for the mothers of children, and good for communities where involved fathers live. Now there is qualitative data to support theoretical and anecdotal accounts so that it is possible to say with confidence that good fathering is perceived by fathers to be good for men's adult development. Although the data are unable to unequivocally demonstrate that it is fathering per se that is responsible for developmental change in fathers, the nearly unanimous perception of fathers is that it is involvement in fathering that has facilitated their developmental maturity in personal, social, familial, and career realms. In many ways, the child is father to the man.

Appendix 1

Interview Schedule

Following is the "normal" sequence of questions and their forms for interviews conducted with each of the 40 study participants. In each interview, this schedule was used as a flexible guide for talking with study participants about the central issues of the research project. If men spontaneously began to discuss an area that was scheduled for later exploration, the "natural" flow of the conversation was allowed to progress, and the interviewer brought the participant back toward the planned sequence of questions as appropriate. Levels of language were adjusted to individual father's educational or communication style. Because demographic questionnaires were filled out by participants prior to the interview, and because the interviewer reviewed those questionnaires with each father to clarify the information and establish rapport (a process requiring approximately 20 minutes of interaction), the interviewer had a basis for understanding communication styles and language levels prior to beginning the interview.

INTERVIEW GUIDE: THE EFFECTS OF PARENTING ON MEN'S DEVELOPMENT

How old were you when you had your first child?

Please describe and extenuating or qualifying circumstances concerning your children: planning, timing, illnesses, developmental disabilities, etc.

Sometimes you hear men make statements like "I am really a different person than I would otherwise be because I have children." Other men may feel that fatherhood has had little or no impact on who they are as people. Do you feel that fatherhood has played a major or minor role in shaping who you are? Please elaborate ...

If you feel that your life is significantly different than it would be if you didn't have children, please be specific in describing how you think it is different.

Aside from how you spend time and money (quantitative differences), do you feel that fatherhood has made you a qualitatively different person? That is, has it caused you to develop differently than you would have developed had you never been a father? Has it significantly affected *who* you are, your skills, your personality, or the quality of your life course? If so how? If not, why not?

Do you feel that fatherhood has in any way affected your maturity? Please explain.

How has fatherhood changed you in regards to the way you approach and view responsibility, if at all?

What are the primary feelings/emotions, both positive and negative, that you associate with fatherhood?

Do you believe that these feelings/emotions can be experienced in the same way in another context, like work or another relationship? Why or why not?

Do you believe that fatherhood has influenced the way you experience, control, and express emotions? If so, how? Are you an emotionally different person?

In terms of your career or work history, what impact, if any, has fatherhood had on your work?

Are there any specific ways that fatherhood has influenced your work history?

Do you feel that you would be further along, just about where you are now, or less far advanced in your work situation if you had never had children?

Any further comments about fathering and work?

How does/has parenthood impacted your relationship with your spouse/partner?

What impact has fatherhood had on your sexuality?
—frequency?
—quality?
—other aspects?

How has parenthood affected your relationship to other relatives?
—your view of your own parents?

Have you become more or less understanding or critical?

How has fatherhood effected your feelings about your own childhood?

Have you thought over how your parents brought you up?
—positive or negative events you experienced?
—reflected on your interests or viewpoints?

How has fatherhood affected your social life or friendships?
—the number of people you interact with?
—network size?
—the types of people you spend time with?
—composition? How often you get together?
—frequency of contact?

Please describe any effect fatherhood has had on your involvement in your community/or in organizations:

Has fatherhood had any significant effect on your ability or desire to take the perspective of others?

Has fatherhood influenced your perceptions of individual differences or diversity in other people?

How, if at all, has fatherhood changed the way you think about and plan for the future?

Has fatherhood influenced what you view to be the main priorities, or what is important in life?

Has fatherhood influenced your views of moral issues?

Has fatherhood influenced your commitment to religion?
—in terms of religious faith?
—in terms of religious behavior/expression?

Has fathering resulted in any shifts in your values?

If so what may those shifts be?

How did fathering interact with these shifts?

What impact, if any, has fathering had on your health habits?
—diet?
—exercise?
—smoking/drinking/drug usage?
—access to medical care (the way you view benefits packages)?
—other?

What impact has fathering had on where you live?

The way your living space is organized, divided, maintained?

Do you feel that fatherhood causes one to experience more conflicting demands than would be the case if you did not have children? Please elaborate …

Has fatherhood brought about any changes in your own competence/self-esteem?

Are there specific areas of competence or ability that you would not have developed had you not been a father?

Are there other areas you would have developed or pursued had you not been a father? Are there different choices you would have made or different interests you would have developed?

Overall, would you say that fatherhood has made you more or less flexible? How so?

How has fatherhood changed you in regards to the way you approach and view problem solving?

What do you view to be the primary benefits of fatherhood?
—the primary costs?

Overall, do you view fatherhood to be a positive or negative shaper of your life and why?

If you had a "magic wand" and could change the number, spacing, timing of children, etc., what would you change and why?

Please describe how you view the father's role.

In everyday terms, what makes a good father?

What do you see as a father's main responsibilities/jobs:
—with regard to his children?
—with regard to his wife?

Are there some things only a dad can do?

Are there some things only a mom can do?

What's the toughest part of being a dad?

Some men are primarily involved as fathers by being a provider. Others may take more active roles in direct involvement with the daily activities of their children. Some men are the primary caregivers for their children. Please describe your pattern of involvement with your children.

In terms of rough percentages, how do you split the following things with your spouse/partner?
—time spent in parenting (overall time doing things with or for the kids)?
—number of parenting tasks?
—responsibility of parenthood (making appointments/arrangements for children ... making sure they have what they need ... clothing, food, supervision, education)?

Has it always been this way, or has your involvement changed over time? If so, how?

Is there anything I should know about your background to help me understand who you are as a dad?

How did you learn to be a father?

Do you have any closing thoughts on fatherhood? Any areas that we haven't discussed that you feel are important to consider?

We have now explored a lot of areas of your life and development. You have stated that you thought that fatherhood has had a major influence on your development in a number of areas (review those areas where the participant had expressed significant perceived changes). How can you be sure that it was fatherhood that brought about those changes/differences, and not just aging or maturity or other life circumstances?

In terms of rough percentages, how much of who you are is due to fatherhood? What percent of you is there because you have children?

Do you have any questions or comments about this interview? Suggestions for making it a better/easier experience?

Appendix **2**

Biographical Sketches of Study Participants

Each man who participated in the study was assigned a pseudonym. In this appendix, men are listed by increasing age within different groups of fathers, determined by their age at their first transition to fatherhood (early timing, on time, and late timing fathers). All information provided about participants is intended to assist the reader in understanding some elements that have been shown in previous research to be important contexts for fathering and to represent the diversity of fathering situations represented by men in the study. The brief sketches provided here were constructed from information provided by the fathers on demographic questionnaires that they completed just prior to the interview. Some sketches also include clarifying information that was shared during the interview. Because income information was collected in "bands" of $10,000 increments (e.g., $20,000–$30,000), midpoints of those bands were arbitrarily selected as figures to report for family income in these sketches.

EARLY TIMING FATHERS

John was a 22-year-old, Caucasian, single parent of two sons, ages 3 and 6. He made his first transition to fatherhood at age 16. He and his former partner had never married. They cohabited for 3½ years before splitting up. His former partner was currently cohabiting at the time of the interview, and John had been living alone with custody of his two sons for the past 2½ years. For the first month after their separation, the children had gone to live with their mother, but returned to live with John continuously from that time on. John had taken some college coursework, but did not have a college degree. He had state support for child care while he attended college courses. He was self-employed approximately 15 hours per week at the time of the interview in "international distribution" and reported a household income below $20,000 per year. John listed his religious identity as "Christian" and explained that he did not participate in organized religion, but taught his children about "religious happenings" and read to his children from the Bible.

Alan was a 23-year-old, Caucasian, married father of two daughters, ages 2 years and 8 weeks. He was 21 at the time of his first transition to fatherhood. Alan had completed some college coursework, but did not hold a degree or certificate. His wife was a high school graduate as well. Alan worked full time as an authorization clerk at a bank and his wife had been home full time since the birth of their first child. Alan reported their household income to be below $20,000 per year. Identified as a Methodist, Alan estimated spending 1 hour per week in religious services.

Donald was a 23-year-old, Caucasian, married father of a 4-year-old son and a 3-year-old daughter. Donald's partner became pregnant prior to their marriage, when he was 18 years old. They had been married for 4 years at the time of the interview. Donald had taken some college courses, but had neither earned a college degree nor completed an advanced certificate program. He had deferred a desire to pursue higher education so that he could support his wife and children. Donald was working 40 hours per week in the health care field. His wife had taken some college coursework as well and was working full time. Their family income was approximately $45,000. Donald reported no religious preference and no time in weekly religious activities.

Michael was a 26-year-old, African American father, who was separated with a divorce pending. At the time of the interview, he was engaged to a woman who had three children from a previous relationship. He considered himself to be a stepfather to those children. His first child was born when he was 16. He was a the biological father of three children, a 10-year-old daughter, an 8-year-old daughter, and a 5-year-old son. His stepchildren were a 14-year-old daughter, an 11-year-old son, and a 9-year-old daughter. At the time of the interview, he was cohabiting with his fiancé and his stepchildren and regularly saw his biological children every other weekend. Michael had completed some college coursework, but held no degree. He was employed half time and his fiancé worked full time. He reported a household annual income of $35,000. Michael reported no religious preference and no time in weekly religious activities.

Craig was a 27-year-old, Caucasian father of three daughters, ages 2, 4, and 9. Craig and his wife were both in their first marriage. They married after they became pregnant when Craig was 18 years old. Craig had completed high school and had taken "a few" college courses, but held no advanced degree. Craig was the sole provider for the family, working more than 40 hours per week as a printer. Craig described his wife as being "employed full time" as a stay at home mother. He reported an annual family income of approximately $45,000. Craig listed "Roman Catholic" as a religious preference, and indicated that he did not spend any time on a regular basis attending services.

Randy was a 33-year-old, Caucasian father of four children. He had two daughters, ages 5 and 8, and two sons, ages 1 and 4. His first child had been born when Randy was 21. Randy and his wife had been married for 12 years at the time of the interview. Randy had completed high school and his wife had taken "a few" college courses after completing high school. Randy was self-employed as a building contractor, and his wife stayed home full time. Randy reported earning approximately $25,000 per year. He listed "Pentecostal" as a religious preference and reported 4 hours per week in religious activities. Randy reported that he and his wife had experienced 3 miscarriages. Two had occurred between the births of their first two children, and the last had occurred after the birth of his youngest son.

Steve was a 35-year-old, Caucasian father of a 16-year-old daughter, an 8-year-old son, and a 2-year-old son. Steve had been married for 10 years, followed by 8 years of separation. He did not have a legal divorce, and had been cohabiting with his girlfriend for the 3 years prior to the interview. His former wife had custody of their 16-year-old daughter, and his 8-year-old son spent half time residing with Steve. Steve's 2-year-old son was born to his cohabiting girlfriend. In addition, his never-married girlfriend had a 7-year-old daughter from a previous relationship. She co-resided with Steve and his partner. Steve had completed high school and had taken some college coursework without obtaining a degree or certificate. His partner had completed high school and some college courses as well. His partner was employed full time. Steve had lost his job as a computer operator 3 weeks prior to the interview. He reported a household income of about $45,000. When asked to state his religious preference or identity, Steve responded " passive (non-active) Christian." He did not spend any time in organized religious services on a weekly basis.

James was a 43-year-old, African American father of three children and a stepfather of three children. James was divorced and remarried. His first child, a 23-year-old daughter, was born before his first marriage. He had also fathered a son (age 17 at the time of the interview) with his first wife, and a daughter (age 13) with his second wife. Although his current wife had three children from previous relationships (daughters ages 17 and 20, and a son, age 15), this was her first marriage. James had dropped out of high school to support his family, and had spent 10 years prior to the interview unemployed. He reported being disabled ("hip problems"). His spouse had also been unemployed for the past 6 years, but was scheduled to begin work the week following the interview. James reported an annual family income of less than $10,000 per year. James stated "Pentecostal" as a religious preference and reported 10 hours per week in religious services.

ON TIME FATHERS

Peter was a 23-year-old, Caucasian, married father of a 1-year-old son. It was the third marriage for his wife, who was 14 years older than Peter. It was Peter's first marriage. Peter had completed high school and had taken some college coursework without completing a degree or certificate program. His wife was a high school graduate as well. At the time of the interview, both Peter and his wife were unemployed. Peter had been laid off for 2 weeks. He was currently seeking a better position. Peter reported a household income of $25,000. He listed "Christian" as his religious identity and indicated that he spent between 0 and 2.5 hours per week in attending religious services.

Chris was a 25-year-old, African American father of a 3-year-old and stepfather of a 13-year-old son and a 12-year-old daughter. Chris reported that he was never married, and currently cohabiting with his "girlfriend" (his second serious relationship). She had been previously married. Both Chris and his partner had high school degrees. Chris was working 10 hours per week at the time of the interview, and his partner was unemployed. Chris stated that he had a total disability from a back injury sustained in a bus accident. He reported an annual family income of less than $10,000. Chris listed "Baptist" as a religious preference, but indicated that he did not invest any time in weekly religious services.

Tim was a 27-year-old, European American, married father of a 1-year-old son. He was currently pursuing Ph.D. studies, while working full time. Both he and his wife were in their first marriage. Tim's wife held a 4-year degree and was working full time as well. Tim reported a household income of $35,000 annually. He listed his religious identity as "Dissenting Catholic" and did not report any weekly involvement in religious services.

Vicente was a 27-year-old, African American father of an infant daughter. He had previously been married for 3 years, but was separated from his first wife. At the time of the interview, he had been cohabiting with the mother of his daughter for 4 years. His partner had been married and divorced, with no children from her first marriage. Vicente had completed some college coursework, but held no college degree. His partner had graduated from high school. Vicente had been employed full time as a production worker and had been unemployed for one week at the time of the interview. He was working 60 hours per week through temp agencies. His partner was working full time. He reported their household income to be $35,000. For religious identity, Vicente listed "Christian" and reported 1 hour of engagement in services on a weekly basis.

Mark was a 28-year-old, Caucasian, married father of a 10-month-old son. It was the first marriage for both he and his wife, and both held 4-year college degrees. At the time of the interview, Mark was working two jobs: full time at a large bank and 19 hours per week as a finance manager of a food bank. His wife was also working full time. Mark reported an annual household income of $65,000. He stated "Lutheran" as a religious preference and estimated that he spent 5 hours per week in religious services.

Scott was a 29-year-old, Caucasian, married father of two daughters, ages 3 and 5. Both Scott and his wife held high school diplomas. At the time of the interview, Scott was working two jobs (approximately 60 hours per week total) and his spouse was working full time. Scott reported a family income of approximately $35,000 per year. He listed "Orthodox" as his religious preference, and estimated spending 1 hour per week in religious services.

Charles was a 32-year-old, African American father of a 4-year-old son, and stepfather to 16- and 19-year-old daughters. His wife's daughters were from previous relationships. Charles held a high school diploma, and his wife held a 2-year degree. Both Charles and his wife worked full time, and reported a family income of approximately $35,000 per year. Charles described himself as a Pentecostal who spent approximately 6 hours per week in religious activities.

Nelson was a 32-year-old, Hispanic, divorced father of a 7-year-old daughter and a 5-year-old son. At the time of the interview, Nelson had been divorced for 1 year and 8 months. He had been a single parent father for the past 3 years. He had completed some college coursework, but held no degree or certificate. Nelson reported that he worked part time in his father's store, was active in the National Guard, was a landlord, and collected unemployment. He estimated that he worked approximately 10 hours per week, and had a household income of less than $20,000. Nelson listed "Catholic" as his religious identity and attended services 1.5 hours per week.

Clifford was a 33-year-old, African American father of an 8-year-old daughter and a 7-year-old son. He also reported being the stepfather of a 1-year-old daughter, who was born to his current fiancé. Clifford had separated from his former spouse 2½ years prior to the interview and had finalized a divorce 5 months prior to his participation in the study. He was currently cohabiting with his fiancé. Clifford had completed high school and some college course work, but held no advanced degrees or certificates. He was employed full time by the state and worked approximately 10 hours per week in a funeral home as well. His fiancé had completed some college coursework and worked full time. Clifford reported his annual household income to be approximately $45,000. He reported spending approximately 2 to 3 hours per week in religious services as a Methodist.

Manuel was a 33-year-old, African American father of 2 children and a stepfather of 4 children. Neither Manuel nor his current partner had ever married. Manuel had relationships with multiple partners prior to his current partner. He had fathered two daughters, ages 4 and 10, at the time of the interview. His oldest daughter was born to a previous partner, and his youngest daughter to his current partner. Although not married, he perceived himself to be the stepfather to 2 sons (ages 8 and 10) and 2 daughters (ages 6 and 17) of his current partner. Manuel reported that he and his current partner had "split up" for a year after their daughter was born, but they had reunited and had been together for a total of 3 years. Manuel had completed high school, but his partner had dropped out and did not hold a GED. At the time of the interview, Manuel was self-employed, working full time as a telemarketer. His partner was working approximately 20 hours per week. Manuel reported a prior history of long-term gang activity, drug trafficking, and incarceration. Manuel reported a combined family income of less than $10,000 per year. He reported a religious conversion experience and listed "Christian" as a religious preference, and estimated that he spent approximately 5 hours per week in religious services.

Thomas was a 33-year-old, "white Anglo," married father of a 2-year-old son. Thomas held a Ph.D. in sociology, and his wife held a Ph.D. and had done postdoctoral training as well. Both Thomas and his wife were employed full time. Their reported family income was $70,000. Thomas identified himself as an agnostic and did not spend any time in religious activity on a weekly basis.

Glen was a 34-year-old, Italian American father of a 6-year-old daughter and a 2-year-old son. Glen and his wife were both in their first marriage. Glen was working on a masters' degree in business, and was employed 45 hours per week as a marketing executive. His wife had a 4-year college degree and worked 20 hours per week at the time of the interview. Glen reported a household income of approximately $85,000 per year. As a Roman Catholic, Glen estimated spending approximately 2 hours per week in religious services.

Neil was a 34-year-old, White Anglo-Saxon father of two daughters and a son. His first daughter was born when he was 25. At the time of the interview, his daughters were 7 and 9 years old, and his son was 2. Neil was married. Both he and his wife had completed high school and taken some college coursework, but they held no advanced degrees. Neil was self-employed as a trucking contractor, working "many part time jobs" totaling over 40 hours per week. His wife was working 10 to 15 hours per week as well. Neil described his religious preference as "born-again Christian, non-denominational." He had previously been a full-time youth minister and at the time of the interview reported spending from 3 to 5 hours per week in organized religious services.

Nick was a 37-year-old, Caucasian father of a 6-year-old son. Nick had been married and divorced twice. His first marriage began at age 18 and lasted until he was 20. His second marriage stretched from age 29 to 35. He had been divorced for 2 years at the time of the interview and had not seen his son, born to his second wife, for the past 25 months. His son resided with his wife in another state, and she had threatened court action to prevent Nick from visiting. Nick had graduated from high school and worked full time in a state hospital as a psychiatric attendant. He reported an annual income of less than $20,000. Nick identified himself as a Baptist who spent 0 hours per week in religious services.

Colin was a 38-year-old, Caucasian father of a 9-year-old son, born to his second wife. His first marriage, at age 19, lasted 2 years. He dated his current wife for 6 years. They had been married for 10 years at the time of the interview. It was her first marriage. Colin had completed his baccalaureate degree and had taken some graduate coursework. He was employed full time as a chemical dependency counselor. His wife had a 2-year college degree and worked full time as well. Colin reported a household income of $55,000 per year. Colin had spent a long period of time playing the club scene in a "rock and roll" band and had decided to give up the "party lifestyle" after the birth of his son. He indicated that he was "not involved in religion on an organized level" and spent no time on a weekly basis engaged in religious activities.

Jeff was a 38-year-old, Scottish American, remarried father of a 10-year-old daughter and an 8-year-old son. Both Jeff and his wife had been previously married and divorced, without having children in their first marriages. They had been married for 11 years at the time of the interview. Jeff held a 4-year college degree and his wife had completed high school. Jeff worked full time as a refinery operator and his wife worked 18 hours per week. Their household income was $45,000 per year. Jeff reported his religious identity to be "Full Gospel/Charismatic" and estimated that he spent 3 hours per week in religious services.

Will was a 38-year-old, Caucasian, married father of two teenage children. His son was 13 and his daughter was 11 at the time of the interview. Both Will and his wife had completed graduate-level coursework. Will worked half time (on commission as a salesperson) and his wife worked full time. Will reported his annual family income to be $65,000. Will was a Catholic who spent 1 hour per week in religious services. He and his wife both invested heavily in the athletic pursuits of their children, who were performing at elite levels.

Bill was a 39-year-old, Caucasian, married father of a 15-year-old son and a 10-year-old daughter. He had completed high school and a 2-year degree program and was working full time as a research laboratory technician at a large corporation. His wife had a 2-year college degree and worked 40 hours per week as well. Bill reported a family income of $75,000 per year. His religious identity was "Christian," although he did not report any time in religious services on a weekly basis.

Joseph was a 39-year-old, African American father with three children from his first wife, a 14-year-old daughter, a 13-year-old son, and a 5-year-old son. His first wife was married prior to their relationship, and Joseph was the stepfather of her daughter age 2. Joseph had separated from his second wife 5 years prior to the interview, and did not get custody of the children. He had not had children present in his household until his son had moved in with him 2 months prior to the interview. Joseph had taken some college coursework but did not have a degree. He had been a corrections officer, and at the time of the interview had been unemployed for 8 months. His current partner had separated from her first husband, and was not working due to disabilities. Joseph reported his annual household income to be below $10,000. Joseph identified himself as a Methodist who spent about 4 hours per week in religious services.

Robert was a 39-year-old, Caucasian, married father of three children. Robert and his wife had a 14-year-old son, an 11-year-old daughter, and a 7-month-old daughter. Robert had taken some college credits, but did not hold a baccalaureate degree or certificate. He was employed as a truck driver "delivery person" for roughly 60 hours per week. His wife also worked 40 hours per week. Robert reported a household income of

$35,000. His religious preference was "Presbyterian" and he reported spending about 4 hours per week in religious services. Robert was a recovering alcoholic who had observed many effects of substance abuse on his roles as husband, father, and provider.

Adam was a 41-year-old, separated father of two children. Adam listed his ethnic identity as Irish/Italian/American/Cherokee. His marital history was complicated by the fact that at age 25 he had married a "Chinese woman," who was "friend of a friend" "for immigration purposes." He subsequently divorced her once her immigration status stabilized. He reported being "really married" to "one person" at age 29. His first child was born shortly thereafter, and they stayed together for 2 years, then separated. During a brief reconciliation attempt, Adam and his second wife conceived their daughter. They had been separated for 7 years at the time of the interview. His son was 12 years old and his daughter 9 years old at that time. His children were residing with their mother in a distant state, and Adam was under a restraining order, preventing him from entering the state of their residence. He had not seen his children for 9 months at the time of the interview. Adam had completed high school and some college coursework, but did not hold a college degree or advanced certificate. He was working as an incinerator operator at a large corporation. He reported an annual income of $25,000, no religious preference, and no religious activity on a weekly basis.

David was a 42-year-old, Caucasian, married father of three daughters. David's daughters were ages 14, 17, and 18 at the time of the interview. Both David and his wife held 4-year degrees. David was self-employed in sales, working approximately 50 hours per week. His wife worked about 8 hours per week. David reported a family income of approximately $50,000 per year. As described later (see Leo), David and his family co-resided with Leo and his family for a number of years, and they engaged in numerous business and ministry partnerships. Although not officially "stepparents" of Leo and Deborah's two sons, there were unique fictive kin relationships in the household, consisting of four adults and five teenage children. David's daughters and Leo's sons perceived themselves to be siblings. David described his religious preference as "Assemblies of God/Pentecostal" and estimated spending from 11 to 15 hours per week in religious services.

Gilbert was a 43-year-old, American Hungarian father of a 12-year-old son. Gilbert's wife was previously married, but had no children with her previous husband. Gilbert's son was born when he was 29. Gilbert completed high school and had taken some college credits. He was self-employed as an automobile salesperson. His wife did not work outside of the home. Gilbert's family income was approximately $35,000 per year. Although Gilbert identified himself as a Catholic, he reported no time invested in weekly religious activities.

Leo was a 43-year-old Caucasian, married father of two sons, ages 15 and 18 at the time of the interview. Both Leo and his wife held 4-year college degrees. Leo was self-employed in sales, working approximately 50 hours per week. His wife worked 28 hours a week. Leo reported a family income of $55,000 per year. His religious preference was "Protestant." Leo was an ordained minister, although he was not officially serving in a church setting on staff. He reported spending about 24 hours per week in organized religious activities, most of which was volunteer work through church and para-church organizations. Several years prior to the interview, Leo and his spouse had formed close friendships and business and ministry partnerships with David (see earlier) and his spouse. At the time of the interview, they had shared a large residence for a number of years. Although not officially "stepparents" of David and Esther's three daughters, there were unique extended family relationships in the household.

Tom was a 44-year-old, Caucasian father of two teenage sons, ages 14 and 16. He had also fathered a daughter who died within 24 hours of her birth. Tom had been separated for 1 year and the divorce had been finalized 1 week prior to the interview. His 16-year-old son had chosen to reside with Tom, whereas his 14-year-old chose to live with his former wife in another state, several hundred miles away. Tom held a 2-year degree and reported being "an internship short" of a 4-year college degree. Tom was a dental lab technician and had been laid off 1 week prior to the interview. Tom participated in from 1 to 3 hours of religious services weekly as a Catholic.

Ken was a 45-year-old, Caucasian father of a 21-year-old daughter and a 16-year-old son. He was the stepfather of a 22-year-old son as well. Both Ken and his wife had been previously married, divorced, and remarried. Ken held a masters' degree in business and his spouse had a 2-year college degree. Ken worked about 50 hours per week as an executive in a large corporation and his wife did not work outside of the home. Ken reported an annual income in excess of $100,000. Ken's daughter had continuously remained in the custody of his first wife after their divorce, from the time that she was 1 year old. Ken's step son had lived with him continuously between ages 2 and 18. Ken legally adopted him at age 16. Ken's current spouse suffered from advanced stages of Lupus. Ken's religious preference was "Christian" and he reported 6 hours per week in organized religious activities.

Ned was a 45-year-old, Caucasian single parent of three children. He had been married and divorced three times, and was not in a relationship with a significant other at the time of the interview. His oldest child, a 22-year-old daughter, was from his first marriage, and his other two children, a 14-year-old daughter and an 11-year-old son, were from his second marriage. Ned reported that his second wife had left him and the children when his daughter was 3, and the children had stayed with him continuously from that time. His oldest daughter had lived with his first wife from the time she was 6 until she graduated from high school. At that time, she moved in with Ned for a year, before establishing her own household. Ned had a high school diploma. At the time of the interview he had just been laid off for the fourth time in 12 months. He had been working as a textile operator. Ned reported his household income to be $25,000 per year. He reported from 3 to 4 hours of attendance at religious services per week as a Methodist.

LATE TIMING FATHERS

Roger was a 33-year-old, Caucasian, married father of an infant son. Both Roger and his wife held 2-year degrees from a community college and both were employed full time. Roger reported a combined family income of $75,000 per year. Roger identified himself as a Baptist who invested "very little" time in religious activities weekly.

Anthony was a 39-year-old, Italian American, married father of two daughters, ages 3 and 5, and an infant son. He and his wife had experienced 6 years of infertility before beginning to have children. His son was "unexpected." Anthony's first child was born when he was 34 years old. Anthony had completed some college courses but had not earned a college degree or completed an advanced certificate program. Anthony worked full time as a union auto worker at the time of the interview. Anthony's wife held a masters' degree and worked full time as a nurse. His family income was approximately $85,000 per year. Anthony reported no religious preference and no time invested in weekly religious participation.

Greg was a 40-year-old, Caucasian father of an 8-year-old daughter and stepfather of a 6-year-old daughter. Greg had been married, divorced, and remarried. His second wife had been widowed prior to marrying Greg. Greg held an MBA degree and his wife was taking graduate coursework as well. Greg was working approximately 45 hours per week as a business executive, and his wife worked about 25 hours per week. Greg reported a household income of approximately $50,000. His religious preference was "Evangelical Christian" and he reported engaging in religious services approximately 5 hours per week.

Bruce was a 41-year-old, Caucasian father of two girls, ages 6 and 4. Bruce and his wife were both in their first marriage, and had been married for 9 years at the time of the interview. Bruce had completed a 4-year college degree and his wife had done some college coursework, but held no college degree. Bruce was employed full time as an office manager, and his wife worked full time as well. He reported a household income of $55,000. Bruce listed "Catholic" as his religious preference, spending 1 hour per week in church activities.

Paul was a 41-year-old Caucasian, who listed himself as "universal" in regard to ethnic identity. He was 6 years into his second marriage at the time of the interview, and was the father of a 3-year-old girl, placing his first transition to biological parenthood at age 38. He had also been stepfather to a 17-year-old son from his first marriage. His first marriage occurred when he was 26 years old. He and his first wife separated after 5½ years and later divorced. His current wife was previously married and divorced, but had no children in her prior marriage. Paul held a masters' degree and worked full time. His wife had a Ph.D. and worked full time during the academic year. Paul reported their household income to be $75,000 and listed "United Methodist" as his religious identity. He estimated that he spent 5 hours per week in religious services.

References

Aljadir, L. P. (1988). Dietary habits in the transition to parenthood: Dietary habits before pregnancy, during pregnancy, and in young families. In R. Palkovitz & M. B. Sussman (Eds.), *Transitions to parenthood* (pp. 61–83). New York: Haworth.

Allen, S. M. & Hawkins, A. J. (1999). Maternal gatekeeping: Mothers' beliefs and behaviors that inhibit greater father involvement in family work. *Journal of Marriage and the Family, 61,* 199–212.

Allport, G. W. (1961). *Pattern and growth in personality.* New York: Holt, Rinehart & Winston.

Ambert, A. M. (1992). *The effect of children on parents.* New York: Haworth.

Anthony, E. J., & Benedek, T. (1970). *Parenthood: Its psychology and psychopathology.* Boston: Little, Brown.

Argyle, M., & Beit-Hallahmi, B. (1975). *The social psychology of religion.* London: Routledge & Kegan Paul.

Baltes, P. B. (1979). Life-span developmental psychology: Some converging observations on history and theory. In P. B. Baltes & O. G. Brim, Jr. (Eds.), *Lifespan development and behavior* (Vol. 2, pp. 256–274). New York: Academic Press.

Baltes, P. B. (1987). Theoretical propositions of life-span developmental psychology: On the dynamics between growth and decline. *Developmental Psychology, 23,* 611–626.

Barnett, R. C. (1994). Home-to-work spillover revisited: A study of full-time employed women in dual-earner couples. *Journal of Marriage and the Family, 56,* 647–656.

Baumrind, D. (1975). *Early socialization and the discipline controversy.* Morristown, NJ: General Learning Press.

Bell, R. Q. (1968). A reinterpretation of the direction of effects in studies of socialization. *Psychological Review, 75,* 81–95.

Belsky, J. (1984). The determinants of parenting: A process model. *Child Development, 55,* 83–96.

Belsky, J. & Kelly, J. (1994). *The transition to parenthood.* New York: Delacorte.

Bergman, S. (1991). *Men's psychological development: A relational perspective.* Work in Progress No. 40, The Stone Center, Wellesley College, Wellesley, MA.

Bernard, J. (1981). The good provider role: Its rise and fall. *American Psychologist, 36,* 1–12.

Blankenhorn, D. (1995). *Fatherless America: Confronting our most urgent social problem.* New York: Basic Books.

Bohannon, J. R. (1991). Religiosity related to grief levels of bereaved mothers and fathers. *Omega, 23,* 153–159.

Bolger, N., DeLongis, A., Kessler, R. C., & Wethington, E. (1989). The contagion of stress across multiple roles. *Journal of Marriage and the Family, 51,* 175–183.

Bronstein, P. (1988). Marital and parenting roles in transition: An overview. In P. Bronstein & C. P. Cowan (Eds.), *Fatherhood today: Men's changing role in the family.* (pp. 3–10). New York: Wiley.

Catalfo, P. (1997). *Raising spiritual children in a material world.* New York: Berkley Books.

Cazenave, N. A. (1979). Middle-income Black fathers: An analysis of the provider role. *The Family Coordinator, 28,* 583–593.

Chancey, D. (1996, November). *Developing a measure of religiosity.* Round Table Discussion presented at the 58th annual National Council on Family Relations, Kansas City, MO.

Chartier, M. R., & Goehner, L. A. (1976). A study of the relationship of parent–adolescent communication, self-esteem, and God image. *Journal of Psychology and Theology, 4,* 227–232.

Christiansen, S., & Palkovitz, R. (1998). Exploring Erikson's psychosocial theory of development: Generativity and its relationship to paternal intimacy, identity and involvement in child care. *Journal of Men's Studies, 7,* 133–156.

Christiansen, S. L., & Palkovitz, R. (2001). Why the "good provider" role still matters: Providing as a form of paternal involvement. *Journal of Family Issues, 28,* 84–106.

Clark, C. A., Worthington, E. L., & Danser, D. B. (1988). The transmission of religious beliefs and practives from parents to firstborn early adolescent sons. *Journal of Marriage and the Family, 50,* 463–472.

Cohen, T. F. (1993). What do fathers provide? Reconsidering the economic and nurturant dimensions of men as parents. In J. C. Hood (Ed.), *Men, work, and family* (pp. 1–22). Thousand Oaks, CA: Sage.

Cohen, T. F., & Durst, J. (1996, November). *Daddy's home: The pathways, philosophies, and role attachments of fathers in role-reversed households.* Paper presented at the 58th annual National Council on Family Relations, Kansas City, MO.

Colarusso, C. A., & Neimiroff, R. A. (1982). The father in midlife: Crisis and growth of paternal identity. In S. H. Cath, A. W. Gurwitt, & J. M. Ross (Eds.), *Father and child: Developmental and clinical perspectives* (pp. 315–327). Boston: Little, Brown.

Coleman, A., & Coleman, L. (1988). *The father.* New York: Avon.

Conger, R. D., Elder, G. H., Lorenz, F. O., Conger, K. J., Simons, R. L., Whitbeck, L. B., Hick, S., & Melby, J. N. (1990). Linking economic hardship to marital quality and instability. *Journal of marriage and the Family, 52,* 643–656.

Cooney, T. M., Pedersen, F. A., Indelicato, S., & Palkovitz, R. (1993). Timing of fatherhood: Is "on-time" optimal? *Journal of Marriage and the Family, 55,* 205–215.

Costa, P. T., Jr., & McCrae, R. R. (1988). Personality in adulthoood: A six-year longitudinal study of self-reports and spouse ratings on the NEO Personality Inventory. *Journal of Personality and Social Psychology, 54,* 853–863.

Cowan, C. P., & Cowan, P. A. (1987). Men's involvement in parenthood: Identifying the antecedents and understanding the barriers. In P. W. Berman & F. A. Pedersen (Eds.), *Men's transitions to parenthood: Longitudinal studies of early family experience* (pp. 145–174). Hillsdale, NJ: Lawrence Erlbaum Associates.

Cowan, P. (1988). Becoming a father, a time of change, an opportunity for development. In P. Bronstein & C. Cowan (Eds.), *Fatherhood today: Men's changing role in the family* (pp 13–35). New York: Wiley.

Cowan, P. A. (1991). Individual and family life transitions: A proposal for a new definition. In P. A. Cowan & M. Hetherington (Eds.), *Family Transitions* (pp. 3–30). Hillsdale, NJ: Lawrence Earlbaum Associates.

Cox, M., Owen, M., Lewis, J., & Henderson, V. K. (1989). Marriage, adult adjustment, and early parenting. *Child Development, 60,* 1015–1024.

Dalbey, G. (1988). *Healing the masculine soul.* Dallas: Word.

Daly, K. J. (1995). Reshaping fatherhood: Finding the models. In W. Marsiglio (Ed.), *Fatherhood: Contemporary theory, research, and social policy* (pp. 21–40). Thousand Oaks, CA: Sage.

Daly, K. J. (1996a). *Families and time: Keeping pace in a hurried culture.* Thousand Oaks, CA: Sage.

Daly, K. J. (1996b). Spending time with the kids: Meanings of family time for fathers. *Family Relations, 45,* 466–476.

Daly, K. J., & Dienhart, A. (1997, November). *Stepping in time: The dance of father involvement.* Paper presented at the National Conference on Family Relations, Crystal City, VA.

Daniels, P., & Weingarten, K. (1982). *Sooner or later: The timing of parenthood in adult lives.* New York: Norton.

Daniels, P., & Weingarten, K. (1988). The fatherhood click: The timing of parenthood in men's lives. In P. Bronstein & C. P. Cowan (Eds.), *Fatherhood today: Men's changing role in the family* (pp. 36–53). New York: Wiley.

Degler, C. (1980). *At odds: Women and the family in America from the revolution to the present.* New York: Oxford University Press.

Demos, J. (1982). The changing faces of fatherhood: A new exploration of American family history. In S. H. Cath, A. R. Gurwitt, & J. M. Ross (Eds.), *Father and child: Developmental and clinical perspectives* (pp. 425–445). Boston: Little, Brown.

Demos, J. (1986). The changing faces of fatherhood. In *Past, present, personal: The family and the life course in American history* (pp. 41–67). New York: Oxford University Press.

Dienhart, A. (1998). *Reshaping fatherhood: The social construction of shared parenting.* Thousand Oaks, CA: Sage.

Dienhart, A., & Daly, K. (1997). Men and women cocreating father involvement in a nongenerative culture. In A. J. Hawkins & D. C. Dollahite (Eds.), *Generative fathering: Beyond deficit perspectives* (pp. 147–164). Thousand Oaks, CA: Sage.

Dinnerstein, X. (1976). *The mermaid and the minotaur.* New York: Harper & Row.

Dixon, R. A., Lerner, R. M., & Hultsch, D. F. (1991). The concept of development in the study of individual and social change. In P. Van Geert & L. P. Moss (Eds.), *Annals of Theoretical Psychology* (Vol. 7, pp. 279–323). New York: Plenum.

Doherty, W. J., Kouneski, E. F., & Erickson, M. F. (1998). Responsible fathering: An overview and conceptual framework. *Journal of Marriage and the Family, 60,* 277–292.

Dollahite, D. C., & Hawkins, A. J. (1998). A conceptual ethic of generative fathering. *Journal of Men's Studies, 7,* 109–132.

Dollahite, D. C., Hawkins, A. J., & Brotherson, S. E. (1997). Fatherwork: A conceptual ethic of fathering as generative work. In A. J. Hawkins & D. C. Dollahite (Eds.), *Generative fathering: Beyond deficit perspectives* (pp. 17–35). Thousand Oaks, CA: Sage.

Elder, G. H. (1985). Perspectives on the lifecourse. In G. H. Elder (Ed.), *Life course dynamics: Transitions and trajectories* (pp. 23–49). Ithica, NY: Cornell University Press.

Elder, G. H. (1991). Family transitions, cycles, and social change. In P. A. Cowan & M. Hetherington (Eds.), *Family transitions* (pp. 31–57). Hillsdale, NJ: Lawrence Erlbaum Associates.

Erikson, E. (1950). *Childhood and society.* New York: Norton.

Erikson, E. (1964). *Insight and responsibility.* New York: Norton.

Erikson, E. (1968). *Identity, youth and crisis.* New York: Norton.

Erikson, E. (1980). *Identity and the life cycle.* New York: Norton.

European Commission Network in Childcare. (1993). *Men and careers: Report of an international seminar in Ravenna, Italy, 21–22 May.* Brussels: European Commission Network on Childcare.

Farrell, M. P., & Rosenberg, S. D. (1981). *Men at midlife.* Boston: Auburn House.

Festinger, L. (1957). *A theory of cognitive dissonance.* Stanford, CA: Stanford University Press.

Francis, L. J., & Gibson, H. M. (1993). Parental influence and adolescent religiosity: A study of church attendance and attitude toward Christianity among adolescents 11 to 12 and 15 to 16 years old. *International Journal for the Psychology of Religion, 3,* 241–253.

Freud, S. (1964). New introductory lectures in psychoanalysis. In J. Strachey (Ed. & Trans.), *The standard edition of the complete psychological works of Sigmund Freud* (Vol. 22, pp. xxx–xxx). London: Hogarth. (Original work published 1933)

Futris, T., & Pasley, B. K. (1997, November). *The father role identity: Conceptualizing and assessing within role variability.* Paper presented at the meeting of the Theory Construction and Research Methodology Workshop, National Council on Family Relations, Arlington, VA.

Garbarino, J. (2000). The soul of fatherhood. *Marriage and Family Review, 29,* 11–21.

Gerson, K. (1993). *No man's land: Men's changing commitments to family and work.* New York: Basic Books.

Gillespie, R. (1999, October). *Transforming femininity discourses: Voluntary childlessness and the emergence of a childless femininity.* Paper presented at the second biennial feminism(s) and rhetoric(s) conference, "Challenging rhetorics: Cross-Disciplinary Sites of Feminist Discourse," Decatur, IL.

Gilligan, C. (1982). *In a different voice: Psychological theory and women's development.* Cambridge, MA: Harvard University Press.

Grimm-Thomas, K., & Perry-Jenkins, M. (1994). All in a day's work: Job experiences, self-esteem, and fathering in working-class families. *Family Relations, 43,* 174–181.

Griswold, R. L. (1993). *Fatherhood in America: A history.* New York: Basic Books.

Griswold, R. L. (1997). Generative fathering: A historical perspective. In A. J. Hawkins & D. C. Dollahite (Eds.), *Generative fathering: Beyond deficit perspectives* (pp. 71–86). Thousand Oaks, CA: Sage.

Gutmann, D. (1991). *The father and the masculine life cycle.* Publication No. 13, Institute for American Values Working Paper for the Symposium on Fatherhood in America, retrieved from http://www.cfyc.umn.edu/Documents/A/B/AB1008.html 9/20/01.

Haas, L. (1993). Nurturing fathers and working mothers: Changing gender roles in Sweden. In J. C. Hood (Ed.), *Men, work, and family* (pp. 238–261). Newbury Park, CA: Sage.

Hall, D. T., & Richter, J. (1988). Balancing work life and home life: What can organizations do to help? *Executive, 2,* 213–223.

Hareven, T. K. (1977). Family time and historical time. *Daedalus, 106,* 57–70.

Havinghurst, R. J. (1953). *Human development and education.* New York: Longman.

Hawkins, A. J., Christiansen, S. L., Sargent, K. P., & Hill, J. E. (1993). Rethinking fathers' involvement in childcare: A developmental perspective. *Journal of Family Issues, 14,* 531–549.

Hawkins, A. J., & Dollahite, D. C. (1997a). Beyond the role-inadequacy perspective of fathering. In A. J. Hawkins & D. C. Dollahite (Eds.), *Generative fathering: Beyond deficit perspectives* (pp. 3–16). Newbury Park, CA: Sage.

Hawkins, A. J., & Dollahite, D. C. (1997b). *Generative fathering: Beyond deficit perspectives.* Thousand Oaks, CA: Sage.

Hawkins, A. J., & Palkovitz, R. (1999). Beyond ticks and clicks: The need for more diverse and broader conceptualizations and measures of father involvement. *Journal of Men's Studies, 8,* 11–32.

Heath, D. (1978). What meaning and effects does fatherhood have for the maturing of professional men? *Merrill Palmer Quarterly, 24,* 265–278.

Heath, D. (1991). *Fulfilling lives.* San Francisco: Jossey-Bass.

Heider, F. (1958). *The psychology of interpersonal relations.* New York: Wiley.

Hewlett, B. S. (2000). Culture, history and sex: Anthropological contributions to conceptualizing father involvement. *Marriage and Family Review, 29,* 59–73.

Hill, R., & Mattesich, P. (1979). Family development theory and life-span development. In P. B. Baltes & O. G. Brim, Jr. (Eds.), *Life span development and behavior* (Vol. 2, pp. 161–204). New York: Academic Press.

Hochschild, A. R. (1997). *The time bind: When work becomes home and home becomes work.* New York: Metropolitan Books.

Hoffman, M. L. (1981). The role of the father in moral internalization. In M. E. Lamb (Ed.), *The role of the father in child development* (2nd ed., pp. 359–378). New York: Wiley.

Hoffman, M. L., & Manis, J. D. (1979). The value of children in the United States: A new approach to the study of fertility. *Journal of marriage and the Family, 41,* 583–596.

Hood, J. C. (1986). Meaning and measurement of the provider role. *Journal of Marriage and the Family, 48,* 349–360.

Hooker, K., & Fiese, B. H. (1993, March). Temporal perspectives on changes in self related to parenting. Society for Research in Child Development, New Orleans, LA.

Horna, J., & Lupri, E. (1987). Father's participation in work, family life and leisure: A Canadian experience. In C. L. Lewis & M. O'Brien (Eds.), *Reassessing fatherhood: New observations on fathers and the modern family* (pp. 54–73), London: Sage.

Hultsch, D. F., & Plemons, J. K. (1979). Life events and life-span development. In P. B. Baltes & O. G. Brim, Jr. (Eds.), *Life span development and behavior* (Vol. 2, pp. 1–36). New York: Academic Press.

Hwang, C. P. (1987). The changing role of Swedish fathers. In M. E. Lamb (Ed.), *The father's role: Cross cultural perspectives* (pp. 115–138). Hillsdale, NJ: Lawrence Erlbaum Associates.

Ihinger-Tallman, M., Pasley, K., & Buehler, C. (1993). Developing a middle-range theory of father involvement postdivorce. *Journal of Family Issues, 14,* 550–571.

Johnson, R. C. (1992). Fathers and cultural influence. In the Minnesota Fathering Alliance (Eds.), *Working with fathers: Methods and perspectives* (pp. 47–58). Stillwater, MN: Nu Ink Unlimited.

Johnson, W. B. (1993). Father uninvolvement: Impact, etiology and potential solutions. *Journal of Psychology and Christianity, 12,* 301–311.

Kieren, D. K., & Munro, B. (1987). Following the leaders: Parents' influence on adolescent religious activity. *Journal for the Scientific Study of Religion, 26,* 249–255.

Klenow, O. J., & Bollin, R. C. (1989). Belief in afterlife: A national survey. *Omega, 20,* 63–74.

Kotre, J. (1984). *Outliving the self: Generativity and the interpretation of lives.* Baltimore: Johns Hopkins University Press.

Kuhn, T. S. (1962). *The structure of scientific revolutions.* Chicago: University of Chicago Press.

Lamb, M. E. (1981). Fathers and child development: An integrative overview. In M. E. Lamb (Ed.), *The role of the father in child development* (2nd ed., pp. 1–70). New York: Wiley.

Lamb, M. E. (1987). Introduction: The emergent American father. In M. E. Lamb (Ed.), *The father's role: Cross cultural perspectives* (pp. 3–25). Hillsdale, NJ: Lawrence Erlbaum Associates.

Lamb, M. E. (1997). Fathers and child development: An introductory overview. In M. E. Lamb (Ed.), *The role of the father in child development* (3rd ed., pp. 1–18). New York: Wiley.

Lamb, M. E. (2000). The history of research on father involvement: An overview. *Marriage and Family Review, 29,* 23–42.

Lamb, M. E., Pleck, J. H., & Levine, J. A. (1987). The role of the father in child development: The effects of increased paternal involvement. In C. Lewis & M. O'Brien (Eds.), *Reassessing fatherhood: New observations on fathers and the modern family* (pp. 109–125). Beverly Hills, CA: Sage.

LaRossa, R. (1988). Fatherhood and social change. *Family Relations, 37,* 451–457.

LaRossa, R. (1997). *The modernization of fatherhood.* Chicago: University of Chicago.

LaRossa, R., & Reitzes, D. C. (1993). Continuity and change in middle class fatherhood, 1925–1939: The culture–conduct connection. *Journal of Marriage and the Family, 55,* 455–468.

Latshaw, J. (1998). The centrality of faith in fathers' role construction: The faithful father and the Axis Mundi paradigm. *Journal of Men's Studies, 7,* 53–70.

Lawton, C. (1991, May 26). Baby beckons: Why is daddy at work? *New York Times,* pp. C1, C8.

Lerner, R. M., & Spanier, G. B. (1978). A dynamic interactional view of child and family development. In R. M. Lerner & G. B. Spanier (Eds.), *Child influences on marital and family interaction* (pp. 1–22). New York: Academic Press.

Levine, J. A., & Pittinsky, T. L. (1997). *Working fathers: New strategies for balancing work and family.* Reading, MA: Addison-Wesley.

Lewis, C., & O'Brien, M. (1987). Constraints on fathers: Research, theory and clinical practice. In C. L. Lewis & M. O'Brien (Eds.), *Reassessing fatherhood: New observations on fathers and the modern family* (pp. 1–19). London: Sage.

Marks, S. R. (1977). Multiple role strain: Some notes on human energy, time and commitment. *American Sociological Review, 42,* 921–936.

Marsh, M. (1990). Suburban men and masculine domesticity, 1870–1915. In M. C. Carnes & C. Griffen (Eds.), *Meanings of manhood: Constructions of masculinity in Victorian America* (pp. 111–127). Chicago: University of Chicago Press.

Marsiglio, W. (1995). Fathers' diverse life course patterns and roles: Theory and social interventions. In W. Marsiglio (Ed.), *Fatherhood: Contemporary theory, research and social policy* (pp. 78–101). Thousand Oaks, CA: Sage.

Marsiglio, W., Day, R. D., & Lamb, M. E. (2000). Exploring fatherhood diversity: Implications for conceptualizing father involvement. *Marriage & Family Review, 29,* 269–293.

McAdams, D. P., & de St. Albin, E. (Eds.). (1998). *Generativity and adult development: How and why we care for the next generation.* Washington, DC: American Psychological Association.

McAdoo, J. L. (1988). Changing perspectives on the role of the Black father. In P. Bronstein & C. P. Cowan (Eds.), *Fatherhood today: Men's changing role in the family* (pp. 79–92). New York: Wiley.

McAdoo, J. L. (1993). The roles of African-American fathers: An ecological perspective. *Families in Society: The Journal of Contemporary Human Services, 74,* 28–35.

McKeown, K., Ferguson, H., & Rooney, D. (1998). *Changing fathers?: Fatherhood and family life in modern Ireland.* Cork, Ireland: Collins Press.

Minton, C., & Pasley, K. (1996). Fathers' parenting role identity and father involvement: A comparison of nondivorced and divorced nonresident fathers. *Journal of Family Issues, 17,* 26–45.

Mott, F. L. (1990). When is a father really gone? Paternal–child contact in father-absent homes. *Demography, 27,* 499–517.

Mueller, D. P., & Cooper, P. W. (1986). Religious interest and involvement of young adults: A research note. *Review of Religious Research, 27,* 245–254.

Neugarten, B. L., & Weinstein, K. K., (1964). The changing American grandparent. *Journal of Marriage and the Family, 26,* 299–304.

Newman, P. R., & Newman, B. M. (1988). Parenthood and adult development. In R. Palkovitz & M. B. Sussman (Eds.), *Transitions to parenthood* (pp. 313–338). New York: Haworth.

Nock, S. L. (1982). The Life-Cycle Approach to Family Analysis. In B. B. Wolman (Ed.), *Handbook of developmental psychology* (pp. 636–651). Englewood Cliffs, NJ: Prentice-Hall.

Nock, S. L. (1998). *Marriage in men's lives.* New York: Oxford University Press.

Osofsky, J. D., & Connors, K. (1979). Mother–infant interaction: An integrative view of a complex system. In J. D. Osofsky (Ed.), *The handbook of infant development* (pp. 519–548). New York: Wiley.

Palkovitz, R. (1980). Predictors of involvement in first-time fathers. *Dissertation Abstracts International, 40,* 3603B–3604B. (University Microforms No. 8105035)

Palkovitz, R. (1984). Parental attitudes and fathers' interactions with their five-month-old Infants. *Developmental Psychology, 20,* 1054–1060.

Palkovitz, R. (1987). Consistency and stability in the family microsystem environment. In D. L. Peters & S. Kontos (Eds.), *Annual advances in applied developmental psychology* (Vol. 2, pp. 40–67). New York: Ablex.

Palkovitz, R. (1988). Predictors of change in parental role prescriptions and self esteem across the transition to parenthood. *Family Perspective, 22,* 15–28.

Palkovitz, R. (1992a, April). *Parenting as a generator of adult development: Is the child parent to the adult?* Paper presented at the meeting of the Conference on Human Development, Atlanta, GA.

Palkovitz, R. (1992b, November). *Parenting as a generator of adult development: Conceptual issues and implications.* Paper presented at the meeting of the Theory Construction and Research Methodology Workshop, National Council on Family Relations, Orlando, FL.

Palkovitz, R. (1994, November). *Men's perceptions of the effects of fathering on their adult development and lifecourse.* Paper presented at the meeting of the National Council on Family Relations, Minneapolis, MN.

Palkovitz, R. (1996a). Parenting as a generator of adult development: Conceptual issues and implications. *Journal of Social and Personal Relationships, 13,* 571–592.

Palkovitz, R. (1996b). The recovery of fatherhood? In A. Carr & M. S. Van Leeuwen (Eds.), *Religion, feminism and the family* (pp. 310–329). Louisville, KY: Westminster John Knox Press.

Palkovitz, R. (1997). Reconstructing "involvement": Expanding conceptualizations of men's caring in contemporary families. In A. J. Hawkins & D. C. Dollahite (Eds.), *Generative fathering: Beyond deficit perspectives* (pp. 200–216). Thousand Oaks, CA: Sage.

Palkovitz, R. (1999, October). *Fathers' involvement with children and men's development: Good fathering is good for everyone.* Paper presented at the annual meeting of the Pennsylvania/Delaware Council on Family Relations, "Men in Families." Grantham, PA.

Palkovitz, R. (2000, November). The bottom line: Men's perceptions of costs and benefits of active fathering. National Council on Family Relations, Minneapolis, MN.

Palkovitz, R., Christiansen, S. L., & Dunn, C. (1988). Provisional balances: Father's perceptions of the politics and dynamics of involvement in family and career development. *Michigan Family Review, 3,* 45–64.

Palkovitz, R., & Copes, M. (1988). Changes in attitudes, beliefs and expectations associated with the transition to parenthood. *Marriage and Family Review, 12,* 183–199.

Palkovitz, R., & Palm, G. (1998). Fatherhood and faith in formation: The developmental effects of fathering on religiosity, morals and values. *Journal of Men's Studies, 7,* 33–51.

Palkovitz, R., & Sussman, M. B. (Eds.). (1988). *Transitions to Parenthood.* New York: Haworth.

Palm, G. (1993). Involved fatherhood: A second chance. *Journal of Men's Studies, 2,* 139–155.

Palm, G. (1997). Promoting generative fathering through parent and family education. In A. J. Hawkins & D. C. Dollahite (Eds.), *Generative fathering: Beyond deficit perspectives* (pp. 167–182). Newbury Park, CA: Sage.

Parke, R. D. (1981). *Fathers.* Cambridge, MA: Harvard University Press.

Parke, R. D., & Brott, A. A. (1999). *Throwaway dads: The myths and barriers that keep men from being the fathers they want to be.* New York: Houghton Mifflin.

Pasley, K., & Minton, C. (1997). Generative fathering after divorce and remarriage: Beyond the "disappearing dad." In A. J. Hawkins & D. C. Dollahite (Eds.), *Generative fathering: Beyond deficit perspectives* (pp. 118–133). Thousand Oaks, CA: Sage.

Peterson, G. W., & Rollins, B. C. (1987). Parent-child socialization. In M. B. Sussman & S. K. Steinmetz (Eds.), *Handbook of marriage and the family* (pp. 417–507). New York: Plenum.

Piotrkowski, C. S., Rapoport, R. N., & Rapoport, R. (1987). Families and work. In M. B. Sussman & S. K. Steinmetz (Eds.), *Handbook of marriage and the family* (pp. 251–284). New York: Plenum.

Pipher, M. (1999). *Another country: Navigating the emotional terrain of our elders.* New York: Riverhead Books.

Pleck, J. (1987). American fathering in historical perspective. In M. S. Kimmel (Ed.), *Changing men: New direction in research on men and masculinity* (pp. 83–97). Beverly Hills, CA: Sage.

Pleck, J. H. (1993). Are "family-supportive" employer policies relevant to men? In J. C. Hood (Ed.), *Men, work, and family* (pp. 217–237). Newbury Park, CA: Sage.

Pleck, J. H. (1997). Paternal involvement: Levels, sources, and consequences. In M. E. Lamb (Ed.), *The role of the father in child development* (3rd ed., pp. 66–103). New York: Wiley.

Popenoe, D. (1996). *Life without father.* New York: The Free Press.

Promise Keepers. (1995, July). *Raise the standard 1995.* Conference booklet, Men's Conference, Minneapolis, MN.

Pruett, K. D. (1989). The nurturing male: A longitudinal study of primary nurturing fathers. In S. Cath, A. R. Gurwitt, & L. Gunsberg (Eds.), *Fathers and their Families* (pp. 389–405). Hillsdale, NJ: Analytic Press.

Riegel, K. L. (1976). The dialectics of human development. *American Psychologist, 31,* 689–700.

Robinson, B. E., & Barret, R. L. (1986). *The developing father: Emerging roles in contemporary society.* New York: Guilford.

Rodgers, R. H. (1973). *Family interaction and transaction: The developmental approach.* Englewood Cliffs, NJ: Prentice-Hall.

Roof, W. C. (1993). *A generation of seekers: The spiritual journeys of the baby boom generation.* San Francisco: Harper.

Rossi, A. (1984). Gender and parenthood. *American Sociological Review, 49,* 1–19.

Rossi, A. S. (1980). Aging and parenthood in the middle years. In P. B. Baltes & O. G. Brim, Jr. (Eds.), *Life span development and behavior* (Vol. 3, pp. 138–207). New York: Academic Press.

Rossi, A. S., & Rossi, P. H. (1992). *Of human bonding.* New York: Aldine deGruyter.

Rotundo, E. A. (1985). American fatherhood: A historical perspective. *American Behavioral Scientist, 29,* 7–25.

Rotundo, E. A. (1993). *American manhood: Transformations in masculinity from the revolution to the modern era.* New York: Basic Books.

Russell, G. (1978). The father role and its relation to masculinity, femininity, and androgyny. *Child Development, 49,* 1174–1181.

Sachs, B. E. (1983). *Paternal generativity: The influence of the transition into fatherhood on first-time fathers' relationships with their own fathers and their definitions of their generative identities.* Unpublished doctoral dissertation, University of Maryland, College Park.

Sagi, A., & Sharon, N. (1983). Costs and benefits of increased paternal involvement in childrearing: The societal perspective. In M. E. Lamb & A. Sagi (Eds.), *Fatherhood and social policy* (pp. 219–233). Hillsdale, NJ: Lawrence Erlbaum Associates.

Santrock, J. W. (1997). *Life span development* (6th ed.). Dubuque, IA: Brown & Benchmark.

Scanzoni, J. H. (1975). *Sex roles, life styles and childrearing: Changing patterns in marriage and the family.* New York: The Free Press.

Schor, J. B. (1992). *The overworked American: The unexpected decline of leisure.* New York: Basic.

Schwab, R., & Petersen, K. U. (1990). Religiousness: Its relation to loneliness, neuroticism, and subjective well-being. *Journal for the Scientific Study of Religion, 29,* 335–345.

Seltzer, J. A. (1991). Relationships between fathers and children who live apart: The father's role after separation. *Journal of Marriage and the Family, 53,* 79–101.

Seltzer, J. A., & Bianchi, S. M. (1988). Children's contact with absent parents. *Journal of Marriage and the Family, 50,* 663–677.

Shelton, B. A., & John, D. (1993). Ethnicity, race, and difference: A comparison of white, black and hispanic men's household labor time. In J. C. Hood (Ed.), *Men, work and family.* New York: Sage.

Snarey, J. (1993). *How fathers care for the next generation: A four-decade study.* Cambridge, MA: Harvard University Press.

Snarey, J., Son, L., Kuehne, V. S., Hauser, S., & Vaillant, G. (1987). The role of parenting in men's psychosocial development: A longitudinal study of early adulthood infertility and midlife generativity. *Developmental Psychology, 23,* 593–603.

Speicher-Dubin, B. (1982). Relationships between parent moral judgement, child moral judgement and family interaction: A correlational study. *Dissertation Abstracts International, 43,* 1600B. (University Microfilms International Order no. 8223231)

Stearns, P. N. (1991). Fatherhood in historical perspective: The role of social change. In F. W. Bozett & S.M.H. Hanson (Eds.), *Fatherhood and families in cultural context* (pp. 28–52). New York: Springer.

Stier, H., & Tienda, M. (1993). Are men marginal to the family?: Insights from Chicago's Inner City. In J. C. Hood (Ed.), *Men work and family* (pp. 23–44). Thousand Oaks, CA: Sage.

Teachman, J. D., Call, V.R.A., & Carver, K. P. (1994). Marital status and the duration of joblessness among white men. *Journal of Marriage and the Family, 56,* 415–428.

Thurnher, M. (1974). Goals, values and life evaluations at the present stage. *Journal of Gerontology, 29,* 85–96.

Uttal, D. H., & Perlmutter, M. (1989). Toward a broader conceptualization of development: The role of gains and losses across the life span. *Developmental Review, 9,* 101–132.

Vaillant, G. E. (1977). *Adaptation to Life.* Boston: Little, Brown.

White, J. M. (1991). *Dynamics of family development: A theoretical perspective.* New York: Guilford.

Whitehead, B. D. (1993). Dan Quayle was right. *Atlantic Monthly,* April, 47–78.

Wordsworth, W. (1802/1992). My heart leaps up when I behold. In N. Roe (Ed.), *William Wordsworth selected poetry* (p. 172). New York: Penguin Books.

Zinsmeister, K. (1991). *The nature of fatherhood.* An Institute for American Values Working Paper for the Symposium on Fatherhood in America. Publication W.P.11.

Zussman, R. (1987). Work and family in the new middle class. In N. Gerstel & H. E. Gross (Eds.), *Families and work* (pp. 338–346). Philadelphia: Temple University Press.

Author Index

A

B

C

D

Subject Index

H

I

J

L

M

U

V

W

Y

Participant Quote Index